Cultural Mapping and Musical Diversity

Transcultural Music Studies
Series Editors
Simone Krüger Bridge, Liverpool John Moores University
Britta Sweers, University of Bern

Monographs and edited collections on contemporaneous explanations surrounding the nature of music and human beings in a (post-)global world. Books in this series encompass a comprehensively wide selection of subject matters alongside a shared interest in fieldwork—physical, virtual, historical—and its complex challenges and fascinations in a postcolonial age. Topics include music's use in social, collective and psychological life; musical individuals; music in globalization and migration; music education; music, ethnicity and gender; and environmental issues.

Published

Provincial Headz: British Hip Hop and Critical Regionalism
Adam de Paor-Evans

The Lifetime Soundtrack: Music and Autobiographical Memory
Lauren Istvandity

Forthcoming

Bikutsi: A Beti Dance Music on the Rise, 1970–1990
Anja Brunner

Türkü and Halay between Gent and Turkey: Turkish Folk Music in a Transnational Context
Liselotte Sels

Cultural Mapping and Musical Diversity

edited by
Britta Sweers and Sarah M. Ross

equinox

SHEFFIELD UK   BRISTOL CT

Published by Equinox Publishing Ltd.

UK: Office 415, The Workstation, 15 Paternoster Row, Sheffield,
       South Yorkshire, S1 2BX
USA: ISD, 70 Enterprise Drive, Bristol, CT 06010

www.equinoxpub.com

First published 2020

British Library Cataloguing-in-Publication Data
A catalogue record for this book is available from the British Library.

ISBN-13 9781781797587 (hardback)
         9781781797594 (paperback)
         9781781797600 (ePDF)

Library of Congress Cataloging-in-Publication Data
Names: Sweers, Britta, 1969- | Ross, Sarah M.
Title: Cultural mapping and musical diversity / edited by Britta Sweers and
   Sarah M. Ross.
Description: Sheffield, South Yorkshire ; Bristol, CT : Equinox Publishing,
   2020. | Series: Transcultural music studies | Includes bibliographical
   references and index.
Identifiers: LCCN 2019021253 (print) | LCCN 2019021875 (ebook) | ISBN
   9781781797600 (ePDF) | ISBN 9781781797587 (hb) | ISBN 9781781797594 (pb)
Subjects: LCSH: Ethnomusicology. | Cultural property--Protection. |
   Intangible property--Protection. | Unesco. Intangible Cultural Heritage
   Section.
Classification: LCC ML3798 (ebook) | LCC ML3798 C83 2020 (print) | DDC
   780.89--dc23
LC record available at https://lccn.loc.gov/2019021253

Typeset by S.J.I. Services, New Delhi, India

Contents

List of Figures

Preface and Acknowledgements

Britta Sweers and Sarah M. Ross
University of Bern, Switzerland
Hannover University of Music, Drama, and Media, Germany

The chapters presented in this book emerged during the 29th meeting of the European Seminar in Ethnomusicology (ESEM) that took place in Bern from September 4–8, 2013. ESEM—a platform for scholars and advanced students—was initially founded by the late John Blacking (1928–90) as a European network for ethnomusicologists in Belfast in 1981. With approximately 250 members in 2019, ESEM is comparably small, yet, at the same time, a highly international network for European ethnomusicology. Since its foundation, ESEM has become a central exchange platform for ethnomusicology's localized variants in Western and Eastern Europe, while welcoming scholars and topics from all over the world. This background is reflected in the different perspectives presented in this volume. In a way, ESEM's disciplinary focus reflects the topic of this book, as ESEM is an associated member of the International Music Council, which is also connected to UNESCO, and which provides a central thematic thread in this book.

We are grateful to our Swedish colleague and former ICTM President Krister Malm, who suggested the initial idea of that year's theme "Cultural Mapping and Musical Diversity" at the 2012 ESEM meeting in Ljubljana. Reflections on our relevant keywords ("musical mapping" and "cultural diversity") revealed that the theme touched upon several under-addressed methodological questions. It may not be surprising that the strongest international response to our conference call focused on "Intangible Cultural Heritage," which informs Parts III and IV of this book. How strongly this theme resonated with the practical side of conference organization became apparent in our musical choices: What music do we want to experience at an ethnomusicological meeting? Those traveling from afar often expect to hear some grassroots or local traditions, global developments notwithstanding. Yet, particularly in Switzerland, this is often questioned by locals, who do not necessarily identify with Swiss folk music, and its internationally marketed iconicity as an expression of Swissness. The compromise was to bridge iconic tradition and modernity by offering, on the one hand, traditional Swiss experiences, for example a yodeling workshop that might, however—as in the case of the Quartet Alphorn Experience—also merge this "tradition" with modern elements, such as jazz, funk, blues, or unusual grooves, and, on the other hand, "modern" music experiences. This also became evident with the audiovisual performance *Sonic Traces: From Switzerland* by Norient. Performed by Michael Spahr and Simon Grab during the seminar, this performance presented a contradictory and complex electronic audiovisual experience of twenty-first-century Switzerland with artists such as trash-blues musician Reverend Beat-Man, and composer and musician Ruedi Häusermann from Zürich. This combination between local and global, traditional and modern, acoustic and electric, points to the central challenges of mapping local traditions and cultural diversity in a modern context, the very issues that were addressed at the 2013 ESEM Seminar, and which inform the central core of this book.

Our first thanks go to the financial sponsors, without whom the event would not have been possible: The Schweizerische Nationalfonds (SNF); the Burgerstiftung Bern; the University of Bern, particularly the Philosophisch-historische Fakultät, and the Center for Cultural Studies (CCS) and Center for Global Studies (CGS), who each supported this event generously. We are also grateful to the Institute of Musicology, the Institute of Geography, and the Institute for Advanced Studies in the Humanities (IASH) for providing the space to host this event. Further thanks go to the local organizing team, especially Theresa Beyer, who was also supported by Maša Marty and IT specialist Patrick Kraus, as well as to Janina Neústupný and her team of student helpers. Additional thanks go to Brigitte Bachmann-Geiser, Werner Schmitt, Frieda Stauffer, Gurbachan Singh, and Korbinian Seitz. We are also extremely grateful for donations from generous sponsors, especially Christoph Streubel with Präsenz Schweiz, Christian Strickler (Swissinfo), the SAGW (Schweizerische Akademie der Geistes- und Sozialwissenschaften), Bern Tourimus, and Ewa Dahlig-Turek (European Science Foundation). Finally, special thanks go to Simone Krüger Bridge and everyone at Equinox Publishing.

Introduction: Cultural Mapping and Musical Diversity

Britta Sweers and Sarah M. Ross

Founded in the twelfth century on a hill site surrounded by the river Aare, Bern, the federal city of Switzerland with around 140,000 inhabitants, became a UNESCO World Heritage Site in 1983. Hosting the 29th meeting of the European Seminar in Ethnomusicology (ESEM) from September 4–8, 2013, the city of Bern thus indirectly invited such a topic as "Cultural Mapping and Musical Diversity," the theme which served as the basis of this book's collection. When the initial call for papers was sent out, we had indeed expected a number of papers addressing the theme of UNESCO Intangible Cultural Heritage (ICH). Yet we were then surprised to note how strongly the ICH theme actually dominated, which indicated the need for intellectual exchange about it. Recent years saw a number of ethnomusicological publications on UNESCO-related topics, as apparent, for instance, in Howard's (2012) pioneering reflection on ICH policies in Japan, China, and Korea; and the ICTM (International Council for Traditional Music) conference in Astana (July 16–22, 2015) with its focus on ICH issues (see also Serafimovska et al. 2016; Grant and Sarin 2016). The ESEM meeting not only highlighted specific gaps in research and discourse within the broader discipline of ethnomusicology itself, and thus also the need for scholarly attention on the UNESCO-related debate, but it also pointed to the lack of research about its relation to the environment and landscape, and related research methods, in particular the method of mapping in ethnomusicology. The chapters and case studies present relevant insights that are, in some instances, still further to be explored, yet even so we hope to make a contribution to the ongoing debate on heritage, cultural mapping, and diversity.

Returning briefly to Bern as a case study of tangible cultural heritage, the city's UNESCO status has led to various not-always-easy debates related to cultural heritage and sustainability. "Heritage" might be understood here as "the legacy of physical artefacts and intangible attributes of a group or society that are inherited from past generations, maintained in the present and bestowed for the benefit of future generations" (UNESCO n.d.a.), or, in other words, as a selection from a selection—a small subset of history that relates to a given group of people in a particular place at a specific time (cf. Dann and Seaton 2001: 26), which obtains further value and visibility due to its status as UNESCO Cultural Heritage. So how can selected systems, environments, objects, or traditions be maintained within a continuously transforming world? In other words, how can they be sustained?

How strongly such questions have played a role in UNESCO's selection process becomes apparent in the criteria list. As is stated with regard to Bern, "The Old City of Berne [sic] is a positive example of a city that has conserved its medieval urban structure whilst responding, over time, to the increasingly complex functions of a capital city of a modern State" (criterion 3) (UNESCO n.d.b.). Fulfilling the criteria of integrity and authenticity with regard to urban living in the twenty-first century, Bern, on the one hand, seems to convey a well-balanced model of heritage preservation, and yet, as warned by Entente Bernoise (2005), this also implies dangers, such as musealization due to the perfectionalization or complication of necessary private renovation, thereby threatening the central issue of sustainability. While the realization of UNESCO's tangible cultural heritage imperative (i.e. "buildings and historic places, monuments, artifacts, etc., which are considered worthy of preservation for the future," UNESCO n.d.a.) is clearly problematic, its selection framework of intangible cultural heritage of immaterial nature has been even more complex. ICH is defined by UNESCO as

> the practices, representations, expressions, knowledge, skills—
> as well as the instruments, objects, artefacts and cultural spaces
> associated therewith—that communities, groups and, in some
> cases, individuals recognize as part of their cultural heritage.
> (UNESCO 2003)

Items of intangible cultural heritage have faced additional challenges as compared to tangible cultural heritage (cf. Titon 2015: 168–72 for a broader discussion). As the case studies presented in this book illustrate, the difficulties not only relate to questions of preservation—and possible musealization—of local music traditions, but are shaped by its invisible boundaries, and questions around inclusion and exclusion. The challenges posed by the immaterial nature of culture—and music—were indirectly reflected in the delayed implementation of relevant UNESCO resolutions, which are a focal theme of the second part of this book (Figure 1.1).

At the same time, and as stated in the initial call for papers for the ESEM meeting, the challenges in the case of intangible cultural heritage are further evident in the methods used to study ICH, particularly in the specific process of mapping and cartographic methods. Moreover, challenges are also apparent within the broader contextualization of music and sound in regards to landscape and environment. A major basis for identifying intangible cultural heritage in general has been the process of "cultural mapping," which has become, as outlined in the Introduction to Part I, a central keyword in the UNESCO strategy to protect world cultural and natural heritage. Cultural mapping can be described as a tool to enhance awareness of cultural diversity. As the South African sociolinguist Nigel Crawhall (2009) pointed out, cultural mapping was initially considered to represent the "landscapes in two or three dimensions from the perspectives of indigenous and local peoples."

May 14, 1954: *Convention for the Protection of Cultural Properties in the Event of Armed Conflict* (The Hague)

Nov. 14, 1970: *Convention on the Means of Prohibiting and Preventing the Illicit Import, Export and Transfer of Ownership of Cultural Property* (Paris)

Nov. 16, 1972: *Convention Concerning the Protection of the World Cultural and Natural Heritage* (Paris)

August 6, 1982: *Mexico City Declaration on Cultural Politics* (Mexico City)

Nov. 15, 1989: *Recommendation on the Safeguarding of Traditional Culture and Folklore* (Paris)

Nov. 2, 2001: *Universal Declaration on Cultural Diversity* (Paris)

Oct. 17, 2003: *Convention for the Safeguarding of the Intangible Cultural Heritage* (Paris)

since **Nov. 2003**: Convention open for signature

Oct. 20, 2005: *Convention on the Protection and Promotion of the Diversity of Cultural Expression* (Paris)

April 2006: Convention enters into force (after ratification by 30 states)

2016: Convention has been ratified by 171 members

Figure 1.1: Key dates for the implementation of UNESCO Intangible Cultural Heritage resolutions.

It thus transforms intangible cultural heritage into visible objects by establishing profiles of cultures and communities, including music traditions. As Crawhall (ibid.) outlined further, cultural mapping has been used for a variety of purposes as broad as peace building, adaptation to climate change, sustainability management, heritage debate and management, and it can also become highly useful in the analysis of conflict points. This book's chapters also highlight that related concepts of "diversity" often only become apparent at second sight. Rather, they need to be distilled from concepts and keywords such as hybridity, identity, or inclusion/exclusion.

How far has cultural mapping been transferred into the field of music? A major part of this book investigates the impact of cultural mapping on ethnomusicological research, and vice versa. For instance, Bern's architectural value can be measured and verified by geographical and architectural maps, material analysis, and the cataloging of physical artifacts (UNESCO n.d.b.). Yet how can intangible cultural heritage—and musical traditions—be mapped? Can they be mapped at all? Moreover, cultural mapping is connected to political impact on various levels, given that the UNESCO Intangible Cultural Heritage lists clearly shape the public visibility or invisibility of selected musical traditions. This is evident at all levels, ranging from local-national lists (Should the central Swiss *Betruf* ("call to prayer") be included, or not?), to officially ratified representative traditions, such as flamenco. Cultural mapping also touches on questions with regards to the interrelation of music and landscape: What role does diversity play in the sustainability of musical environments and landscapes? While this topic has been particularly discussed in the context of applied ethnomusicology and sustainability (e.g. Schippers 2015), it still lacks a more detailed discussion. The focus on environment and landscape also points to mapping approaches in ethnomusicology more generally, because mapping initially served to create geographic representations of surfaces and landscapes. So how can musical and cultural landscapes be related to these physical-environmental concepts?

Based on these preliminary thoughts, the book is subdivided into four main parts, each preceded by comprehensive introductions.

Part I: The Method of Cultural Mapping

Promoted by UNESCO as a key tool for identifying cultural assets and uncovering diversity within a specific region, cultural mapping, the often promotional descriptions notwithstanding, appears as an essential modern means for implementing sustainable developments. The mapping of intangible cultural assets, particularly music, has a long history. For instance, during the period of comparative musicology, as outlined by Marcello Sorce Keller (Chapter 1), the creation of maps—in a variety of forms—has been a central element in early ethnomusicological research. Yet, despite comprehensive discourse around mapping in other fields, such as cultural area studies, the process of mapping per se—maybe because it was often seen as a means of illustration—has received little attention in later ethnomusicology. This also applies to more current uses of cultural mapping, which so far lacks broader methodological reflections, as apparent in geography, for instance (see also Introduction to Part I for a broader discussion). The method of musical cartography and mapping clearly calls for further reflections, not only within ethnomusicology, but also in the UNESCO conceptualization of cultural mapping. Going beyond a purely UNESCO-related focus, the chapters in Part I thus provide a stimulus for further reflection on the method of musical cartography and mapping, asking questions such as: What approaches and research techniques have been used so far to establish musical maps? What kinds of maps have been developed (and, for example, how far do these correspond to indigenous mental maps that have only been transmitted orally)? How do current approaches differ from earlier cultural mapping (as in cultural area studies) that informed Alan Lomax's *Cantometrics* (1968)? How far do the methods of cultural mapping and ethnomusicological fieldwork differ, and how can they benefit from each other?

Part II: Cultural Landscape and Music

In its original meaning, mapping was interrelated with the representation or cartography of the earth surface or physical landscape. A more specific feature has been cultural landscape, which can be understood, as defined by the World Heritage Committee, as a distinct geographical area representing the "combined work of nature and man" (UNESCO 1968). The preservation of cultural landscapes has also been a major focus of the UNESCO tangible and—increasingly—intangible cultural heritage programs. At the same time, the growing interest in soundscape studies has opened up research on the interrelation between sound and environment (Schafer 1977). Going beyond these pioneering approaches, more recent ethnomusicological studies, following Feld (2012), have not only re-integrated music and performance into their investigations, but they have also focused on the impact of particular environments and (physical and cultural) landscapes on human music and performance. Based on varied case studies, the chapters in Part II both explore the relation between nature/landscape and music/sound (and their definitions), and add broader contextualization, asking questions such as: How exactly is landscape interrelated with music and identified (and vice versa)? How is this interrelation applied and exploited in an (inter-)national context? As shown in the chapters presented here, each environment casts a specific impact on local musical behavior, be it with regard to the interaction and festival cultures of pastoralist and agriculturalist groups in northwest China; the impact of the Palestinian environment on art and scholarly writing; pilgrimage music in the Bolivian Highlands that is related to specific places; or the transformation of musical practices due to the alteration of cultural landscapes. The first three chapters reflect more extreme environments, similar to Feld's (2012) rainforest or the high Alpine Swiss environment. The final chapter calls for further attention to the interrelation between human music making and environment in general, which affects nearly all sociocultural stratospheres, including the so-called Western hemisphere. While these transformations might be more apparent in the case of folk or traditional contexts, they have also influenced art music spheres (cf. Allen 2011 for a broader discussion). Similar to the chapters in Part I, these case studies, too, invite further studies in the future.

Part III: The Politics of Intangible Cultural Heritage

As the 2003 UNESCO Convention for the Safeguarding of the Intangible Cultural Heritage pointed out in Article 12, each state that signed the declaration "shall draw up, in a manner geared to its own situation, one or more inventories of the intangible cultural heritage, present in its territory and monitor these" (UNESCO 2003). In the course of ten years, UNESCO established a growing number of officially acknowledged criteria in three categories (a) List of Intangible Cultural Heritage in Need of Urgent Safeguarding; (b) Representative List of Intangible Cultural Heritage of Humanity; and (c) Good Safeguarding Practices. As suggested earlier, the critical analysis of ICH lists began with Howard's (2012) publication on Intangible Cultural Heritage lists, and several ethnomusicologists have since been involved in their nominations and scientific committees (e.g. Salwa El-Shawan Castelo-Branco (Portugal/Fado), Ursula Hemetek (Austria), Sanubar Baghirova

(Azerbaijan)), although this has not always been the case. Ten years after the implementation of the UNESCO Convention, the 2013 ESEM meeting provided an ideal starting point for a retrospective look at UNESCO's preceding initiatives and campaigns. For instance, the UNESCO website in 2016 provides challenges for researchers: the website is rich with material, yet difficult to navigate. Documents are often hidden, and processes "behind" the lists are often difficult to access. Moreover, despite a search engine, it is often difficult to locate specific names and music genres, while the related film material on ICH traditions is extremely heterogeneous, ranging from ethnomusicological documentaries and uncommented film segments to advertising material. Part III of this book thus focuses on the process of creating the actual lists of TCH and ICH. This not only includes the cultural- and national-political contexts of the selection process, but also the role of archives, for instance, without which the creation of heritage lists would be even more difficult. As shown in the chapters included here, none of the lists has resulted from a "neutral" selection process, but have been shaped by the interests of various political, local, and other interest groups. This has not only led to conflicts early on in the selection process, but also has led to an imbalanced representation. This raises questions such as: What is actually selected? On which basis have the repertoires been chosen and categorized? What is excluded—and why? What is deemed representative? Who are the decision makers and, as is illustrated in the case of Switzerland, how does the exchange work between different interest groups (e.g. ethnomusicologists, locals, politics). As Chapter 12 by Ross illustrates, Switzerland is a particularly interesting case, as it raises critical questions about transnational cultures (such as the Jewish communities) in the mostly national-oriented selections. As becomes apparent, the UNESCO campaign, meant to protect local traditions, can also easily become a means of exclusion due to its national orientation.

Part IV: Intangible Cultural Heritage: Case Studies

The chapters in the final part re-assess some hitherto established UNESCO Intangible Cultural Heritage lists in order to highlight the sensitive nature and effects of various heritage representations. By analyzing selected case studies in more detail, Part IV thus extends the discussions in Part III about the selection process and its long-term impact, albeit with concrete examples. This section thereby casts a critical eye on existing lists and their impact, including *flamenco* and *verbuňk*, adding concrete case studies to the broader theoretical discourse (see also Boyu 2015; Schippers 2015; Titon 2015). What are the strategies to resolve these questions? To what extent have traditions been strengthened and protected due to their UNESCO status? What has happened to traditions that were excluded? How far have they become less visible, as in the case of the musical life of the UNESCO-protected Jemaa el Fnaa Square? How is the issue of diversity, which has been so strongly emphasized in the UNESCO declarations, reflected and realized? How might diversity be represented in future? How has the selection process affected musical canonization (and exclusion)? What is the role of ethnomusicology in the UNESCO Intangible Cultural Heritage program? Have the ICH lists indeed supported traditions with regard to sustainability, or have traditions been fixed, as feared in the case of Bern, as a museum-like object that blocks rather than supports development? A critical assessment of UNESCO'S ICH is still missing, including considerations of the marginalization of groups outside the official heritage lists, but that also need protecting. How far have communities articulated the need for altered approaches? Are they being heard or ignored? These questions invite critical reflection, both within ethnomusicology and beyond.

About the Editors

Britta Sweers is Professor of Cultural Anthropology of Music at the Institute of Musicology (since 2009) and Director of the Center for Global Studies (since 2015) at the University of Bern (Switzerland). She has been President of the European Seminar in Ethnomusicology (ESEM) since 2014. Major publications include *Electric Folk: The Changing Face of English Traditional Music* (2005), *Polyphonie der Kulturen* (CD/CD-ROM, 2006/8), *Grenzgänge–Gender, Race und Class als Wissenskategorien in der Musikwissenschaft* (ed.; with Cornelia Bartsch, 2015). She is co-editor of the *European Journal of Musicology* and of the Equinox book series Transcultural Music Studies.

Sarah M. Ross is Professor of Jewish Music Studies and Director of the European Center for Jewish Music at Hannover University of Music, Drama, and Media, Germany. She obtained her PhD in 2010 at the University of Music and Theatre, Rostock, Germany. She is the author of *A Season of Singing: Creating Feminist Jewish Music in the United States* (Brandeis University Press, 2016), co-editor of *Judaism and Emotion: Texts, Performance, Experience* (Peter Lang, 2013), and editor of the book series *Jewish Music*

Studies (Peter Lang). Her main fields of research are Jewish music, ethnomusicological gender studies, and music and sustainability.

References

Allen, Aaron S. 2011. "Ecomusicology: Ecocriticism and Musicology." *Journal of the American Musicological Society* 64(2): 391–94.
https://doi.org/10.1525/jams.2011.64.2.391

Boyu, Zhang. 2015. "Applied Ethnomusicology in China." In *The Oxford Handbook of Applied Ethnomusicology*, edited by Svanibor Pettan and Jeff Todd Titon, 735–71. New York and Oxford: Oxford University Press.
https://doi.org/10.1093/oxfordhb/9780199351701.013.24

Crawhall, Nigel. 2009. "The Role of Participatory Cultural Mapping in Promoting Intercultural Dialogue—'We are not Hyenas.'" Concept paper. Paris: UNESCO.
http://unesdoc.unesco.org/images/0019/001907/190753e.pdf (accessed 15 October 2018).

Dann, Graham M. S., and A. V. Seaton. 2001. "Slavery, Contested Heritage and Thanatourism." *International Journal of Hospitality & Tourism Administration* 2(3–4): 1–29. https://doi.org/10.1300/J149v02n03_01

Entente Bernoise. 2005. "Denkmalschutz: Die Stadt Bern auf dem Weg nach Ballenberg?!" http://ententebernoise.ch/recherchen/2005_03_Denkmalpflege.pdf (accessed 15 October 2018).

Feld, Steven. 2012. *Sounds and Sentiment: Birds, Weeping, Poetics, and Song in Kaluli Expression.* 3rd edn. Durham, NC and London: Duke University Press.
https://doi.org/10.1215/9780822395898https://doi.org/10.1215/9780822395898

Grant, Catherine, and Chhuon Sarin. 2016. "Gauging Music Viability: Three Cases from Cambodia." *Yearbook for Traditional Music* XLVIII: 25–47.
https://doi.org/10.5921/yeartradmusi.48.2016.0025

Howard, Keith, ed. 2012. *Music as Intangible Cultural Heritage: Policy, Ideology, and Practice in the Preservation of East Asian Tradition.* Farnham: Ashgate.

Schafer, Raymond Murray. 1977. *The Tuning of the World.* Toronto: McClelland and Steward.

Schippers, Huib. 2015. "Applied Ethnomusicology and Intangible Cultural Heritage." In *The Oxford Handbook of Applied Ethnomusicology*, edited by Svanibor Pettan and Jeff Todd Titon, 134–56. New York and Oxford: Oxford University Press.
https://doi.org/10.1093/oxfordhb/9780199351701.013.7

Serafimovska, Velika Stojkova, Dave Wilson, and Ivona Opetčeska Tatarčevska. 2016. "Safeguarding International Cultural Heritage in the Republic of Macedonia." *Yearbook for Traditional Music* XLVIII: 1–24.
https://doi.org/10.5921/yeartradmusi.48.2016.0001

Titon, Jeff Todd. 2015. "Sustainability, Resilience, and Adaptive Management." In *The Oxford Handbook of Applied Ethnomusicology*, edited by Svanibor Pettan and Jeff Todd Titon, 157–95. New York and Oxford: Oxford University Press. https://doi.org/10.1093/oxfordhb/9780199351701.013.8

UNESCO. 1968. "Final Report of the Meeting of Experts to Coordinate, with a View to their International Adoption, Principles and Scientific, Technical and Legal Criteria Applicable to the Protection of Cultural Property, Monuments and Sites." Paris, December 31, 1968. SCH/CS/27/8.

—2003. "Text of the Convention for the Safeguarding of the Intangible Cultural Heritage, Art. 2." http://www.unesco.org/culture/ich/en/convention#art2 (accessed 15 October 2018).

—n.d.a. "Tangible Cultural Heritage."
http://www.unesco.org/new/en/cairo/culture/tangible-cultural-heritage/ (accessed 15 October 2018).

—n.d.b. "Old City of Bern." http://whc.unesco.org/en/list/267 (accessed 15 October 2018).

Part I
The Method of Cultural Mapping

Introduction to Part I

Britta Sweers
University of Bern, Switzerland

Cultural mapping is regarded by UNESCO as one of the most central method-ological resources for safeguarding cultural diversity, as is similarly expressed on the UNESCO Bangkok website:

> *Cultural mapping* has been recognized by UNESCO as a cru-cial tool and technique in preserving the world's intangible and tangible cultural assets. It encompasses a wide range of tech-niques and activities from community-based participatory data collection and management to sophisticated mapping using *GIS* (*Geographic Information Systems*). (UNESCO n.d.)

Before addressing UNESCO's specific approach and ethnomusicological perspectives toward mapping, it is worth recollecting the main features of maps in general. Roughly defined as "a representation usually on a flat sur-face of the whole or a part of an area,"[1] maps are always symbolic abstrac-tions of reality, as is evident with topographic or geographical maps that have to represent the three-dimensional global surface in two dimensions. This abstraction is also apparent on other levels, as maps, while seemingly conveying authentic representations, need to minimize, reduce, or generalize complex systems and structures. At the same time, they need to be complete, precise, and understandable with regard to, for instance, symbols, colors, or aesthetics, which has constituted a challenge for cartographers until the pres-ent day (MacEachran 1994).

The term "cultural mapping" has been particularly used within the applied context of UNESCO-related projects (e.g. UNESCO 2009), but has subsequently also been adapted by other institutions, academic disciplines, and community projects. A central reference point is the keynote speech by Clark, Sutherland, and Young from a 1995 cultural mapping workshop in Australia (1995a). As is pointed out here, "The most fundamental goal of cultural mapping is to help communities to recognize, celebrate, and support cultural diversity for economic, social and regional development" (Clark, Sutherland, and Young 1995b: 2). Further specified by Crawhall and Rambaldi (2013: 31), "Cultural mapping is a way of defining what culture means to the community, identifying the elements of culture that add value (both social and economic), recording, preserving or building on these elements in new and creative ways." That the UNESCO concept goes beyond mere documentation is also evident in the following: "This mapping, together with an investigation performed following a wide conception of culture, produces a document including guidelines for a cultural plan, but also for a sustainable development of the examined context" (Clark, Sutherland, and Young 1995b).[2]

In contrast to conventional maps, cultural mapping not only comprises landscape features, but "also other cultural resources and information recorded by alternative technique," with musicological resources being explicitly mentioned here (Clark, Sutherland, and Young 1995b). Contrary to pure documentation, the intention of cultural mapping is clearly geared towards change, which indicates parallels to the approaches of applied ethnomusicology that emphasize the action and inclusion of the community (Pettan 2008). Cultural mapping could also include the simultaneous usage of multiple forms of documentation and maps:

> Mapping may be just one component of a broader inventory process, which could include other components such as genealogies, oral history, image archiving, research and documentation of specific cultural and environmental knowledge and practices. (Crawhall and Rambaldi 2013: 47)

As sociolinguist Crawhall points out in a UNESCO paper on "The role of participatory cultural mapping in promoting intercultural dialogue" (2009: 6), an equally significant document for this debate, cultural mapping is a "(re)presentation of landscapes from perspectives of indigenous and local people." The approach thus sets a strong emphasis on the inclusion of communities. Consequently, and due to the intention of reflecting multiple local perspectives rather than abstract ones, cultural mapping reveals highly subjective perspectives (cf. Duxbury, Garrett-Petts, and MacLennan 2015: 16).

Crawhall (2009: 10) elaborates further that "Mapping as such does not ensure in full understanding and/or consent of local and indigenous communities. What counts is the approach, the process, and good practice," with the aim of making the intangible tangible or the invisible visible, while also bridging communication and intergenerational knowledge (cf. Duxbury, Garrett-Petts, and MacLennan 2015; Porelli, Talone, and Tommarchi 2010). Assuming that, if applied widely, cultural mapping could help to reach UNESCO objectives, Crawhall indicates a broad range of approaches, including mental maps, personal concepts of vegetation, etc., yet also land issues. Supporting locals in being able to express their views can thus become central to the identification of intangible cultural heritage and related issues of its safeguarding, issues that also apply to ethnomusicological approaches.

Cultural mapping has become a particularly prominent feature in projects with an (urban) planning dimension (e.g. Pillai 2013) and many other applied projects across different disciplines. However, often described as a method or toolkit in many—especially online—handbooks that emerged since the mid-1990s (e.g. Rowe 2012), most approaches to cultural mapping remain relatively vague, rarely ever reflecting on the actual set of methods being used. As a form of symbolic representation, maps are shaped by processes of selection, generalization, and design. Furthermore, they are projections of political and cultural concepts, which have rarely been questioned. It is also striking that the lack of neutrality has rarely been discussed in a UNESCO-related context. As the chapters in this volume indicate, ethnomusicological discourse can make an important contribution to these debates.

Within the discipline of ethnomusicology, the tool of mapping played a particular role in comparative musicology. Roughly speaking, one can make out two perspectives: the first perspective, as Marcello Sorce Keller outlines in his historical overview (Chapter 1), represents the traditional approach of collecting and establishing cultural boundaries, which has been associated with the perspective by the early American anthropologist and cultural relativist Alfred Louis Kroeber (1876–1960) and which subsequently influenced early research. Yet while mapping became criticized due to its connection with the so-called *Kulturkreislehre*, it influenced comparative musicology from the 1920s and 1930s until the 1960s, which first depicted transregional and global maps of musical styles and instruments. Despite the popularity of the highly debated Cantometrics approach (1968) by Alan Lomax (1915–2002), mapping has only recently been taken up again, for instance in the context of Systematic Musicology, to express measured data in maps (e.g. Savage and Brown 2014). Sorce Keller's chapter provides a concise introduction to mapping concepts and approaches in ethnomusicology, thereby providing a deeper insight into critical issues and analyzing what actually constitutes a map. Sorce Keller comes to the conclusion that there is still a need for ethnomusicology to engage more deeply with the tool of mapping and its concepts, processes, and approaches, which remains strongly under-researched.

While mapping saw some growth in its use by and critical reflections in ethnomusicology (see, for instance, St. Patrick's College 2015), the discipline is, as Michelle Bigenho (2008: 24–32) mused, still occupied with mapping the world in the "old" style. Rejecting mapping in reference to Clifford Geertz's "we don't study places, but rather study in places" (Geertz 1973: 22), Bigenho questioned mapping approaches that lead to ideas of Andeanism, Orientalism, and regional perception, thereby pointing to the problem of mapping objectification. This criticism notwithstanding, new critical approaches have emerged, such as Riley and Hunter's *Mapping Landscapes for Performance as Research* (2009), emphasizing a mapping that combines geographies, institutions, histories, and practices; or Savage and Brown's "Cluster Analysis of Song-Type Frequencies" (2014), with their focus on visualizing patterns in music. Yet in tune with Bigenho (2008) and Savage and Brown (2014), it is important to point to the prevailing problem of the equation of "one" culture to "one" music culture.

A more positive perception emerged in the use of mapping in applied ethnomusicology, and most strongly related to UNESCO's Intangible Cultural Heritage program, and the issue of cultural mapping that might or could lead to a new comparative musicology, as was suggested by Savage and Brown (2013). While further reflection is needed here, Chapters 2–4 make some fruitful critical attempts to highlight aspects of cultural mapping in ethnomusicological research in general, including particular mapping approaches and processes. Svend Kjeldsen (Chapter 2) provides a practical example of mapping in an urban context with regard to musicians of Irish descent in Manchester, highlighting how mapping can reveal a so-called third space. Pekka Suutari (Chapter 3) points to the multi-layeredness of mapping by combining musical devices with linguistic aspects. This combination, in particular, allows for deeper insights into multi-ethnic contexts and identities, as in the case of Karelia, the border region between Russia and Finland. Suutari shows that associations of language are not only related to everyday life (e.g. with regard to vocabulary in peasant life), but also that modern fusion forms can provide new spaces in this context. Finally, Ana Hofman's chapter provides a case study of counter-mapping. Focusing on musical examples from former Yugoslavia, Hofman highlights how mapping can bring out issues that are easily overlooked in conflicted political situations, while asking about the alternative voices in the construction of modern nation-states.

Notes

1 Merriam Webster Dictionary, "Map." Available at http://www.merriam-webster.com/dictionary/map (accessed October 15, 2018).
2 As is pointed out further by Clark, Sutherland, and Young (1995b), "The mapping of indigenous cultural resources carried out by indigenous communities is a crucial step toward demonstrating that cultural diversity is a means to enrichment for society. As such, UNESCO will continue to support pilot projects at work in the field."

References

Bigenho, Michelle. 2008. "Why I'm Not an Ethnomusicologist." In *The New (Ethno) musicologies*, edited by Henry Stobart, 28–39. Lanham, MD: Scarecrow.
Clark, Ian, Johanna Sutherland, and Greg Young. 1995a. Keynote speech, Cultural Mapping Symposium and Workshop, Australia.
—1995b. "Mapping of Indigenous Cultural Resources." In *Mapping Culture—A Guide for Cultural and Economic Development in Community.* Canberra: Commonwealth Department of Communications and the Arts. http://www.unesco.org/new/en/culture/themes/culture-and-development/unesco-and-indigenous-peoples-partnership-for-cultural-diversity/cultural-mapping/ (accessed October 15, 2018).
Crawhall, Nigel. 2009. "The Role of Participatory Cultural Mapping in Promoting Intercultural Dialogue—'We are not Hyenas.'" Concept paper. Paris: UNESCO. http://unesdoc.unesco.org/images/0019/001907/190753e.pdf (accessed October 15, 2018).
Crawhall, Nigel, and Giacomo Rambaldi. 2013. "What is Cultural Mapping." In *A Contemporary Guide to Cultural Mapping: An ASEAN-Australian Perspective*, edited by Ian Cook and Ken Taylor, 29–54. Jakarta: ASEAN.
Duxbury, Nancy, Will F. Garrett-Petts, and David MacLennan. 2015. *Cultural Mapping as Cultural Enquiry.* New York: Routledge. https://doi.org/10.4324/9781315743066
Geertz, Clifford. 1973. *The Interpretation of Cultures.* New York: Basic Books.

Lomax, Alan. 1968. *Folksong Song Style and Culture*. Washington DC: American Association for the Advancement of Science.

MacEachran, Alan. 1994. *Some Truth with Maps: A Primer on Symbolization and Design*. Washington, DC: Association of American Geographers.

Pettan, Svanibor. 2008. "Applied Ethnomusicology and Empowerment Strategies: Views from across the Atlantic." *Musicological Annual* 44(1): 85–100. https://doi.org/10.4312/mz.44.1.85-99

Pillai, Janet. 2013. *Cultural Mapping: A Guide to Understanding Place, Community, and Continuity*. Malaysia: Strategic Information and Research Development Center.

Porelli, Antonio, Antonio Talone, and Enrico Tommarchi. 2010. "Cultural Mapping: Sustainability and Interoperability for Local Development." (October 15, 2010). *ESA Research Network Sociology of Culture Midterm Conference: Culture and the Making of Worlds*. https://doi.org/10.2139/ssrn.1692722.

Riley, Shannon Rose, and Lynette Hunter, eds. 2009. *Mapping Landscapes for Performance as Research: Scholarly Acts and Creators*. Basingstoke and New York: Palgrave Macmillan.

Rowe, Johanna. 2012. *What's Your Story? Cultural Mapping—Best Practices Manual for Rediscovering Small Town Canada*. N.p.: Wawa Cultural Mapping Project. http://www.creativecity.ca/database/files/library/Cultural_Mapping_Best_Practices_Manual_May_2012.pdf (accessed October 15, 2018).

Savage, Patrick E., and Steven Brown. 2013. "Toward a New Comparative Musicology." *Analytical Approaches to World Music* 2(2): 148–97.

—2014. "Mapping Music: Cluster Analysis of Song-Type Frequencies within and between Cultures." *Ethnomusicology* 58(1): 133–35. https://doi.org/10.5406/ethnomusicology.58.1.0133

St. Patrick's College, Dublin. 2015. *Mapping Popular Music in Dublin*. https://mappingpopularmusicindublin.wordpress.com/ (accessed October 15, 2018).

UNESCO. 2009. "Building Critical Awareness of Cultural Mapping: A Workshop Facilitation Guide." http://unesdoc.unesco.org/images/0019/001903/190314e.pdf (accessed October 15, 2018).

—n.d. "Cultural Mapping." *UNESCO Bangkok: Tools for Safeguarding Culture*. https://bangkok.unesco.org/content/cultural-mapping (accessed June 7, 2019).

Chapter 1

Kulturkreise, Culture Areas, and Chronotopes: Old Concepts Reconsidered for the Mapping of Music Cultures Today

Marcello Sorce Keller

> Terms are like horses on the old post roads of Europe and America.
> When one animal gets tired, you should give it a rest and mount
> a fresh steed, which itself can only go so far. (Slobin 2007: 109)

The word "mapping" rarely appeared in music studies, not even back in the days of comparative musicology, when it was, however, quite frequently implied. Comparative musicologists such as Erich Moritz von Hornbostel (1877–1935) were, in fact, keenly aware of cultural diversity. And whenever diversity is recognized, the next step is, automatically, to imagine its location in both space and time. That is not at all to say that ethnomusicology today is less aware of cultural diversity than comparative musicology was. One difference is, however, that the latter had the ambition (among others) to compare every musical style or practice with every other; whereas when ethnomusicology took over, the order of priorities dramatically changed. For one thing, ethnomusicologists realized the necessity for specialization and for getting into participant observation (which appropriately gives priority to context but, by its very nature, is only feasible in small and circumscribed environments). Moreover, cultural relativism as professed by the Boas School (Margaret Mead (1901–1978), Ruth Benedict (1887–1948), and their associate Gregory Bateson (1904–1980) was at times interpreted as saying that cultures are so intrinsically different as to make comparison futile. Victor Grauer has a point when he observes that in ethnomusicology:

> One is expected to study the manner in which various aspects of culture function within a narrowly defined social context ... [and] one cannot, and in fact must not, compare a certain practice in one place with what might look or sound like something similar in another place because that would entail the removal of both practices from their "context." (Grauer 2011: xvi–xvii)

And yet similarities exist, diversities exist as well, and in perceiving how they mix, inevitably, in some way or another, we are actually mapping them— although not necessarily on paper, with colored areas or graphs.

One of the merits of the theme chosen for the 2013 Conference of the European Seminar in Ethnomusicology is that it makes very clear how the evaluation of musical diversity goes hand in hand with some form of "mapping," that is, of conceptual representation. It was a very timely theme, because we are right now, at the beginning of the twenty-first century, confronted with musical phenomena that exert global impact, and make it more difficult than ever to identify or trace borderlines. So it is more challenging than ever—if we wish to develop some comprehensive idea of what the social use of sound is like on a global scale—to develop new and more sophisticated forms of mapping. That is why I thought I would, as a starting point, share some general considerations about concepts, ideas, and categories used for musical mapping throughout the history of our field. Some of them still have, in my view, potential. In other words, they could be advantageously refined and updated.

Fishing Nets

I believe it is quite useful to re-visit concepts that the social sciences used in the past, even those that were at some point dropped or forgotten when their limitations became apparent. Re-visiting them is useful because old concepts can often be rejuvenated and may even turn out to be apt to describe situations that did not exist at the time of their making. We are in a way condemned to constantly refine our conceptual tools, as well as come up with new ones, because the world out there is not only more complex than we imagine but, probably, even more complex than we may possibly imagine. No single concept, category, or mental construct is likely ever to fully describe and comprehend any single aspect of reality. And yet, inadequate as all concepts and mental categories are bound to be, they are far from useless—as long as we are aware they can only bring us so far. Inadequate as they are in a general sense, they all highlight some aspects of reality that otherwise might escape our attention. In other words, concepts and categories developed as tools for gaining knowledge are in a way like fishing nets: a fisherman chooses which one to use, depending on the kind of fish he is after. Whenever a net is needed to catch tuna, it helps remember that the lighter ones, useless for the purpose, may come in handy the day we wish to catch sardines; so let us not throw them away. When cultural practices are the object of our interest, like music for instance, a variety of "fishing nets" can be used, including some of those that in the course of time may have been discarded while—to be sure—new ones constantly need to be developed at the same time.

The Subjective Art of Mapping

It was about 150 AD when Claudius Ptolemy (ca. 100–160 AD) published his famous world-map, in a book titled *Geography*, containing the mathematics needed to represent a three-dimensional earth on a two-dimensional surface. It has remained to this day one of the most famous ancient texts on the science of map-making. A recent publication by historian Brotton (2012) well underscores how Ptolemy, like mapmakers before and after him, operated in environments of subjective knowledge, and were influenced by politics, religion, and ideologies. All such ideas and beliefs inevitably interacted with their science, and helped shape what their maps would look like and could be used for. In other words, mapmakers are scientists, artists, and storytellers all at once. They may even be to some extent propaganda writers—whether they realize it or not. Maps are ultimately the product of both science and value systems, and reveal much about the intellectual horizon of their makers.[1]

Maps are especially revealing of their makers, when they concern cultures. Identifying the meaningful aspects of culture, those deserving to be singled out (over others that may be less distinctive), is in fact problematic— it entails judgment, and it is with judgment that our biases enter the stage. It helps that anthropology and ethnomusicology take into consideration the objective nature (up to a degree) of political borders. Unfortunately, the influence of political borders on cultural practices cannot easily be represented by colored areas on a map and, if we try to make that influence visible, we almost always discern a center, a periphery, and many fuzzy areas.[2] Difficult to do as that is, there have been numerous attempts to map musical traditions in their relation to physical space—to geography (Lomax 1968; Collaer and

Linden 1968). All of them are quite intriguing, not only as historical documents, but also because one could say of them all what Mark Twain once wrote at the end of one of his stories: "Now, then, that is the tale. Some of it is true" (Gooden 2002: 44).

The Geography of Culture

Napoleon once stated that "the politics of nations originates in their geography"—a variant, if you will, of the much older theory of climates (in so far as geography is, at least in part, also a result of climate).[3] Throughout the nineteenth century this idea was very seriously considered, well beyond the realm of politics. Best known of all in this respect is Friedrich Ratzel (1844–1904), one of the initiators of "cultural diffusionism." His book, *Anthropogeographie: Die geographische Verbreitung des Menschen* ["Anthropogeography: The Geographic Distribution of the Human"], was at the time of its publication a remarkable achievement (Ratzel 1902). In France, almost at the same time, the school of *géographie humaine* was developed by Paul Vidal de la Blache (1845–1918) and Jean Brunhes (1869–1930), who also tried to connect physical geography to cultural patterns. Ratzel, de la Blache, and Brunhes were the founders of what later came to be known as "cultural geography" (Brunhes 1910; de la Blache 1922).

Somewhat later still, in 1932, Georges Reynard De Gironcourt (1878–1960) published a little book, intriguingly titled *Une science nouvelle: la géographie musicale* (De Gironcourt 1932). He was no musician or musicologist, but only a well-traveled agronomist, whose work consisted in investigating prospective developments of agriculture in the French, English, and German colonies.[4] Notably, he paid attention to the unfamiliar sounds that reached his ears during his adventurous trips, and deemed it worthwhile to describe them. De Gironcourt, however, a complete outsider to musical scholarship, was totally unaware of comparative musicology and his book failed to attract scholarly attention and become the beginning of something. More or less at the same time, students of musical folklore and comparative musicology, even though they never explicitly spoke of "musical geography," did however take into consideration relationships between musical styles and practices on the one hand, and the "territory" or "landscape" in which they take place, on the other. They all developed concepts suitable to describe what, at the time, were perceived to be the more significant aspects of such relationships.

Kulturhistorische Schule

The approach of the *Kulturhistorische Schule* ("Cultural-Historical School [of Thought]"), or geographical-historical method, developed by Fritz Graebner (1877–1934), Wilhelm Schmidt (1868–1954), and Bernard Ankermann (1859–1943), appeared in its full formulation in Fritz Graebner's *Methode der Ethnologie* (Graebner 1911). It is only seldom remembered by anthropologists today, although its historical importance is undeniable; if nothing else, because scholars such as Werner Dankert (1900–1970), Walter Wiora (1906–1997), Marius Schneider (1903–1982), and Curt Sachs (1881–1959) were all strongly influenced by it (Schneider 1976). Herbert Hübner (1903–1989) who was associated to the *Schule*, even made an attempt at classifying vocal styles that in some way anticipates what Alan Lomax did some twenty years later (Hübner 1938).[5] The main contention of the School is that the territorial distribution of cultural traits reveals not just former contacts among distant regions but, actually, veritable layers of culture history or, in its terminology, *Kulturkreise*. In other words, what the geographical-historical method calls a *Kulturkreis* is a geographical entity (whose component parts are not necessarily contiguous), characterized by a cluster of traits representing distinctive forms of culture—where such clusters of traits make up a layer of historical significance. Here we are talking about "layers," pretty much like geologists do. The *Kulturkreislehre* was formulated at a time when cultural evolutionism was generally accepted. From that standpoint, a view of culture made up of layers representing evolutionary stages appeared both significant and convincing. For instance, the *Kulturhistorische Schule* considered Alphorn signals, cattle calls, and yodel singing not only as characteristic of the alpine area but, further, as an archaic layer in the history of music, still remaining visible here and there (like in the Balkans and parts of Central Africa).[6]

At any rate, there is no question that the *Kulturhistorische Schule* has to be credited for making a courageous attempt to link ethnography with geography and history. It was an attempt that, to my knowledge, was never proven fundamentally wrong. It was tacitly abandoned after World War II, when scholars grew specialized to such a degree as to make large-scale comparisons difficult to achieve. In my view, the concept of *Kulturkreis* remains potentially useful, because even when stripped of its evolutionary underpinnings, one has to admit that cultural layers nonetheless exist: human groups and societies are stratified in all sorts of ways; and furthermore, layers belonging to one given group are often shared by other groups, which appear not to have been in contact with the first one. It also has to be granted that the

Kulturhistorische Schule was far from naïve or simplistic. It was quite aware that a variety of *Kulturkreise* may co-exist in the same region. However—nobody is ever perfect—Graebner, Schmidt, and Ankermann did not consider the possibility that *Kulturkreise* might interact with one another, and were not especially informed on contemporary linguistics. For instance, they appear not to have been aware of the "theory of background" by Graziadio Isaia Ascoli (1829–1907). Thanks to Ascoli, it is today largely accepted that whenever a language is replaced by another language,[7] the ghost of the one that disappeared remains somewhat active in the background and influences phonology and syntax of the newcomer language. It would seem plausible to extend this idea to the musical domain. Whenever a musical style is imported and becomes dominant in a given area, in the process of adapting to local needs and customs, quite possibly it can be influenced by "habits" belonging to previous styles or repertoires that are now extinct or pushed to the margins of social awareness.[8] The *Kulturhistorische Schule* also did not consider what help might have come from Matteo Giulio Bartoli (1873–1946) and his "spatial linguistics," which consisted in establishing relationships among languages, not just on the basis of their morphology and grammar but, also, of the cultural attitudes they express (Bartoli 1946).[9] All that escaped the attention of the *Kulturhistorische Schule*[10] could well be used today to improve upon its (only partly outdated) conceptual tools.

Culture Areas

Before World War II, at a time when fieldwork was beginning to characterize anthropology, Franz Boas (1858–1942), Alfred Louis Kroeber (1876–1960), and Clark Wissler (1870–1947) developed the "culture area" concept. A culture area, building upon the definition of culture given by E. B. Tylor (1958), was defined at the time as a "geographically circumscribed group of people (a defined population)[11] who at a particular time share a body of knowledge, beliefs, and attitudes toward each other and the world."[12]

The concept of "culture area" appears at first sight simpler and more straightforward than that of *Kulturkreis*. And yet on a closer examination it is no less problematic, because it is always difficult to choose the culture unit. Scale, in fact, has been a constant problem in anthropology; once we change the scale of observation, what first appeared to be a well-defined entity, may become blurred and maybe even a marginal sub-set of a larger entity. Yet the concept of "culture area" has been extremely important to anthropology (and ethnomusicology): arguably as important as that of historical "period" to music history ("periods" suffer just as much from the "scale problem," a temporal scale in this case).

Music historians also deserve to be mentioned. Because they need to deal with geography as well as with the time dimension, they often came quite close to what Mikhail Bakhtin (1895–1975) called "chronotope" (Bakhtin 1981);[13] and anthropologists came quite close to it as well, as I will indicate in the following paragraph.

The concept of "chronotope" is an intriguing one, referring to the space-time matrix providing base conditions for narratives and language of a certain kind.[14] According to Bakthin, specific chronotopes correspond to particular genres, representing worldviews and ideologies. Mikhail Bakhtin and his followers knew little about music history, and presumably nothing about the *Kulturhistorische Schule*, as well as of Anglo-American anthropology where "culture areas" were often paired with so-called "age areas"—for instance, by Clark Wissler (Kroeber 1931). Had Bakhtin and his followers been familiar with anthropology, they would have realized that the chronotope concept was not quite as new as they thought it was, and could be refined on the basis of musical knowledge. Bakhtin was of course primarily concerned with literary genres. Genres are equally crucial to musicking as well. Musical "genres" are remarkably more numerous than literary genres, less culture-specific, and more ephemeral. How people experience in their consciousness the *longue durée* of literary genres and, at the same time, the *brève durée* of musical genres is quite intriguing, since in both domains, genres carry ideological connotations (that usually have a long life span).[15] It is a fact of our time that much knowledge has been accumulated in fields of intellectual endeavor that are not conversant to each other, and existing knowledge is more and more often ignored in good faith.[16] So we often do not know things that, in principle, are knowable because the knowledge that would explain them is available elsewhere. But that is, of course, another story. Going back to areas and periods, it is worth observing how just like historical periods give us the impression that Western music can be captured in a single chronological narrative, so the "culture area" concept gives the over-simplistic impression that culture traits may be neatly distributed on a map, and color-coded for convenience—thus under-emphasizing local differences within the chosen unit. In fact, that is pretty much what George P. Murdock (1897–1985) did when he examined and classified 565 different cultures, on the basis of thirty specific traits, and put them together in a grand scheme (Murdock 1967, 1969).

"Culture areas," moreover, as well as "historical periods," are discrete conceptual entities; and what lies in the center tends to be considered more typical, and deserving more attention, than what lies at the margins (one possible reason why "pre-classical" composers such as Giovanni Battista Sammartini or C. P. E. Bach attracted less interest than Haydn; one reason why the Kalulis singing their traditional songs in the rainforest of New Guinea appear to us more anthropologically significant than other Papua New Guinea people who live in Port Moresby, watch television and learn to play country music). In other words, once we have a "period" automatically we have its forerunners and its later imitators; once we locate an "area," automatically we have "central" and "pure" examples representing it, as well as "marginal" and "hybrid" examples, which—supposedly—less well represent the area, and so tend to be overlooked. It would probably be possible to produce an improved, more dynamic, definition of *Kulturkreis* as well as of "culture area": For instance, by using a model derived from Vittore Pisani (1899–1990) who effectively described Indo-European languages as "lakes" of a sort, whose basin is alimented by linguistic rivers bringing them waters of different color and mineral make-up—the mix of waters they may contain at point in time X can be almost completely replaced by another mix, once point in time 2X is arrived at (Pisani 1940)—and all intermediate stages of the process deserve equal attention.

Lomax and Beyond

More or less at the time Bakhtin introduced the term *chronotope*, Alan Lomax (1915–2002) was the author of the most ambitious effort—so far—in making cross-cultural comparisons of musical style and behavior (Lomax 1968). In a way not very different from Murdock's, and certainly inspired by his work, Lomax tried to correlate musical profiles of 233 musical cultures with some of their social and cultural traits (Lomax 1968).[17] His study of territorial distribution of musical practices, in relation to fundamental cultural attitudes concerning social interaction, still remains controversial. Such controversy is however immaterial for the purpose of this chapter. It is on the contrary relevant to recall one perceptive observation Lomax made, in a way, on the margin: that the "sound" factor appeared to him to be the most stable and lasting aspect of musical cultures; in other words, singing style changes more slowly than the content of songs, both musical and textual. Intuitively that seems to be the case in many cultures known to this writer and, quite probably, worthy of empirical verification. Lomax also observed that forms of vocal production (blend, vibrato, etc.) appear to exist independently from the geographic distribution of other elements of style (melody, rhythm, form, etc.). That is another observation which, if systematically verified, would appear quite relevant for future assessments of the geographic distribution of style characteristics.

Lomax's *Cantometrics*, like Murdock's *Atlas*, today engender misgivings for the conviction they express that large and identifiable culture areas exist across our planet. This notion that culture is linked to particular territories or places was later strongly challenged, at least since the early 1990s, by a growing interest in the mobility of cultural forms. It was James Clifford who first blew the whistle and suggested the geographic distribution of cultures is more complex than hitherto imagined and, furthermore, it considerably changes in the course of time (Clifford 1992). Indeed, that is the case. Today we inhabit a world where the Japanese go and study Buddhism in the United States, where branches of Sufi mysticism are born in Europe or America and remain there (Westerlund 2004), where South Korea produces the largest proportion of Christian missionaries and where Mormonism, only a small Church in the US, enjoys a huge following in Africa. And, as far as music is concerned, today we come across Turkish music in Frankfurt or in Melbourne, Indo-Pakistani Bhangra in London, Yodel choirs in New Zealand, as well as Alphorn players in Japan. Not only immigrants bring along their own music, but often music travels on its own, quite independently from the people who originally made it, and it develops in unexpected ways in the new territories it reaches, in the hands of people who learn it, in a way similar to how they learn a foreign language.[18] With so many traditions exported and transplanted, the sonic profile of the planet undergoes constant change, and it is today more problematic than ever to speak of music only in terms of "roots" and "native soil." Indeed musical areas (like historical "periods") do not tell us the entire story. There are territories, no doubt, that remain culturally and musically insular—probably as a result of some effort to remain so. In such ever-changing panorama, insularity or, as some prefer, "islandness" may be possibly described as the ability to ignore and defy communication possibilities that are so easily available.

Of Soundscapes and Soundgroups

Back in the 1970s Raymond Murray Schafer gave us a wonderful new word: "Soundscape" (Schafer 1977). With his copious writings he made us all aware of how important it is to understand the relationship between man and the sound environment. Schafer also pointed out how the relationship between natural sounds and human sounds has changed in the course of human history, and how the ever-mutable soundscape impacts music practice itself. There is music that needs to stand out from the background soundscape in order to make itself noticeable (no wonder so much of it today is so very loud in Western culture); and there is music which, on the contrary, wishes to blend into the pre-existing sonic cloud. A soundscape-oriented mapping of the world would certainly not suffice to make sense of the multiverse of sound-clouds we cross in our daily life (layered like veritable *Kulturkreise* and, at the same time, juxtaposed like "culture areas," and often overlapping each other). It would not suffice, but it surely would help us better understand where, when, how, and why the sound-clouds we inhabit can be functional or dysfunctional to our well-being or to the activities we wish to pursue. The new field of "ecomusicology" is very promising in that respect.

In the late 1980s, realizing how many musical processes spread across geographical and national borders, and how today we no longer have societies tidily related to specific musics, as one reads in textbooks, John Blacking first and Tullia Magrini later, suggested the concept of "sound group" (Blacking 1995: 232; Magrini 2003: 29–30). A sound group is essentially an affinity group, made up of people who are often not in touch with each other but, intriguingly—scattered as they may be across the planet—independently choose (sometimes literally fall in love with) the same musical genre, whether they are old and young, rich and poor, country people or city people.[19] Sound groups, therefore, may easily be transnational entities of people, unaware of each other, who like the same music because they identify with the values connected to it (or which they suppose are connected to it—right or wrong that they may be).[20] In other words, contrary to generational groups, sound groups are open and the choice to belong to one or another usually is a powerful statement for self-representation.

C-Maps

Concept Maps (or C-Maps) are diagrams highlighting relationships between concepts—a graphical tool helping to organize and structure knowledge. They typically represent ideas and information as boxes or circles, connected by labeled arrows in a downward-branching hierarchical structure. Their use and impact have increased considerably over the past several years: from educational contexts, to business, science and technology, medicine, and so on. C-Maps are quite effective in organizing forms of knowledge that are intertwined. One can easily imagine them summarizing forms of musical practice, knowledge, taste, as well as their distribution in space. I see them as a useful tool to highlight how *Kulturkreise* and culture areas may relate to one another.

Conclusions

All such concepts I have been recalling, old and new, possess potential. *Kulturkreis*, too often interpreted more narrowly than originally intended, reminds us that traditions are more frequently layered than simply juxtaposed, and that culture traits that appear typical in one area are frequently found elsewhere too. The "culture area" concept reminds us that cultural traits (very much like religions) tend to cluster in some areas more than in others. Difficult as such areas may be to identify, they usually have a center and it is mostly their periphery that is fuzzy and problematic. If used in conjunction with recent knowledge about migrant and transplanted traditions, with ever-changing soundscapes, the coming and going of sound groups, even old concepts such as *Kulturkreis* and "culture area" still appear useful. To be sure, none of them can comprehensively describe musical cultures in relationship to their space-time dimensions, and that is where there is room for improvement as well as for new conceptualizations. Fishing nets often need to be repaired, or be used more skillfully—sometimes they just need to be replaced by better ones. In other words, while it is undeniable that ever new metaphors are needed to explain reality, still it pays to remember —for instance—that back in the seventeenth century the universe was seen as a "great watch," designed, wound, and set by a divine watchmaker; that during the industrial revolution the "steam engine" became the favorite metaphor for anything perceived to be moving; and later still, under Darwin's influence, the universe became an "evolving organism." Today the computer metaphor of the World Wide Web is invoked to explain things as diverse as consciousness and DNA. All such metaphors bring us to a point where another one has to take over.

It seems important to stress how, whatever concept, metaphor or model we wish to use, they all become more powerful when in conjunction, and supplemented with, information that was not available at the time they were in fashion. For instance, in conjunction with information about what motivates cultural choices, while others equally possible are rejected. Cultures are distinctive not so much because they may use the "*sitar*" rather than the "*koto*" or the "mandolin": that is only the surface of things. Important as such choices are, more important is how they are arrived at, and that is where we know the least.[21] In other words, cultures essentially differ in how they make their own choices, and handle change. So the fundamental question to ask is: how much is this or that culture changing? How fast? And how does change affect its geographic reach?[22] The in-depth study of local cases is fundamental, and its importance cannot be overemphasized. I like to think that much of it that is available will not remain local knowledge, and will be used for meta-analysis leading to ever-new forms of mapping the planet. Just as we wish to know in what world we live in, in terms of geography, climate, social environments, etc., we also wish and need to have updated views and understanding of the sonic make-up of this planet we inhabit. I am actually surprised that, with the astonishing development of tourism during the twentieth century, no "Musical Guide to Planet Earth" was ever published so far! Such a guide would probably have to be updated on a yearly basis, as we know today that some traditions are very territorial, others less so, and others still are easily deterritorialized. I see many good reasons why the musical mapping of the world could become one of the priorities for contemporary scholarship.

About the Author

Marcello Sorce Keller, originally a pop music arranger who later repented and became a music scholar, is the author of *What Makes Music European* (Scarecrow, 2012) and, with Linda Barwick, of *Italy in Australia's Musical Landscapes* (Lyrebird, 2012). Sorce Keller graduated in composition and social sciences in Milan. He later obtained a PhD in musicology at the University of Illinois, Urbana-Champaign, and taught in conservatories and universities in Switzerland, Italy, the USA, Australia, and Malta. Now retired, he spends much of his time playing and composing frivolous music.

Notes

1   Even contemporary satellite images are not bias-free and do not yield an entirely objective view of the world. Google Earth and other digital mapping applications necessarily express national priorities and cultural norms.

2   While working on a map showing the counties of England, mathematician Francis Guthrie, in 1852, postulated that four colors would be sufficient, so that in any map no two regions sharing a common border were the same color. Only in 1976 Kenneth Appel and Wolfgang Haacken, at the University of Illinois, proved this is actually the case.

3   Since the time of Hippocrates, many writers attributed the differences among people to environmental conditions. A most influential advocate of climatic theories was Georges-Louis Leclerc, Comte de Buffon (1707–1788), who published his landmark multi-volume study of natural history in the mid-eighteenth century. Also in the eighteenth century Montesquieu, in considering all the social and cultural differences in the world, tried to account for them in terms of climate, topography, or race.

4   On De Gironcourt's expeditions and earlier career, see De Gironcourt et al. 1920.

5   It is worth noticing that whereas many classificatory systems have been developed in the course of time for musical instruments (the Sachs-Hornbostel is one out of many), very few attempts have been made to classify vocal styles and modes of vocal production, and none of them has gained widespread acceptance. The result is that we do not have a rigorous terminology allowing us to compare voices. That is nearly impossible to do at an inter-cultural level (for instance, comparing the voice of a Javanese Gamelan singer with that of someone singing Japanese Noh), as well as within single cultures: music critics just use adjectives when describing the singing of Maria Callas in contrast to that of Renata Tebaldi, or that of Willie Nelson in contrast to that of Kenny Rogers.

6   The *Kulturhistorische Schule* also believed in monogenesis and diffusion. Today, although archaeologists usually rely on monogenetic assumptions, anthropology and ethnomusicology feel more comfortable with the idea that monogenesis and polygenesis combine.

7   Such as, for instance, when Spanish replaced many native languages in South America after the arrival of Columbus; when Middle English replaced Anglo-Saxon after the Norman invasion of 1066; when English replaced Gaelic in the larger part of Ireland after eight centuries of British presence.

8   A whole society can sometimes entirely substitute one musical system for another, of which the wholesale adoption of Western music by most of the population of South Korea is a good example.

9   Here we are only a few steps away from what, later in the twentieth century, came to be called "sociolinguistic."

10 Just like Anglo-American scholars today seldom read contributions not written in English or translated into English, German-speaking scholars of a century ago seldom read much that was not written in German.

11 A "defined" population, or group, is a population that is somewhat geographically self-contained—an island is an extreme example—and where people do not generally go outside of their area, except for very short periods of time. Other factors, besides geographical isolation, may contribute in keeping a population self-contained, for instance intermarriage and/or a strong sense of ethnic identity.

12 Edward Burnett Tylor's classic definition of "culture" was "the sum of the lived experience and stored knowledge of a discrete population that differs from neighboring groups" (Tylor 1958: 6).

13 For instance, Gerhard Nestler (1962) who wrote a history of music focusing on places where at particular times more musically significant events happened than elsewhere, and William Weber (1975).

14 The term is concocted out of ancient Greek: *chronos* (Χρόνος) for "time" and *topos* (τόπος) for "place" and "location."

15 Here I am speaking about definable genres such as "ballad," "lyric song," Sardinian "tenores," Icelandic "tvisongur," and not of ideologically invented genres, to be ranked along the low-brow–high-brow continuum ("classical music," "folk music," "popular music," etc.). How "universal" literary genres are (stories, biographies, epics, essays, etc.), appears quite clearly—although that is not the point Northrup Fry directly addresses (Fry 1957).

16 Historians of science Robert Proctor and Londa Schiebinger intriguingly suggest that not all-existing knowledge is always ignored in good faith. Much of it is screened out by our ideological mental prejudices. In fact, they call the study of why we do not know, or no longer know, or pretend not to know, or forget we know something, "Agnotology," and make the point that part of our ignorance is culturally produced (Proctor and Schiebinger 2008).

17 Lomax argued that different technological systems represented by the cultures of the world correlate well with their systems of music and dance. Interestingly, in his *Cantometrics* project, based on sound recordings rather than transcriptions, which is an important distinction between his approach and the techniques most other analysts employed, musical style is described according to thirty-seven parameters (pertaining to melodic shape, range, ornamentation, accentuation, vocal blend, the nasality of the singing, the ratio of words to music, the use of rubato, etc.). The overall conclusion is that "song style symbolizes and reinforces certain important aspects of social structure in all cultures" (Lomax 1968: vii). On the basis of the sampling he did, Lomax came to the conclusion that, as far as Europe goes, broad areas exist: Mediterranean Europe, Central and Eastern Europe (the so-called shatter belt), and Northern and Oceanic Europe.

18 One example of huge planetary impact is that of jazz, of how—throughout the world—people who have no Afro-American background took it over and made it their music.

19 Let us consider how many fans of Elvis there are across the globe, from Jogjakarta to Cuba or Sweden, etc., or how many people today, across the planet, learn to play djembe or didgeridoo.

20 Here I am thinking of the almost exclusively political interpretation of jazz made in Europe during the 1960s and 1970s, which was only seldom shared by jazz musicians in the USA.

21 For instance, in studying how, where, and how much "classical music" can be accessed, it is significant to consider that many people who profess a fondness for it are really more attracted by its image, staking a snobbish claim to what is perceived as an elite activity. Adorno (1962: 21–32) labeled such people *Kulturkonsumenten* ("culture consumers").

22 Economists understand the question better than most. They speak, for instance, of "inflation," which is a form of change; but they also consider the "rate of inflation," meaning how fast change is changing. In mathematics that would be the "second derivative." This is a conceptual tool we have not yet learned to use in music studies. So we are unable to produce forms of mapping that describe cultural dynamics.

References

Adorno, Theodor W. 1962. *Einleitung in die Musiksoziologie.* Frankfurt am Main: Suhrkamp.

Bakhtin, Mikhail M. 1981. "Forms of Time and of the Chronotope in the Novel." In *The Dialogic Imagination: Four Essays*, edited by Michael Holquist, 84–258. Austin: University of Texas Press.

Bartoli, Matteo Guido. 1946. *Saggi di linguistica spaziale.* Torino: Rosenberg & Sellier.

Blacking, John. 1995. *Music, Culture and Experience: Selected Papers of John Blacking*, edited by Reginald Byron. Chicago and London: University of Chicago Press.

Brotton, Jerry. 2012. *A History of the World in Twelve Maps.* London: Allen Lane.

Brunhes, Jean. 1910. *La géographie humaine. Essai de classification positive. Principes et exemples.* Paris: Alcan.

Clifford, James. 1992. "Traveling Cultures." In *Cultural Studies*, edited by Laurence Grossberg, Cary Nelson, and Paula Treichler, 96–117. New York: Routledge.

Collaer, Paul, and Albert Vander Linden. 1968. *Historical Atlas of Music: A Comprehensive Study of the World's Music—Past and Present.* London: Harrap.

de la Blache, Paul Vidal. 1922. *Principes de la géographie humaine. Publiés d'après les manuscrits de l'auteur par Emmanuel de Martonne.* Paris: Librairie Armand Colin.

De Gironcourt, Georges Reynard. 1932. *Une science nouvelle: la géographie musicale.* Nancy: André.

De Gironcourt, Georges R., et al. 1920. *Missions de Gironcourt en Afrique occidentale, 1908–1909, 1911–1912*. Documents scientifiques. Paris: Société de Géographie.

Fry, Northrop. 1957. *Anatomy of Criticism*. Princeton: Princeton University Press.

Gooden, Philip, ed. 2002. *The Mammoth Book of Literary Anecdotes: Over Five Centuries of Recollections, Essays and Quotes*. London: Robinson.

Graebner, Fritz. 1911. *Methode der Ethnologie*. Heidelberg: Winter.

Grauer, Victor. 2011. *Sounding the Depths: Tradition and the Voices of History*. Self-published via CreateSpace.

Hübner, Herbert. 1938. *Die Musik im Bismark-Archipel. Studien zur Kulturkreislehre und Rassenforschung*. Berlin: Bernhard Hahnenfeld.

Kroeber, Alfred Louis. 1931. "The Culture-Area and Age-Area Concepts of Clark Wissler." In *Methods in Social Science: A Case Book*, edited by Stuart A. Rice, 248–65. Chicago: University of Chicago Press.

Lomax, Alan. 1968. *Folksong Song Style and Culture*. Washington DC: American Association for the Advancement of Science.

Magrini, Tullia. 2003. "Villaggio globale e sound group." In *Il giudizio estetico nell'epoca dei mass media. Musica, cinema, teatro*, edited by Anna Rita Addessi and Roberto Agostini, 25–30. Lucca: Libreria Musicale Italiana.

Murdock, George P. 1967. "Ethnographic Atlas: A Summary." *Ethnology* VI: 109–236. https://doi.org/10.2307/3772751

—1969. *Ethnographic Atlas*. Pittsburgh: University of Pittsburgh Press.

Nestler, Gerhard. 1962. *Geschichte der Musik. Die großen Zeiträume der Musik*. Gütersloh: C. Bertelsmann.

Pisani, Vittore. 1940. *Geolinguistica e indoeuropeo*. Rome: Giovanni Bardi.

Proctor, Robert N., and Londa Schiebinger, eds. 2008. *Agnotology: The Making and Unmaking of Ignorance*. Stanford, CA: Stanford University Press.

Ratzel, Friedrich. 1902 [1891]. *Anthropogeographie: Die geographische Verbreitung des Menschen*. 3rd edn. Stuttgart: Verlag von G. Engelhorn.

Schafer, Raymond Murray. 1977. *The Tuning of the World*. Toronto: McClelland and Steward.

Schneider, Albrecht. 1976. *Musikwissenschaft und Kulturkreislehre: Zur Methodik und Geschichte der vergleichenden Musikwissenschaft*. Bonn-Bad Godesberg: Verlag für systematische Musikwissenschaft.

Slobin, Mark. 2007. "Musical Multiplicity: Emerging Thoughts." *Yearbook for Traditional Music* XXXIX: 108–16.

Tylor, Edward Burnett. 1958 [1871]. *Primitive Culture*. Reprint. New York: Harper & Row.

Weber, William. 1975. *Music and the Middle Class: The Social Structure of Concert Life in London, Paris and Vienna between 1830 and 1848*. New York: Holmes and Meier.

Westerlund, David, ed. 2004. *Sufism in Europe and North America*. London: Routledge Cuzron, Taylor & Francis Group.

Chapter 2

Mancunian Irish: Identity, Cultural Intimacy, and Musical Hybridization—Urban Ethnomusicology and Cultural Mapping

Svend Kjeldsen

Cultural mapping is a helpful method that is employed in diverse disciplinary contexts with different purposes, and via the application of a broad spectrum of tools and techniques. Mapping in itself draws attention to the existence and importance of cultural resources of a socio-musical nature. Mapping can, for example, appear productive for the analysis of disagreements and cultural tensions. It can prove useful for the development of strategies for cooperation, peace building, and musical enrichment in particular regions or cities. The main aim of this chapter is to study subtle points of conflict during processes of identity production within the context of the nation-state when citizens reject state-sanctioned cultural and legal norms. The chapter explores how meaning is created among citizens, as they utilize discursive resources in creative ways, with music being crucial, generating what is often referred to as musical hybridization.

The production of cultural identity is based on a certain social poetics or "cultural intimacy" that provides the glue in everyday life. This was described by anthropologist Herzfeld as "embarrassment and rueful self-recognition" (2005: 6–8) through various common frameworks of memory and, what might appear as, stereotypes. Identity production involves everyday games of hide-and-seek played only by "natives," along with unwritten rules of behavior, jokes (understood in "half a word"), and a sense of complicity. Herzfeld explains the relevance of "cultural intimacy" within anthropology in the following way:

I suggest that the model of cultural intimacy is a particularly apt concept for anthropologists to contribute to the study of nationalism (as well as other idioms of identity formation), because it typically becomes manifest in the course of their long-term fieldwork, a site of social intimacy in the fullest sense. (Herzfeld 2005: 3; see also Stokes 2010: 32–33, 190–193)[1]

The Irish Community in Manchester South

My point of musical departure is the investigation of music performance practices among Irish musicians in Manchester, UK. The performers in the Manchester Irish community are remarkable in the way they fuse their music with other musics within the city, not found anywhere else in Britain. The precondition for my work is my own life as a professional musician, having performed, traveled, and recorded with second-generation Irish musicians from London, Birmingham, and Manchester for more than twenty years. Today's Manchester lies within the Greater Manchester urban area; it is the UK's second largest city, with a population of 2.5 million. Manchester is multicultural. The Manchester results from the UK 2011 census, published in February 2013 by the British Office for National Statistics (ONS), are shown in Figure 2.1.

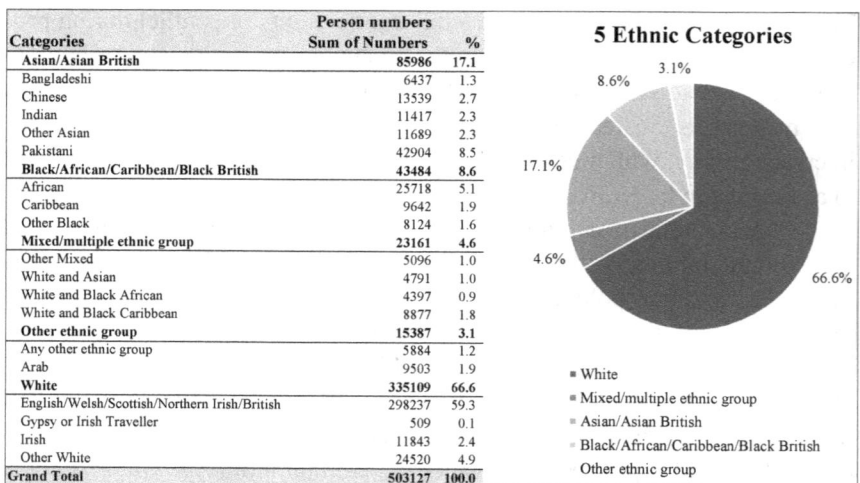

Categories	Person numbers Sum of Numbers	%
Asian/Asian British	**85986**	**17.1**
Bangladeshi	6437	1.3
Chinese	13539	2.7
Indian	11417	2.3
Other Asian	11689	2.3
Pakistani	42904	8.5
Black/African/Caribbean/Black British	**43484**	**8.6**
African	25718	5.1
Caribbean	9642	1.9
Other Black	8124	1.6
Mixed/multiple ethnic group	**23161**	**4.6**
Other Mixed	5096	1.0
White and Asian	4791	1.0
White and Black African	4397	0.9
White and Black Caribbean	8877	1.8
Other ethnic group	**15387**	**3.1**
Any other ethnic group	5884	1.2
Arab	9503	1.9
White	**335109**	**66.6**
English/Welsh/Scottish/Northern Irish/British	298237	59.3
Gypsy or Irish Traveller	509	0.1
Irish	11843	2.4
Other White	24520	4.9
Grand Total	**503127**	**100.0**

5 Ethnic Categories

- White
- Mixed/multiple ethnic group
- Asian/Asian British
- Black/African/Caribbean/Black British
- Other ethnic group

Figure 2.1: The UK 2011 Census: Manchester (ONS).[2] Data analysis: Svend Kjeldsen.

The census contains five main ethnic categories. I point to the fact that 66.6 percent of the population is "white." People of Irish descent can identify themselves as either "Northern Irish," "Irish Traveller," or "Irish." As we shall see shortly, these categories do not correspond with the identities found among second-, third-, and fourth-generation Irish in Manchester. The pie chart generated from data on the ONS website clearly presents the "white" part of the population as a unity, while the already limited ethnic differences disappear (Hickman 2011). Irish people have lived, worked, and performed their music in Manchester for 260 years. The most important influxes were related to the Industrial Revolution (1750–1850), the Great Irish Famine (1845–1852), Manchester's mobilization during World War II (1935–1945), and the rebuilding of the city after WWII in the 1950s–1960s. The war-related influxes of migrants make up, what is primarily understood as, the present first-generation Irish, being the forefathers of the subsequent second-, third-, and fourth-generation Irish in Manchester. These are the demographic groups in which I identified the musicians, who contributed to my ethnography and on which this chapter is based.

About Diaspora

In current, predominantly British readings of diaspora, the term is used by anthropologists and cultural critics to express modes of *hybrid* consciousness and identity (Hall 1990; Gilroy 1993; Clifford 1994; Brah 1996). In this postmodern version of the diasporic, the contemporary hallmark of the experience is of a process of unsettling, recombination, and hybridization. The meaning of diaspora can denote a social condition: the experience of being *from* one place and *of* another. Or it could be of other places; diasporas are about multiple traveling across geographical, cultural, and psychological borders. One consequence is that a diasporic space is created, which transgresses the boundaries of ethnicity and nationalism. Gilroy (1993) observes that diaspora provides a "third space," an alternate public sphere, which includes both identification outside, and permanent living inside, the national time-space. The value of the concept of diaspora lies in its simultaneous qualities of disruptiveness and inclusiveness. Diaspora, in this definition, highlights multi-generations, multi-connections across diaspora, a global imagined community of, as in my research, Irishness, and the contradictory relationship between the so-called "homeland" and diaspora. It also undermines nation-state identities and profiles hybrid identities.

Locating the Irish Diaspora in Britain and Manchester

Let me locate the Irish diaspora in the UK and, more specifically, Manchester, to identify the preconditions for the production of identity among people living there. The situation is obviously complicated by the fact that identity production takes place in a zone between the so-called homeland and host nation, which, in this research, is a former colonizing power. In the Republic of Ireland, there has been a historical denial of diaspora, although not of emigration. Prior to the 1990s, there was little discussion about diaspora in the public sphere, although in public discourse reference was and is made to "Irish Wannabees" and "Plastic Paddies," indicating the lack of "authenticity" and the relative Irishness of the Irish in Britain (Arrowsmith 2000; Campbell 2000). Historically, anti-Irish racism in the UK has comprised two elements: firstly, the Irish were constructed as inferior, and secondly as alien in the articulation of a racist discourse underpinned by anti-Catholicism (Hickman and Walter 1997: 228–30; Hickman 1998: 290–91). In modern British history, anti-Irish racism has been implemented into a new political strategy for the construction of the UK as a national community. The idea of *assimilation* of the Irish and the myth of *homogeneity* was introduced, based on the assumption that religion and national identity no longer distinguish the Irish from the British native population. Another premise was that racism is not relevant in the case of the Irish, as race is a question of skin color. The Irish share whiteness with their hosts (Hickman and Walter 1995: 6; Hickman 1998: 289), and were largely invisible as an ethnic group, but continued to be radicalized as inferior and alien others (Hickman and Walter 1995: 9). The forced inclusion of the Irish in Britain deprived them of their rights to be an ethnic group with their own identity. The borderline between their Irish identity and British identity became blurred and indefinable.

Hybridization, Third Space, Non-Hyphenated Identity

The Irish diaspora in Britain occupies a classic "third space," one that does not have access to a recognized hyphenated identity. There has never been a way to be Irish-British or British-Irish in the UK in the way in which people can acceptably claim to be Irish-American. Among people born in England to Irish-born parents, only about 20–25 percent claim to be English/British with no reference to their Irish heritage. Instead, they make use of all sorts of phrases to represent their identity, such as second-generation Irish, half-Irish and half-British, or London Irish, Birmingham Irish, or, in this research, Manchester Irish. The labels emerge due to the agency of the Irish in the UK when constructing their own identity definitions. The following excerpt from an interview with Mancunian[3] Irish fiddle player Andrew Dinan (18 March 2014) is an ethnographic documentation of Manchester Irish identity:

> You know if you are American-Irish, it's fine. It's sound, because that's kind of cool, if you are Australian-Irish that's great ... if you are Nepalel ... if you are Nepalese-Irish that's brilliant, that's just fantastically intriguing,—but if you are English Irish, you're a tanner.[4] And it's just ... it's that ... that, that type of thing annoys me ... you know it's ... I've also met these ... I just want people to know is I don't want ... If you're looking at me like somebody who wants to be Irish, you got it wrong ... 'cause I don't want to be Irish, and I'm not coming to you playing the music want you to turn round and say: "God, he's, fucking hell ... isn't he so Irish?"

> I just want to sit in the session and play tunes and play top-tunes and play them really well, and I don't want anyone to mention: "Who the hell? ... is wha'? or where? ... where are you from?" ... I don't care! ... It doesn't ... it really doesn't matter ... And it won't matter in the future, when everybody involved's passed this non-sense, and the lines are taken off the maps ... It really won't ...

> I was raised by Irish parents so I kind of ... you know ... there's Irish anyway ... there's definitely a massive Irish infl ... Irish influence in me ... but ... I'm a Mancunian ... and I was born and raised here and I live here ... and I ... I love Man ..., I love Manchester ... can't imagine living anywhere else ... including Ireland. (p/c, Andrew Dinan, 18 March 2014)

With Herzfeld in mind, I interpreted Dinan's agency within the realm of social poetics, as I read the specific objective of social poetics as focusing analysis on lived, historical experience, and thereby restoring awareness of the social, cultural, and political grounding—the cultural intimacy—of even the most formal power and most abstract knowledge. Local identities can be adopted without the binary clash that hybrid names would have entailed, given the history of Britishness as an encompassing identity (Hickman 2000a, 2000b). Within hyphenated identities, the hyphen is the third time-space, the imaginary homeland. The question to ask here is: How do the Irish in Manchester, in their "third space," and without access to a recognized hyphenated identity, create meaning by utilizing discursive musical resources in creative ways? In the following, this question will be explored through two musical readings.

Musical Reading 1: Ríoghnach Connolly and Black Lung's 'Black is the Colour'

Ríoghnach Connolly, born in 1984, is a fourth-generation Mancunian Irish singer, songwriter, and flute player, performing with both Irish traditional and contemporary lineups. Her band Black Lung specializes in hybrid musical repertoires consisting of common traditional songs found in Ireland, Scotland, Wales, and England, as well as contemporary songs written by Connolly, Ellis Davies, Cheryl Wheeler, Robert Petway, and others. A sixteen-strong hybrid ensemble[5] performs this repertoire, which is an expression of hybridization in a number of ways, as it consists of jazz, rock, and classical musicians, plus musicians from Irish and Indian music traditions. The group's eclecticism is further reflected in its comprehensive hybridized instrumentation, consisting of vocals, flute, backing vocals, *uilleann* pipes, fiddle, mandolin, banjo, button accordion, tenor saxophone, acoustic and electric guitars, cellos, piano, keyboard, *bodhrán*, *tabla*, double bass, and drum kit. The sixteen musicians represent different national relations to countries such as Ireland, India, Scotland, Wales, and England. In the following, I will discuss Connolly and Black Lung's interpretations of the folk song 'Black is the Colour (Of My True Love's Hair),' a traditional folk song first collected and registered by Cecil J. Sharp and Olive Dame Campbell (Campbell and Sharp 1917: 255) in the Appalachian mountain region of the United States in 1916, where it was sung by Mrs. Lizzie Roberts at Hot Springs, North Carolina. The song most probably originates from Scotland, as it refers to the River Clyde in the song's lyrics.

Many different versions of this song exist. It is an ongoing discussion which version should be considered the "original." The version registered by Sharp and Campbell had six verses and was addressed to a male, but many versions are addressed to females.[6] Over the years, 'Black is the Colour' has been classified within the commoditized category "Celtic music" (Taylor 1997; Stokes and Bohlman 2003), and many popular singers (e.g. Nina Simone, Joan Baez, Hamish Imlach, Judy Collins, Karan Casey, Pete Seeger,

Black is the Colour

Traditional

Black is the colour of my true love's hair
His lips are like some roses fair
He has the sweetest smile and the gentlest hands
And I love the ground whereon he stands.

I love my love and well he knows
I love the ground whereon he goes
I wish the day it soon would come
When he and I could be as one.

I go to the Clyde and I mourn and weep
For satisfied I never can be
I'll write him a letter just a few short lines
And suffer death a thousand times.

Black is the colour of my true love's hair
His lips are like some roses fair
He has the sweetest smile and the gentlest hands
And I love the ground whereon he stands.

Figure 2.2: Sheet music and text for 'Black is the Colour' (transcription: Svend Kjeldsen)

Christy Moore, Phil Coulter, Katherine Jenkins, and Brian McFadden) have recorded their rendition of the song.

In 2012, Connolly launched an album titled *Black Lung* on which she recorded 'Black is the Colour,' interpreted as a slow jazz-ballad. This version has clear rhythmical and improvisatory inspiration from Nina Simone's *Black Gold* (RCA Victor, LSP-4248, 1970), an LP featuring two versions of the song. The first, sung by Simone, was a piano-based male version without meter. The second sung by her guitarist, Emile Latimer, was a guitar-based female version in 3/2 time. Both renditions were based on a modified edition created by Latimer. The melody-line in Connolly's version corresponds to the rendition collected by Sharp. She sings four verses (see Figure 2.2). The song is a hybrid version of Simone and Latimer's work. It is a male version, maintaining the 3/2 time, accompanied by both piano and guitar, plus a rhythm section consisting of double bass and drum kit.[7] Connolly's studio recording of 'Black is the Colour' is different to her many live-performances of the folk song, which express a high degree of homogeneity and uniformity. To demonstrate this, I will analyze one specific performance taking place at the Manchester Jazz Festival on 20 July 2012. The narrative of the song is about love and separation, solidarity and harmony that never became a reality. In that sense, the song evokes nostalgia, a symptom of our age and a historical emotion. Boym defines nostalgia as follows:

> Nostalgia (from *nostos*—return home, and *algia*—longing) is a longing for a home that no longer exists or has never existed. Nostalgia is a sentiment of loss and displacement, but it is also a romance with one's own fantasy. Nostalgic love can only survive in a long-distance relationship. (Boym 2001: xiii–xiv)

Boym offers a tentative typology and distinguishes between two main types of nostalgia: the restorative and the reflective. Restorative nostalgia is at the core of national and religious revivals and contains two main plots— the return to origins and the conspiracy. Reflective nostalgia does not follow a single plot, but explores ways of inhabiting many places at once and imagining different time zones. It loves details, not symbols. At best, it can present an ethical and creative challenge, not merely a pretext for melancholies. Restorative nostalgia takes itself seriously. Reflective nostalgia, on the other hand, can be ironic and humorous. It reveals that longing and critical thinking are not opposed to one another, just as affective memories do not absolve one from compassion, judgment, or critical reflection (Boym 2001: 41–45).

The core scenario in 'Black is the Colour' is about the painful separation between a male and a female, but in Ríoghnach Connolly's context, it seems obvious to interpret this image within Boym's framework, which is the Irish migrant who will never experience the solidarity and coherence with the so-called homeland. In Connolly's performance at the Manchester Jazz Festival, the longing for the homeland was emphasized by her singing in *sean-nós* style with its melismatic ornamentation and intervallic variation, developed through song-performance in the Irish language.[8] Manchester-based Indian singer and *tabla* player Utam Gilly Singh performs the third verse. According to Singh, his performance in Urdu involves a vocal approach known as *gáyakí* in Hindustani music, in which he adds ornamentation (*gamaka*) to improvisations based on the lyrics and melody of 'Black is the Colour.' *Gáyakí*, invoking melancholy, love, and longing, is the art of singing the *ghazal* (guzzle), a popular form of music in India and Pakistan. *Ghazal* is commonly understood as a poetic expression of both the pain of loss or separation and the beauty of love in spite of that pain—in other words, expressions parallel to the nostalgic narrative identified within the song.[9]

While Singh's performance refers to nostalgia, which seems similar to Ríoghnach Connolly's singing, this does not lead to a mawkish doubling of sentimentalism, and instead becomes a form of critical reflection through a shared exploration of different places, times, and cultures. Having two singers from two different Mancunian ethnic minorities performing their different versions of separation and pain, points towards a common space of solidarity and coherence, a space that can simply be labeled Manchester. Furthermore, the musical arrangement of 'Black is the Colour' allows the musicians to express both the ethnic and the musical diversity that prevails within Manchester. Ríoghnach Connolly's Manchester acts as a nexus for fusion and hybridization, as Irish musical forms combine with other Mancunian and Mancunian-ethnic music gestures. Connolly and Black Lung's performance also illustrates Boym's viewpoint: "Nostalgia is not always about the past; it can be retrospective; but also prospective" (Boym 2001: xvi). The fantasies of the past, determined by the needs of the present, have a direct impact on the realities of the future. Considerations about the future make Connolly, Singh, and their colleagues take responsibility for their nostalgic tales. Unlike melancholia, which confines itself to the planes of individual consciousness, nostalgia is about the relationship between the biography of individuals and of groups, between personal and collective memory. While futuristic utopias might be an outmoded option, nostalgia itself has a utopian dimension— though it is no longer directed toward the future. Sometimes it is not directed toward the past either, but rather *sideways*. In the case of Connolly and her Black Lung colleagues, the music expresses a sideways utopian perspective within a joint, relational space in contemporary Manchester.

Musical Reading 2: Michael McGoldrick Big Band, 'The Jolly Tinker & Edinburgh Rock'

Michael McGoldrick, born in 1971, a third-generation Mancunian Irish, is a renowned multi-instrumentalist, composer, and band-leader, best known for his performances on flute, whistles, and *uilleann* pipes. McGoldrick has written melodies in traditional Irish style with rural references and pre-modern orientation. In parallel, there is material pointing toward postmodern aesthetics, borrowing elements from many different ethnic and popular musics. McGoldrick has recorded five solo albums to date,[10] all a blend of Irish traditional music and several other musics. An urbanized sound is created by employing grooves from popular musics in combination with loops, samples, industrial sound effects, and electro-acoustic instrumentation. The created sound picture could be interpreted as ethno-techno, as well as post-ethnic music. McGoldrick also integrates compositions in his repertoire, written by musicians from other ethnic minorities living in Manchester. Good examples are the pieces 'The Bunny's Hat,' and 'Edinburgh Rock' composed by *uilleann* piper David Lim, a Mancunian of Singaporean descent. In the following, I focus on a set of reels,[11] 'The Jolly Tinker & Edinburgh Rock.' It was recorded on McGoldrick's third solo-album *Wired*, but here I analyze the reels as they were performed by Michael McGoldrick Big Band in the Old Fruitmarket, Celtic Connections, 27 January 2013 in Glasgow, Scotland.[12]

'The Jolly Tinker' is a traditional dance-tune within the Irish traditional repertoire.[13] The key is A Dorian, which equals G Major, but starting on A. The tune is unusual as it consists of five unrepeated 8-bar parts, given that most Irish dance tunes consist of two repeated 8-bar parts (see note 11). The latter applies to the subsequent tune 'Edinburgh Rock' (in B Dorian, which equals A Major, but starting on B), composed by Dave Lim, thereby representing a structural and historical continuity in the Irish music tradition. The entire set was arranged with two rounds of 'The Jolly Tinker,' followed by three rounds of 'Edinburgh Rock,' 16 bars of trumpet improvisation, and finally two rounds of Dave Lim's tune. The melody-line of the pre-modern 'The Jolly Tinker' was performed on low whistles, accompanied by

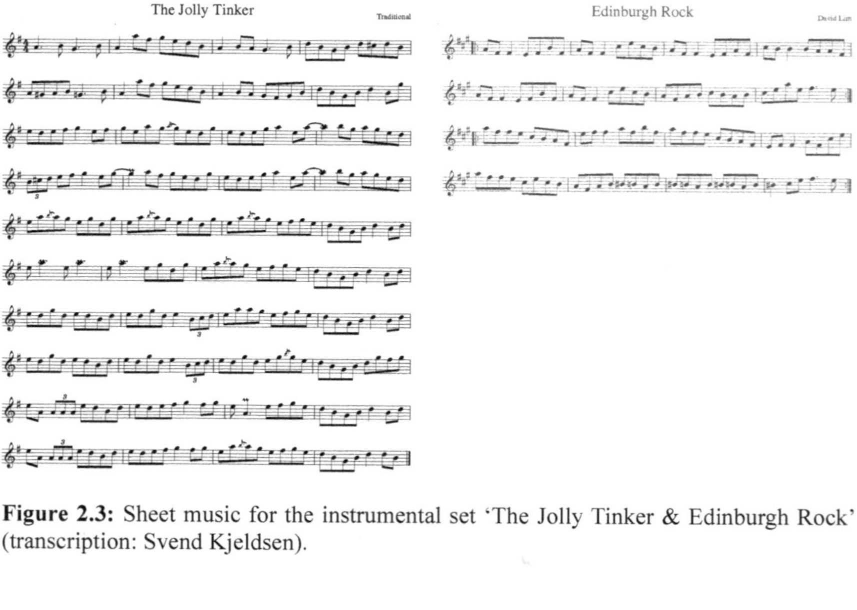

Figure 2.3: Sheet music for the instrumental set 'The Jolly Tinker & Edinburgh Rock' (transcription: Svend Kjeldsen).

the *bodhrán* (the Irish frame drum), acoustic guitar, and supported by an accompaniment performed on drum kit and electric bass. This accompaniment resembles a type of folk-rock fusion developed in the 1970s and 1980s by Irish bands such as Stockton's Wing (Keegan 2011: 665–66) and Moving Hearts (O'Regan 2011: 468).[14]

The unrepeated, flowing quality of 'The Jolly Tinker' ceased with a break before the band continued into 'Edinburgh Rock,' a tune which in contrast opened up energetic, groovy playing. Two whistles and two fiddles now performed the melody-line. The rhythm section was expanded with instruments reflecting urban Manchester: keyboard, electric rhythm guitar, *tabla* and funk/jazz trumpet. Within the Irish idiom, three rounds of a dance tune are commonly performed before moving on to three rounds of the next tune. This structural organization of pre-modern, rural, West of Ireland material was changed here in favor of a postmodern format, liberated from the traditional number of rounds. The melodic material was performed as a unity, inducing a feeling of high and euphoria, similar to, for example, trance, a 1990s genre of electronic dance music. While both tunes are meant and suitable for Irish traditional set dancing, neither set nor *sean-nós* dancing was performed in the Old Fruitmarket that night. However, there was a groove-related urban club dance feel, which undoubtedly had something to do with the tempo. A traditional Irish reel is typically performed for dance with an average tempo of 112–120 bpm (Vallely 2011b: 680), whereas the music in the Old Fruitmarket was performed at a tempo of 125, which is similar to, for example, trance (4/4: 125–150 bpm), techno (4/4: 120–150 bpm), and house (4/4: 118–135 bpm) (Borthwick and Moy 2004). The macro-arrangement of the performance demonstrates the fusion of a pre-modern and postmodern Irish musical piece, hybridized in a postmodern urbanized format, which is reflective of the multiple influences of other musics in Manchester, such as rock, folk rock, jazz, funk, trance, techno, and house. Through this hybridization, the original structure and traditional qualities of the melodic material were dissolved and suspended in favor of qualities derived from urban musics.

As mentioned above, I noted that while Connolly and her colleagues take responsibility for their nostalgia, they are constructing a sideways utopia within contemporary Manchester. With this in mind, I wanted to examine whether nostalgia and such utopian perspective were similarly at play in McGoldrick Big Band's performance of the Irish instrumental set. Yet I found that in his artistic effort, McGoldrick moves away from nostalgia as an exploration of a vertical past consisting of national and religious symbols and undercurrents, and instead creates a reflective and creative sideways horizon of the present with its many visible and accessible Mancunian musical dimensions in everyday life. His creative maneuver generates a utopian perspective, because several musical dimensions are present elsewhere in the Irish diaspora and other diasporas. In this way, McGoldrick's work serves to invite Manchester Irish citizens to take up positions within the global imagined community linked together by a shared sense of Irishness.

As likewise indicated earlier, McGoldrick's urbanized sound is created by employing grooves from popular musics, such as rock, jazz funk, and soul. This is also the case when it comes to 'The Jolly Tinker & Edinburgh Rock.' Groove can be described as syncopated music with a prominent, regular beat. Groove is a way of organizing the temporal aspect of music, a particular approach to rhythm and meter (Abel 2014: 1–2). It is known that Irish traditional dance music has a metronomic pulse and is regular at a number of metrical levels. Ó Súilleabháin has pointed out that "traditional players give a longer durational value to the first of each group of two quavers" (Ó Súilleabháin 1984: 8). This performance technique creates a swing rhythm related to jazz and its "democratization" of rhythmic values (Schuller 1968: 8–10). In other words: there is a backbeat in Irish dance music. Syncopation understood as strong displacement of rhythmic energy is, however, idiosyncratic and less common in Irish traditional dance music, but the metronomic pulse in combination with the backbeat may explain why Irish dance music is so receptive to groove within the Mancunian Irish context. However, in the above analysis of 'The Jolly Tinker & Edinburgh Rock' performance, I found that all rhythmical elements resembled groove: a strict metrical pulse, a strong backbeat, extensive application of syncopations, and a general leveling of meter throughout the entire arrangement. The temporal regularity found in 'The Jolly Tinker & Edinburgh Rock' and universally found in groove qualifies as genuine mimesis. It takes as its starting point the temporal reality of the modern world, with its rigid production rhythm and infiltration of the clock in every facet of life. Groove does, however, not simply incorporate clock time into its forms. Instead, it seeks to humanize the rigid and reified temporality through a process of mimesis. Groove can be recognized as a mimetic response to the highly measured temporality of the modern world, capable of effecting a critique of it. Groove bears within itself an aesthetic critique of the alienated temporality of neoliberalism and figures a demand for the collective control of time and history. Groove humanizes measured time and presents a utopian picture of liberated existence. In this sense, groove might belong within the tradition of working-class resistance. As demonstrated, when McGoldrick and his Mancunian Irish colleagues perform 'The

Jolly Tinker & Edinburgh Rock,' they release a utopian perspective at a musical macro level. By executing the inherent groove, they also release a utopian perspective at a musical micro level. Hence, Mancunian Irish performances of hybridized groove music articulate utopian perspectives at two interconnected levels.

Conclusions

Musicians of Irish descent, born in Manchester, live in a third space with little or no access to a recognized hyphenated identity. Instead, they create their own local identity: Manchester Irish, hence avoiding the pain and embarrassment evoked by national hybrid identities. In their self-defined third space, identity and meaning are produced through creative, hybridizing musical ownership, as Irish musical forms combine with Mancunian and Mancunian-ethnic music gestures. By doing so, Mancunian musicians are able to handle their nostalgia in different ways. In the first example, I found that a sideways utopian perspective was revealed through the creation of a city intimacy as a celebration of the music makers' own locality. In my second example, nostalgia was also mastered sideways through a broad creative exploration of the musical horizontality of the Mancunian present, providing relatedness to the entire Irish diaspora and other diasporas. This paved the way for a utopian perspective of potential membership in the global imagined community, offering a shared sense of Irishness for the Mancunian Irish. The global, utopian perspective at the musical macro level was further reinforced through its interconnectedness with the utopian dimension within the groove at the musical micro level. The resulting musical hybridization also points to the possibility of global diasporic solidarity based on personal experiences of immigration and multiculturalism.

About the Author

Svend Kjeldsen, PhD, is a musician, ethnomusicologist, and psychologist. For more than twenty years, he worked as a composer, recording artist, and toured as a professional musician all over Europe. Kjeldsen has taught at Aarhus University, the University of Limerick, and at music schools all over Europe. He has done research on the *bodhrán*, *lilting*, and on British-Irish music. Publications have focused on topics such as music and migration, cultural politics, regional and local Irish music traditions, trends on the European-Celtic music scene, contemporary *bodhrán* playing techniques, the origins of *bodhrán* and *bones*, and other organological subjects.

Notes

1   In Andrew Shryock's edited book, *Off Stage/On Display* (2004), cultural intimacy is employed as a theoretical platform for the study of mass mediation of socio-cultural identities and cultural forms. Through a number of different approaches, it investigates the zones of intimacy that mass mediation inevitably seems to require and subsequently obscures.

2   Data-source: Table KS201EW, subset for Manchester (Area code E08000003). Data analysis: Svend Kjeldsen. Data from ONS (Office for National Statistics, https://www.ons.gov.uk) are freely available under
http://www.nationalarchives.gov.uk/doc/open-government-licence/version/3/

3   "Mancunian" is the adjective and demonym of Manchester.

4   The Black and Tans were a force of Temporary Constables recruited to assist the Royal Irish Constabulary during the Irish War of Independence. The force was the brainchild of Winston Churchill, then British Secretary of State for War, and was recruited in Great Britain in late 1919. Due to the ferocity of the Tans' behavior in Ireland and the atrocities committed, feelings continue to run high regarding their actions. "Black and Tan," "Tan," or, as in this case, "Tanner" remain pejorative terms for the British in Ireland, and the Irish in the UK. The term can still stir bad reactions because of their remembered brutality. One of the most famous Irish Republican songs is Dominic Behan's 'Come out Ye Black and Tans' (Bennett 1976).

5   Ríoghnach Connolly (vocals, flute), Utam Gilly Singh (vocals, *tabla*), Zoe Chiotis (vocals), Fiona Browne (*uilleann* pipes), Angela Durcan (banjo, mandolin), Emma Sweeney (fiddle), Steve Prosol (button accordion), Ben Cashell and Hannah Miller (cello), Angus Fairbairn (tenor saxophone), Feilimí Devlin (*bodhrán*), Ellis Davies (electric guitar), Joe Bardwell (acoustic guitar), John Ellis (piano, keyboard), Nick Blacka (double bass), and Rob Turner (drum kit).

6   The American song collector, songwriter, and composer John Jacob Niles composed a new melody to 'Black is the Colour' between 1916 and 1921 to which he adapted the traditional lyrics. He recorded this version on the album *American Folk Lore Vol. 3* (RCA Red Seal Musical Masterpiece Series M-824, 1941) and three subsequent albums in his own name. Niles's version became popular on the American continent for some decades. It has very little resemblance to the traditional version discussed in this chapter.

7   Connolly's studio recording of 'Black is the Colour' is performed by a smaller
     jazz lineup consisting of Connolly (vocals, flute), Ellies Davies (electric guitar),
     John Ellis (piano), Matt Owens (double bass), and Rick Weedon (drum kit).
8   *Sean-nós* means "old style." It is a way of singing developed over the centuries in
     Irish-speaking Ireland and Gaelic-speaking Scotland. The term is somewhat mis-
     leading. Since the line of singing has never been broken, the style is as modern
     as it is old. It has been passed on from generation to generation and is therefore
     referred to as "traditional"; it is the traditional way of singing a song in Irish in
     Ireland and in Gaelic in Scotland. The style is deeply rooted in the rhythms of the
     Gaelic language and in the meters of and rhythms of Gaelic poetry. In Ireland it
     has survived wherever the Irish language itself has survived in areas known as
     Gaeltachts. Songs in English are also sung in this style. Good examples of this
     are the singing of Paddy Tunney as heard on his albums *The Man of Songs* (Folk
     Legacy FSE 1, 1962) and *A Wild Bee's Nest* (Topic 12T139, 1965), and obvi-
     ously the singing of Ríoghnach Connolly analyzed in this chapter. Performance
     technique in *sean-nós* consists of a number of interrelated elements. Tone quality,
     or "timbre," may vary from extreme nasality, to a hard or constricted tone, to a
     relaxed, "open" one. Vocal registration may exclusively use the chest voice or
     have a preference for the highest register, or head voice. Melodic ornamentation
     or variation is the technical feature most frequently associated with *sean-nós*
     singing. This includes melismatic ornamentation and intervallic variation. In
     melismatic ornamentation, a single syllable is sung to several notes. Intervallic
     variation involves the varying of intervals between specific notes of a melody.
     Rhythmic variation is another important aspect of *sean-nós*, especially the use of
     rubato, a designation, which includes the varying of the value of notes within a
     musical phrase. Of particular importance is the management of "phrasing," the
     way in which the musical phrases are presented, both individually and in relation
     to each other (Mac Con Iomaire 2011: 625–28; Ó Canainn 1993: 41–89).
9   Utam Gilly Singh undoubtedly makes use of artistic freedom in his *ghazal-*
     inspired *gáyakí* performance of verse three in 'Black is the Colour,' for which
     reason it makes sense to identify his point of reference. The Urdu term *ghazal*
     literally means "talk of love" and primarily refers to a North Indian genre of
     love songs, originally associated with Sufism, a concept often defined as the
     inner, mystical dimension of Islam. *Ghazal* is a poetic form consisting of rhym-
     ing couplets and a refrain, with each line sharing the same meter. The form is
     ancient, originating in ancient Arabic poems long before the birth of Islam. The
     ghazal spread into South Asia in the twelfth century due to the influence of Sufi.
     Although the *ghazal* is most prominently a form of Urdu poetry, it is today found
     in the poetry of many languages of the Indian sub-continent. The *ghazal* tradi-
     tionally deals with just one subject: love, specifically an unconditional and supe-
     rior love, interpreted for a higher divine love or for a mortal beloved. The love
     is always viewed as something that will complete a human being. A *ghazal* is

commonly written from the point of view of the unrequited lover whose beloved is portrayed as unattainable. The lover is aware and resigned to this fate but continues loving nonetheless; the lyrical impetus of the poem derives from this tension. The *gáyakí*, i.e. the singing performance of *ghazal*, is a very old art form in the Hindustani tradition. Singers such as Ustad Barkat Ali Khan and many other singers in the past used to practice it, but due to the lack of historical records, many singers are unknown. It was especially with Akhtari Bai Faizabadi that classical rendering of *ghazal*s became popular amongst the masses (Pesch 2009; Baily 2011).

10 *Morning Rory* (Aughrim Records, AUGH01, 1996); *Fused* (Vertical Records, VERTCD051, 2000); *Wired* (Vertical Records, VERTCD074, 2005); *Aurora* (Vertical Records, VERTCD090, 2010); *ARC* (Vertical Records, VERTCD111, 2018).

11 The reel is the most popular tune-type in the Irish tradition. Typically notated in 4/4 time it consists largely of quaver movement with an accent on the first and third beats of the bar. Most reels follow the standard AABB from where the first 8-bar part of the tune is repeated before the second 8-bar part—the turn—is introduced and repeated. This 32-bar "round" is repeated usually two or three times before a second reel is introduced. The grouping of two or more tunes together in this manner is typical. It is likely that the reel originated in France in the early 1500s as the "haye." It was being played as "reill" in Scotland in 1590 and its modern form was brought to Ireland from there in the late 1700s (Ó Súilleabháin 1990).

12 Michael McGoldrick Big Band had the following lineup in the Old Fruitmarket: Michael McGoldrick (flute, whistles, low whistles, *uilleann* pipes), Emma Sweeney (fiddle), Colin Farrell (fiddle), Neil Yates (trumpet), Ed Boyd (acoustic guitar), Ian Fletcher (electric guitar), Donal Shaw (keyboard), Ewen Vernal (electric bass), John Joe Kelly (*bodhrán*), Parvinder Bharat (*tabla*), James Mackintosh (drum kit), and guest musician Ross Ainslie (low whistle).

13 'The Jolly Tinker' (in Irish *Ealaín an Tincéara*) was noted and indexed by Breandán Breathnach. His source was Michael "The Master" McDermott (d. 1947), a schoolteacher and fiddler from Pomeroy and Carrigmore, County Tyrone, Ireland. The tune is registered as number 186 in Breathnach's *Ceol Rince na hÉireann* (1996), Vol. 4: 86. A different version is registered as number 751 in O'Neill's *1001 Gems: The Dance Music of Ireland* (1907/1965): 131. 'The Jolly Tinker' has been recorded on a number of well-known Irish traditional albums such as Martin O'Connor's *The Connachtman's Rambles* (Mulligan, LUN027, 1979), The Chieftains' *An Irish Evening* (RCA, 09026-60916-2, 1991) and Paddy Glackin & Robbie Hannan's *The Whirlwind* (Shanachie, 79093, 1995).

14 Stockton's Wing and Moving Hearts were inspired by Irish interpreters of "Celtic rock" (Mathieson 2001: 4–9), the Horslips (Vallely 2011a: 352), and Thin Lizzy (Mathieson 2001: 52), together with British folk rock bands such as Fairport Convention (Klitgaard 1989a: 75–77) and Steeleye Span (Klitgaard 1989b: 208).

References

Abel, Mark. 2014. *Groove: An Aesthetic of Measured Time*. Leiden: Brill.

Arrowsmith, Aidan. 2000. "Plastic Paddy: Negotiating Identity in Second-generation 'Irish-English' Writing." *Irish Studies Review* 8(1): 35–43. https://doi.org/10.1080/09670880050005093

Baily, John. 2011. *Songs from Kabul: The Spiritual Music of Ustad Amir Mohammad*. Farnham: Ashgate.

Bennett, Richard. 1976. *The Black and Tans*. London: Severn House.

Borthwick, Stuart, and Ron Moy. 2004. "Funk: The Breakbeat Starts Here." In *Popular Music Genres: An Introduction*, Stuart Borthwick and Ron Moy, 23–41. Edinburgh: Edinburgh University Press.

Boym, Svetlana. 2001. *The Future of Nostalgia*. New York: Basic Press.

Brah, Avtar. 1996. *Cartographies of Diaspora: Contested Identities*. London: Routledge.

Breathnach, Breandán. 1996. *Ceol Rince na hÉireann* IV ["The Dance Music of Ireland IV"]. Baile Atha Cliath: An Gum.

Campbell, Sean. 2000. "Beyond 'Plastic Paddy': A Re-examination of the Second-Generation Irish in England." In *The Great Famine and Beyond*, edited by Donald MacRaild, 266–88. Dublin: Irish Academic Press. https://doi.org/10.1080/02619288.1999.9974977

Campbell, (Dame) Olive, and Cecil Sharp. 1917. *English Folk Songs from the Southern Appalachians*. New York: C. P. Putnam's Sons.

Clifford, James. 1994. "Diasporas." *Cultural Anthropology* 9: 302–38. https://doi.org/10.1525/can.1994.9.3.02a00040

Gilroy, Paul. 1993. *The Black Atlantic*. London: Verso.

Hall, Stuart. 1990. "Cultural Identity and Diaspora." In *Identity: Community, Culture, Difference*, edited by Jonathan Rutherford, 222–37. London: Lawrence and Wishart.

Herzfeld, Michael. 2005. *Cultural Intimacy: Social Poetics in the Nation-State*. 2nd edn. New York: Routledge.

Hickman, Mary. 1998. "Reconstructing Deconstructing 'Race': British Political Discourses about the Irish in Britain." *Ethnic and Racial Studies* 21: 288–307.

—2000a. "'Binary Opposites' or 'Unique Neighbours': The Irish in Multi-Ethnic Britain." *Political Quarterly* 7(1): 50–58.

—2000b. "A New England through Irish Eyes." In *The English Question*, edited by Selina Chen and Tony Wright, 96–110. London: Fabian Society.

—2011. "Census Ethnic Categories and Second Generation Identities: A Study of the Irish in England and Wales." *Journal of Ethnic and Migration Studies* 37(1): 79–97. https://doi.org/10.1080/1369183X.2011.523005

Hickman, Mary, and Bronwen Walter. 1995. "Deconstructing Whiteness: Irish Women in Britain." *Feminist Review* 50 (summer): 5–19. https://doi.org/10.1057/fr.1995.18

—1997. *Discrimination and the Irish Community in Britain*. London: Commission for Racial Equality.

Keegan, Niall. 2011. "Stockton's Wing." In *The Companion to Irish Traditional Music*, edited by Fintan Vallely, 665–66. Cork: Cork University Press.

Klitgaard, Alan. 1989a. "Fairport Convention." In *Politikens Folkemusik leksikon. Den nye folkemusiks navne gennem 30 år*, edited by Alan Klitgaard, 75–77. København: Politikens Forlag.

—1989b. "Steeleye Span." In *Politikens Folkemusik leksikon. Den nye folkemusiks navne gennem 30 år*, edited by Alan Klitgaard, 208. København: Politikens Forlag.

Mac Con Iomaire, Liam. 2011. "Song." In *The Companion to Irish Traditional Music*, edited by Fintan Vallely, 625–30. Cork: Cork University Press.

Mathieson, Kenny. 2001. *Celtic Music*. San Francisco: Blackbeat Books.

Ó Canainn, Toman. 1993. *Traditional Music in Ireland*. Cork: Ossian Publications.

Ó Súilleabháin, Micheál. 1984. *The Bodhrán*. Dublin: Waltons.

—1990. "The Creative Process in Irish Traditional Dance Music." In *Irish Musical Studies: Musicology in Ireland*, edited by Gerard Gillen and Harry White, 117–30. Dublin: Irish Academic Press.

O'Neill, Francis. 1965 [1907]. *1001 Gems: The Dance Music of Ireland*. Dublin: Waltons.

O'Regan, John. 2011. "Moving Hearts." In *The Companion to Irish Traditional Music*, edited by Fintan Vallely, 468. Cork: Cork University Press.

Pesch, Ludwig. 2009. *The Oxford Illustrated Companion to South Indian Classical Music*. Oxford: Oxford University Press.

Schuller, Gunther. 1968. *Early Jazz: Its Roots and Musical Development*. New York: Oxford University Press. https://doi.org/10.2307/3392329

Shryock, Andrew. 2004. "Other Conscious/Self Aware: First Thought on Cultural Intimacy and Mass Mediation." In *Off Stage/On Display: Intimacy and Ethnography in the Age of Public Culture*, edited by Andrew Shryock, 3–28. Stanford: Stanford University Press.

Stokes, Martin. 2010. *The Republic of Love: Cultural Intimacy in Turkish Popular Music*. Chicago: University of Chicago Press. https://doi.org/10.7208/chicago/9780226775074.001.0001

Stokes, Martin, and Philip V. Bohlman. 2003. "Introduction." In *Celtic Modern: Music at the Global Fringe*, edited by Martin Stokes and Philip V. Bohlman, 1–26. Oxford: Scarecrow Press.

Taylor, Tim. 1997. *Global Pop: World Music, World Markets*. New York: Routledge.

Vallely, Fintan. 2011a. "Horslips." In *The Companion to Irish Traditional Music*, edited by Fintan Vallely, 352. Cork: Cork University Press.

—2011b. "Tempo." In *The Companion to Irish Traditional Music*, edited by Fintan Vallely, 680. Cork: Cork University Press.

Discography

The Chieftains. 1991. *An Irish Evening.* RCA, 09026-60916-2.
Connolly, Ríoghnach. 2012. *Black Lung.* http://rioghnachconnolly.bandcamp.com/
Glackin, Paddy & Robbie Hannan. 1995. *The Whirlwind.* Shanachie, 79093.
McGoldrick, Michael. 1996. *Morning Rory.* Aughrim Records, AUGH01.
McGoldrick, Michael. 2000. *Fused.* Vertical Records, VERTCD051.
McGoldrick, Michael. 2005. *Wired.* Vertical Records, VERTCD074.
McGoldrick, Michael. 2010. *Aurora.* Vertical Records, VERTCD090.
McGoldrick, Michael. 2018. *ARC.* Vertical Records, VERTCD111.
Niles, John Jacob. 1941. *American Folk Lore Vol. 3.* RCA Red Seal Musical
    Masterpiece Series M-824.
O'Connor, Martin. 1979. *The Connachtman's Rambles.* Mulligan, LUN027.
Simone, Nina. 1970. *Black Gold.* RCA Victor, LSP-4248.
Tunney, Paddy. 1962. *The Man of Songs.* Folk Legacy FSE 1.
Tunney, Paddy. 1965. *A Wild Bee's Nest.* Topic 12T139.

Other Sources

Dinan, Andrew (Mancunian Irish fiddle player), interview by Svend Kjeldsen,
    March 18, 2014, transcript.
ONS. "2011 Census, United Kingdom Submission for United Nations Questionnaire
    on Population and Housing Censuses." http://www.ons.gov.uk/ons/index.html
    (accessed October 15, 2018).

Chapter 3

Dying Language, Multi-Identity, and Music for the Young

Pekka Suutari

While looking at the geography of autochthonous (indigenous) minorities, one is faced with problems of definition and consistency in population cohesion (Markusse 2011). Different individuals relate differently to their minority status, and flexibility and multi-ethnicity are typical terms to describe their belonging to several ethnic groups simultaneously. Living in urban areas and moving in and out of home regions and countries induces a sense that cultural traditions and activities are more important than geographical place. Cultural affinities are mental rather than local. The writings of Stuart Hall in the 1990s brought the question of diversity and fragmentation of identities ("more than one") into the focus of cultural research. According to Hall (1996a: 116), identity is about groups and cultures, which are symbolically and functionally intertwined. Traditionally, ethnic identities—by which I mean associations with national minorities—are placed on the margins of state culture. Even so, Hall considered himself to be at the center with a multiple identity, which strengthened and described modern experience (Hall 1996a: 114). Hall's stance toward flexible ethnicity of everyday life illustrates the current situation not only of migrants, but also more generally of small linguistic groups in Eastern Europe.

During the formation of nation states and modernization, it was essential to define and differentiate nationalities (Brown 2004). The nation-state project embraced the idea that minorities will assimilate and finally disappear in the modernization process and especially with the rise in educational level. Yet in the 1980s, anthropologists realized that, contrary to these expectations, minorities were not disappearing, but had began to claim the protection of and support for their own language and cultural heritage (Roosens 1989). In line with Edward Bruner (1986), instead of recording disappearing tribal culture, researchers began describing the active struggles for civil rights and faith in the future awakened by ethnic awareness. There was a mental shift from the preservation of the blooming past to envisioning the future as "the golden era" for ethnic groups. The task of researchers was not to promote the political interests of minorities, but to locate them within (postmodern) cultural processes. This meant that research on ethnic groups did not aim to record the remnants, but to observe the beginnings and analyze cultural changes during "becoming," rather than "being" (Hall 1996b: 16).

The Landscape of Languages in Eastern Europe

The status of minority language groups has changed due to their integration into urbanized societies. For example, the border regions of Eastern Europe were formed through nationalizing processes from originally diverse and multiethnic relationships. According to Brown (2004), the borderlands of Poland, Ukraine, and Belarus were until the nineteenth century typically undefined and fuzzy in terms of ethnicity. Brown studied how, during Soviet times and its top-down nationalizing process, mixed language populations were made to represent certain nationalities on the one hand, and Soviet people on the other. Yet the "old" heterogeneity was still alive in people's memories and stories: while the "nationalized" people knew their official nationality, they were unable to speak their own national language (Brown 2004). So as regional minorities become multiple in their identities, the use of minority languages often disappears. And while forms of national heritage may adapt to the changing circumstances, there is a constant struggle in the existence and status of minority cultures at micro and macro levels. In practice, the pressure of homogeneity and assimilation changes cultural situations, inhibiting the reaping of the benefits that come from multilingualism and multiculturalism (cf. Slezkine 1994). The everyday lives of families, as experienced by different generations, convey different ways of making sense of and defining ethnicity, and the space to express it. At the same time, ethnicity manifests itself differently through the practices of surrounding groups and societies. Traditions are not mediated as such, but they represent the minority culture at individual, group, and governmental levels in these new situations and contexts. Therefore it is important to study identities in the light of local activities: Whose needs are taken into account? In which ways are language and culture plugged into the expression of multiple identities of individuals? What is the role of civic organizations and other actors in producing traditions?

Folklorist Arno Survo (2001: 16–18) speaks about national or ethnic categories as "empty models of explanations." He studied the complex and blurred ethnicity of the Ingria in the Leningradskaya Oblast, a federal district in northwestern Russia, through direct contact with people from diverse origins. When everyday ethnicity escapes official definitions, there appears a situated dialogue-conflict between the "own" and the "other." Idealized signifiers, such as atheist, Soviet, Lutheran, Finnish, or Russian, are "empty" and unable to depict the ethnicity that arises during everyday encounters. Moreover, ethnicity is produced both in inter-group as well as in in-group contacts. Linguist Riho Grünthal (2009) has studied three generations in relation to the attrition of the languages of small nations: The generation living in village communities and speaking the minority language as their first language is in danger of losing contacts with the third, Russian-speaking generation. The second generation born after World War II and brought up in the societal transition of reconstruction is more attached to Russian than to the minority language. The third generation speaks mainly Russian, but there is variation between individuals and families as to the extent to which and how knowingly they identify with their ethnic lineage and maintain its multilingualism. A large part of third-generation small ethnic groups has learned their language through formal study, and rarely as a natural language spoken at home or within the village community.

How are multi-ethnic identities formed in cases when minority language and culture are not an integral part of people's everyday lives? How does music produce different linguistic and ethnic identities? The sociocultural context allows researchers to study mixed and situated linguistic identities in cases where the ability to communicate in a language and identify through it diverge (Iskanius 2006: 77). This raises questions about language use in situations where a person's own minority language is no longer the primary means of communication within his/her minority group, while not maintaining solely symbolical meanings either. Observations were conducted by means of fieldwork and repeated field visits in the capital of the Republic of Karelia, Petrozavodsk, in Russia. Petrozavodsk is a city of nearly 300,000 inhabitants, of which less than 10 percent are ethnic Karelians (Folk census 2012; Suutari 2010: 9).

Music and the Nuori Karjala ("Young Karelia") Association

I have studied musical change in Russian Karelia since 2003. This included traveling there two to three times per year, while also working there on a research exchange for four months during the autumn of 2011. In this chapter, I will concentrate on interviews with the chair of the Nuori Karjala association and the musicians linked to its activities. Partially, the interviews mirror my experiences while attending the *ethnovetsherinka* (live music) evenings arranged by Nuori Karjala in the nightclubs Extreme Bar, Heikkonen, and Post Modern. The evenings have been held twice a year since 2006, and their purpose is to attract young Baltic Finnish people to become members of the association. For musicians, the evenings are important as they potentially create an (ethnic) Karelian city audience for Baltic Finnish pop and folk rock in Petrozavodsk. The Nuori Karjala ("Young Karelia") association was established in the early 1990s in order to promote the use of Baltic Finnish languages among youth in the Republic of Karelia. It gathers young people from Karelian, Veps, and Finnish ethnic groups, which all face the same problem: assimilation into the Russian language. Similar to many other national regions in Russia, their ethnic background is mixed and the notion of identity is strongly linked to local circumstances (cf. Olson 2004). Around the year 2006, the activities of the association changed considerably, when its chair Natalia Antonova started new activities in order to increase young people's use of Baltic Finnish[1] languages in their everyday life. Initially, she obtained information about its members, and noticed that more than half of the original members had moved to the neighboring country Finland. She thus sought out new members to join the association by not only talking to people (which she believed was not enough for activating them), but by mobilizing the folk music scene by organizing joint music events in Petrozavodsk.

In Petrozavodsk, there are six or seven well-established bands, which play Karelian, Finnish, and Veps folk rock (such as Sattuma, Talvisovat, D'Airot, or Noid). Some of these have garnered an international reputation and are of semi-professional quality. The first Karelian rock songwriter was Santtu Karhu, who started in 1988 to write his own songs in his home dialect livvi Karelian (of Vedlozero). He was inspired by Soviet Estonian rock of the 1980s, and the ethno futuristic movement and ideology there, and thought that if Estonians can make contemporary music in their own language, why not also Karelians (Bogdanov 2009). His contacts in Finland were also important, and he made his first three single records in Helsinki with his group Talvisovat in 1989–1991. This gave him the opportunity to attract the best rock musicians from Petrozavodsk to join his band (Suutari 2014). Besides Santtu Karhu, there were also "outcasts" from the Soviet folkloric scene. The most important was the group Myllärit, whose musicians left the State Song and Dance Ensemble Kantele in the early 1990s (due to the economic crisis) in order to tour in Central Europe and Finland. Myllärit played initially acoustic folk music, *pelimanni* style Finnish and Karelian tunes, but within a few years their music grew louder and became more rock-oriented, and thus featured on big festival concert stages. Myllärit also established commercial music studios and festivals in Petrozavodsk, and influenced the development of rock music and musical life more generally in the city.

Music became an important part of the association's activities. The *ethnovetsherinkas* evenings created a pleasurable atmosphere, and attracted around 20–30 new members during each gathering. Most of the active members of Nuori Karjala have been students or recent graduates studying Baltic Finnish languages at Petrozavodsk State University, and its membership is constantly changing due to new generations of students in the language department. In an interview, Antonova explained that the association does not engage in political work, and that its purpose is not to draw "an army of thousands of members," but instead to find and support young people interested in maintaining Baltic Finnish languages, who may likely have roots within Karelian, Finnish, or Veps families. To provide some context, Soviet Karelian schools focusing on local languages were abolished and, since the 1950s, Russian has been the main language taught in schools. It is therefore difficult to find people who are under the age of 70 and able to speak Karelian fluently. In some villages, Karelian has survived as a spoken language, but assimilation into Russian took over in most places and families by the early 1980s. The status of Karelian is still very low, even among Karelians themselves (Kunnas 2013: 320–24). In the cities, the number of people who can speak Karelian is even smaller, and there are very few social occasions that help to maintain this and other minority languages. In Petrozavodsk, the Karelian ethnic minority is invisible along with a few cultural activities that reflect ethnic identity, as per Stuart Hall's argument about articulating cultural activities to experiencing ethnicity.[2] At its peak, the Nuori Karjala association had 280 members. Unexpectedly Russian authorities accused them of acting as a "foreign agent" against the Russian Federation. Following the Sankt Petersburg court decision in September 2015, the association was obliged to close down (see Suutari and Davydova-Menge 2017: 11–12). In 2016, a smaller group of its activists started a new association with the same name. Its activities have been considerably smaller, but the music evenings still attract 50–100 members.

In Petrozavodsk there is a choir for veterans in the Republic Center for National Cultures and half a dozen musical groups for small children. Russians usually treat all citizens equally. Yet, while language is the most important marker of ethnic difference, in Karelia the young speak Russian as their first language. So being Karelian (or Veps) results in a complicated process of conscious search for personal roots and family traditions. Being a Karelian means adopting a multicultural identity within the monolingual Russian context (p/c, Antonova, 2010). Even specialists do not usually speak Karelian with one another. Hence, cultural activities, such as theatre, literature, and music, are important means to activate the use of their own language, while social media (such as VKontakte.ru) provides an important means of communicating in Karelian to "test"[3] it.

The Karelian language has strong associations with villages and house-hold traditions. Its vocabulary is rich when talking about the peasant life context or nature in Karelia. Newer phrases adapted to city surroundings are unknown to most Karelians, and thus political speeches or discussions on contemporary topics are difficult to comprehend. Antonova therefore highly respects singer-songwriter Santtu Karhu, who expanded the scope of his lyrics to include topics about modern life and minority political questions, while creating new expressions in the Karelian language in his songs, rather than borrowing words from Russian or Finnish. Antonova suggested that this is proof that Karelian could potentially be used as a means of communication in modern life, even though it does not guarantee that Karelian would be understood, let alone used, by young urban people who normally speak in Russian.

The purpose of youth activities, such as those of Nuori Karjala, is even more important as governmental institutions with their official policies of representing national arts and culture are unable to maintain local minority languages and identities. Indeed, artists of state ensembles or folkloric youth groups of the Ministry of Culture in Karelia do not speak local languages, and the target audience for their music is Russian and international, rather than local and ethnic audiences (p/c, Ivanov, 2004). Antonova (p/c, 2010) suggested that deception is widespread, as official organizations falsely claim that the Karelian language is still well managed, and ensembles are able to sing and work in minority languages. Public celebrations may start with welcome phrases in the Karelian language ("Terveh teillä hyvä rahvas"); however, the remainder of the speeches is usually in Russian (Knuuttila 2010: 54). Antonova and others who I interviewed would like to see Karelian life maintained; however state ensembles combine the local repertoire with pre-dominantly Russian musical stylistic traditions (p/c, Antonova, 2010; p/c, Karhu, 2006 and 2011). The result is colorful and entertaining, but not very helpful from the point of view of language revitalization.

Of particular interest is the coexistence (even hybridization) of different Baltic Finnish languages, Karelian, Veps, and Finnish, and, in the case of Karelian, the use of three different dialects that are standardized as literal variants of Karelian in the Republic of Karelia. Young people do not feel lim-ited in their home dialects as much as with previous generations; as Karelian is taught at the university, it is easier to understand each other's linguistic variants (p/c, Karlova, 2014). This shows that the disagreements by lead-ing linguists who have pioneered the development of literal Karelian in the early 1990s (Õispuu 2013) can be overcome, at least in everyday relations. Therefore, the Nuori Karjala association emphasizes the importance of bring-ing together young Baltic Finnish people, regardless of their linguistic (or dialectic) background, even if some linguistic variants are difficult to under-stand. While, in practice, Russian is the common language for Finno-Ugrians in Russia, the symbolic power of Finno-Ugric languages is not dependent on these subtle differences in vocabulary and dialect.

Folk Rock

Natalia Antonova feels that language is an important part of musical activ-ities, and she is disappointed that the Karelian language is not taught at the Finno-Ugric Folk Music Department of the Petrozavodsk State Conservatory, which is deeply involved in the development of folk music in Karelia with graduates mastering the traditional styles of Karelian folk music. Yet, as they are unable to speak or understand the language, something is missing from their art education: "As Karelian, I personally think that to understand and know the words in a song is the most important to me. And how the performer can master the language in which he or she is singing" (p/c, Antonova, 2010). The conservatory has educated a large number of specialists in folk music, and credit is due to their deep-level engagement in fieldwork and first-hand knowledge of local material, yet the language is only taught at the university and not the conservatory. Specialists who have mastered the various tradi-tional cultural activities are rare, but are important for the survival and devel-opment of rich local traditions:

Antonova: They speak about the national culture in Russian language, and we [the Nuori Karjala association] try to speak about our own culture in Karelian language. There is such a difference.

Suutari: Are these two different things?

Antonova: I think they are completely different. Completely different things. Many Karelians and many people that live in Karelia have such a belief that we can talk about these things without knowing the language in question. This is reality. (p/c, Antonova, 2010)

Natalia Antonova's personal mission is to revive the use of the Karelian language, and she criticizes the state ensemble Kantele for not improving the linguistic situation in Karelia:

I think that if a band or ensemble considers itself a national ensemble, a Karelian or Veps, it is obligatory that there are people who speak or who know the language in which they are singing. And in this sense I like and respect for example Volodya Solovyev, who can Veps. And Santtu Karhu, who speaks livvi Karelian. Enska Jakobson, who sings in his mother tongue. And Arto Rinne also. (p/c, Antonova, 2010).

When Santtu Karhu (b. 1967) started his career, his main motivation was to raise interest among young people to revive their Karelian roots and to strengthen their Karelian identity: "Many times I have said that, as long as there is even one child who speaks Karelian, I will make music. Thereafter we will retire" (p/c, Karhu, 2006). In the early 1990s, when Santtu Karhu was less than thirty years old, he and his band Talvisovat had few opportunities to perform in the Karelian Republic due to the economic crisis in Russia, instead performing frequent festival and club gigs in Finland. Performing for younger audiences motivated him to play rock, while noting that music in the Karelian language was dominated by folkloristic performances, which he criticized for bringing Russian musical styles into Karelia (p/c, Karhu, 2006). He released records in Finland and produced six albums, while maintaining a critical focus in his lyrics throughout (Suutari 2014: 122). He studied old proverbs, interviewed people, and searched out folklore collections in order to use its rich linguistic expressions in his music. This is admirable as Finnish audiences have a perfunctory understanding of Karelian, while the Karelian audience in Russia only emerged relatively recently due to the Nuori Karjala evenings in Petrozavodsk.

Another singer, Vladimir Solovyev (b. 1979), started to write his own songs via an initiative of EBLUL (European Bureau for Lesser-Used Languages), who invited him to participate in a song contest in Pajala, northern Sweden. EBLUL organized European-level song contests for minority languages, with the North European semifinals being held in Sweden, where Saami, Finnish-Swedes, Roma, and others participated. Solovyev created music in the Veps language as "a bit of a joke," but the surging international music movement in support of European minority languages led him to think about it more seriously (p/c, Solovyev, 2007). He has since led his Veps folk rock group Noid for more than ten years, motivated by the desire to show the local youth in Petrozavodsk that "this ethnic group exists," and to propagate its traditional music in modern form in order to raise the status of Veps culture among young audiences, and especially among the Veps themselves.

Meanwhile, Enska Jakobson (b. 1973) was inspired by the music of local rock group Revolver when he saw them play in a street café. Jakobson soon formed his own band, D'Airot, with his classmates, initially struggling to source musical instruments and learning to play from scratch. D'Airot have published five albums in total, with Jakobson writing the lyrics, which on the one hand reflect national romantic traditions of the Republic of Karelia, and on the other express the current misery of Baltic Finnish society in a sarcastic style. He is not afraid of censorship, but is careful nonetheless about including political content in the lyrics:

> Well, I won't write hard line texts, where the truth would be plain. These texts are difficult to interpret. One likes to say as indirectly as possible. When in the family the relatives have gone ten years in Siberia [in prisoners' camps], an anxiety is certainly somewhere there inside. One has something to lose. I think that this is a very common phenomenon for everyone. Because most of the families have lost someone. And I also have responsibilities: I have my family and children. This is a practical matter too. With a means of art, I have a right and even responsibility to express. And I want to express. I don't accept everything, but I try to do it as indirectly as possible. (p/c, Jakobson, 2011).

The musicians in D'Airot do not understand Jakobson's lyrics as they are in his home language, Finnish, a situation similar to Santtu Karhu's Talvisovat. In any case, the message is important: the minorities' way of life is troublesome, their self-esteem is low, and many societal and personal problems result from this situation.

The Nuori Karjala association has also organized another musical initiative in the form of a techno pop group called Anna Tulla, which was put together upon sending out an open call to its members. It resulted in wide attention, with many young people showing an interest in participating in the band. Several people have written lyrics for the group in all variants of Baltic Finnish languages, while one of its singers, Darya Kuznetsova (b. 1987), has composed material on her guitar. Darya's background is typical: her mother was Karelian with a background in the livvi dialect, but Darya started to study the Viena dialect at school in Petrozavodsk and later at university. She became a teacher of Viena Karelian, despite her background as *livvikkö*, but even so she did not notice the difference in variants until her studies at the university. For her, the differences do not matter, and instead what matters is linguistic usefulness.

Constructing a Nation

The essence of Nuori Karjala's work lies in its focus on identity, which it instills among the young. Its member musicians have received encouragement to compose music for an ethnic audience. The new modes of using language are important for language revival and revitalization (Munne 2013; Grenoble and Whaley 2006), and they are essential for societal development too. Young people's identity is dependent on the opportunities for group membership and having positive group experiences. While identifying as Karelian, Finn, or Veps (Baltic Finnish) does not dissociate them from being Russian, given that many groups across various places in Eastern Europe have proven this flexibility in their identities (Brown 2004), this minority identity, however, needs locations where their sense of life as Baltic Finnish youth can be articulated and expressed in contemporary culture and music (cf. Hall 1996b: 3). The simultaneous use of three Baltic Finnish languages in Karelia and three Karelian dialects has become an essential part of identity production for members of the Nuori Karjala association in Petrozavodsk. Naturally, this is carried out and reflected in their musical practices: if music was performed by Soviet-style folklore groups only (e.g., on the grounds of "friendship between peoples"), the situation would resemble "empty" spaces, just as Arno Survo (2001) has described. New kinds of musical styles have emerged (rock, folk, techno, rap) that bring young people together in the Republic of Karelia. The coexistence of Baltic Finnish languages may be the continuation of old practices, but it also aims politically to raise people's consciousness about identity questions and differences among the various ethnic groups in northwest Russia.

About the Author

Pekka Suutari is professor of cultural studies at the Karelian Institute of University of Eastern Finland (Joensuu). He has studied musicology (ethnomusicology) at the Universities of Helsinki and Gothenburg, and he has acted as a visiting professor at the Karelian Research Centre of the Russian Academy of Sciences in Petrozavodsk, Russia. His main research interests are the music of the borderland between Finnish and Russian Karelia, and the ethnic activities of these areas. His current article is a result of a joint research project, "Flexible Ethnicities," that hosted researchers from UEF, Joensuu, and KRC, Petrozavodsk.

Notes

1   Baltic Finnish is a linguistic umbrella concept for Finnish, Karelian, and Veps languages in Karelia. Antonova held evening gatherings where these three minority languages were used together (besides Russian, of course). Although the audience did not know these minority languages very well, the audience tended to regard them as part of their own identity. Antonova's speeches and other presentations were conducted in a variety of these languages and in Russian.

2   According to Stuart Hall's articulation theory, ethnic identity is fragmented and is constructed of articulations of culture and ethnicity. Articulation means not just emphasizing something but also connecting cultural activities, experiences, stories, histories etc. to identity categories, which are separated from the others. Thus, cultural activities and events have a big role in processing identity (Hall 1996b).

3   They do not only test their language proficiency, but also the suitability of the language itself, because the less-used minority language is not fully developed and needs further development to be able to express (post)modern concepts and experiences.

References

Bogdanov, Evgenii. 2009. "Grani Karel'skogo etnofuturisma: Zametki o tsennostnom i ideinom mire rok-lirika Santtu Karhu." In *Kantele, runolaulu ja itkuvirsi*, edited by Pekka Huttu-Hiltunen, Frog, and Eila Stepanova, 75–84. Kuhmo: Juminkeko.

Brown, Kate. 2004. *A Biography of No Place: From Ethnic Borderland to Soviet Heartland*. Cambridge, MA: Harvard University Press.

Bruner, Edward. 1986. "Ethnography as Narrative." In *The Anthropology of Experience*, edited by Victor W. Turner and Edward M. Bruner, 139–55. Urbana and Chicago: University of Illinois Press.

Folk census. 2012. Владение языками населением наиболее многочисленных национальностей по субъектам Российской федерациию. [Language ability of population of the most numerous nationalities in regions of the Russian Federation.] http://www.gks.ru/free_doc/new_site/perepis2010/croc/Documents/Vol4/pub-04-07.pdf (accessed June 14, 2019).

Grenoble, Lenore A., and Lindsay J. Whaley. 2006. *Saving Languages: An Introduction to Language Revitalization*. Cambridge: Cambridge University Press. https://doi.org/10.1017/CBO9780511615931

Grünthal, Riho. 2009. "Kieliyhteisön rapautuminen ja kielellisen identiteetin muutos." In *Kielissä kulttuurien ääni*, edited by Anna Idström and Sachiko Sosa, 265–89. Helsinki: Suomalaisen Kirjallisuuden Seura.

Hall, Stuart. 1996a [1987]. "Minimal Selves." In *Black British Cultural Studies: A Reader*, edited by Houston A. Baker Jr., Manthia Diawara, and Ruth H. Lindeborg, 114–19. Chicago: University of Chicago Press.

—1996b. "Introduction: Who Needs 'Identity'?" In *Questions of Cultural Identity*, edited by Stuart Hall and Paul du Gay, 1–17. London: Sage Publications. https://doi.org/10.4135/9781446221907.n1

Iskanius, Sanna. 2006. *Venäjänkielisten maahanmuuttajaopiskelijoiden kieli-identiteetti*. PhD dissertation. Jyväskylä: University of Jyväskylä. https://jyx.jyu.fi/bitstream/handle/123456789/13433/9513925234.pdf?sequence=1&isAllowed=y (accessed October 15, 2018).

Knuuttila, Sanna-Riikka. 2010. "Public Attitudes towards Language Use: Karelian Language at 'Congresses of Karelians'." In *Karelia Written and Sung: Representations of Locality in Soviet and Russian Contexts*, edited by Pekka Suutari and Yury Shikalov, 50–58. Helsinki: Kikimora Publications.

Kunnas, Niina. 2013. "Vienankarjalaisten kielikäsityksiä." In *Karjala-kuvaa rakentamassa*, edited by Pekka Suutari, 289–330. Helsinki: Suomalaisen Kirjallisuuden Seura.

Markusse, Jan D. 2011. "National Minorities in European Border Region." In *The Ashgate Research Companion to Border Studies*, edited by Doris Wastl-Walter, 351–71. Farnham: Ashgate.

Munne, Timoi. 2013. "Karjalan kielen voimavarat Suomessa." In *Karjala-kuvaa rakentamassa*, edited by Pekka Suutari, 386–403. Helsinki: Suomalaisen Kirjallisuuden Seura.

Õispuu, Jaan. 2013. "Painettu sana pitää kansaa koossa: vertaileva katsaus Aunuksenkarjalan ja Vironkirjallisuuden historiaan." In *Karjala-kuvaa rakentamassa*, edited by Pekka Suutari, 108–21. Helsinki: Suomalaisen Kirjallisuuden Seura.

Olson, Laura J. 2004. *Performing Russia: Folk Revival and Russian Identity*. London and New York: Routledge. https://doi.org/10.4324/9780203317570

Roosens, Eugeen. 1989. *Creating Ethnicity: The Process of Ethnogenesis*. London: Sage.

Slezkine, Yuri. 1994. *Arctic Mirrors: Russia and the Small Peoples of the North*. Ithaca, NY: Cornell University Press.

Survo, Arno. 2001. *Magian kieli. Neuvosto-Inkeri symbolisena periferiana*. Helsinki: Suomalaisen Kirjallisuuden Seura.

Suutari, Pekka. 2010. "Introduction: Locality: Representations and Practices." In *Karelia Written and Sung: Representations of Locality in Soviet and Russian Contexts*, edited by Pekka Suutari and Yury Shikalov, 5–14. Helsinki: Kikimora Publications.

—2014. "Santtu Karhu: Laulaja-lauluntekijä rajalla." In *Etnomusikologian vuosikirja* 26, edited by Saijaleena Rantanen and Meri Kytö, 102–29. Helsinki: Suomen etnomusikologinen seura. http://julkaisut.etnomusikologia.fi/EVK/EVK_Vol_26_2014.pdf (accessed October 15, 2018). https://doi.org/10.23985/evk.66790

Suutari, Pekka, and Olga Davydova-Menge. 2017. "Predislovie." In *Gibkie etnitshnosti. Etnitsheskie protsessy v Petrozavodske i Karelii v 2010-e gody*, edited by Pekka Suutari and Olga Davydova-Menge, 5–30. Sankt-Peterburg: Izdatel'stvo Nestor-Istoriya.

Interviews

Antonova, Natalia. Petrozavodsk (25 March 2010). Interviewer: Pekka Suutari.

Ivanov, Vyatsheslav. Petrozavodsk (20 February 2004 and 26 May 2014). Interviewers: Pekka Suutari and Ilya Moshnikov.

Jakobson, Enska. Petrozavodsk (14 September 2011). Interviewer: Pekka Suutari.

Karhu, Santtu. Petrozavodsk (7 June 2006 and 7 October 2011). Interviewer: Pekka Suutari.

Karlova, Olga. Helsinki (23 May 2014). Interviewer: Ilya Moshnikov.

Kuznetsova, Darya and Yulya Maksimova. Petrozavodsk (20 May 2010). Interviewer: Pekka Suutari.

Solovyev, Vladimir. Petrozavodsk (30 October 2007). Interviewer: Pekka Suutari.

Chapter 4

Mapping "Inconvenient" Music Heritage[1]

Ana Hofman

> There is no such thing as "heritage" ... These practices, as well as
> the meaning of the material "things" of heritage, are constituted
> by the discourses that simultaneously reflect these practices while
> also constructing them. (Smith 2007: 13; Harvey 2001)

Although scholars agree that every process of heritage production is contested, the concept of so-called "inconvenient heritage" (Dearborn and
Stallmeyer 2010: 34) or contested and dissonant heritage (Tunbridge and
Ashworth 1996) raises particular problems around such issues as ownership,
control, and representation. Heritage management generally promotes the
dominant or authorized interpretations of contested heritage by obscuring or
removing the politically inexpedient parts (see Smith 2007).

Critical heritage studies illustrate the mechanisms of heritage production,
point to heritage as a process, and argue that heritage is best defined as "heritagization" rather than as an abstract noun (Harvey 2001). When it comes
to UNESCO's protocols on heritage, these criticize the World Heritage
Convention for legitimizing a particular Western (if not Western European)
perception of heritage in terms of both policy and practice (see Byrne 1991;
Pocock 1997; Cleere 2001; Sullivan 2004, among others). The World Heritage
List has shown to not only be Eurocentric in its composition, but that it is also
dominated by monumentally grand and aesthetic sites and places (Arizpe
2000: 36; Cleere 2001; Yoshida 2004: 109).[2] Such approaches to heritage
management pose questions around the dominant paradigm, namely that
cultural heritage is focused on objects or events, but not on individuals or
communities (see Kirshenblatt-Gimblett 1998). Regarding the management

of music and dance heritage, a rather small number of ethnomusicological accounts deal critically with the ways in which UNESCO recognizes, authorizes, and validates certain cultural expressions (see Ceribašić 2009; Graeff 2014). Nina Graeff (2014), for example, challenges the conceptual duality between tangible and intangible, while pointing toward the intangible dimensions of tangible objects and vice versa, such as found in musical instruments, or in the materiality of intangible music heritage. Similar to critical heritage studies, the approach of cultural mapping, although often maintaining the division between intangible and tangible heritage, shifts the focus toward more self-reflexive, community-led heritagization practices. In particular, "counter mapping" (Duxbury et al. 2015: 6), which is associated with the traditions of critical cartography (Crampton and Krygier 2005), proposes more critical analyses of the processes surrounding enclosure, partitioning, coding, and ranking of expressive culture (Mannion et al. 2007: 19). Critical cartography focuses more closely on communities that challenge the state's formal mapping by adapting its official techniques for representation and creating subversive, radical, alternative mapping practices. Drawing on these tendencies, approaches, and theories, which examine heritage as a political and cultural process of remembering/forgetting (Dicks 2000; Graham 2002; Peckham 2003; Smith 2007), this chapter focuses on the political dimension of musical heritagization with particular focus on a case study of Yugoslav partisan songs.

Mapping Music Heritage after 1989

"Suddenly, cultural heritage is everywhere," writes Lowenthal in his book *Possessed by the Past: The Heritage Crusade and the Spoils of History* about the "heritage boom" that occurred during the 1990s (Lowenthal 1998: ix). The fact that the so-called heritage boom coincided with the collapse of socialism in the Soviet Union and Eastern Europe triggered important transformations, not just in the practices of heritage, but also via epistemological shifts in framing the historical past as heritage after 1989. In post-socialist societies, the dominant discourses of heritage management proved to be particularly contested when concerns over cultural practice related to the socialist past. Scholarly accounts usually employed a totalitarian paradigm when addressing the socialist past, which is based on the understanding that cultural production in "Eastern" societies was state-imposed, state-controlled, and rigid. Yet this perspective offers only a one-dimensional interpretation of socialist culture, centered on the opposition between state-controlled cultural politics, on the one hand, and dissident, counter-state activities on the other. In such analyses, the public sphere is treated as being overwhelmed by the state's restrictive practices, while private or semi-private spaces are seen as the only niches for "freely uncensored activities" (for a critique of such approaches, see Yurchak 2006; Hofman 2011, 2016). Accordingly, socialist culture is predominantly understood through the prism of the ideological canon, that is, as not lived, experienced, and shaped by the people, but imposed by party authorities and state cultural politics. This has resulted in narratives of socialist expressive practices as ideologically burdened (with the problem of ownership); as non-original/non-real/fake expressions of reality (with the problem of value); and as non-attached to the past and hence decontextualized (with the problem of continuity).

As some scholars have shown, the totalitarian paradigm was not ideologically neutral or unproblematic, but related to the ideologies of nationalism (and revisionism) and neoliberal capitalism, which emerged in "Eastern" societies after the end of socialism (see Buchowski 2004; Buden 2009; Petrović 2012; Prica 2007; Kirn 2010). These voices questioned the earlier approaches for excluding people—the real protagonists and practitioners— as active receivers and bearers of cultural practices, while neglecting their life histories, and the role of personal and family narratives (see Petrović 2012). Challenging the totalitarian paradigm, they placed instead an important emphasis on non-institutional and informal cultural practices. They proposed to understand heritage as a mode of cultural production and living practice associated with everyday activities. They also pointed to the paradox of how "life becomes heritage" (Kirshenblatt-Gimblett 1998), raising questions about synchronizing the heritage clock with the historical clock,[3] and asserting that sometimes the past becomes heritage even before it had a chance to be lived.

In the sections that follow, I will engage with the controversies surrounding the heritagization of the socialist music legacy in a post-Yugoslav context. I will refer to the practice of cultural mapping, which can be particularly useful in the context of uneven power relations, while articulating marginalized voices and perspectives in society (Duxbury et al. 2015: 4).

Partisan Songs

During the 1980s, and particularly after the fall of the Berlin Wall, the socialist legacy provoked contested approaches and heritage narratives in public discourses. The "traumatic past" became the most contested historical period. On traumatic history and music in Eastern Europe, Maria Cizmic writes, "memories of traumatic events regularly circulate in relationship to politics and power" (Cizmic 2012: 5). Lynn Meskell describes such traumatic memory as "negative heritage," which is at the opposite spectrum of an otherwise often uncritical, positive understanding of heritage (Meskell 2002: 557).[4] After the break-up of Yugoslavia in 1991, the negative heritage that potentially carried socialist connotations was considered "inconvenient" and part of an "unwanted totalitarian past" and "a heritage of *the State* and not of the *time*" (Kovačević 2012: 17). Moreover, being symbolically related to former Yugoslavia, such cultural practices carried inherent *multicultural* connotations and associations with its former co-nations (which, after the break-up of the country and during the civil war, became enemies). Due to the dominance of national-oriented heritage discourses in post-Yugoslav societies, cultural practices from the socialist period were regarded as even more contested.

Within this socio-political climate, the legacy of antifascist resistance during World War II (National Liberation Struggle, or NOB) has been a recurrent theme in the newly founded post-Yugoslav states. In the light of rising militant nationalism and neoliberal politics, the partisan resistance[5] became part of the problematic socialist past and a subject of negation and revisionism in public discussions. As a result, partisan songs as the main musical genre of antifascist resistance were placed at the margins of public discourses as an ideologically burdened, formalized music genre, and as an ideological construction of the communist regime devoid of any "real" social significance and potential. Also, the revisionist attempts, which sought to examine World War II music practices such as "ustashas" or "chetnics" songs,[6] positioned them as a part of totalitarian legacy utilized for political purposes by the former Yugoslav communist party (see Ceribašić 1998). What was the most important historical moment of triumph against fascism during World War II became re-interpreted as communist manipulation and totalitarian propaganda.[7]

After World War II, partisan songs became one of the strongest media in the memorialization of World War II, and in the process of mythologization of NOB and the creation of the partisan myth—the foundational grand narrative of socialist Yugoslavia. From the more spontaneous settings of battlefields, village, or town squares in the liberated territories, this music entered the official elite culture, and started being performed at formal events, commemorations, and celebrations. Thus in the period after the Second World War, much of this musical production was staged, occupying an important place in "official" culture. Partisan songs became the regular repertoire of choirs that were central in official public rituals as an important part of the official memory politics. Partisan songs in choral performances formed the main part in state holidays and commemorations. At the same time, such musical content gradually entered the sphere of popular music, first in the genre of so-called entertainment music, while later being transferred to other genres as well (see Hofman and Pogačar 2017). The usage of musical or textual motifs from partisan songs was customary, particularly during the 1960s when "pop-culturalization" was presented as having an "educational" function, while bringing this content closer to younger generations. In such compositions, the "formal and commemorative type" of presentation typical in partisan songs was changed in favor of dealing more flexibly with the music material (ibid.).

Due to the highly ritualized context of state celebrations and commemorations, as well as the official policy-led cultural popularization of partisan songs, it could be expected that during socialism, this music was glorified due to its revolutionary content and its potential for building a united socialist Yugoslavia. Yet to the contrary, the musical production provoked contested discourses among Yugoslav folklorists and ethnomusicologists. They often examined partisan songs critically, particularly regarding issues of creation, artistic quality, and added value (all mentioned in the second part of this chapter). An analysis of relevant scholarly accounts illustrates the contested position of partisan songs within dominant heritage discourses during socialism, but what is even more interesting is that scholarly analyses point to similar concerns and debates raised by this music today, almost thirty years after the dissolution of Yugoslavia.

Folkloristic Narratives

Because of the many specificities of the music performed during the NOB, folklorists and ethnomusicologists found the genre of partisan songs particularly complex. Dominant discourses that shaped the concept of "revolutionary folklore" were not univocal, but often multi-vocal and controversial.

From its nationalistic background to its revolutionary disposition, partisan songs were investigated along two dominant approaches: first, as a carefully planned concept that was imported to the masses, and second, as a romantic paradigm of the "singing masses" underpinned by the claim that partisan songs were spontaneously created. From its very beginning, this genre was deliberated neither within the framework of artistic production nor of folkloristic form (Komelj 2009: 13), and positioned in-between artistic and folkloric production. This is embodied in the term *narodno stvaralaštvo* ("national creativity"), instead of heritage, an inclusive concept used for various forms of expressive culture. With the exception of the early post-World War II years, these songs were rarely systematically recorded, systematized, and archived. Although some organized song collecting along with musical notation had already started during the NOB, after World War II there was no serious scholarly interest in systematic collection and preservation (Nedeljković 1960: 140). The largest collecting project was conducted by Dušan Nedeljković in 1950, affiliated to the Ethnographic Institute of the Serbian Academy of Sciences and Arts, when approximately 20,000 partisan and *pesme obnove i izgradnje* (songs of renewal and reconstruction) were collected on the territory of Serbia. According to Jelena Jovanović, a researcher at the Musicological Institute of the Serbian Academy of Sciences and Arts, these songs were not collected during specialist fieldwork because researchers searched for the "more archaic," "older" musical forms. This was echoed by colleagues from the Institute for Ethnomusicology (*Glasbenonarodopisni inštitut*) of the Slovenian Academy of Sciences and Arts, where no separate collection of partisan songs exists, but only the recordings that were part of the "usual" fieldwork collecting of folk music. Therefore, it is possible to track partisan songs, but only when they are performed as part of the singer's "usual" repertoire. The marginalization of partisan song collecting was also criticized by scholars who reported on the marginal position of this genre in dominant research protocols, and the fact that partisan songs were not recognized by music scholars as "real music heritage" that can stand up along with other cultural heritage forms:

> Folk art creation from the time of our national revolution has so far been much neglected. It was approached mainly from the perspective of party propaganda, and only in exceptional cases researchers considered it as an equivalent form of folk oral creation. (Bošković-Stulli 1960: 251)

Despite the large number of scholarly conferences, meetings, and articles dedicated to the musical production of NOB,[8] no serious study has been undertaken that addresses the genre of partisan songs in the entire territory of former Yugoslavia. The usual approach taken by music scholars was to present material, insights, and conclusions concerning their own Republic. Studies that offer a synthetized approach dedicated to the music in NOB are rather rare, as also reported by scholars:

> So far, only a few individuals are devoted to the scientific research
> of partisan songs but still mostly just casual. Several years ago,
> a representative of the competent scientific institutions even said
> that time has not yet come for such work. (Hrovatin 1960: 257)

Although from today's standpoint, such critiques can be regarded as the result of the ideological climate at the time, they certainly reflect a lack of consensus about and a controversial stance toward this music. Accordingly, it is not possible today to find systematic collections or archives dedicated to partisan songs in scholarly institutions, such as the musicological and ethnomusicological institutes or music academies. Interestingly, national radio and TV stations in post-Yugoslav countries have archives of partisan song recordings and the music performed during World War II, yet they show a lack of interest in the systematic categorization or digitalization of this music.[9]

Consonant Sounds of a Dissonant Heritage

What were the main obstacles for giving this "highly ideological" musical content its rightful place within scholarly accounts during socialism? Why was this music not seen as worthy enough, despite its visibility in public and official discourses? In this section, I illustrate four dominant narratives, which shaped scholarly discourses on partisan songs as inappropriate heritage during socialist Yugoslavia: heterogeneity of the musical material; utilized/short-lived folkloric tradition; political/propaganda content; and partisan songs as a living practice.

The heterogeneity of the musical material presented obvious difficulties and was the main obstacle in deliberations of partisan songs as heritage (Nedeljković 1960: 138). Songs with the purpose of encouraging, supporting, and mobilizing soldiers to fight and cope with personal problems at the front originated in different socio-cultural environments. Existing songs were often adjusted to fit marching and fighting, and shaped by the aesthetics of military (*borbene*) mass songs. Many songs also emerged from the interactions between fighters, and eventually contained political, militant, and revolutionary content: "With a higher form of partisan struggle, the initial spontaneous and disorganized singing in the squad and hiking was transformed in better quality" (Cvetko 1960: 5). In addition, NOB revived existing rebel songs and felt strengthened by their content: songs of peasant uprisings, international worker's songs, songs from the French and October Revolutions, and songs from the Spanish Civil War. Scholars defined partisan songs as one broader category, which does not only include songs created within the partisan units, but also other revolutionary and resistance songs "from all times and nations," which were performed in authentic or rearranged versions during NOB:

> In the broad sense, the partisan songs are not only those that have occurred in the partisan units in the liberated territories but also other rebel and revolutionary songs from various times and nations, which are in the original or modified forms performed during NOB (folk fighting songs, stylized folk songs, awaking, rebel, labor and revolutionary). (Cvetko 1960: 5)

Folklorists recognized the overlapping of two main groups of songs, folk and mass combat songs, as one of the important features of this music. In general, an array of dichotomies such as local/international, individual/collective and spontaneous/ideological contributed toward discourses on partisan songs as "inconvenient" heritage. New songs created during NOB, regardless of being composed by famous composers or poets[10] who were active participants in the war or among the fighters themselves, were often based on "traditional" aesthetics. Composers often intentionally opted for folk tunes and composed in the "folk spirit" in order to come closer to "folk expression" and more effectively mobilize the broad masses. Nikola Hercigonja, a composer and partisan fighter himself, warned that traditional music practices are the exact element that made it possible for "new" songs to come close to the masses (Hercigonja and Karaklajić 1962: xi). This raised a question about the relationship between individual and collective authorship, and ideological guidance and spontaneity, as one of the central issues in addressing the complexity of this music genre. Several intellectuals and composers asserted that the time of the anonymous folk heritage is over, and that songs created by soldiers and peasants during the fight cannot be seen as "folk creations."[11]

Moreover, in folklorists' writings, partisan songs were identified as a "short-lived music tradition" that occurred suddenly and had an "intensive life only for a moment," usually with a production that "is not so easy to follow" (Škrbić 1961: 307). The fact that partisan songs were often collected, written, and canonized in the very moment of their performance affected the "quality of the material," which did not have the time to evolve to be selected and revised: "The most valuable songs in the printed songbooks are not always, but quite often in a certain way lost within the mass of poetic worthless verses" (Bošković-Stulli 1960: 252). Four years during NOB was not enough time for the songs' intergenerational "active transmission" and the development of musical variants, a process crucial for the "quality" of heritage. According to dominant scholarly accounts, only those songs that resisted the advancement of time and continued to be actively performed after World War II were worthy of being considered as "real" heritage.

Scholars also outlined the aesthetic-political relationship and ideologization of art in questions concerning partisan songs. From the very beginning, many partisan units had organized groups responsible for cultural programs, and some of them even had choirs, which performed at organized cultural events (Križnar 1992: 13–14). A key moment highlighted by scholars is the year 1943, after which the balance between spontaneity and direction in performing partisan songs was challenged, as the original spontaneity was lost and overtaken by acquisition-oriented implementation and dissemination of partisan songs (Karakaš 1974: 12). During the post-World War II years, and despite the ideology of Marxism-Leninism as the main framework for folkloristic accounts, the question of "artistic value," quality, and politics in "folk revolutionary songs" (*narodne revolucionarne pesme*) persisted as the most controversial. Despite insisting on the ideological role of these songs in strengthening socialist society, scholars regarded these ideological elements as contamination of authentic folklore and criticized the explicit political instrumentalization of partisan art. Partisan songs tended to be seen as subordinate to politics and propaganda, which contaminate their artistic autonomy and aesthetic value. In addition to highlighting the social functions of partisan songs, some authors even apologize for these being aesthetically inferior and simplistic (Hrovatin 1960: 255).

Such narratives about ideological vs. artistic purity reveal controversial stances toward aesthetic quality of partisan folklore: "Partisan folk song, which we have today, cannot be seen as art in general" (Škrbić 1961: 307).

Concurrently, some scholars have advocated the thesis that the political nature of partisan songs lies in the very conditions of their making. They argued that it is impossible to understand partisan songs without considering the specific war-related and revolutionary moment of its creation, with its intensity, atmosphere, and challenges: "It is difficult to understand them without understanding the environment in which they occurred and lived" (Čubelić 1960: 279). Partisan songs were seen as free, natural, and impulsive expressions in the extraordinary moment of fighting for freedom, which could not easily be grasped in intellectual, rational ways. Such difficulties in theorizing dynamic expressive practices during World War II were also reflected by scholars themselves: "Wrong assumptions about our folk poetry of revolution create a lot of misunderstanding for today's readers; often even for educated people" (ibid.). However, even those authors, who suggested that we have to experience the suffering and atmosphere of the partisan struggle in order to comprehend the tragic beauty of these songs, argued that only "selected songs of national revolution have specific and clear aesthetic quality" (ibid.).

An additional obstacle in dealing with partisan songs as heritage was posed in the scholarly emphasis that these songs were not part of the past, but an omnipresent element in building a socialist society and mobilizing the masses via its educational function. The official discourses based on ideas of continuous revolution and continuous transformation of Yugoslav society into a "communist classless society" depicted partisan art not as a part of history, but as an ongoing revolutionary present:

> It is a partisan song which is still needed today. Evoking the
> memory of the victims of glorious battles and deserved victories,
> it promotes and leads the working masses to a new success on the
> difficult path toward a brighter future. (Hrovatin 1960: 255)

Accordingly, scholars deployed the narrative of liveliness of partisan artistic production and its relevance for the current moment, being aware of the dangers of regarding partisan songs as "artifacts":

> Ethnological scholarship should not operate solely with historical
> documents, which are covered with the sediment of the past, but
> must use more live material ... Slovenian partisan songs are even
> today something as alive and needed as they were in the time of
> WWII. Because of that they have also often performed in public

manifestations, at conventions, work actions, at school, on the radio, concerts, etc. Also, they are still published in newer song-books, magazines and other publications. (ibid.)

Illustrating the multiple scholarly views has served to survey the specific positions of partisan songs as a simultaneously "inconvenient" and omni-present cultural form. While this summary is a highly condensed and selected view of folkloristic accounts, many parallel voices and paradigms have been reduced here in favor of more dominant views. However, the discussions presented here enable us to track the interesting continuity of contested nar-ratives and multiple accounts and practices that have surrounded the genre of partisan songs since the end of World War II.

Inconvenient Music Heritage: Mainstreamed or Future-Oriented Memory

As deliberated in the introductory part of this chapter, after the break-up of Yugoslavia, performances of partisan songs moved away from stage and official celebrations during socialism toward performing in informal, private settings, and as part of individual memories and family histories. Performing partisan songs was reduced to NOB veterans' celebrations of important anni-versaries connected to World War II, or reserved for private occasions during late hours:

> "When Slovenia became independent, we were no longer rel-evant," said Elena Legiša, a member of Trieste partisan choir. "After Slovenia gained independence, this content was rejected for a certain time. Gradually, it has returned." (Hladnik-Milharčič 2011)

At the beginning of the 2000s, the dominant ideas surrounding partisan songs gradually changed, since the partisan movement started to be framed within the context of the broader European heritage of antifascist resistance and negotiating "Europeanness" in post-Yugoslav nation-states (see Petrović 2012; Perica and Velikonja 2012). In such reinterpretations, emphasis was put on regional resistance as part of the wider European antifascist movement. Consequently, partisan songs started to be re-legitimized, re-narrated, and incorporated in the national musical corpuses (see Hofman 2015, 2016).[12]

In the last few years, new debates about the Yugoslav antifascist resistance and partisan songs started occupying public discourses in post-Yugoslav societies (see Hofman 2015, 2016; Hofman and Pogačar 2014, 2017). Interest in the socialist past has re-entered the public sphere in response to both the post-socialist transformations and the current global crisis of neoliberal capitalism, and their effects on societies. New approaches to Yugoslav antifascism have tried to prove that this legacy has not been an ideologically contaminated myth or "communist fabrication" (*komunistička izmišljotina*). They also expressed a clear disagreement with the historical revisionism of World War II history that excludes the music heritage of NOB from official and public discourses. Instead of focusing on partisan songs as a canonized genre of the socialist past, they directed attention to understanding them as real and "authentic" legacies of antifascist resistance: heroism, sacrifice for one another, morality, and solidarity (see Hofman 2015, 2016). At the same time they openly called for the valorization of beliefs in this legacy and its detachment from the historical view, thereby advocating a "sincere approach" toward its perception during the rise of the far right, racism, and xenophobia, not just in the region, but also worldwide. Such revitalizing and re-narrating of partisan songs as the leading genre of the socialist music legacy occupies a significant place in the emergence of new discourses about the socialist experience, and plays an important role in current sonic (re)conceptualizations of alternative cultural expressions in post-Yugoslav societies.[13]

In that sense, proactively revisiting this musical past may be seen as a new form of "counter mapping" of the socialist legacy, and as part of more general tendencies that use the arts in socially-engaged public practices of cultural mapping worldwide (see e.g. Bishop 2012). Yet can we rethink the mapping of partisan songs in post-Yugoslav heritage management as a vehicle for community empowerment? Can "counter mapping" provide new strategies for building new alliances and networks across national borders? In 2015, the Franja Partisan Hospital in Slovenia was included in UNESCO's Tentative List of World Heritage and received the European heritage label. Due to its symbolic value as a unique example of healthcare in the dramatic conditions of World War II, this site became a symbol of humanity, solidarity, and comradeship among local people, hospital staff members, and wounded soldiers, who fought against fascism and Nazism in World War II. Its designation reflects UNESCO's interests in cultural sites, which, since 1989, were largely neglected and abandoned. However, how "alternative voices" and the "counter mapping" of the legacy of World War II, including partisan songs, will correlate with dominant development and sustainability policy, planning, and advocacy in UNESCO's official heritage narratives is still to be seen.

About the Author

Ana Hofman, PhD, is a senior research fellow at the Institute of Culture and Memory Studies of the Slovenian Academy of Science and Arts in Ljubljana. Her research focuses on the intersection of memory, music, and sound studies, with a focus on activism and the social meaning of resistance in the past and present. She uses both archival and ethnographic methods to examine musical sound during socialism and the present-day conjuncture of neoliberalism and postsocialism in former Yugoslavia. She has published many articles and book chapters, including two monographs: *Staging Socialist Femininity: Gender Politics and Folklore Performances in Serbia* (2011) and *Music, Politics, Affect: New Lives of Partisan Songs in Slovenia* (2015), which deals with the sonic reactualizations of cultural memory on antifascism in the post-Yugoslav context. She is currently working on the monograph *Socialism, Now! Music and Activism after Yugoslavia*.

Notes

1   This article is a result of the project "Music and Politics in the Post-Yugoslav Space: Toward a New Paradigm of Politics of Music at the Turn of the Century" (ID J6-9365) which is financially supported by the Slovenian Research Agency.

2   The 2003 Convention for the Safeguarding of the Intangible Cultural Heritage (Intangible Cultural Heritage Convention; ICHC) has been characterized by some as a counterpoint to the World Heritage Convention (WHC), and as an attempt to acknowledge and privilege non-Western manifestations and practices of heritage (Kurin 2004).

3   Different temporalities of things, persons, or events provide tensions between the contemporary and the contemporaneous (Kirshenblatt-Gimblett 1998).

4   Mass graves constitute an extreme case of negative heritage.

5   The partisan movement and the very term "partisan" gained more specific and complex connotations in other resistance movement in France and Italy (Komelj 2009).

6   In 1941, Ustashas were appointed to rule a part of Axis-occupied Kingdom of Yugoslavia as the Independent State of Croatia (NDH), a quasi-protectorate established by Fascist Italy and Nazi Germany during World War II. During NDH, hundreds of thousands of Serbs, Jews, and Roma were killed. Chetnics

(Chetnik Detachments of the Yugoslav Army) was a World War II movement led by Draža Mihailović, which started as an anti-Axis movement but engaged in tactical or selective collaboration with the occupying forces during almost all of the war.

7   Visible also in formal acts, which equated fascism with communism.
8   Particularly the Federation of Associations of Yugoslav Folklorists (*Saveza udruženja folklorista Jugoslavije*). Its sixth congress in Bled (1959) and eighth congress in Titovo Užice (1961) were specifically dedicated to the folklore of the socialist revolution.
9   According to a personal communication with staff at Radio Ljubljana and Radio Belgrade.
10 Such as Oskar Danon, Nikola Hercigonja, Matej Bor, and Radovan Gobec.
11 Milan Apih, a Slovenian poet, wrote one of the most popular partisan songs, 'Bilećanka'.
12 For more information about the "nationalization of the partisan legacy" in the context of Slovenia, see Perica and Velikonja (2012: 123).
13 About the role of the genre of partisan songs in the new practices of music activism in post-Yugoslav societies, see Hofman (2016).

References

Arizpe, Lourdes. 2000. "Cultural Heritage and Globalization." In *Values and Heritage Conservation*, edited by Erica Avrami, Randall Mason, and Marta de LaTorre, 32–37. Los Angeles: The Getty Conservation Institute.

Bishop, Claire. 2012. *Artificial Hells: Participatory Art and the Politics of Spectatorship*. London and New York: Verso.

Bošković-Stulli, Maja. 1960. "Neki problemi u proučavanju folklora iz NOB." *Rad Kongresa Folklorista Jugoslavije, VI, Bled 1959*, 251–54. Ljubljana: Savez udruženja folklorista Jugoslavije.

Buchowski, Michal. 2004. "Hierarchies of Knowledge in Central-Eastern European Anthropology." *Anthropology of East Europe Review* 22(1): 5–14.

Buden, Boris. 2009. *Zona prelaska. O kraju postkomunizma*, Edicija Reč. Belgrade: Fabrika knjiga.

Byrne, David. 1991. "Western Hegemony in Archaeological Heritage Management." *History and Anthropology* 5: 269–76.
https://doi.org/10.1080/02757206.1991.9960815

Ceribašić, Naila. 1998. "Heritage of the Second World War in Croatia: Identity Imposed upon and by Music." In *Music, Politics, and War: Views from Croatia*, edited by Svanibor Pettan, 109–29. Zagreb: Institute of Ethnology and Folklore Research.

—2009. "New Wave of Promoting National Heritage: UNESCO's 'Convention for the Safeguarding of the Intangible Cultural Heritage' and its Implementation."

In 6th International Symposium "Music in Society." Sarajevo, October 28–30, 2008, 124–37. Sarajevo: Musicological Society of the FB-H/Academy of Music in Sarajevo.

Cizmic, Maria. 2012. *Performing Pain: Music and Trauma in Eastern Europe.* Oxford: Oxford University Press. https://doi.org/10.1093/acprof:oso/9780199734603.001.0001

Cleere, Henry. 2001. "The Uneasy Bedfellows: Universality and Cultural Heritage." In *Destruction and Conservation of Cultural Property*, edited by Robert Layton, Peter G. Stone, and Julian Thomas, 22–29. London: Routledge.

Crampton, Jeremy W., and John Krygier. 2005. "An Introduction to Critical Cartography." *ACME: An International E-Journal for Critical Geographies* 4(1): 11–33.

Čubelić, Tvrtko. 1960. "Stilsko izražajne karakteristike narodnih pjesama iz razdoblja narodne revolucije." In *Rad Kongresa Folklorista Jugoslavije, VI, Bled 1959*, 279–83. Ljubljana: Savez udruzenja folklorista Jugoslavije.

Cvetko, Dragotin. 1960. *Zgodovina glasbene umetnosti na Slovenskem (III).* Diploma, University of Ljubljana.

Dearborn, Lynne, and John C. Stallmeyer. 2010. *Inconvenient Heritage: Erasure and Global Tourism in Luang Prabang.* Walnut Creek, CA: Left Coast Press.

Dicks, Bella. 2000. *Heritage, Place and Community.* Cardiff: University of Wales Press.

Duxbury, Nancy, William F. Garrett-Petts, and David MacLennan, eds. 2015. *Cultural Mapping as Cultural Inquiry.* New York and London: Routledge. https://doi.org/10.4324/9781315743066

Graeff, Nina. 2014. "Experiencing Music and Intangible Cultural Heritage: Some Thoughts on Safeguarding Music's Intangible Dimension." *El oído pensante* 2(2). http://ppct.caicyt.gov.ar/index.php/oidopensante/issue/view/303 (accessed October 15, 2018).

Graham, Brian. 2002. "Heritage as Knowledge: Capital or Culture?" *Urban Studies* 39(5–6): 1003–1017. https://doi.org/10.1080/00420980220128426

Harvey, David C. 2001. "Heritage Pasts and Heritage Presents: Temporality, Meaning and the Scope of Heritage Studies." *International Journal of Heritage Studies* 7(4): 319–38. https://doi.org/10.1080/13581650120105534

Hercigonja, Nikola, and Đorđe Karaklajić, eds. 1962. *Zbornik partizanskih narodnih napeva.* Belgrade: IP Nolit.

Hladnik-Milharčič, Ervin. 2011. "'Smrt fašizmu!,' reportaža Zbori in pesmi upora." https://www.dnevnik.si/1042440353/magazin/reportaza/1042440353 (accessed October 15, 2018).

Hofman, Ana. 2011. *Staging Socialist Femininity: Gender Politics and Folklore Performance in Serbia.* Balkan Studies Series 1. Leiden: Brill.

—2015. *Glasba, politika, afekt: novo življenje partizanskih pesmi v Sloveniji* ["Music, Politics, Affect: New Lives of Partisan Songs in Slovenia"], Zbirka Kulturni spomin, Ljubljana: Založba ZRC.

—2016. *Novi život partizanskih pesama* [*The New Lives of Partisan Songs*]. Belgrade: Biblioteka XX.

Hofman, Ana, and Martin Pogačar. 2014. *Partizanski upor danes? Muzičke prakse NOB in družbena angažiranost.* Ljubljana: Borec.

—2017. "Partisan Resistance Today? The Music of the National Liberation Struggle and Social Engagement." In *Sounds of Attraction: Yugoslav and Post-Yugoslav Popular Music*, edited by Miha Kozorog and Rajko Muršič, 21–39. Ljubljana: Ljubljana University Press, Faculty of Arts.

Hrovatin, Radoslav. 1960. "Slovenska partizanska pesem kot predmet znanosti." In *Rad Kongresa Folklorista Jugoslavije, VI, Bled 1959*, 255–58. Ljubljana: Savez udruzenja folklorista Jugoslavije.

Karakaš, Branko, ed. 1974. *S'pesmom do slobode s'pesmom u slobodi* (CD). Beograd: Muzičko odeljenje sekretarijata za narodnu odbranu.

Kirn, Gal. 2010. "Od primata partizanske politike do postfordistične tendence v socialistični Jugoslaviji." http://www.mirovni-institut.si/data/tinymce/Publikacije/postfordizem/MI_politike_postfordizem_203-244_kirn2.pdf (accessed 15 October 2018).

Kirshenblatt-Gimblett, Barbara. 1998. *Destination Culture: Tourism, Museums, and Heritage.* Berkeley: University of California Press.

—2004. "Intangible Heritage as Metacultural Production." *Museum International* 56(1–2): 52–65. https://doi.org/10.1111/j.1350-0775.2004.00458.x

Komelj, Miklavž. 2009. *Kako misliti partizansko umetnost.* Ljubljana: Založba cf*.

Kovačević, Ivan. 2012. *Ogledi o jugoslovenskom kulturnom nasleđu.* Belgrade: Univerzitet u Beogradu, Filozofski fakultet (etnološka biblioteka knj. 61).

Križnar, Franc. 1992. *Slovenska glasba v narodnoosvobodilnem boju.* Ljubljana: Znanstveni institut Filozofske fakultete.

Kurin, Richard. 2004. "Safeguarding Intangible Cultural Heritage in the 2003 UNESCO Convention: A Critical Appraisal." *Museum International* 56(1–2): 66–76. https://doi.org/10.1111/j.1350-0775.2004.00459.x

Lowenthal, David. 1998. *The Heritage Crusade and the Spoils of History.* Cambridge: Cambridge University Press.

Mannion, Greg, Ivanič, Roz, and the Literacies for Learning in Further Education (LfLFE) Research Group. 2007. "Mapping Literacy Practices: Theory, Methodology, Methods." *International Journal of Qualitative Studies in Education* 20(1): 15–30. https://doi.org/10.1080/09518390600924063

Meskell, Lynn. 2002. "Negative Heritage and Past Mastering in Archaeology." *Anthropological Quarterly* 75(3): 557–74. https://doi.org/10.1353/anq.2002.0050

Nedeljković, Dušan. 1960. "Narodno stvaralaštvo u periodu narodne revolucije oslobodilačkog rata i izgradnje socijalizma Jugoslavije." In *Rad Kongresa Folklorista Jugoslavije, VI, Bled 1959*, 137–60. Ljubljana: Savez udruzenja folklorista Jugoslavije.

Peckham, Robert Shannan, ed. 2003. *Rethinking Heritage: Cultures and Politics in Europe.* London: I. B. Tauris & Co.

Perica, Vjekoslav, and Mitja Velikonja. 2012. *Nebeska Jugoslavija: interakcija političkih mitologija i pop-kulture*. Belgrade: Biblioteka XX vek.

Petrović, Tanja. 2012. *Yuropa: jugoslovensko nasleđe i politike budućnosti u postjugoslovenskim društvima*. Belgrade: Fabrika knjiga.

Pocock, Douglas. 1997. "Some Reflections on World Heritage." *Area* 29(3): 260–68. https://doi.org/10.1111/j.1475-4762.1997.tb00028.x

Prica, Ines. 2007. "Problem interpretacije tranzicije iz 'nerealnogsocijalizma'" ["A Problem of Interpretation of Transition from 'UnrealSocialism'"]. In *Antropologija postsocijalizma* [*Anthropology of Postsocialism*], edited by Vladimir Ribić, 24–50. Belgrade: n.p.

Škrbić, Milan. 1961. "Problem vrednovanja partizanske narodne pjesme." In *Rad VIII kongresa folklorist Jugoslavije u Titovom Užicu 1961*, 307–308. Belgrade: Naučno delo.

Smith, Laurajane. 2007. "Empty Gestures? Heritage and the Politics of Recognition." In *Cultural Heritage and Human Rights*, edited by Helaine Silverman and Fairchild D. Ruggles, 159–71. New York: Springer. https://doi.org/10.1007/978-0-387-71313-7_9

Sullivan, Sharon. 2004. "Local Involvement and Traditional Practices in the World Heritage System." In *Linking Universal and Local Values: Managing a Sustainable Future for World Heritage*, edited by Eléonore de Merode, Rieks Smeets, and Carol Westrik, 49–58. Paris: World Heritage Centre.

Tunbridge, John E., and Gregory John Ashworth. 1996. *Dissonant Heritage: The Management of the Past as a Resource in Conflict*. Chichester and New York: J. Wiley.

Yoshida, Kenji. 2004. "The Museum and the Intangible Cultural Heritage." *Museum International* 56(1–2): 108–12. https://doi.org/10.1111/j.1350-0775.2004.00464.x

Yurchak, Alexei. 2006. *Everything was Forever, Until It was No More: The Last Soviet Generation*. Princeton, NJ: Princeton University Press.

PART II

Cultural Landscape and Music

Introduction to Part II

Britta Sweers
University of Bern, Switzerland

As highlighted in Part I, the activity of musical mapping includes a large range of multi-layered perspectives. This variety notwithstanding, it has particularly been intertwined with human perceptions of surrounding environments and landscapes. Moving beyond technical questions, Part II focuses on the interrelation between music and landscape by addressing another central issue in UNESCO-related discourses, the so-called "cultural landscapes." Similar to "cultural mapping," the term "cultural landscape" has a divided history: While an etymological focus on the term "landscape" provides insights into historical, transforming concepts on the relationship between humans and surrounding environments, the concept of "cultural landscape," particularly in its differentiation to unpopulated nature, only dates back to the twentieth century.

A linguistic perspective, particularly in English and German languages, reveals central defining aspects, such as the interrelation between humans or human perception and environment, which have already been inherent in early etymological concepts. Most likely first used in the fifth century as *landscipe/ landscaef* (German: *Land-schaffen/-formen*), the expression "land" was defined, from a legal perspective, as "any part of the earth's surface that can be owned as property," which is similar to the French *paysage* and the Spanish *paisaje* that relate to the old Roman concept of *pagus*, a rural district that includes the notion of ownership (cf. Costello 1991). The suffix "-scape" (German: *-schaft*), in particular, points to the deliberate process of artificial formation (German: *schaffen*; English: "create"). Contrary to this legal understanding of landscape, the arts-related perception in the sense of "a section or expanse of natural scenery" or art "representing national inland or coastal scenery" dates back to 1598, when it was borrowed into the English language from Dutch painting (ibid.; Makhzoumi and Pungetti 1999).

While the term "cultural mapping" was initially coined in a UNESCO-related context, the application of "cultural landscape" dates further back. Apparently, it was first used in 1908 by German geographer Otto Schlüter (1872–1959), who described the human-shaped *Kulturlandschaft* ("cultural landscape") in opposition to the so-called *Urlandschaft* ("primeval landscape"), thereby, on the one hand, establishing an opposition between humans and their environment, and, on the other hand, pointing toward the interaction between humans and nature (Schlüter 1906: 26). This division was subsequently adapted in commonly used definitions of the *natural* environment. The concept of landscape is clearly set apart from "environment," which has been perceived as the "external factors surrounding and affecting a given organism at any time" (Costello 1991: 447). In contrast, the idea of "landscape" (that is similarly differentiated from the concept of "scenery" as "all the features that give character to a landscape"; cf. Costello 1991: 1199) might simply be described as the visible characteristics of a region, which includes physical elements of land, form, vegetation, animals, and humans, yet also absorbing forms and buildings. In other words, and as Nora Mitchell, Mechthild Rössler, and Pierre-Marie Tricaud from the Division for Heritage and the UNESCO World Heritage Centre pointed out, "Cultural landscapes are those where human interaction with natural systems has, over a long time, formed a distinctive landscape. These interactions arise from, and cause, cultural values to develop" (UNESCO n.d.a.; Mitchell, Rössler, and Tricaud 2009: 5).

As is evident here, the idea of a polarized division between a human-less environment and a culturally-shaped landscape was also taken up by UNESCO in 1992 when the World Heritage Convention was established as "the first international legal instrument to recognize and protect cultural landscapes." Understanding cultural landscapes as the "combined works of nature and of man" (Art. 1 of the Convention, 2012, pt. 47: 14), UNESCO perceived those regions included in the Heritage List as

> illustrative of the evolution of human society and settlement over time, under the influence of the physical constraints and/or opportunities presented by their natural environment and of successive social, economic and cultural forces, both external and internal. (UNESCO n.d.)

In fact, UNESCO's concept points to a large range of landscape categories, particularly those (1) *"clearly defined landscape designed and created intentionally by man,"* which also includes garden and parkland landscapes, and those regions "associated with religious or other monumental buildings and ensembles," and (2) *"organically evolved landscape(s)"* resulting from a constant, process-like interaction of humans with their environment. These two main categories are further subdivided into (a) "relict (or fossil) landscape in which an evolutionary process came to an end at some time in the past," and (b) "continuing landscape ... which retains an active social role in contemporary society closely associated with the traditional way of life." The List distinguishes a further category (3), the *associative cultural landscape,* valued due to the "religious, artistic or cultural associations of the natural element" (UNESCO n.d.).

Given the regional context of the ESEM Cultural Mapping Seminar, UNESCO's differentiation can be illustrated in the case of Switzerland, which ratified the UNESCO Convention on September 17, 1975. For example, the Lavaux vineyard landscape on Lake Leman, which was inscribed in 2007, was recognized particularly due to criterion 3 of the World Heritage List (UNESCO World Heritage Centre n.d.b) (as representing a past tradition, in other words "to bear a unique or at least exceptional testimony to a cultural tradition or to a civilization which is living or which has disappeared"); criterion 4 (the specific human-environmental feature, i.e. "to be an outstanding example of a type of building, architectural or technological ensemble or landscape which illustrates (a) significant stage(s) in human history"); and criterion 5 (representing an exceptionally harmonic interaction of humans and environment[1]):

> The Lavaux vineyard landscape is a thriving cultural landscape that demonstrates in a highly visible way its evolution and development over almost a millennia [*sic*], through the well preserved landscape and buildings, and also the continuation and adaptation of longstanding cultural traditions, specific to its locality. It also illustrates very graphically the story of patronage, control and protection of this highly valued wine growing area, all of which contributed substantially to the development of Lausanne and its Region and played a significant role in the history of the geo-cultural region; and has prompted, in response to its vulnerability next to fast-growing settlements, exceptional popular protection. (UNESCO World Heritage Centre n.d.b)

The concept of "cultural landscape" thus intertwines with human-natural interaction. Yet even in explicitly environmentally-focused cases, as in the case of the Jungfrau-Aletsch-Bietschhorn area that was first inscribed as World Heritage Property in 2001, interactions with humans are recognized as a significant element, as is further evident in the following quote related to criterion 7:

> The impressive landscape within the property has played an important role in European art, literature, mountaineering and alpine tourism. The area is globally recognised as one of the most spectacular mountain regions to visit and its aesthetics have attracted an international following. (UNESCO World Heritage Centre n.d.c)

Clearly, the UNESCO concept goes far beyond mere agricultural techniques, biological diversity, and issues of environmental sustainability by pointing to the "specific spiritual relation to nature," which is similarly reflected in the various forms of cultural expressions, including music. At the same time, it also intertwines with the concept of sustainability. Derived from the Latin term *sustinere* ("maintain," "endure"), the concept of sustainability, which is a further criterion in the decision process, relates to a biological process of "how biological systems endure and remain diverse and productive" by "involving methods that do not completely use up or destroy natural resources" (Costello 1991), of which music has been a marker as well.

Consequently, the chapters in this part focus on the interconnection between landscape and music performance within cultural and environmental landscapes. Steven Feld's frequently quoted *Sounds and Sentiment: Birds, Weeping, Poetics, and Song in Kaluli Expression* (1982) might be viewed as the most prominent example in ethnomusicology. Yet in reality the concept of cultural landscape has been used in highly diverse ways, as evident in recent music-related publications dealing with the concept of cultural landscape. To quote just a few examples that illustrate the variety within ethnomusicological research shows that this literature includes investigations of other natural environments. For example, Benjamin Koen (2011) investigated the interaction of human music performance in the Pamir Mountains, while Theodore Levin (2013) pointed to the interaction between music making and the non-human environment in the steppe context of Tuvinian overtone singing. The literatures also include different concepts of cultural landscape. For instance, Jeffrey Paul Melnick, in *A Right to Sing the Blues* (2001), related the concept not so much to the natural environment but to (urban) traditional music cultures, while other publications added further political dimensions to this concept: Angela Impey (2002) addressed the conflict between external criteria on environmental protection, which led to the removal of local settlements, and the traditional local human interaction with the environment in the context of State Parks in South Africa, while questioning Western standards of environmental sustainability established in the creation of human-less environments. Similarly, Kirsty Gillespie (2013) focused on the interaction of mining, environment, and music making in Australia. The latter examples, in particular, point to the growing importance of ethnomusicological research with regard to environmental discourses.

Notwithstanding these exemplary studies, there is still a critical need for further comparative work, particularly through a close-up focus on the precise process involved in the interactions between humans with their surrounding landscape, as well as of the impact of the environment on the formation of cultural landscapes. The following four chapters not only focus on different landscapes each, but they also provide examples of in-depth studies of different human-music-environment relations and interactions. As the case studies will show, these relations become apparent on multiple sociocultural levels that not always appear to be interconnected directly with the natural environment, at least at first sight. However, these partly hidden connections become particularly evident through the study of these musical practices and perspectives.

Lukas Park (Chapter 5) analyzes the correlation between music and landscape as an intersection between nature and culture. Focusing on the change and preservation of Tibetan *hua'er* music traditions located in the Chinese part of the region, Park provides an example of not only how geographic and harsh environmental conditions shape singing and performance styles, but also how music changes in line with the transformation of the region's cultural landscapes, which raises issues that have similarly been tied to the UNESCO debate on Intangible Cultural Heritage. Shai Burstyn (Chapter 6) reminds us of the importance of re-opening analyses of historical concepts surrounding music and landscape, while casting a historical perspective on the Jewish-Zionist comparative musicologist A. Z. Idelsohn and his emphasis on the "natural environment and climate as shaping forces on music in general and on national folksong in particular" (p. 109). Connecting landscape, climate, and musical style, Idelsohn argued that microtonal intervals could only emerge in this specific pure air of the desert regions, while repetitions are likewise a reflection on the desert environment, thereby also explaining the specific nature of the Hebrew melody. While Idelsohn's line of argument was clearly shaped by the political context of his time, it is nevertheless an interesting example of the interrelatedness between music and environment, a perspective that maintains strong presence in popular science and also partly in UNESCO-related debates.

In contrast, Thomas Solomon's chapter moves on to the Highland of Bolivia and highlights how specific tunes related to pilgrimage interconnect with the natural landscape, but also how this interaction has shaped the broader perceptions about cultural landscape. For instance, Solomon's chapter reveals that the natural geographic environment (including soil types and vegetation) is constantly culturally (re-)defined and imbued with specific meaning through music. Music can thus be understood as a mediator, revealing the relationship between natural geography and social identity. Finally, Vincenzo della Ratta (Chapter 8) returns to Asia by focusing on the Central Highlands of Vietnam, which are inhabited by twenty different ethnic groups that are related to one another via similar traditions and music. In 2005, gong culture was recognized as Intangible Cultural Heritage by UNESCO, and della Ratta reflects the pre-history of this process as it is intertwined with issues relating to the environment and is closely interconnected with tourism as well. While not so much focusing on the environment *per se*, della Ratta directs the reader to the specific cultural landscape and the related space that has been generated by UNESCO in this process, made visible through music and gong culture.

Note

1   "[To] be an outstanding example of a traditional human settlement, land-use, or sea-use which is representative of a culture (or cultures), or human interaction with the environment especially when it has become vulnerable under the impact of irreversible change" (UNESCO 2019).

References

Costello, Robert B. 1991. *Random House Webster's College Dictionary*. New York: Random House.
Feld, Steven. 1982. *Sounds and Sentiment: Birds, Weeping, Poetics, and Song in Kaluli Expression*. 3rd edn. Durham, NC and London: Duke University Press, 2012. https://doi.org/10.1215/9780822395898

Gillespie, Kirsty. 2013. "Ethnomusicology and the Mining Industry: A Case Study from Lihir, Papua New Guinea." *Musicology Australia* 35(2): 178–90. https://doi.org/10.1080/08145857.2013.844486

Impey, Angela. 2002. "Culture, Conservation and Community Reconstruction: Explorations in Advocacy Ethnomusicology and Participatory Action Research in Northern Kwazulu Natal." *Yearbook for Traditional Music* 34: 9–24. https://doi.org/10.2307/3649187

Koen, Benjamin. 2011. *Beyond the Roof of the World: Music, Prayer, and Healing in the Pamir Mountains*. New York and Oxford: Oxford University Press.

Levin, Theodore with Valentina Süzükei. 2013. *Where Rivers and Mountains Sing: Sound, Music, and Nomadism in Tuva and Beyond*. Bloomington, IN: Indiana University Press.

Makhzoumi, Jala, and Gloria Pungetti. 1999. *Ecological Landscape Design and Planning*. New York: Routledge.

Melnick, Jeffrey Paul. 2001. *A Right to Sing the Blues: African Americans, Jews, and American Popular Music*. Cambridge, MA: Harvard University Press.

Mitchell, Nora, Mechtild Rössler, and Pierre-Marie Tricaud. 2009. "World Heritage Cultural Landscapes: A Handbook for Conservation and Management." *World Heritage Papers 26*. Paris: UNESCO.
http://whc.unesco.org/documents/publi_wh_papers_26_en.pdf (accessed October 15, 2018).

Schlüter, Otto. 1906. *Die Ziele der Geographie des Menschen*. Munich: Oldenbourg.

UNESCO. n.d. "Cultural Landscapes." https://whc.unesco.org/en/culturallandscape/ (accessed October 15, 2018).

—2019. "Criteria for Selection." https://whc.unesco.org/en/criteria/ (accessed June 7, 2019).

UNESCO World Heritage Centre. n.d.a. "The Criteria for Selection." http://whc.unesco.org/en/criteria/ (accessed October 15, 2018).

—n.d.b. "Lavaux, Vineyard Terraces: Description." http://whc.unesco.org/en/list/1243 (accessed October 15, 2018).

—n.d.c. "Swiss Alps Jungfrau-Aletsch: Description." http://whc.unesco.org/en/list/1037 (accessed October 15, 2018).

Chapter 5

Landscapes and Flower Songs: Proposing the Hypothesis of Agriculturalist-Pastoralist Coalescence as the Origin of *Hua'er* Festivals

Lukas Park

This chapter is concerned with *hua'er*, a vocal folk music style sung in China's ethnically diverse northwest. During field research in 2012, one of my informants, himself being an expert researcher on *hua'er* culture, offered a hypothesis of the probable origin of *hua'er* music: He proposed that *hua'er* and especially *hua'er* festivals are a result of the intermixing of pastoral and agricultural societies. Land-tilling agriculturalists were largely bound to one place throughout the annual farming cycles; the inhabited space determined the locality of religious and musical festivals. On the other hand, pastoralists roamed different natural and cultural landscapes within the annual seasons, and even over adjacent years; the visited localities and contact-points with settled populations may have been chosen by environmental factors (such as accessibility or vicinity to current nomadic routes), and may even have been chosen based on individual preference. The emergence of grand festivals is based on these dynamics between different perspectives and usages of the surrounding environment and landscapes.

Despite the apparent obviousness of the hypothesis, it has not been published anywhere to date (2019). The lyrics of *hua'er* songs are frequently connoted with sexual topics and activities, and the actual coalescence of nomad and farming cultures might indeed have happened during the *hua'er* festivals. At these annual gatherings, many singers of different ethnic groups, cultural backgrounds, religions, and geographical areas meet and engage in singing with each other. Occasionally, sexual activities apart from the main performances have been accounted for. This chapter aims to scrutinize the feasibility of these activities being a probable driving force for the origin of *hua'er* festivals. Furthermore, the circumstance surrounding why so far nobody has published this theory, albeit being very obvious, is scrutinized. Drawing on expert interviews and social media inquiries as research methods, results point to both academic as well as ideological grounds as the reason why scholars are hesitant to publish this hypothesis of origin.

Setting the Field

In summer 2012, I conducted field research in southern Gansu. Besides recording *hua'er* singers at various festivals of different sizes, and recording semi-professional singers in specially arranged recording sessions, I also conducted interviews with experts. Interviews with prolific *hua'er* researchers Ke Yang, Li Lin, and Zhang Junren proved to be the most fruitful and informative, which is why I chose them as case studies for this chapter.[1] Coupled with unrecorded statements at private meetings with these scholars, the assertions given in the interviews have to be examined under a new light, one that does not only reflect and analyze the statements *per se*, but also sheds light on interpretations seen in the wider context of Chinese academic politics and its ideological influence on personal choices.

The interviews conducted with experts on *hua'er* were semi-guided and conducted entirely in Chinese. I prepared eight questions for the interviews, while question three was explicitly on the history of *hua'er*, particularly not so much on the "when" but more on the "why" did it start. I offered examples for reasons of relaxation, communication, or entertainment.[2] I hoped, and this was also disclosed to my interview partners, that in personal communication different information would be given than in official publications about *hua'er*. Only the parts of the interviews in which we talked about the origin and history of *hua'er* are analyzed for this chapter. I kept in contact via social media applications (namely QQ and WeChat 微信) with Ke Yang and Zhang Junren. Li Lin, however, does not use a computer or social media apps on his mobile phone. As well as the interviews, clarifying WeChat conversations with Zhang Junren were held in order to verify and summarize some of my points.

At one of our numerous meetings and conversations, the following hypothesis emerged: When nomadic or semi-nomadic herders were coming down from their summer pastures in the slack season, they lured village dwellers out with singing. The villagers replied by singing, while the two parties approached each other, and, giving mutual consent, the engagement would lead to sexual encounters right there and then. The Chinese term for "*hua'er* festival," namely *hua'er hui* 花儿会, also allows for the translation and/or meaning of "*hua'er* meeting," thus implying a smaller-scale occurrence. The Chinese character used, *hui* 会, translates as "festival, meeting, gathering, get together, assembly." These early *hua'er* meetings may well have been the only opportunity for herders to meet other people, as usually they were locked away in remote mountain areas for most of the year. *Hua'er* and *hua'er* meetings/festivals may have served as an important outlet for people, resulting in an intermixing between pastoralist nomads and agriculturalist farmers. This proves to be an interesting example of how landscapes influence an entire culture, and may have helped to form an interesting mix of respective landscape-affiliated cultures, namely, agricultural lifestyles in wide basins and valleys, and nomadic lifestyles associated with mountainous areas.

This hypothesis, which shall be coined the Pastoralist-Agriculturalist Coalescence Hypothesis, or PACH, for the remainder of this chapter, was never published or even mentioned in existing *hua'er* literature. I received the consent from my interview partners to publish it in the present format. For various reasons, the above-described nature of *hua'er* meetings/festivals might provoke controversy in China. Beside the academic objection that *hua'er* festivals are widely believed to have originated together with and out of religious temple fairs 庙会, there may yet be ideological reasons why the PACH remains unpublished to date. In China, some guidelines proposed by Mao Zedong at the Yan'an Forum on Literature and Art 延安文艺座谈会 in 1942 regarding musical practices are still in place. These guidelines firmly place workers and farmers at the center of attention of all artistic creation. Therefore, music too must serve proletarian politics and support the popular masses (McDougall 1980). Until now, scholars who oppose these fundamentals are running the risk of ruining their academic careers (Yang 1994a).

Furthermore, *hua'er* became a strong representative force in recent years, especially due to its recognition by the United Nations Educational, Scientific, and Cultural Organization (UNESCO), and its inclusion on national and international Intangible Cultural Heritage (ICH) lists since 2009 (Ding 2010). Since then, *hua'er* has become the center of attention for state-owned media, and is being closely observed under the pretense of protection and safeguarding.[3] This chapter aims to work on two levels, while embracing two distinctive, but interdependent research questions: First it asks about the feasibility of the PACH in general; and second it asks why this idea surrounding *hua'er* origin is not part of the academic discourse, regardless of its feasibility.

Ethnography of *Hua'er*

Hua'er literally means flower, and indeed, flower names such as white peony 白牡丹 or lotus 莲花 are frequently used as synonyms for young women in the song lyrics. An alternative label for this music is *shaonian* 少年, which is used synonymously for young men. Occasionally, Chinese scholars also talk about *hua'er* as *yequ* 野曲, meaning wild tunes. *Hua'er* are a sub-genre of the widely dispersed mountain songs, or *shan'ge* 山歌, an umbrella term applied to many folk musics all over China. Written sources indicate that the mountain songs as a term and as a genre are at least 1,300 years old (Yang 1981). *Hua'er* itself is most commonly divided into the Taomin branch and the Hezhou branch. Taomin *hua'er* 洮岷花儿 are sung in the south of Gansu around the Lotus 莲花山 and Erlang Mountains 二郎山. Hezhou *hua'er* 河州花儿 are affiliated with certain ethnic groups and are sung primarily in the north of the *hua'er* region. Due to improved means of transportation, nowadays many Hezhou *hua'er* can also be heard at *hua'er* festivals in south Gansu, as *hua'er* singers tend to travel to far-away festivals that may have been too remote before the development of traffic infrastructure in the region.

Hua'er is traditionally sung without much instrumental accompaniment, although occasionally *erhu* 二胡 or *sanxian* 三弦 are used. Its lyrics touch upon aspects of sexuality, life, death, environment, family, health, and much more. The region where *hua'er* is sung is on the border between the Tibetan and the Loess plateaus, in the provinces Qinghai, Gansu, and Ningxia. This region is commonly termed as Northwest in China, evoking not only geographical connotations, but also taking into account socioeconomic and historical factors. The motherland of *hua'er* is often said to be around the counties Linxia, Gannan, and Huangnan in the south of Gansu. This region has a significant Muslim Hui and Tibetan populace.

There are eight ethnic groups residing in the *hua'er* region, who sing *hua'er*.[4] The largest minority group in the *hua'er* region are the Muslim Hui 回 Chinese, mainly living in Gansu, Qinghai, and Ningxia. They are also the only recognized minority group that adopted Standard Chinese as its first language. The Dongxiang 东乡 are Muslim people of Mongolian descent. They mainly live in Gansu and speak a Mongolic language. The Sala 撒拉

mainly live in Qinghai, speak a Turkic language, and believe in Islam. The Tu 土 mainly live in Qinghai, speak a Mongolic language and believe in Vajrayana Buddhism. The Muslim Bao'an 保安 mainly live in Gansu and speak a Mongolic language. The Yugu 裕固 mainly live in Gansu and believe in Vajrayana Buddhism. Depending on where they live, they speak either a Mongolic or a Turkic language. A large number of Tibetans 藏, also believers of Vajrayana Buddhism, live in Qinghai and Gansu. The majority Han 汉 people believe in Chinese folk religion, which blends Daoist, Mahayana Buddhist, and Confucian elements in a way that appears to be practically impossible to separate (Yang 1998: 215–22). In several autonomous regions in Gansu, the respective ethnic minority group may be the local majority, as is the case in Linxia Hui and in Gannan Tibetan autonomous prefectures.

There have been violent conflicts and clashes between Muslim groups, Han Chinese, and Tibetans. Interethnic relationships remain uneasy, but despite tensions all these groups sing *hua'er* together and attend the same *hua'er* festivals. The entire region was originally the territory of Tibetan pastoralists, but the influx of Han Chinese from the fourteenth century onwards gradually pushed the Tibetans out, making the Ming dynasty 明朝 (1368–1644) the formative period of Han domination in the region (Kouwenhoven 2013). Still, tunes and lyrics of Tibetan and Han groups are partly similar, suggesting inter-cultural contact over a long period of time. Most of the groups in the region are somewhat sinicized 汉化, meaning that they can speak Chinese as a second or third language, or have adopted it as their first language. *Hua'er* appears to be sung in the local Mandarin Chinese dialect, even though only the Han and Hui speak it in their daily lives, while all other groups have their own respective languages. However, most of the ethnic minority groups mentioned above are capable of understanding and speaking the local dialect (Yang 1994b: 101).

The main performance contexts of *hua'er* are the *hua'er* festivals. These festivals can take many forms, from an informal meeting of a few people during one afternoon to bigger gatherings with tens of thousands of people over many days. Most *hua'er* festivals are held in the fifth and sixth lunar month, approximately July and August each year, the slack season before the harvest. All ethnic groups participate in the *hua'er* festivals, although the social meaning and function might be different for each group. The Muslim population, for example, does not share the polytheistic world of Chinese and Tibetan worshippers, and participate as pleasure-seekers or as merchants, selling drink and food. In recent years, there are also government-organized *hua'er* festivals, with official competitions, media coverage, and modern technical equipment on huge performance stages.

The origin and historical development of *hua'er* and *hua'er* festivals are highly controversial issues, hence many different and conflicting theories exist. According to one popular idea, *hua'er* emerged in the Zhou dynasty 周朝 (1046–256 BC), when the *Classic of Poetry* 诗经 was written, a collection of poems and songs containing lyrics only and no transcriptions of melodies. Lyrics and poetic forms of *hua'er* songs are frequently compared with the folk songs of that book, the so-called *feng* 国风, which are apparently of similar content and style. Another opinion is that *hua'er* was formed in the Tang dynasty 唐朝 (618–907) due to the manifold international relations at the time. There were many foreign orchestras at court, the Silk Road being one of the most frequented. In this multicultural scenario, *hua'er* songs were formed (Yang 1994b: 105–107). Others, like Ke Yang (1983) for example, posit that *hua'er* evolved in the Ming dynasty 明朝 (1368–1644). Supporters of this theory rely on records in *hua'er* researcher Zhao Zongfu's *Treatise on Hua'er* 花儿通论 (Feng and Stuart 1990). According to Zhao, *hua'er* originated with Han migrants from central China during the Ming dynasty, and later developed through cultural interaction between the different peoples in the *hua'er* region. The first written records mentioning *hua'er* are commonly believed to have been made in the Qing dynasty 清朝 (1644–1911) by poet Wu Zhen, who lived from 1721 to 1792 around present-day Lintao and described *hua'er* festivals in his poems.

Results from Interviews

Hua'er as Prayer to the Gods

The interview with Ke Yang (born 1935), professor emeritus of Chinese literature at Lanzhou University, was conducted on August 26, 2012 at his home on campus. His son was present at the beginning of the interview, took pictures, and brought tea, but left the room after the conversation commenced. For Ke Yang, the origins of *hua'er* lie at the end of the Yuan dynasty 元朝 (1271–1368) and the beginning of the Ming dynasty 明朝 (1368–1644). For him, theories of *hua'er* originating in the Tang dynasty 唐朝 (618–907), or its affiliations with the *Classic of Poetry*, are merely conceptions that may or may not be possible, but in any case lack scientific, that is, written evidence. Ke Yang noted that *hua'er* festivals are frequently held in the vicinity of temples, and he mentioned the general importance of temple fairs. Like *hua'er* festivals, most temple fairs take place in the slack season between weeding and harvesting, and they often happen on the same day. In agricultural societies, people pray for good weather, or for having children if they do not yet have any. Ke Yang postulated that at the very beginning, *hua'er* was sung as a "prayer to the gods, not to people."

The Hua'er Workers

Li Lin (born 1938) was head of Min county in the south of Gansu, a position from which he retired in 1998. Before that, he was a middle school history teacher, and he has been a private scholar of *hua'er* throughout his life, specializing in the Taomin branch of *hua'er* and especially the *hua'er* festival on the Erlang Mountain at the foot of which he lives. Present at the interview on August 12, 2012 was his daughter, who provided tea, took pictures, and after the interview offered a delicious lunch. Li Lin thinks that there is simply no material that can clarify when *hua'er* emerged. He further mentioned that there are some who say it emerged in the Ming dynasty 明朝 (1368–1644), because there were a few poets that mentioned *hua'er* in their poems, even directly using the term *hua'er*. However, for Li Lin it is clear that *hua'er* existed long before even the Song dynasty 宋朝 (960–1279), but there are no written records. In Chinese literature, poems by scholars and in folk songs stem from the same source. They evolved from very old folk songs, which were used by poets to turn into poems. On the question of when he dates this source, Li Lin pointed to the *Classic of Poetry*, but for him, mountain songs existed even before the *Classic of Poetry*.

Li Lin dismissed scholars who argue in favor of the Ming dynasty theory as lacking the capacity for logical deduction, because they apparently only accept direct written records. For him, the first time the term *hua'er* was used for describing folk songs was at the time of the Southern and Northern dynasties 南北朝 (420–589): In the collection of poems, *Songs from the Jade Terrace* 玉台新咏, there is a folk song called 'Embroidered Collar' 领边绣. In the lyrics, the singer of the song is "agreeing to be a *hua'er* worker, all year around to be carried around your neck." *Hua'er*, in this case, is synonymous with flower, which is also used to describe the embroidered patterns on clothes. Li Lin's logically deducted explanation is that the singer calls himself a *hua'er* worker. Therefore, if a *hua'er* worker is somebody who sings folk songs, the songs themselves must be called *hua'er*.

The Pastoralist-Agriculturalist Coalescence Hypothesis

The interview with Zhang Junren (born 1962) was conducted on August 21, 2012 at his home on the campus of the Northwestern Normal University in Lanzhou. Two of his master students were also present and recorded the whole interview on video. Zhang Junren saw the earliest function of *hua'er* in its communicative features: "The *hua'er* region was originally nomad's land, not farmer's land, *hua'er* was originally sung by nomads and herders. When people are away all year around, then in their loneliness they start to sing—to themselves, to anybody they meet, or even to people over the next hilltop." He further mentioned:

> Sometimes I think a bit cruder: My betrothed, my wife and I, we are on the mountain all year round. That sounds so boring, doesn't it? A person sometimes needs this verbal dalliance, which is also a kind of human emotional need, so he needs this kind of thing. Only through singing *hua'er*, only at the *hua'er* festivals can they have this time, can they be happy. And then he goes back, and then he's gone again. So, I think it is quite possible that the origin of *hua'er* has to do with this specific human communication.

Zhang Junren was sure that the Hezhou style of *hua'er* developed during the Yuan dynasty 元朝 (1271–1368), although he noted the problem that the available written sources are of course by scholars. When something is written down, it means that it has already reached such a level of popularity that scholars become interested in it. A verifying online communication was held with Zhang Junren via WeChat on October 17, 2014:[5]

> Park: "Maybe you remember, once you said that *hua'er* and *hua'er* festivals are a result of nomads mixing with farmers. When the nomads were coming down from their summer pastures on the mountains, they lured the village girls out of the villages to play."

> Zhang: "There is no evidence for this, it is only a feeling I got after investigating for a very long time."

On the question why nobody had proposed this hypothesis yet, Zhang Junren answered that "guessing is no problem, but for academic matters we must have evidence. This is a common problem of Chinese academic research at the moment." He went on to substantiate this assertion by citing

Nietzsche's "God is Dead" as something that simply cannot be proven. We both agreed that sometimes it is hard for ethnomusicologists to provide written evidence of historical events. I then bluntly summarized my points and laid out my assumption "why nobody has proposed that theory yet, namely that *hua'er* is very famous at the moment, it is watched by national and international protection programs. For a Chinese scholar or cultural worker, it would be hard to imagine that such a venerable tradition actually developed out of such a vulgar function. I think nobody has proposed this hypothesis because it is too vulgar, it does not conform to the existing point of view." Zhang Junren replied very briefly but was affirmatively positive. The main hypothesis from our conversations in Lanzhou has been repeated and verified.

Conclusion

As mentioned in the introduction, a widely accepted assumption of the origins of *hua'er* festivals is that they originated from religious gatherings and temple fairs, even though Chinese scholars remain divided about possible connections between *hua'er* and temple fairs (Zhao 1989; Du 1997; Xi 1989). Scholars who ignore or deny connections between *hua'er* and temple worship may do so not out of real conviction, but possibly in order to protect *hua'er* culture from too much state intervention. Yang Mu describes *hua'er* festivals as a type of folk activity, of which the ultimate goal is lovemaking that may or may not lead to marriage (Yang 1998: 199). He calls those folk activities Erotic Musical Activities, or EMA. Traditionally, due to its sexual nature, *hua'er* was forbidden to be sung in the vicinity of villages; only in more remote mountain areas was it allowed. For Yang Mu, *hua'er* singing is not for marriage partner seeking, as it is known in other parts of China and how it is propagated by the Communist Party. It is sung solely to find a short-term pre- or extramarital sexual partner.

Mountain songs, and thus also *hua'er*, are not merely a pastime activity during outdoor work, or idle entertainment during festivals. They play an active and relevant role in courting and in the creation of offspring. Furtive love affairs, which take place during festivals, may occasionally result in pregnancy. This may be a welcome gift to women whose marriages have not been blessed with children. If women whose marriages remain childless try to get pregnant by strangers, they risk public derision, but to remain childless might result in even more public shame for them. A husband, if pragmatic, will choose to remain silent about such efforts to extend the family line

(Kouwenhoven 2013: 115–25). This observation caters toward the PACH, for the biological father of the offspring—quite possibly a nomadic herder—would be away in remote mountain areas for most of the year. In any case, he did not travel to a *hua'er* festival to seek settled family life, and therefore would not interfere with the domestic peace.

According to official party line, sexual practices connected with the *hua'er* festivals are so-called bad customs 陋俗 that have to be changed into good customs 良俗. The capacity of *hua'er* festivals to serve as a temporary refuge and public outlet for private emotions is also particularly important for women, who are tied to their domestic lives for much of the year. The festivals provide them with a fairly safe environment, and a rare opportunity to speak out. Furthermore, they are a way of escaping gender norms, where typical behavior patterns usually expected from women may be disregarded. With the growing impact of government interference through organized song competitions, complete with the handing out of awards, and additional musical entertainment by professional pop singers, much of the singing now takes place primarily as a harmless pastime. The multitude of functions of *hua'er* festivals is and was so vast that they hardly can be reduced to either sexual activities, nor solely religious activities, nor a simplified mixture of the two.

The PACH conceptualizes *hua'er* and *hua'er* festivals as a result of the mix between pastoralist and agriculturalists, i.e. nomads and farmers. When herders came down from their summer pastures in the slack season they "lured" the villagers out with their singing, which was possibly the beginning of *hua'er* festivals. This chapter set out to answer the question whether the PACH is a feasible explanation for the possible origin of *hua'er* festivals, and also why there is no publication yet that proposes this theory of origin. First, I proposed that it is widely believed that *hua'er* emerged out of religious activities. Second, academics might impose a kind of self-censorship in order not to fall out of party line. The proposition of the PACH is very clear. It also converges with the most acknowledged theory of *hua'er* origin, namely that it came about in the Ming dynasty 明朝 (1368–1644) with the immigration of Han people into the hitherto largely Tibetan population. *Hua'er* is believed to have been created in this multicultural setting. Scholars stay quiet on the details, but generally the PACH is solid, because it merely adds detail to an already existing theory, and does not necessarily pose a new theory in itself.

The lyrics of *hua'er* have sexual connotations, and are traditionally used for partner-seeking. Chinese academics have regarded love songs as something that solely exists for courting, with a prospect to monogamous marriage. Love songs are not recognized as a means for achieving premarital or extramarital sex (Yang 1994b: 110). Among the people in the *hua'er* region, the activity of *hua'er* singing is carried out in public, but the related sexual relationship that may follow is clandestine, and therefore hard to research. One does not need to subscribe to the idea that *hua'er* emerged from religious ceremonies in order to recognize their relevance in religious contexts. Temple fairs are a convergence of religious and secular customs that became intertwined (Kouwenhoven 2013: 143–44). Both sex and religion are politically sensitive topics in China. Scholars have to be careful not to run against party line, and often prefer to conduct morphological music studies 音乐形态学 than musical ethnographies 音乐民族志 that touch upon the complex relations in the region.

The designation of *hua'er* music as national and international Intangible Cultural Heritage elevated it from backward 落后 and coarse 土 toward folk art 民间艺术 and traditional culture 传统文化; the performers are not mere singers 歌手 anymore, they have become folk artists 民间艺人 and transmitters of authentic culture 原生态传承人. From the standpoint of a modern society, it may be unthinkable for official government bodies, culture workers, and academics to place such a prestigious "art" form like *hua'er* upon the coalescence of agriculturalists and pastoralists, making it implicitly vulgar and backward. To accept an entire musical style as being based on sexual intermixing between nomads and farmers might be hard to tolerate for the so-called cultural and political elites in China. The Pastoralist-Agriculturalist Coalescence Hypothesis does not fit into China's current ideological mainstream, as it would represent a picture of *hua'er* that is not accepted by authorities.

Appendix: WeChat Conversation

Park: "I have a problem regarding the origin of *Hua'er*: maybe you remember, once you said that *Hua'er* and *Hua'er* festivals are a result of nomads mixing with farmers. When the nomads were coming down from their summer pastures on the mountains, they lured the village girls out of the villages to play. Do you have sources for that? Did you publish something about it?"	卢：我有个关于花儿的渊源的问题：你可能还记得，你一次说过了，花儿与花儿会是牧民和农民的混合过程出来的。夏天时，牧民从山上牧场下来，到了乡村就开始唱花儿，把村里的姑娘勾引出来玩儿。你关于这方面有没有材料？你自己出版过吗？

Zhang: "There is no evidence for this, it is only a feeling I got after investigating for a very long time."	张：这个没有什么证据，之是我在做了很长时间考察之后的感觉。
Park: "Yes. But I think it is a justified argument, even though there is no evidence. So then nobody else published it?"	卢：恩。可是我觉得很有道理，虽然没有证据。所以呢，也没有人提出这个观点吗？没有出版？
Zhang: "Yes."	张：是的。
Park: "Pity. But I think that is very strange. This would be a very obvious, very logical theory of origin. Of course it is only a possible hypothesis. Why do you think nobody has proposed this yet?"	卢：倒霉。但是我觉得很奇怪。这个很明显的，很逻辑的一个渊源理论。当然只一个有可能性的假说。你觉得为什么还没有人提出这个？
Zhang: "Guessing is no problem, but for academic issues we must have evidence, this is a common problem of Chinese academic research at the moment. In fact there simply are some things which cannot be proven, can Nietzsche's 'God is Dead' be proven?"	张：作为猜想是没有问题的，作为学术问题是需要证据的，这是中国目前学术研究的通病。事实上有些东西是没法正明的，尼采的"上帝死了"能证明马？
Park: "Ah, I see. Chinese scholars have to provide 'written evidence,' right? But that is hard for us ethnomusicologists."	卢：哦。明白了。中国的学士需要提供"文字证据"是吗？我们民族音乐学家无法提供这些！
Zhang: "Yeah."	张：也。
Park: "Okay. I have another guess why nobody proposed that theory yet: *Hua'er* is very famous at the moment, it is watched by national and international protection programs etc. For a Chinese scholar or cultural worker it would be hard to imagine that such a valuable tradition actually developed out of such a vulgar function."	卢：恩。我还有另外的猜想，为什么还没有人提出这个：花儿呢，现在很有名有国家和国际性的保护项目等。对中国学者和文化工人是无法想象的，一个那么有价值的传统从一个那么下流的，"牧民搞农民"的功能发展出来的。
Zhang: (Smiles)	张：（表情符号）
Park: "I think nobody uttered this hypothesis because it is too vulgar, it doesn't fit in with the contemporary point of view."	卢：我觉得，没有人提出这个假说，因为太下流，不适合目前的看法。
Zhang: "Yes."	张：是的。
Park: "Maybe I am just speaking nonsense."	卢：有可能我在废话。
Zhang: "No."	张：No。

About the Author

Lukas Park is currently an independent researcher. From 2015 to 2018 he was assistant professor of ethnomusicology at the Soochow University School of Music in China. He completed his PhD in musicology in 2015 at the University of Vienna, with specializations in the fields of ethnomusicology and sinology, and further studied at Fudan University and Qiqihar University. His academic interests focus on Chinese culture and music, especially rock and folk music

Notes

1   That is not to say that other interviews were not as informative, but their contents touched upon different aspects and different areas of research than this chapter aims to scrutinize.
2   3、花儿的历史：为什么开始（散心、交流、娱乐等）？
3   A discussion of the UNESCO-ICH initiative is not the topic of this chapter, but I suggest Mountcastle (2010) for a study of how ICH initiatives may inadvertently contribute to the further marginalization and demise of the very culture they aim to safeguard.
4   For a critical discussion of this statement, please refer to Yang (1998), and my dissertation (Park 2015). The often-cited "eight ethnic groups" have to be viewed in light of the official classification of the fifty-five ethnic minority groups, termed minority "nations" by the Chinese government. The classifications largely follow the definition of nation as laid out in the 1913 essay by Joseph Stalin, Marxism, and the National Question, and are highly problematic.
5   Please refer to the Appendix for the full conversation.

References

Ding, Zuoshu 丁作枢. 2010. *New Compilation of Lotus Mountain Hua'er* 莲花山花儿新编. Lintan 临潭: Kangle Culture and Sports Bureau 康乐县文化体育局.

Du, Yaxiong 杜亚雄. 1997. "Taomin *Hua'er* and Fertility Worship Cults 洮岷花儿和生殖崇拜文化." *Folk Culture Forum* 民间文学论坛 4: 14–20.

Feng, Lide, and Kevin Stuart. 1990. "'On *Hua'er*' by Zhao Zhongfu and 'Selections of Traditional Qinghai Folk Songs' by Zhou Juangu and Zhang Gengyou (Review)." *Asian Ethnology* 49(2): 344–46. https://doi.org/10.2307/1178052

Ke, Yang 柯杨. 1983. "Tracing the Roots of *Hua'er* 花儿溯源." In *Collection of Essays on Hua'er* 花儿论集 2, edited by Ke, Yang 柯杨, 86–105. Lanzhou 兰州: Gansu People's Press 甘肃人民出版社.

Kouwenhoven, Frank. 2013. "Love Songs and Temple Festivals in Northwest China: Musical Laughter in the Face of Adversity." In *Music, Dance and the Art of Seduction*, edited by Frank Kouwenhoven and James Kippen, 115–62. Delft: Eburon Publishers.

McDougall, Bonnie S. 1980. *Mao Zedong's "Talks at the Yan'an Conference on Literature and Art": A Translation of the 1943 Text with Commentary*. Ann Arbor: University of Michigan Center for Chinese Studies.

Mountcastle, Amy. 2010. "Safeguarding Intangible Cultural Heritage and the Inevitability of Loss: A Tibetan Example." *Studia ethnologica Croatica* 22(1): 339–59.

Park, Lukas. 2015. *Tonality of Hua'er: The Collective Intentionality of Sound Bodies*. PhD dissertation. Vienna: University of Vienna.

Xi, Huimin 郗慧民. 1989. *Survey on Hua'er Studies* 花儿学通论. Lanzhou 兰州: Lanzhou University Press 兰州大学出版社.

Yang, Mu. 1994a. "Academic Ignorance or Political Taboo? Some Issues in China's Study of Its Folk Song Culture." *Ethnomusicology* 38(2): 303–20. https://doi.org/10.2307/851742

—1994b. "On the *Hua'er* Songs of North-Western China." *Yearbook for Traditional Music* 26: 100–16. https://doi.org/10.2307/768246

—1998. "Erotic Musical Activity in Multiethnic China." *Ethnomusicology* 42(2): 199–264. https://doi.org/10.2307/3113890

Yang, Yinliu 杨荫浏. 1981. *Draft History of Ancient Chinese Music* 中国古代音乐史稿. Beijing 北京: People's Music Publishing House 人民音乐出版社.

Zhao, Zongfu 赵宗福. 1989. *Survey on Hua'er* 花儿通论. Xining 西宁: Qinghai People's Press 青海人民出版社.

Chapter 6

Climate and Environment in Idelsohn's *History of Hebrew Music*

Shai Burstyn

The landscape of the Holy Land figured prominently in the published accounts of nineteenth-century travelers touring Palestine. Indeed, the early decades of that century are considered a golden age of travel literature to the Holy Land. These travel books laid the foundation for the scientific study of the geography, archeology, demography, and fauna and flora of the region (Röhricht 1890). At the same time, a different kind of landscape descrip-tion of the Holy Land thrived in the associative, pseudo-historic writings of Jewish authors, many of whom had never set foot in the Middle East. They concocted their—at times amazingly detailed—nature descriptions by mixing paraphrases of biblical verses with utopian, pseudo-realistic scenes, which were in fact the figments of their fertile imagination.

In 1913, the seventh year of his stay in Jerusalem, Abraham Zvi Idelsohn, the central figure of this chapter, published five short impressionistic sketches of his wanderings around the Holy Land (Idelsohn 1913). Their content and style reveal that he was greatly influenced by the associative-historic genre, even though his descriptions were veritable eyewitness reports. His sketches, though unrelated to his musical concerns, shed light on the emotional-ideological stance that sustained both his research and its findings. As I hope to show in this chapter, they provide the researcher with an insightful backdrop against which Idelsohn's ethnomusicological writings are better understood.

In spite of the general recognition of Idelsohn's writings as seminal for the research of Jewish music, no in-depth attempt has been made to date to view them as a whole. Future studies of his work tackling this ambitious goal

Figure 6.1: Abraham Zvi Idelsohn (1882–1938). Source: A. Z. Idelsohn Archives at the JNUL, Mus. [Jewish National and University Library, Music] 9 (16), reprinted with permission.

will have to scrutinize Idelsohn's extensive oeuvre, analyze and summarize his findings and claims, and proceed to identify the ethnomusicological and historiographic trends and undercurrents that influenced his thinking, as well as the ideological forces that set it in motion and provided its underpinning. The reflections in this chapter provide a modest contribution to the groundwork necessary before an exhaustive study can be accomplished. Its specific topic concerns Idelsohn's views on the importance of natural environment and climate as shaping forces on music in general, and on national folksong in particular.

Idelsohn was born in 1882 in Latvia and received a Jewish Orthodox education, which included some musical instruction and cantorial training. Before turning twenty, he moved to Germany and studied music in Berlin and Leipzig. Trained as a professional cantor, and armed with both Jewish national fervor and musical know-how, the twenty-five-year-old Idelsohn settled in Ottoman Jerusalem in 1907, determined to uncover the ancient roots of Hebrew music, which he believed had survived over two millennia in the religious biblical cantillation of various Jewish communities—especially the Eastern ones—in spite of the fact that the Jewish people had been scattered all over the globe for so long. In 1921, Idelsohn left Palestine and settled in the United States, where he continued his research activities as best as he could, having become severely restricted by a debilitating ailment. He died in 1938.

> תולדות
> # הנגינה העברית
> מהותה יסודותיה והתפתחותה
>
> מאת
>
> אברהם צבי אידלזון
>
> כרך ראשון
>
> ברלין תרפ"ד
>
> הוצאת "דביר" תל-אביב – ברלין

Figure 6.2: Idelsohn, *The History of Hebrew Music.* Title page.

In 1924, Idelsohn published the first volume of *Toldot Hanegina Ha'Ivrit* (*The History of Hebrew Music*). The comprehensive project was to comprise four volumes but due to poor sales, the other volumes, though written, were never published.

Idelsohn's scholarly orientation was thoroughly German. It is no surprise, therefore, to find that his views on the origins and initial development of Jewish music were rooted in contemporaneous German scholarly thought in general, and in those of *Vergleichende Musikwissenschaft* in particular. This is clearly evident in his frequent allusions to the strong connection between the *Volk* and the environment in which it was born and developed. Furthermore, he believed that once established, national traits leave upon a person a permanent stamp, regardless of whether he lives in his homeland or elsewhere. In the terminology current among scholars of nationality, this would classify him as an "organic primordialist" (Smith 2000). At the very beginning of *History*, Idelsohn makes his main point:

> Each nation has its music, which was created under the influence
> of the nature and climate in which it developed, and out of its par-
> ticular life conditions. There are two types [of music] among cul-
> tured people: Eastern and European, and they are different from
> each other in their foundations and forms. (Idelsohn 1924: 1–2)

His first thesis, then, declares the centrality of nature and climate as shaping forces on music. The second thesis, positioning East and West as cultural and musical poles, brings up perforce the issue of race: by East, Idelsohn meant Semitic; by West, he meant Aryan. In the early twentieth century, race was still a central, legitimate topic of scientific discussion and investigation, as it had been throughout the eighteenth and especially the nineteenth centuries. Race also played an important role in contemporaneous theories of comparative musicology, long before genetic anthropology and ethnomusicology were contemplated. It was from these discourses that Idelsohn must have drawn some of his central ideas. In the wake of the horrific events of European history in the 1930s and 1940s, the entire topic had become highly problematic and was largely avoided.[1]

As stated, Idelsohn adopted the opinion that the musical essence of each race was essentially determined by the natural conditions, climate, and geography of the region in which it developed. Nevertheless, these initial musical traits were susceptible to radical modification when, due to external circumstances (such as famine or war), branches, or tribes, of that race were forced to migrate to other, at times very different, geographical zones. There, under the influence of their new natural environment, their musical characteristics changed drastically:

Who would say now that the music of the Finns and Turks, or of the Germans and the people of India, are close in spirit to each other? Turkish and Indian music is Eastern, while Finnic and German music is European. This is so because Eastern nature and climate dictate a certain type of music, as does the tempered West ... Once separated from their race, the Finns settled on the lakes near the Northern part of the Baltic sea, where fog and moisture cover the sky and fill the air, where rain and snow are plentiful, winters are long and cold, nights are prolonged and days are short and dark, full of wailing winds and gushing storms ... furious seas and dark forests. This description typifies the landscape and climate not only of Finland, but also of Sweden, Norway and Scotland. Therefore there is similarity in the music of these nations. In their music one seems to hear stormy rains, gusty winds on the lakes and in the forests ... But the Turks, who belong to the same race, migrated Eastward and settled in Asia minor, where the skies are clear and pure, the air clean and the sun awakens sensuality; in a barren desert, among rocky mountains, where echo repeats itself 7 to 12 times. As a result, their music

is monotonous, sensuous, desert-like. Its sounds glitter like the
bright skies ... it is as if in every tune an exhausted, thirsty soul
wails and sighs: I'm parched! In short—Turkish music is Eastern
in character, and Finnic music is North-European in character,
even though both stem from the same race. (Idelsohn 1924: 1–2)

It is both engaging and revealing that when describing Oriental music,
Idelsohn tends to assume the tone of the impressionistic, romantic, and poetic
musician, rather than that of the restrained, factual ethnomusicologist he is
when describing European music. Note his language when comparing the
effects of nature, landscape, and climate on Semitic and "Aryan" people:

Arabic "night music" (Layl) could come to life only while riding
a camel on a full moon shining over vast desert expanses. Just
as a Scandinavian is incapable of appreciating the night songs
of the Arabic desert, so a prairie man, a desert wanderer, cannot
fathom the sea music of the Scandinavians. How can a Northern
man living on vast waters comprehend the craving of the thirsty
desert Bedouin for water? And contrarywise, how can a dweller
of icy, foggy lands perceive a serenade sung on a magic Italian
night? ... How can the sons of desert tribes sing the marches of
the Roman-Germanic military tradition while returning from the
battlefield, when all their wars are fought riding horses and cam-
els? Likewise, how can one compare the yearnings of a son of
Arabia to his beautiful beloved, hidden away in her father's tent
and may be glimpsed at only through its narrow slits, without
hope of a closer approach; how could this be compared to the
love of the Aryan, whose beloved is readily accessible and attainable? (Idelsohn 1924: 2)[2]

In order to expose the origins of Jewish music and reconstruct its ancient
history, Idelsohn hypothesized a three-stage developmental theory of a
sociology of music: a primordial racial stage, advancing through a tribal
stage (e.g. the spreading out of racial branches Eastward and Westward), and
finally, and most importantly, reaching a national stage, in which each nation
crystallized its unique musical character. This is of course the stage that interested Idelsohn the most, for here he saw the uniqueness of Jewish music.

In constructing his three-stage theory—race, tribe, nation—Idelsohn may
have been influenced by the pioneering work of Wilhelm Wundt (1832–1920),
one of the founding fathers of modern psychology, who in his monumental

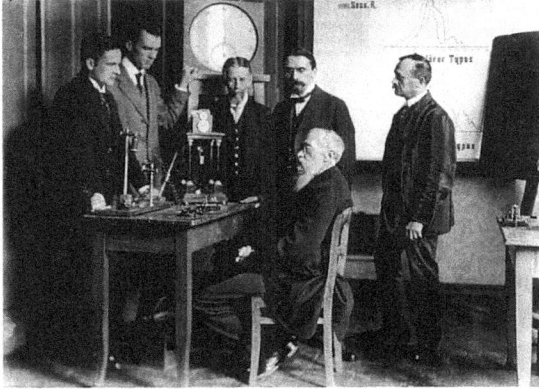

Figure 6.3: Wilhelm Wundt at his lab (ca. 1908). Wikipedia. Original source: http://psy.uniklinikum-leipzig.de/eng/geschi-e.htm. Photo: public domain.

ten-volume *Völkerpsychologie* ("People's Psychology") (1900–1920), which Idelsohn knew and cited, offered a social-psychological overview of people's cultural development.[3] Wundt studied the development of human culture within its social context, placing great emphasis on language, art, myth, and religion, elements that Idelsohn used while formulating a feasible history of Jewish music from its primordial racial and tribal roots to its mature national form. It is obvious that for Idelsohn, who strove to define Jewish music as a *communal* enterprise, Wundt's distinction between individual and communal spiritual creation was a significant source of support. Idelsohn insisted on the anonymity of folk music on the grounds that "when the identity of the creator is known, it is no longer folk music, but rather the music of a particular individual." He cited Wundt as claiming that "each property whose creator is known belongs to the domain of cultural history rather than to that of folk properties" (Idelsohn 1924: 242, n. 1; see also Wundt 1904, vol. 1: 3).

In his *History of Hebrew Music*, as well as elsewhere, Idelsohn outlined essential differences between Eastern and Western cultures, especially between their musics, by way of generalizing two opposing racial psychological portrayals: Western culture was typified by dynamism, development, and enlargement of kernel ideas, and by rationality and individual artistic achievement. Conversely, Eastern culture was characterized by its static nature and preference for narrowness and fixity, as well as by excitedness and simple folk, communal art. While European music developed, adopted harmony, and reached artistic peaks, Oriental music, from which Occidental music has originated, remained unchanged. This difference, argued Idelsohn, is an outcome of the nature of these races—the Semitic race and the Aryan race—and the nature of their lands. The nature [hot climate] of the East saps the strength and makes one sleepy to the extent of becoming hallucinatory and dreamy; European [cold] climate awakens and forces one to act, to overcome the obstacles of nature, and that makes one strong, vital and clear-minded. This is why Eastern music, the fruit of excited imagination and hallucination, remained dreamy and excited like Oriental people, while European music has developed, together with its makers, and received its final form by rules founded on rationality more than on imagination and feeling. (Idelsohn 1909: 454)

Idelsohn did not dream up these ideas about the influence of climate on human nature and culture. Such notions hailed back to the Hellenistic era and beyond, though in the course of centuries these ideas have assumed varying forms and shades.

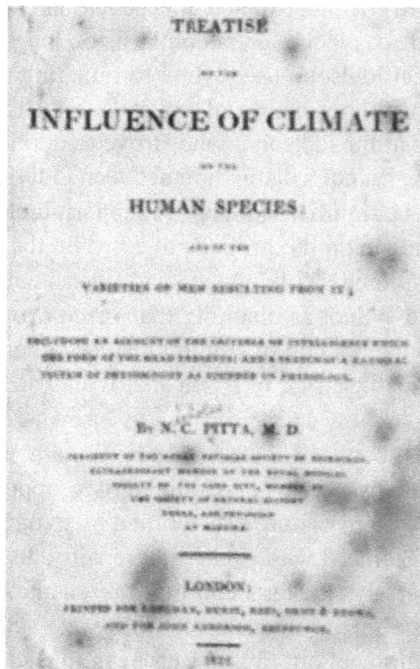

Figure 6.4: Nicholas C. Pitta, *Treatise on the Influence of Climate on the Human Species* (1812). Title page.

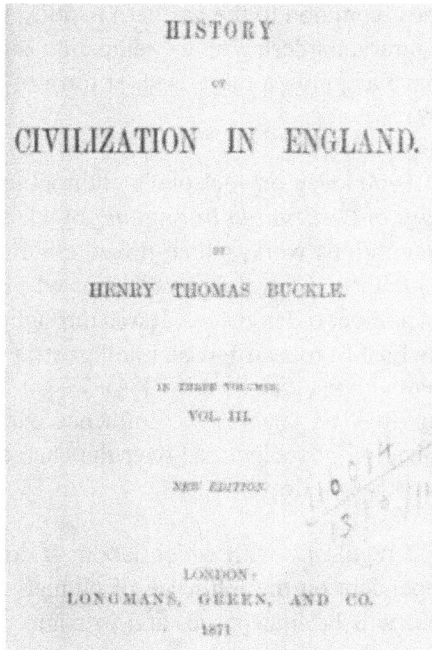

HISTORY

OF

CIVILIZATION IN ENGLAND.

BY

HENRY THOMAS BUCKLE.

IN THREE VOLUMES.

VOL. III.

NEW EDITION.

LONDON:
LONGMANS, GREEN, AND CO.
1871

Figure 6.5: H. T. Buckle, *History of Civilization in England* (1871 edition). Title page.

A pertinent example of these ideas was published in 1812 in the *Treatise on the Influence of Climate on the Human Species and on the Varieties of Men Resulting from it* by a Scottish medical doctor:

> Indolence is a striking characteristic of the natives of hot climates, seemingly interwoven into their very constitutions. In many places ... they let their nails grow into claws that all men may see they do not work. Ease with them is the greatest good, and nothing surprises them so much as to see Europeans take pleasure in exercise: they are astonished to see people walk, who have the choice of sitting still. (Pitta 1812: 79)

The same book contains a passage closely reminiscent of what Idelsohn had written about the Finns and the Turks:

> The Hungarians are referred to the same primitive stock with the Laplanders; but the latter, under the northern zone, have assumed

the features most common to the northern nations, while the former, on the contrary, bordering on the temperate zones of Greece
and Turkey, have acquired a more elegant form of countenance.
(Pitta 1812: 19)

A likely source of influence on Idelsohn's anthropological-geographical
thought is the *History of Civilization in England* by Henry Thomas Buckle
(1821–1862). This ambitious work, which linked environment and climate
with material and intellectual development, achieved great popularity and
was translated into a number of languages. It was through its Russian translation that many in the East European Jewish intelligentsia became acquainted
with Buckle's influential book (see Shavit 1984).

An excerpt from Buckle's chapter II, "Influence exercised by physical
laws over the organization of society and over the character of individuals"
(Buckle 1857: 36), reads as follows:

The energy and regularity with which labour is conducted, will
be entirely dependent on the influence of climate ... if the heat
is intense, men will be indisposed, and in some degrees unfit-
ted, for that active industry which in a milder climate they might
willingly have exerted ... Climate influences labour not only by
enervating the laborer or by invigorating him, but also by the
effect it produces on the regularity of his habits. Thus we find that
no people living in a very northern latitude have ever possessed
that steady and unflinching industry for which the inhabitants
of temperate regions are remarkable ... It would be difficult to
conceive a greater difference in government, laws, religion, and
manners, than that which distinguishes Sweden and Norway on
the one hand, from Spain and Portugal on the other. But these
four countries have one great point in common. In all of them,
continued agricultural industry is impracticable. In the two southern countries, labour is interrupted by the heat, by the dryness of
the weather, and by the consequent state of the soil. In the two
northern countries, the same effect is produced by the severity
of the winter and the shortness of the days. The consequence is,
that these four nations, though so different in other respects, are
all remarkable for a certain instability and fickleness of character; presenting a striking contrast to the more regular and settled
habits which are established in countries whose climate subjects

the working-classes to fewer interruptions, and imposes on them the necessity of a more constant and unremitting employment. (Buckle 1857: 39–41)

Ze'ev Jabotinsky (1880–1940), the prominent intellectual and political leader of revisionist Zionism, drew on Buckle when he insisted that the Jewish national rebirth must take place in the same geographical locale where the nation was born:

The uninterrupted development of our Eretz-Israeli [Palestinian] uniqueness is possible only on the same soil and in the same natural environment in which this uniqueness once came into being. Another climate, a different flora, different mountains, will of necessity distort the body and soul formed by the climate, flora and mountains of Eretz-Israel; because the racial body and racial soul are nothing but an outcome of a specific integration of natural forces. (Jabotinsky 1905: 49)

Idelsohn may have been influenced not only by Buckle's book, but also by some of the Zionist writers who enlisted it in their cause. Jabotinsky's dictum finds a strong echo in Idelsohn's vision, stated decades later:

In our ancient Homeland, which is so rich in associations for us, and where we are constantly reminded of the old sources of Israel's inspiration, there will arise the new Jewish song. It will be created, not as the ultra-moderns think, out of the music, which the composer feels in his heart but rather out of that which he hears around him, influenced also to a great extent by traditional music. It is the song of the Jewish peasant singing in the fields that will be the source of the music of the future. (Idelsohn 1929b: 63)

True to the belief in the reality of *volk*, communal music, which resonates in the above quotation, Idelsohn argued, like others at his time, that "the preference of scale is a racial peculiarity rather than the result of social conditions" (Idelsohn 1932: 637). As regards Semitic scales, he outlined a modal system of four main Arabic *maqamat* (from which others could be derived). With certain modifications (mainly the presence or absence of microtones), these were the four main scalar constructions Idelsohn held to be common among Jews wherever they lived. He believed that unlike Oriental Jews, European Jews do not use microtones due to centuries of exposure to European music. His explanation was that their sense of hearing was weakened by 1,800 years of Northern climate, which dulled their originally acute Oriental hearing (Idelsohn 1920: 496). Moreover, his vested interest in the idea of the survival of ancient Jewish music led him to the dubious conclusion that "despite the resultant variance, synagogue song remains identical the world over, because these differences in tonality are of sufficiently minor importance not to change the character of the music" (Idelsohn 1929a [1967]: 26).

In both Arabic and Jewish modes, Idelsohn was less interested in their sca- lar construction *per se*, than in their motivic nature. His insistence that Semitic modes are essentially melody types, rather than scales in the European sense, placed him at the forefront of contemporaneous ethnomusicological think- ing. To Idelsohn, the motive was the fundamental musical building block of any national music, and it too was influenced by climate and environmental conditions. In *History* and other publications, Idelsohn isolated and defined what he took to be typical national motives. "At first," he wrote, "a motive is formed in the soul of the folk musician, or the folk ... a small group of tones expressing a certain mood" (Idelsohn 1924: 241). He provided several exam- ples of short musical motives he believed to emanate from physical work, such as hauling barges on the Nile or in northern rivers:

> The Slavic barge haulers on the Volga pull the ropes while cry- ing F-D-G-D (2 eights followed by 2 quarters) ... These physi- cal movements already reveal the special quality of the nation's spirit, the first buds of original music, music created out of the unique character of the nation's soul as well as of the influence of nature and climate and the living conditions of the said nation. (Idelsohn 1924: 241)

In other studies, Idelsohn analyzed melodies by "identifying" motives of different national origins, at times within the same melody (Idelsohn 1932: 644).

According to Idelsohn, in Hebrew Semitic music, motivic mosaic is the goal, the principal means of melodic construction, whereas in European music it is only the means for generating variations, extensions, and pro- longations. This insightful view was more than an objective observation; it also contained value judgment probably derived from the current demise of

Figure 6.6: Tunes made up by Idelsohn by linking different national motives (printed in Idelsohn 1932: 644).

tonality in Western art music. Thus, European music seeks constant development of its motives, which is never attained, and thereby leads to its degeneration (Idelsohn 1924: 5).

It should be observed that in spite of this rather unflattering view of Occidental music, in his own compositions Idelsohn did not live up to his scholarly bias of Oriental music. His opera *Jephthah* (1922), for example, is thoroughly Western in style, even though it comprises much Oriental melodic material. In his writings, however, Idelsohn's ideological, national fervor led him not only to praise Semitic musical fundamentals and causally link them to regional climate and environment, but he also declared them superior to European musical foundations:

> The extremely pure air of the East greatly sharpens the sense of hearing. This is why the hearing of an Oriental is very acute and can discriminate very small intervals between adjacent tones ... The Oriental does not find pleasure in musical quantity, that is, he does not strive for many simultaneous voice parts [polyphony, harmony]; he finds satisfaction only in the quality of tones. While using a small range of tones—between fifth and octave, the Oriental splits these intervals further into smaller tones, which scholars lately call quarter tones, thereby opening the possibility of forming numerous scales in Oriental music, each one with its own unique intervals. (Idelsohn 1924: 3)

Even if Idelsohn's ideas regarding the influence of environment on music may be taken to be straightforward, he did introduce an unexpected twist:

[The environment] does not always act with equal force to mold human nature and to change character. A nation in its infancy, when historic life has not yet shaped its grain, is nothing but soft matter, open to changes and influences. But when it has consolidated in the mold of the environment and has become one solid piece of matter, covered by a hard crust, its spiritual form has also been crystallized, and it will resist change by new external factors. If a nation already possessing a certain mature spiritual and cultural form would change its territory and move to a different zone and climate, it might be influenced by its new life conditions, but it *will not change or replace the core of its soul, its spiritual capital ... This is especially true of an emotive capital such as music. This is why the Jewish nation has not replaced its Oriental, Semitic music with another one, and has not forgotten it even while living in diaspora, in changing climates.*[4] (Idelsohn 1924: 2–3, emphasis original)

According to Idelsohn, to assert the causal influence of environment on musical traits is very important, and is a fundamental component of his thesis, an essential stepping-stone on which to set down his central claim of the survival of ancient Hebrew music in biblical cantillation. Similar expressions of his atavistic notions were already apparent in earlier writings, notably the claim that

to this day the Jew is not excited by European music ... Even in diaspora, the Jewish audience did not yet change its Semitic preference, let alone in Eretz-Israel [the land of Israel], in Semitic environment and Oriental climate. Due to two reasons I am very doubtful whether European music can take up root in the Jewish nation at the time of its return to its Oriental homeland: because East cannot be turned into West, and because a 3000-years-old staunch Semitic-Hebrew spirit will contradict such an attempt in all its notorious persistence. (Idelsohn 1920: 502–503)

It is evident that Idelsohn's assertion about the unchanging character of national music (once crystallized) is an indispensable ingredient of his theoretical ideas. It is not merely the environment's influence on music that interested him, but rather the way in which it can bolster his claims for the uninterrupted continuity of Hebrew music.

Idelsohn's views on the history of Jewish music evolved within the ideological framework developed by the emerging discipline of ethnomusicology. It was widely accepted that contrary to Western music, which underwent revolutionary changes in the early twentieth century, musics of other cultures were essentially static and stable. Applying this postulation to Jewish music enabled Idelsohn to present the latter as an organic part of awakening Jewish nationalism. Moreover, it also allowed him to play down the significance of surface-level changes in Jewish music, changes which, so he argued, blinded Jews from perceiving the fundamental stylistic unity and continuity of their national music across history.

About the Author

Shai Burstyn, PhD, was professor and senior faculty member of the department of musicology at Tel-Aviv University (1974–2007), including a three-year tenure as chair. He also taught at the Mannes College of Music (New York) and was a Research Fellow at the Society for the Humanities at Cornell University. Burstyn served on the board of ESEM (European Seminar of Ethnomusicology) and chaired the Israeli Society of Musicology. He has published extensively on various aspects of late medieval and early Renaissance music, notably medieval oral polyphony and Arab influence on medieval European music. His interest in oral music practices led him to research the early Israeli folksong (1925–1960), primarily its ambiguous relations with the music of the Middle East and its national-ideological constraints. Burstyn is a founding member of *Zemereshet*, an Internet project dedicated to collecting and preserving the early Hebrew song repertory.

Notes

1   For a blatantly anti-Semitic example from the early 1930s see Eichenauer (1932).
2   I presume Idelsohn ignored here what he must have known about the central theme of unrequited love in the chansons of medieval troubadours and trouvères because it did not fit his argument.
3   In the opening years of the twentieth century, the young Idelsohn was a student at the Mendelssohn conservatory in Leipzig, while Wundt was a prominent professor at the university there.
4   According to this reasoning, the previously mentioned historical split of the Finns and the Turks must have occurred before a typifying musical character had time to crystallize.

References

Buckle, Henry Thomas. 1871 [1857]. *History of Civilization in England*. New York: D. Appleton & Company. https://doi.org/10.2307/25527645

Eichenauer, Richard. 1932. *Musik und Rasse*. Munich: J. F. Lehmanns Verlag.

Idelsohn, Abraham Zvi. 1909. "Neginatenu Hale'umit" ("Our National Music"). *HaShiloah* 21: 446–65 (in Hebrew).

—1913. "Mimahazot Ha'aretz" ("From the Sights of the Land"). *Luah Eretz Yisrael* 18: 31–65.

—1920. "Negina Shemit" ("Semitic Music"). *Hashiloah* 37: 492–503 (in Hebrew).

—1924. *Toldot Hanegina Ha'Ivrit* [*The History of Hebrew Music*]. Berlin: Dvir (in Hebrew).

—1929a. *Jewish Music in its Historical Development*. New York: Henry Holt and Company. [New York: Schocken, 1967].

—1929b. "Kol Nidrei as an Expression of Jewish Life." Interview with Prof. A. Z. Idelsohn. *Ivri Anouchi* (October 1): 61–63.

—1932. "Musical Characteristics of East-European Jewish Folk-Song." *The Musical Quarterly* 18(4): 634–45.

Jabotinsky, Ze'ev. 1905. "Zionut ve'Eretz Yisrael" ("Zionism and the Land of Israel"). *Ideological Writings* I, Tel Aviv 2015: 37–55.

Pitta, Nicholas C. 1812. *Treatise on the Influence of Climate on the Human Species*. London: Longman, Hurst, Rees, Orme & Brown.

Röhricht, Reinhold. 1890. *Bibliotheca geographica Palaestinae. Chronologisches Verzeichnis der auf die Geographie des Heiligen Landes bezüglichen Literatur von 333 bis 1878 und Versuch einer Cartographie*. Berlin: H. Reuther.

Shavit, Yaacov. 1984. "Hashimush shel Maskilim Yehudim Bemizrah Eropa bemishnato shel H.T. Buckle" ("The Use of H.T. Buckle's Thought by East-European Jewish Intellectuals"). *Zion* 49: 401–12 (in Hebrew).

Smith, Anthony D. 2000. *The Nation in History: Historical Debates about Ethnicity and Nationalism*. Hanover: The University Press of New England.

Wundt, Wilhelm. 1904. *Völkerpsychologie: Eine Untersuchung der Entwicklungsgesetze von Sprache, Mythus und Sitte*, vol. 1. Leipzig: W. Engelmann.

Chapter 7

Dancing the Landscape: Music, Place, Collective Memory, and Identity in a Highland Bolivia Pilgrimage

Thomas Solomon

On May 3 every year, on the occasion of the Catholic feast day *Fiesta de la Santa Vera Cruz* (Feast of the Holy True Cross), people from the rural indigenous communities surrounding the town of Chayanta in the north of the department of Potosí in the Andean highlands of Bolivia engage in a pilgrimage, walking together in large groups for up to several hours as they converge on the town from every direction. Central to the pilgrimage is performance on panpipes, which the men in each band of pilgrims play as they move steadily through the landscape. While each community-based group has one emblematic tune it plays while walking along the pilgrimage route, the pilgrims also pause briefly at several significant places along the route to play different tunes from a special repertory associated with those places. The pilgrimage is thus suffused with the music of the panpipes resounding through the landscape, sonically inscribing the presence of each band of pilgrims into overlapping networks of sacred places, making their communities audible and grounding them in sacralized space.

How might music bring into existence relationships between people and landscape? In what ways might music as a sonorous vehicle embody identity and sonically ground it in place? How can movement through sacralized space enabled by music be a vehicle for collective memory? This chapter explores these questions through an analysis of the May 3 pilgrimage, focusing on musical performance and the movement through space it enables. This case study forms the basis for an exploration of how music as embodied expression mediates between people, place, and collective memory. The natural landscape can be understood to afford resources in the form of specific geographical features, distinctive soil types, rock formations, vegetation, etc. These natural features come to be culturally defined and imbued with meaning through practices such as naming them, talking, and singing about them (Solomon 2000, 2004), and movement through them in the form of dance. Even instrumental music can be involved in the cultural construction of landscape, as when specific tunes or repertoires come to be associated with specific culturally defined places. I argue that musical ritual performance, through its production of the physical sensations of musical sound, mediates between the physical bodies of people and physical features of the landscape, inscribing memory and collective identity in place. Repeated ritual performance, as in the annual pilgrimage discussed here, thus serves to recover those embodied memories and continually reestablish in sonorous form those collective identities, reinscribing them in the bodies of the participants.

If cultural landscapes can be considered the "combined works of nature and humankind, ... express[ing] a long and intimate relationship between peoples and their natural environment" (UNESCO World Heritage Convention n.d.), then, in the case discussed here, it is musical sound that through its physical embodiment mediates and articulates nature and culture, effectively doing the cultural work of "combining." Musical performance and the sounds it creates provide the medium for the phenomenological unity of physical environment and people, making them conceptually and experientially parts of a single ecology. The meaning of nature and landscape is thus not just discursively constructed, but given embodied expression through the human breath that causes instruments to sound and reverberate through the space of landscape—making landscape not just visible but *audible*—and through the moving bodies that instantiate the landscape by means of their movement through it. Ritual based on music and movement thus creates a map, not just as a mental representation but as a lived, embodied experience. This map, as an embodied form of indigenous knowledge and experience concretely realized through collective and participatory performance, effectively takes the affordances offered by the material landscape and culturalizes them, saturating them with meaning that is accessed and reinstantiated whenever socialized bodies move through the landscape, both during the heightened states of cyclical rituals and in the mundane movements of everyday life.

My case study comes from ethnomusicological fieldwork carried out during 1993 among indigenous peoples of the region known as Norte Potosí, or northern Potosí, in the Bolivian Andes Mountains. The indigenous people of Bustillo Province live in dispersed peasant communities spread out over an area of approximately 2,250 square kilometers in the eastern range of the Bolivian Andes, at an altitude of between 3,200 and 4,000 meters above sea level (Figures 7.1 and 7.2). The communities are grouped into nine larger units known as *ayllus*.

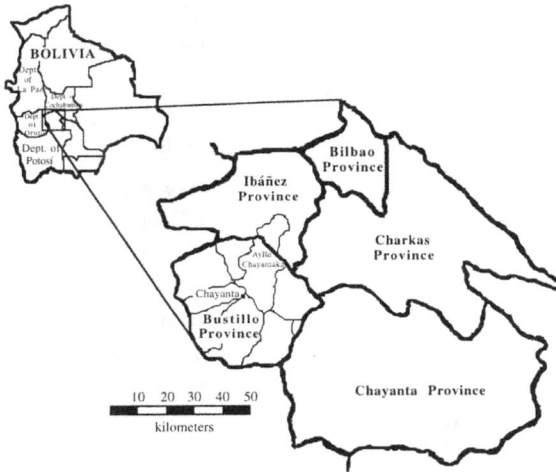

Figure 7.1: Location of Bustillo Province within the region of *Norte Potosí* in Bolivia (Thomas Solomon).

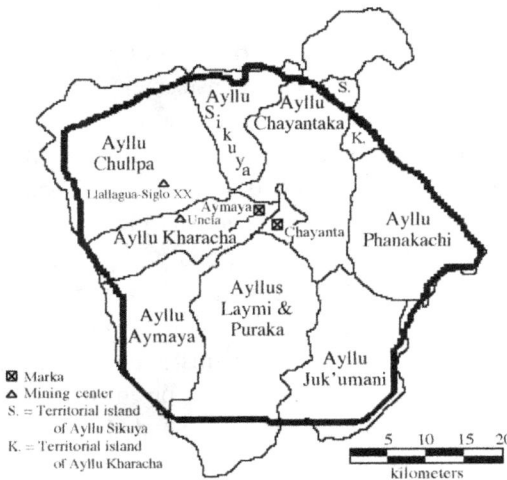

Figure 7.2: The nine *ayllus* of Bustillo Province, with the centrally located town of Chayanta (Thomas Solomon).

While the Quechua- and Aymara-language term *ayllu* has meant different things in different times and places throughout the central Andes (Castelli et al. 1981; Godoy 1985, 1986), in the context of the *ayllus* of Bustillo Province it can be said to evoke a corporate identity based on four inter-related things: (1) common ancestry, (2) a territorial base, (3) a contemporary network of kin relations, and (4) a perceived shared way of life and set of cultural practices (Godoy 1985, 1986; Harris 2000: 97–98).[1] The majority of *ayllu* people live in dispersed rural communities where they engage in a mix of agriculture and pastoralism, although many also do seasonal work outside the community (Kraft 1995: 55) or small-scale mining within their *ayllu*'s territory (Godoy 1990). The population of individual *ayllus* ranges from the approximately 10,500 members of Ayllu Chayantaka, who live in some 45 village communities, to the estimated 2,350 members of Ayllu Sikuya, distributed among about 20 communities (Mendoza et al. 1994). The twin towns of Chayanta and Aymaya, located in the center of the province where the territories of most of the *ayllus* come together like spokes at the center of a wheel, function as the *marka* or ceremonial center, being the site of several inter-*ayllu* fiestas throughout the year, including the feast day that is the focus of this chapter.

The *Julajula* Panpipes and Their Music

On the Feast of the Holy True Cross, people from communities of all nine *ayllus* make a pilgrimage to the central town of Chayanta. During this pilgrimage, the men in each band of pilgrims continuously play a type of panpipe known as *julajula*. Each individual instrument is divided into two parts, one containing four tubes, and the other containing three. By alternating back and forth between the two halves of the instrument, one can produce the successive pitches of a pentatonic scale. But in actual performance, each half of the instrument is played by a different person. Since tunes mostly move stepwise up and down the pentatonic scale, this performance technique results in a continual alternation or hocket back and forth between the players of the two halves. In my musical transcriptions of *julajula* melodies I represent the pitches played on the two parts of the instrument by means of notes with stems pointing in opposite directions: stems up for the four tones produced by the four tubes of the half of the instrument called *yiya* (from Spanish *guía*, "guide") and stems down for the three tones played on the other half, called *arka* (Figure 7.3).

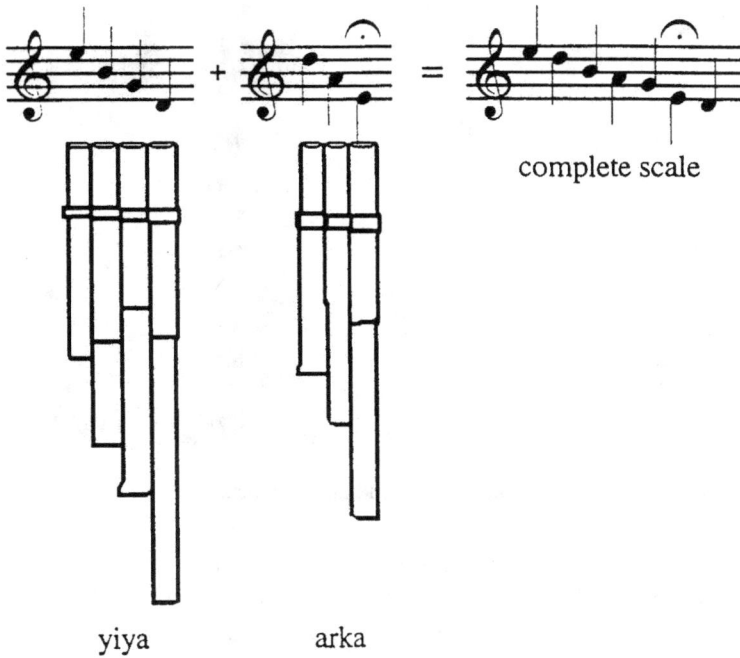

complete scale

yiya   arka

Figure 7.3: Tuning of the *julajula* panpipes, with the pitches of a pentatonic scale distributed among the instrument's two halves, each played by a different player (Thomas Solomon).

There are five sizes of *julajulas*, tuned and played in parallel octaves (Figure 7.4). Thus, in order to have a complete ensemble with five sizes, each size consisting also of two parts played by different people, at least ten players are required. To maximize participation, all the sizes are doubled so that twenty, thirty, or even more men may play together.

There are two stylistically distinct kinds of tunes or genres played on the *julajula*, respectively called *tonada* and *kulwa*, played at different times during the pilgrimage. Both kinds of tunes share certain stylistic features. As already noted, most melodies in both genres alternate pitches between the two halves of the instrument, such that most of the time the same player does not sound two consecutive tones. Exactly one pitch is played on each rhythmic pulse, so there is no syncopation or subdivision of the beat. But there are also significant differences between the two genres, especially having to do with rhythm.

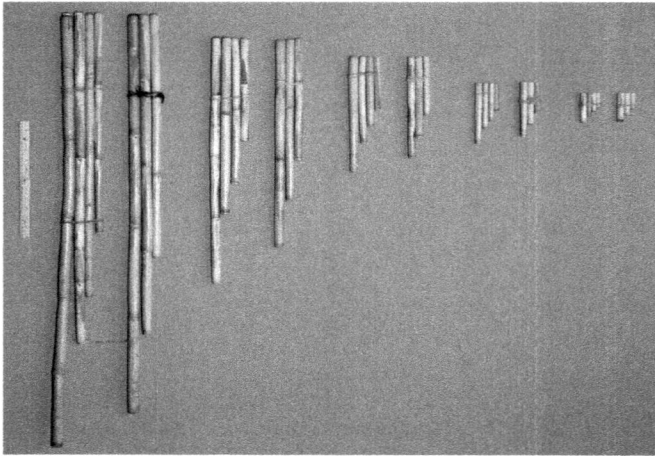

Figure 7.4: The five sizes of *julajulas*, tuned in parallel octaves (Thomas Solomon).

Tonada melodies consist of an irregular series of short phrases of one to nine tones. Within phrases, after articulating each tone the players slowly reduce the amount of breath blown over the tube so that each tone overlaps slightly and blends with the next tone played on the other half of the instrument, resulting in a smoothly undulating melodic line. Players give the last tone of each phrase, however, a short staccato articulation, which contrasts markedly with the smooth connections between tones within phrases. These phrase boundaries always occur between repeated pitches played by the same person; that is, a single pitch is never sounded two consecutive times without a phrase boundary intervening between them. The player has to interrupt the air flow of the first sounding in order to give the tone a second, separate articulation. The resulting break in the melodic flow is lengthened by a very brief interval, so the second sounding of the pitch does not occur where the next pulse would be, as established by the steady pulsation of the preceding phrase. The timing of this very short break between phrases comes not from a subdivision of the pulse, but rather from the use of an independently timed system of pauses. Along with the staccato articulation of the tone just before, these pauses have the effect of marking boundaries between phrases, separating them from each other slightly in time. In my transcriptions of *tonada* melodies, I have indicated these breaks not with a musical rest but with a breath mark, so as not to suggest a relationship between the length of the pause and the pulse established by the basic rhythm of the melody (Figure 7.5).[2]

Figure 7.5: Transcription of a *tonada* melody (Thomas Solomon).

Figure 7.6: Wave form of the first phrase of a *tonada* melody, with transcription (Thomas Solomon).

The graphic representation in Figure 7.6 of the wave form of a line from a *tonada* performance illustrates the contrast between the way pitches are blended into each other within phrases, and the way a brief pause—indicated with breath marks—occurs between repeated pitches, creating a phrase boundary. While the pause is very brief (about 1/8 of a second), it can be easily heard in the performance.

Tonada melodies generally take the form of two repeated sections (labeled A and B in the transcription), in which a single tempo is maintained, followed by a third section (labeled "coda") which is not repeated, and in which the tempo may decrease slightly. The entire melody, including the coda, is played for each repetition, as in the following diagram:

AA BB Coda – AA BB Coda – AA BB Coda ...

The tune may be played continuously for an indefinite number of repetitions, as many times as necessary to keep the music and the band of pilgrims going while walking along the pilgrimage route.

The other genre played on *julajula* is called *kulwa*. This term is derived from the Spanish term *copla*, a poetic couplet. I was told that these tunes used to have words sung by the women among the pilgrims, but the custom of singing *kulwa* has been lost, and the tunes are now performed only in instrumental versions without singing. *Kulwa* melodies are thought to be more serious in character than *tonada* tunes. In contrast to the *tonadas* played while walking, which may change from year to year, *kulwa* tunes are not supposed to ever change, and consequently the *kulwa* repertoire is said to be very old. As one of my field assistants put it, "Since the time of our great-great-grandfathers, they shouldn't change."

Stylistically, *kulwa* differs from *tonada* in several respects. While melodic motion in *kulwa* tunes is mostly stepwise (between the pitches of the pentatonic scale the melodies use) as in *tonada*, leaps upward of larger intervals occur somewhat more commonly in *kulwa* (Figure 7.7). In *tonada*, as

Figure 7.7: Transcription of a *kulwa* melody (Thomas Solomon).

noted above, each section is comprised of several short phrases punctuated by pauses. In *kulwa*, however, each section of the tune consists of a single continuous phrase without pauses. While melodic segments separated by leaps upward sometimes seem to define shorter units, these are not separated from each other by any kind of pause structure and are not marked with a distinct staccato articulation as in *tonada*. The rhythmic pulse and forward "momentum" of the melody are thus not interrupted in *kulwa* as they are in the performance of *tonada* melodies.

Overall, the tempo in *kulwa* performance is somewhat slower than in *tonada*. But tempo is much more flexible in *kulwa* performance than in the performance of *tonada* melodies. While in *tonada* performance the only tempo variation is found in a ritardando during the coda section, within individual repetitions of *kulwa* melodies the tempo may increase and decrease within each section—the tune seems to "speed up" and "slow down." This feature can be seen in the graphic representation in Figure 7.8 of the wave form of two lines from a *kulwa* performance, and my accompanying musical transcription using "real time" proportional spacing between the notes. In the top line, from the A section of the tune, the tempo is held relatively steady and eight pitches with equal duration are sounded over the course of about four seconds. In the second line, from the B section of the tune, the tempo

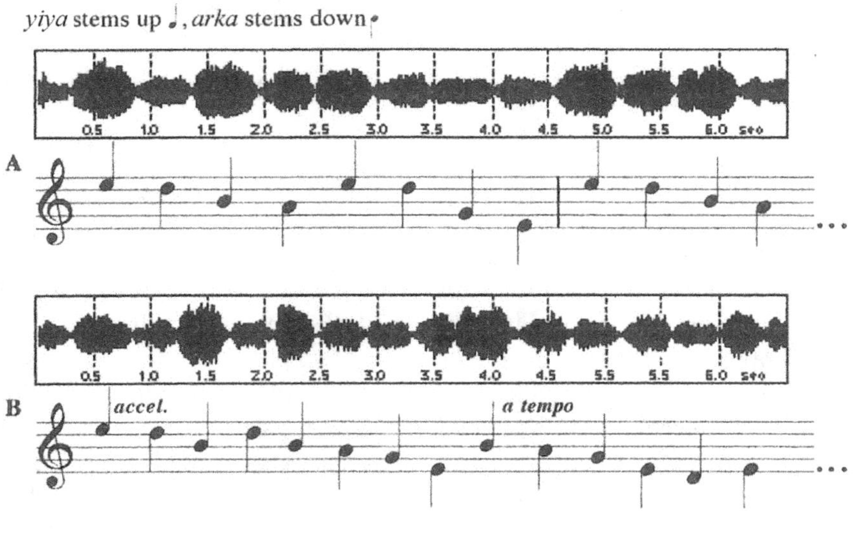

Figure 7.8: Wave form of two phrases from a *kulwa* melody, with transcription (Thomas Solomon).

increases slightly so that ten pitches are sounded within four seconds. The tune then slows back down to the original tempo. The difference may seem slight in this short excerpt, but it is equivalent to a M.M.[3] increase of $\downarrow\ = 30$, and the difference is very audible on my tape recording of the performance. This variation in tempo in *kulwa* performance seems to be facilitated by the fact that when playing this genre, musicians are always at rest, rather than moving along the pilgrimage route, and the tempo is thus not constrained by the speed of the group's walking pace as during performance of the *tonada* genre. These changes in tempo are stylized and made part of tunes themselves, staying the same from one repetition to another, with the result that all the players in a troupe have no problem coordinating among themselves and executing the tempo changes together.

While *tonada* tunes may be played with an indefinite number of repetitions while traversing the pilgrimage route or while entering, walking around, and exiting the plaza in Chayanta, *kulwa* tunes are usually played for just two or three repetitions each time they are performed, whether at an *apachita* on the pilgrimage route, or in front of the church upon arrival in Chayanta (these contexts for *kulwa* performance are more fully discussed below).

Finally, *kulwa* tunes are also realized differently in performance from *tonadas* in terms of form. While *kulwa* tunes, like *tonadas*, have A and B sections and a coda, in *kulwa* performance the coda is not played at the end of each repetition of the melody, but only at the end of the entire *kulwa* performance, as in the following diagram:

AA BB – AA BB – AA BB Coda

Music, Movement, and Place on the Pilgrimage Route[4]

Dozens of communities from the different *ayllus* participate in the fiesta by making the pilgrimage on foot from their home settlements to the town of Chayanta in the form of a group called *wayli* (from Spanish *baile*, "dance"). The core of the *wayli* is formed by male *julajula* players of all ages—from young boys to middle-aged men. In the middle of the group, surrounded by the *julajula* players, walk the *pasantes*, or fiesta sponsors—usually a husband and wife. The *wayli* troupes of most communities also include a male cross-bearer, who carries the community's large cross resting over one shoulder, bringing it from the community's home chapel to the church in Chayanta so that it may "hear" the mass performed by the priest there and be recharged with spiritual power.

Moving about within the *wayli* group is the *mayura*, who keeps the troupe in order by striking with a whip the legs of any of the *julajula* players who do not play well or who otherwise disrupt the group. In front of the players walk two (sometimes three) unmarried girls called *mit'anis*, who wave white flags as they lead the group. Flanking on each side and following behind the group of male *julajula* players are the women of the community, who carry provisions for the overnight stay in town. Depending on the size of the community, the troupe may total up to fifty to sixty people, though the average seems to be around thirty to forty. Only very old or sick people (and perhaps converts to Protestant sects) do not make the pilgrimage, staying home instead in the community throughout the fiesta.

The *tonada* melodies described above are played while actually walking during the pilgrimage journey (Figure 7.9), and it is said that a new melody should be composed each year to be used for the pilgrimage. *Kulwa* melodies constitute a special repertoire played at certain specific moments during the pilgrimage, when the pilgrims stop briefly at certain sacred spots along the pilgrimage route. These are places where it is said that the town of Chayanta—or more specifically, the tower of the church there—can be seen in the distance. To play *kulwa* the men stop walking and stop playing

Figure 7.9: The community in motion: the band of pilgrims traverses the pilgrimage route while the men play *tonada* on the *julajula* panpipes (photo by Willer Flores Aguanta, used with permission)

Figure 7.10: Kneeling posture adopted during the performance of *kulwa* (photo by Thomas Solomon).

the *tonada* melody. They then kneel down facing the direction of the town of Chayanta and begin to play the *kulwa* melody. The kneeling is a sign of reverence and seriousness, adopted from Roman Catholic religious practice (Figure 7.10). They play *kulwa* for two or three complete rounds of the melody, then abruptly stand up and continue on the journey, starting up the *tonada* melody again as they are walking.

While bands of pilgrims from many communities simultaneously make the pilgrimage to the town of Chayanta, I will trace as an example the route taken by people from the community of Irupata, Ayllu Chayantaka, from their home village to Chayanta. As the condor flies, Irupata is only about seven kilometers (a little more than four miles) from Chayanta. The path from the village to the town, however, follows a precipitous topography through ravines and over ridges, and the trip takes about one and a half hours.

The specific route traveled is significant, because the troupe stops at a number of places along the route collectively referred to as *apachitas*. These are places along the path where it is said one can see the tower of the church in Chayanta, on top of which there is a cross. From most of these places the town of Chayanta actually appears as a green and white spot in the distance— the tall trees in the plaza can be seen as green splotches, between which the glint of white buildings is occasionally discernible. The church tower itself is not actually distinguishable, as the tall trees in the plaza in front of the church block it from view. Upon arrival at each *apachita* along the pilgrimage route the *wayli* stops, and the men play a *kulwa* tune as described above.

Each community has its traditional route to the town of Chayanta and its own unique sequence of *apachitas* where its *wayli* stops to play *kulwa*; the paths and *apachitas* of different communities do overlap, however, especially as they converge the closer one gets to the town. During the pilgrimage that takes place during the Feast of the Holy True Cross, the *wayli* from the community of Irupata plays *kulwa* at three different named *apachitas* along the path to town, as well as upon arrival in the town plaza itself. The following description of the pilgrimage during the Fiesta de la Cruz in 1993 is based on my observations and on conversations with Irupateños after the event itself. Like A. Seeger (1987: xvi–xvii), I use the present tense not in order to represent the events described as normative, but to convey the sequential unfolding of events in time and space.

Around 10:00am on the morning of May 3, the *wayli* gathers in the patio of the fiesta sponsors' house. The *mayura* arrives with the *julajulas* in a cloth sack and distributes the instruments among the men who will play. After some time practicing the *tonada* tune that will be played throughout the pilgrimage, a brief meal and a round of ritual libations, the *wayli* exits the house and heads to the path leading out of the community, playing *tonada*.

The first *apachita* where the Irupata *wayli* stops to play *kulwa* is actually at the edge of the settlement of Irupata itself. It is called Q'asa Uray ("descent into the ravine"), as it is where the small plain on which the settlement lies abruptly ends, and the path leads down into a steep ravine through which a road passes. From this high spot the town of Chayanta, the ultimate destination of the group, can be seen in the distance as a green splotch on the landscape (Figure 7.11).

The player of the *urqu* size of *julajula* (the middle size of the five sizes) has to remember tunes and start them, especially *kulwa* tunes. As one of my field assistants explained, the *urqu* player "has greater responsibility to remember, he has to start it. Sometimes he doesn't remember [the *kulwa* melody], and just plays the *tonada*. The people may scold him then because in the *apachitas* you're just supposed to play *kulwa*. After that they play *tonada* again in order to continue along the way."

Thirty-five minutes after leaving Irupata, the *wayli* leaves the road for a footpath that heads straight over a low ridge, at the top of which the group arrives at the second place where the men again stop to kneel down and play *kulwa*. This place is called Janq'u Apachita; the name derives from its

Figure 7.11: Q'asa Uray, the descent into the ravine, site of the first *kulwa* on the journey from Irupata to Chayanta (photo by Thomas Solomon).

singular appearance. Janq'u is the color white in Aymara; this site is an out-cropping of bald white volcanic rock. I am not sure what the significance of this place is—why it is considered an *apachita*. In contrast with other *apachitas*, the town of Chayanta is not actually visible from here, but the bare white rock of the place, probably welded volcanic ash, is striking—almost no vegetation grows there. I asked people if the place has its *kwintu* ("story," from Spanish *cuento*), but I could not find out its significance. Being the highest place around for a few kilometers, it may be a place where lightning frequently strikes, a significant attribute for a place to have. It is also very near the current boundary of Chayantaka territory, and so its significance may lie in something as simple as being the last place the *wayli* can stop briefly to rest before leaving "home" territory on the way to the pilgrimage's final destination.

About forty minutes after leaving Janq'u Apachita, the *wayli* arrives at Kayni Apachita, a small rise just outside the town of Chayanta, and the last place it will stop to play *kulwa* before entering the town itself (Figure 7.12). This place is named for the thorny plant *kayni* that grows there, but it is also important for other reasons. Near the spot where the *wayli* stops to play *kulwa* is a small collection of large stones called *uwija illa* (visible on the far

Figure 7.12: Kayni Apachita, with the town of Chayanta in the background (photo by Thomas Solomon).

right in Figure 7.12). *Uwija* is a Quechua rephoneticization of Spanish *oveja*, "sheep." The word *illa* embodies a much more complex concept.

In the Andeanist ethnographic literature, *illas* are most commonly described as amulet-sized stone effigies of animals. *Illas* may also be boulder-sized rocks, which stand out in the landscape because of their color, shape, or placement in the terrain. Whatever their size, *illas* are "power objects" (Allen 1988: 54), intimately connected with the fertility of fields and animals, but especially the latter. The *uwija illa* near Chayanta, as it contains stones shaped like sheep and sheep's heads, has power over the fertility of sheep. As an elder of Irupata matter-of-factly explained, "It causes the sheep to reproduce." When stopping at Kayni Apachita to play *kulwa*, the people of the *wayli* are just as conscious of being near the powerful *uwija illa* as they are of the view of the town of Chayanta on the plain below.

A few minutes after leaving Kayni Apachita, the *wayli* begins to enter the town of Chayanta itself. On the outskirts of town, the streets that lead into the central plaza are flanked by walls of adobe bricks and stone that enclose the adjacent fields. Once entering the straight lines defined by these walls, the streets guide one into town, giving no choice except to head straight toward the central plaza. The walled streets give the impression that travelers from all directions are drawn to a central point—that all roads cannot help but converge on the plaza.

The streets of Chayanta have Spanish names identified by nameplates attached to the walls of buildings at the four corners of the plaza. The "official" names of these streets refer to the history and geography of the Bolivian state: streets are named after heroes of the war of Bolivian independence from Spain (Sucre, Santa Cruz), the revolutionary patron of the Andean republics (Simón Bolívar), a hero of the War of the Pacific (1879–1884) against Chile (Abaroa), the 1873 treaty of alliance (Alianza) between Peru and Bolivia against Chile prior to that war, other regions of Bolivia (Cochabamba, Tarija), and "commerce" (Comercio). The plaza itself is named after an important date (November 10, 1810) during the war of independence, when in the city of Potosí a group of revolutionaries imprisoned the crown-appointed governor-intendent and set up a junta to rule in place of the royalists.

The people of the *ayllus* may be vaguely aware of the "official" names of the streets entering the plaza, but they conceptualize the town's geography in a very different way. Each *ayllu* has its "own" street, by which the *waylis* of its communities enter the plaza and on which they have their overnight lodging (Figure 7.13). The layout of the streets of the *ayllus* in the town of Chayanta corresponds in a broad way to the relative spatial distribution of the territories of the *ayllus* themselves, and provides for a division of the town itself into "upper" and "lower" parts which correspond to groupings of the *ayllus* into two moieties, separated by one of the sidewalks which cut diagonally through the central plaza. The distribution of *ayllu* streets around the plaza thus recreates and condenses in a small arena the socio-spatial organization of the geography of the *ayllus* in the region.

While the men of the *wayli* may be tired from their journey, they play the *tonada* with renewed vigor for their actual entrance into the town of Chayanta, speeding up the tempo as they walk briskly into the plaza so as to project an aggressive, commanding group presence. For example, the *wayli* of Irupata generally played its *tonada* at a metronome marking of about ♩ = 140 along most of the pilgrimage route, but sped up to about ♩ = 150 for their entrance into the plaza.

The pilgrimage to Chayanta is an occasion for the articulation of *ayllu* territory as a network of sacred places. The places sonically inscribed with *kulwa* performance by the *wayli* from Irupata are ostensibly defined in relation to the church in Chayanta. But, as we have seen, these places may have their own histories and significance, and from one of them the town of Chayanta cannot even be seen. During the journey these sacred places are reinscribed

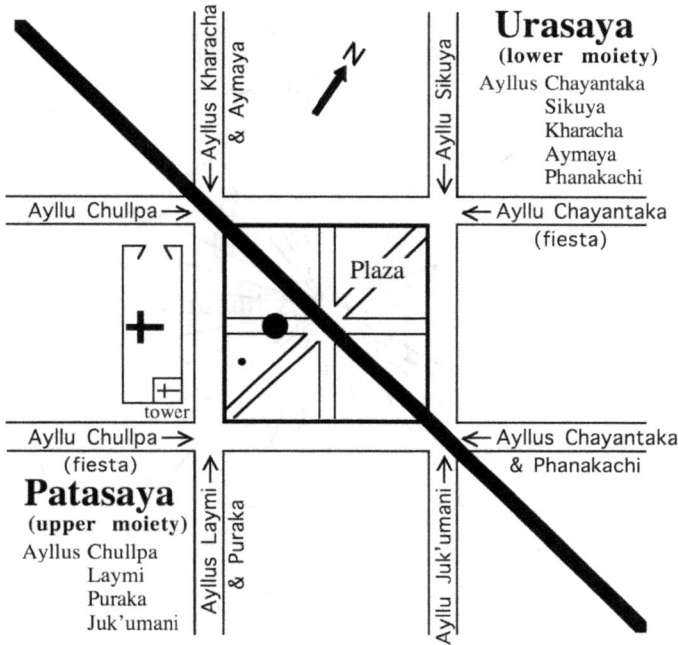

Figure 7.13: Mapping of regional *ayllu* geography onto the town of Chayanta (Thomas Solomon).

as part of a culturally defined landscape through a marked kind of musical performance—the playing of the special *kulwa* melodies, stylistically different from the *tonada* melodies used for walking. The sacredness of these places is also defined by means of a gesture adapted from Roman Catholic religious practice: kneeling. The musical pilgrimage is, then, a journey of the inscription of community, *ayllu*, and moiety identity on the landscape.

While I have followed here the pilgrimage of one community in particular —Irupata, Ayllu Chayantaka—it is important to emphasize that literally dozens of communities from all nine *ayllus* of Bustillo Province also make the pilgrimage to Chayanta, all at the same time. These simultaneous pilgrimages by so many communities, each with its own route, *tonada* and *kulwa* melodies, and set of *apachitas*, effects an articulation of a shared regional space arranged around the town of Chayanta as the *marka*, or ceremonial center held in common by all the *ayllus*. Figure 7.14 models this articulation. The straight lines in the figure do not represent the actual routes of specific communities, and more communities from each *ayllu* than the few

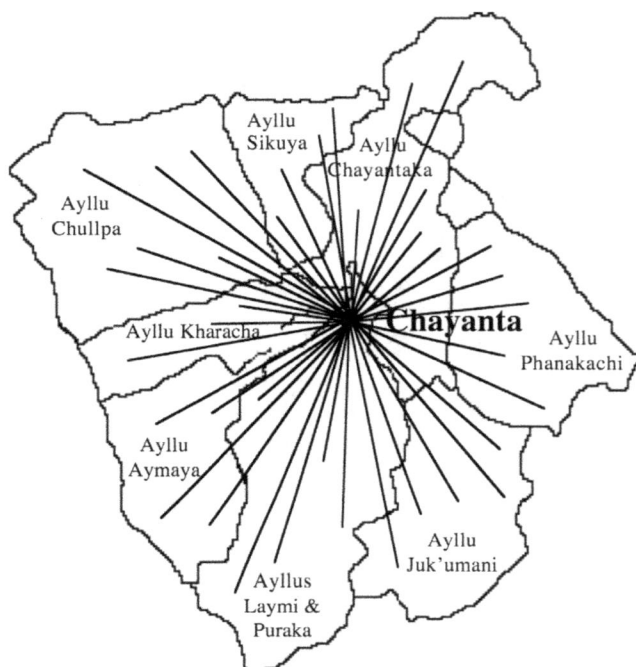

Figure 7.14: Model of the articulation of regional *ayllu* geography during simultaneous community pilgrimages to the *marka* (Thomas Solomon).

represented in the figure may make the pilgrimage to Chayanta, but the figure illustrates how the simultaneous pilgrimages of the individual communities articulate the entire region as a unified space to which they all collectively belong, sharing an identity as "*ayllus* of Chayanta."

Conclusion: The Musical Embodiment of Collective Memory and Identity in Place

In this chapter, I have explored through an ethnographic case study how music can be a vehicle for giving human agency a physical, sensuous form— sound waves traveling through air, land, and people's bodies—that embodies human relationships and inscribes them in a geography saturated with meaning. I suggest that in the case I have described, musical performance enables coordinated sociality in and across a culturally defined landscape, inscribing group identity on the physical features of the land. To say that music *embodies* identity is to say that music's sounds give identity a physical presence appreciable by the senses, that it is experienced as real by living human bodies.

The concept of "collective memory"—or, as Fentress and Wickham (1992) prefer, "social memory"—is also useful in interpreting the case discussed here. The idea of collective memory is credited to the French sociologist Maurice Halbwachs (1980 [1950], 1992). The problem Halbwachs sought to solve was a basic one to the Durkheimian sociological framework in which he was working. Durkheim (1965 [1915]) identified ritual and ceremony as sites for the creation of collectivity through the experience of "effervescence" (similar to what Turner [1977] would later call *communitas*). The question, as Douglas (1980: 8–9) and Coser (1992: 24–25) note, is "where" does the sense of belonging to a collectivity "go" *between* moments of ritual effervescence? How is group consciousness maintained on a day-to-day basis? Halbwachs's answer is that it "resides" in collective memory, a socially constructed negotiation of meaning by individuals as members of a group: "While the collective memory endures and draws strength from its base in a coherent body of people, it is individuals as group members who remember" (Halbwachs 1980 [1950]: 48). Halbwachs also specifically addressed the relationship between memory and the experience of space, suggesting that groups "engrave their form in some way upon the soil and retrieve their collective remembrances within the spatial framework thus defined" (1980 [1950]: 156). From a phenomenological perspective, Casey (1987: 189) similarly argues that the lived body, as both the locus of sensed experience and the repository of memories of those experiences, mediates between memory and place. The case described here suggests that sense-enhancing practices such as musical performance can intensify the active role of the body in inscribing memory on space and place in memory. If "every collective memory unfolds within a spatial framework" (Halbwachs 1980 [1950]: 140), then traversing space as a group also reinscribes the collective memory of groupness on the space traversed. And if "social experience is remapped as mental topography" (Fentress and Wickham 1992: 27–28), I would also suggest that in the case described here, the experience of topographic space is mapped in social terms as well.

Paul Connerton, in his book *How Societies Remember* (1989), follows Halbwachs in stressing the social nature of memory, but adds an important dimension by stressing the roles of performance and of what he calls the "mnemonics of the body" (1989: 74)—ways in which cultural values and categories are literally in*corpo*rated (with emphasis on the Latin root *corpus*, "body") in bodily practices. He describes how conventionalized patterns of bodily movement encode social memory and enact it in performance, arguing that such bodily practices play a crucial role in the diachronic component of collective identity (1989: 103)—preserving such identities through time and re-creating them in cyclical patterns of re-enactment.

In the case described here, musical performance has the effect of heightening the experience of movement through space, turning the steps along the pilgrimage path into a kind of dance. As anthropologist Michael Sallnow argues, in his description of another Andean pilgrimage in southern Peru in which performance on flutes also plays an important role, "any dance routine is itself a formal, kinesthetic mapping of space ... The ritual passage is pervaded by melody and rhythm: the pilgrimage, in a sense, is not so much walked as danced" (1987: 201). Performance on the *julajula* panpipes during the pilgrimage to Chayanta also heightens the experience of *sociality*. The requirement of coordination between the two halves of the instrument, each played by different players, as well as the ensemble organization of five different sizes of *julajulas* played in parallel octaves, are all vehicles for the experience of groupness. Musical performance thus simultaneously embodies and instantiates both space and society—the physicality and sociality of musical performance effectively inscribes community identity on the landscape. Through the pilgrims' dance of inscription across the landscape, the individual pilgrim experiences space as a member of—and, crucially, *in terms of*—the community, and the sounding music gives this identity material form, making it perceptible to the senses and grounding it in the physical landscape.

Acknowledgements

Fieldwork in Bolivia during 1993–1994 was supported by a Fulbright-Hays Doctoral Dissertation Abroad Fellowship.

About the Author

Thomas Solomon, PhD, is Professor in the Grieg Academy-Department of Music at the University of Bergen, Norway. He has previously taught ethnomusicology and popular music studies at New York University, University of Minnesota, and Istanbul Technical University. He has carried out ethnographic research on music, place, and indigeneity in highland Bolivia, and on place and identity in Turkish rap music and hip-hop youth culture in Istanbul. His publications include articles in the journals *Ethnomusicology, Popular Music, European Journal of Cultural Studies*, and *Yearbook for Traditional Music*, as well as numerous chapters in edited volumes.

Notes

1   This paragraph incorporates material published in Solomon (2014).
2   I also do not use time signatures in my transcriptions, in order not to suggest a metrical system or hierarchy of pulses.
3   "Mälzel's Metronome" or "Metronome Marking," a way of indicating tempo in music.
4   The culmination of the pilgrimage on the Feast of the Holy True Cross is a ritual battle known as *tinku* held in the plaza of the town of Chayanta. Due to space limitations, I choose to focus in this chapter on the pilgrimage journey itself and the music associated with it, rather than the *tinku*, which has already been studied extensively by Andeanist anthropologists. For a discussion of the *tinku* in Chayanta, with references to relevant literature on the subject, see Solomon (1997: ch. 8). Some of the material discussed here is also considered, somewhat more briefly, in Solomon (2004).

References

Allen, Catherine J. 1988. *The Hold Life Has: Coca and Cultural Identity in an Andean Community*. Washington DC: Smithsonian Institution Press.
Casey, Edward S. 1987. *Remembering: A Phenomenological Study*. Bloomington: Indiana: University Press.
Castelli, Amalia, Marcia Koth de Paredes, and Mariana Mould de Pease. 1981. *Etnohistoria y Antropología Andina*. Lima: [no publisher].
Connerton, Paul. 1989. *How Societies Remember*. Cambridge: Cambridge University Press. https://doi.org/10.1017/CBO9780511628061
Coser, Lewis A. 1992. "Introduction: Maurice Halbwachs 1877–1945." In Maurice Halbwachs, *On Collective Memory*, 1–34. Chicago: University of Chicago Press.
Douglas, Mary. 1980. "Introduction: Maurice Halbwachs (1877–1945)." In Maurice Halbwachs, *On Collective Memory*, 1–21. New York: Harper & Row.
Durkheim, Emile. 1965 [1915]. *The Elementary Forms of the Religious Life*. New York: Free Press.
Fentress, James, and Chris Wickham. 1992. *Social Memory*. Oxford: Blackwell.

Godoy, Ricardo. 1985. "State, Ayllu, and Ethnicity in Northern Potosí, Bolivia." *Anthropos* 80(1–3): 53–65.

—1986. "The Fiscal Role of the Andean Ayllu." *Man* 21(4): 723–41. https://doi.org/10.2307/2802905

—1990. *Mining and Agriculture in Highland Bolivia: Ecology, History, and Commerce among the Juk'umanis*. Tucson: University of Arizona Press.

Halbwachs, Maurice. 1980 [1950]. *The Collective Memory*. New York: Harper & Row.

—1992. *On Collective Memory*. Chicago: University of Chicago Press.

Harris, Olivia. 2000. *To Make the Earth Bear Fruit: Ethnographic Essays on Fertility, Work and Gender in Highland Bolivia*. London: Institute of Latin American Studies.

Kraft, Karen Elaine. 1995. "Andean Fields and Fallow Pastures: Communal Land Use Management under Pressures for Intensification." PhD dissertation, University of Florida (Gainesville).

Mendoza, Fernando, Willer Flores, and Catherine Letourneux. 1994. *Atlas de los Ayllus de Chayanta. Vol. I: Territorios del Suni*. Potosí, Bolivia: Programa de Autodesarrollo Campesino, Fase de Consolidación.

Sallnow, Michael J. 1987. *Pilgrims of the Andes: Regional Cults in Cuzco*. Washington DC: Smithsonian Institution Press.

Seeger, Anthony. 1987. *Why Suyá Sing: A Musical Anthropology of an Amazonian People*. Cambridge: Cambridge University Press.

Solomon, Thomas. 1997. "Mountains of Song: Musical Constructions of Ecology, Place, and Identity in the Bolivian Andes." PhD dissertation, University of Texas, Austin.

—2000. "Dueling Landscapes: Singing Places and Identities in Highland Bolivia." *Ethnomusicology* 44(2): 257–80. https://doi.org/10.2307/852532

—2004. "Musikalske Konstruktioner af Sted og Identitet i Bolivias Højland." *Jordens Folk* 39(3): 48–53.

—2014. "Performing Indigeneity: Poetics and Politics of Music Festivals in Highland Bolivia." In *Soundscapes from the Americas: Ethnomusicological Essays on the Power, Poetics, and Ontology of Performance*, edited by Donna A. Buchanan, 143–63. Farnham: Ashgate.

Turner, Victor. 1977. *The Ritual Process: Structure and Anti-Structure*. Ithaca, NY: Cornell University Press.

UNESCO World Heritage Convention. n.d. "Cultural Landscapes." http://whc.unesco.org/en/culturallandscape (accessed October 19, 2015).

Chapter 8

The Space of Gong Culture in the Central Highlands of Vietnam: Old and New Directions in Ede Traditional Music

Vincenzo della Ratta

Introduction

The sun was setting over the village of Buon Ako Dhong, on a mid-November day in 2012. A fresh breeze was finally dispelling the heat of the day, rustling the leaves of trees in the gardens around the concrete houses of the village. The asphalted roads with street-lights, the coffee houses, restaurants, and small shops made it hard to imagine that only a few decades ago this area was completely immersed in dense jungle. A great deal had changed since Francis Ford Coppola set his film *Apocalypse Now* (1979), an adaptation of Conrad's novel *Heart of Darkness* (1899), in this remote region straddling the border between Cambodia and Vietnam (although the film was actually shot in the Philippines).

I had sat on a mat inside one of the concrete houses for most of the day, talking with my host Ama H'Loan about the traditions of the Ede people, drinking beer, and smoking cigarettes. I loved to listen to Ama H'Loan, a wise old man in his seventies, with sparkling eyes, always full of energy and willing to answer my questions, even the most complicated ones. After the sun had disappeared from the horizon, he excused himself, stood up, and told me that he had to get ready for the night's performance. At first, it did not occur to me that there was anything strange about his vague reference to taking part in a performance, but when he returned, wearing a traditional coat and loincloth, instead of the western-style clothes he normally wore, I realized that something rather unusual was about to happen. My interest was particularly piqued as it occurred to me that the Ede people do not conceive of music as a show or performance, in the way that it is habitually presented in the West. But Ama H'Loan did not mention a ritual or traditional event; instead he defined it as a "performance." When I asked Ama H'Loan what kind of performance he was about to take part in, he explained that he was a member of a troupe of musicians and dancers that occasionally played for tourists. My curiosity was aroused, and I asked if I too could attend this event. He then left, saying that he would have to ask the chief of the troupe, Ama Y'Pi, to give his permission for me to be present.

As Ede people are traditionally re-named after their children, Ama H'Loan takes his name from his daughter and his name means "the father of H'Loan." His original birth-name is Y Bhiông Niê, and he is a well-known traditional Ede musician, instrument maker, as well as a reliable authority as regards Ede traditional culture. He is often asked to collaborate with the Dak Lak Museum of Ethnology, and he has been invited to perform in many countries, including in Europe. I was aware that Ama H'Loan had already "performed" for audiences in Vietnam and abroad, but I didn't expect him to be part of a troupe engaged in entertaining groups of tourists. I had visited Ama H'Loan at his house many times before that mid-November night, since he was one of the best consultants I had met during years of fieldwork, and there are now few people in the Central Highlands of Vietnam with in-depth knowledge about traditional music and culture. In this region, modernity had a dramatic impact on traditional indigenous cultures, like that of the Ede people. Colonization by the French, three Indochina Wars, government policies of mass resettlement, and the *đổi mới* ("renovation") policy adopted by the central government in 1986 have all drastically affected the traditions of the indigenous ethnic groups of the Central Highlands.

In this chapter, I aim to cast light on the way in which traditional Ede music appears within the modern cultural landscape following UNESCO's declaration as "The Space of Gong Culture" of the Central Highlands of Vietnam as a World Intangible Cultural Heritage in 2005 (UNESCO 2005). To do so, I will first provide a brief historical overview, as the evolution of Ede music belongs to the broader context of the profound changes that have affected the region (the Central Highlands) inhabited by the Ede people, as well as Vietnam as a whole. "Music" (a corresponding term does not exist in the language of the Ede) has undergone many changes in this part of Vietnam, and in order to illustrate them I propose to follow two lines of analysis, the first relating to music that can be defined as vocal, and the second relating to music for ensembles of gongs. To do this, I will use the case study of Ama H'Loan and his troupe from the village of Buon Ako Dhong, which in my view is emblematic. While this chapter will address the changes that have affected the music of the Ede in recent decades, I will also focus on certain aspects of traditional music, particularly the way in which the Ede play gongs traditionally.

Formerly an extemporaneous expression of the emotions of an individual singer, the "vocal music" of the Ede is currently being reconfigured for the performance of pre-established text, either solo or in a group, and often accompanied by a "modern" instrument such as the guitar, and is either performed for tourists, as I will explain later, or for ordinary musical occasions as observed during my fieldwork. Even so, it was particularly the music for gong ensembles that attracted my interest, since it plays an absolutely central role in the musical scenario of the Ede, as well as for other indigenous peoples of the Central Highlands. Music for gongs is, in fact, conceived as a means to communicate with the supernatural world, and is therefore traditionally played only in ritual contexts. The importance of music for the Ede, and especially the importance of rituals with which it is associated, was well understood by the French colonial administration, which invented new rituals for political purposes. The modern state of Vietnam has maintained a similar strategy towards the Ede, but this chapter will be focused above all on the role of gong music in the context of a free market economy within a state characterized by a one-party system, namely the Socialist Republic of Vietnam. This context constitutes the background of the UNESCO declaration of 2005.

The Central Highlands of Vietnam

A Vietnamese saying states that no one has ever really visited the Central Highlands of Vietnam if they have not heard the local gong playing, due to the highly exceptional nature of this particular ancient musical tradition. Yet the problem is that the Central Highlands are still a restricted area, access to which is controlled by the state. In 2005, UNESCO recognized "The Space of Gong Culture" of the Central Highlands of Vietnam as a World Intangible Cultural Heritage (UNESCO 2005), thereby attracting worldwide attention to this area. Tourists have gradually started traveling to the Central Highlands, but they are only allowed to visit a very few selected locations, while the rest of the territory is kept concealed from the eyes of foreigners, as the central authorities have imposed a veto on traveling to remote villages. For this

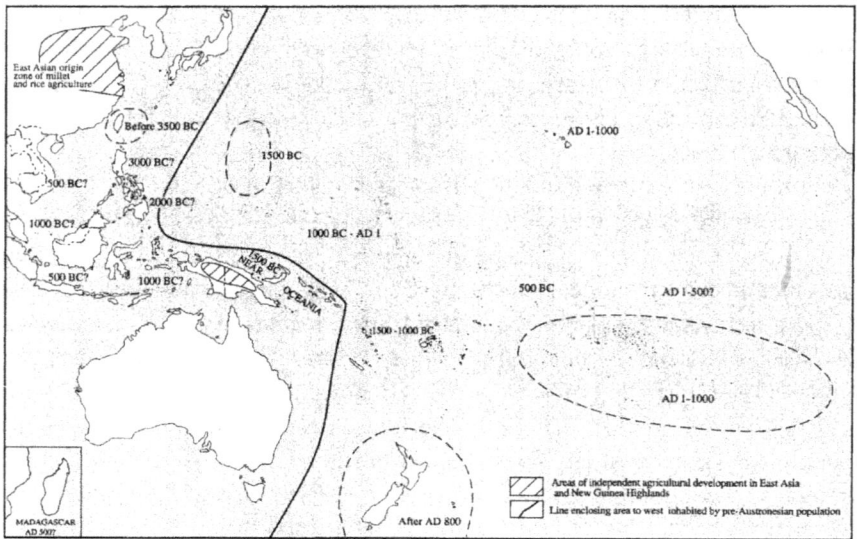

Figure 8.1: Estimated periods of the various phases of Austronesian colonization (Bellwood 1995: 109). Used with permission of ANU Press.

reason, the easiest way—and sometimes the only way—for foreigners to listen to traditional music is to take part in a guided tour, which is limited to a number of selected villages in the Central Highlands.

To understand why access to this part of the country is still substantially restricted, one has to take a look at its history. The region is home to nearly twenty different indigenous ethnic groups, considered as minorities within the Viet (or Kinh) ethnic based nation-state, which belong to two different linguistic families: the Austroasiatic and the Austronesian. The present chapter focuses on the Ede ethnic group (also known as Rhadé), which belongs to the Austronesian linguistic family. The Ede people originated in Northern Borneo, or possibly the Malay Peninsula, around the fifth century BC and were part of the migration movement that took the Austronesian people westward from Taiwan to Madagascar, and eastward to Easter Island (Bellwood 1995: 105–108). The Ede, together with other peoples of the region, lived undisturbed in the Central Highlands for many centuries, although they had various different relations with the neighboring Lowlanders, the Cham, the Laotians, the Khmer, and the Vietnamese (Salemink 2011). This situation ended with the French colonization of Indochina, which triggered various processes that would be disruptive for the cultures of the indigenous people

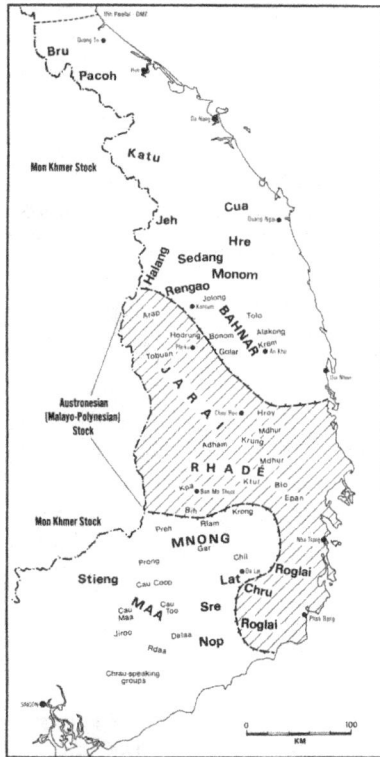

Figure 8.2: Ethnic composition of the Central Highlands (Hickey 1982b: 321).

of this area (Dournes 1977; Hickey 1982a). The increasing colonial interests of the French in this region and its rich natural resources soon led to the end of the independence of the Montagnards, the indigenous people of the Central Highlands.[1]

In 1975, after the first two Indochina Wars, Vietnam became unified under the Communist regime of the North. The Central Highlands were defined as "New Economic Zones," and large numbers of extraneous ethnic groups, mainly ethnic Vietnamese lowlanders, were relocated to this remote and under-populated area, leading to drastic changes in many aspects of the lives and cultures of the indigenous peoples. This process, defined by Evans (1992: 288) as "internal colonialism," led to a series of disputes and controversies regarding the ownership of communal land. In addition to the issue of land tenure, the religious freedom of the indigenous people of the Central Highlands was restricted, and there was a number of episodes of harsh repression of peaceful demonstrations, culminating in the particularly serious incidents of 2001 and 2004 (Human Rights Watch 2002, 2011).

The Gong Culture of the Ede People

In 2005, the UNESCO committee declared the gongs of the Central Highlands of Vietnam a World Intangible Cultural Heritage (UNESCO 2005). The term "Space of Gong Culture" was used to refer to the various different gong cultures of the whole geographic area, since gongs play a key role within all the indigenous traditional societies of the region. The Central Highlands are a very particular case in the context of the gong-chime culture of Southeast Asia, as defined by Hood (1980), as this is the only region, together with Luzon in the Philippines, where both flat and bossed gongs are played.

Gongs have a special value and significance for all indigenous ethnic groups in this region, since these instruments are a status symbol, and, more importantly within the context of the local traditional religion, a medium for communicating with the spirits, which many ethnic groups, no matter which linguistic family they belong to, call *Yang*. Endowed with spiritual power, gongs are exclusively played within ritual contexts, or at least this was the time-honored traditional practice.

The way in which the Ede play their gongs is particularly interesting, and Ama H'Loan explained this to me in detail during our many talks. The Ede gong ensemble, which is simply called *čĭng* ("gongs"), has two different sections, one consisting of bossed gongs, called *čĭng kdor*, the other consisting of flat gongs, called *čĭng knah*. The *čĭng kdor* contains three bossed gongs called *ana*, *mdŭ*, and *mông*, while the *čĭng knah* contains six flat gongs, each one of which has a specific name. The first of these is called *knah* (sometimes *knah phŭn* or *knah di*), the second is *h'liang*, the third is *khôk* (sometimes *knah khôk*), and the other three are *hluê khôk*, *hluê h'liang*, and *hluê khôk diet*. The *čĭng* ensemble is complemented by a big flat gong, *čar*, and a big double-headed drum dug out of a single tree trunk, called *h'gor*.[2]

The largest gongs hang in a row from the ceiling of the longhouse above a bench, called *kban* or *kpan*, where the players sit (see Hauteclocque-Howe 1987: 124). The smallest gongs are often not suspended from the ceiling, as they can easily be held without additional support, and neither does *mdŭ*, which is not played vertically like the others, but horizontally. The gongs called *ana*, *mông*, and *čar* are not played on the bench but hang from the ceiling to one side (see Figure 8.3). When rituals are held in the open air, the

Disposition des gongs dans la "maison longue"

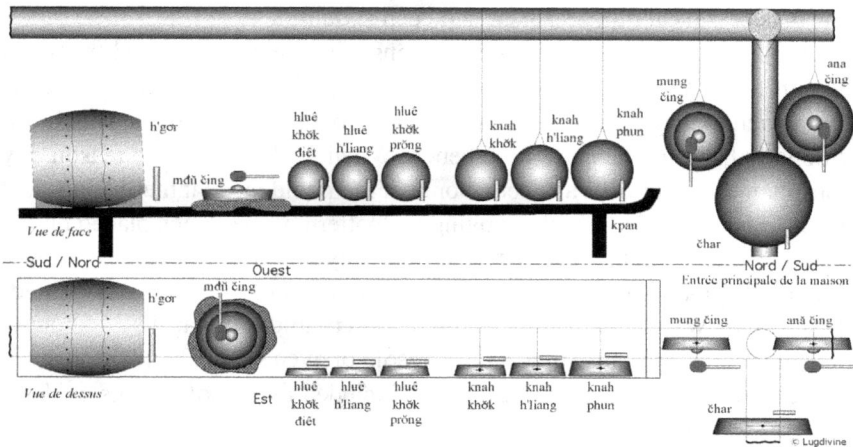

Figure 8.3: Disposition of the gongs in the longhouse (Kersalé 2000: 16–17). All the gongs are played on the bench, except for *ana*, *mông*, and *čar*, which hang to one side. Used with permission of Buda Records.

players sit on simple seats on the ground and the gongs hang from a special wooden or bamboo frame.

The order in which the gongs are positioned in line on the bench is invariable. At one end of the line stands the bossed gong *mdŭ* placed horizontally on a cushion, or something similar, on the player's lap, in order to dampen its sound; then the flat gongs, played vertically, are arranged from the smallest gong to the biggest.

Henri Maître (1909: 128), the French explorer who visited the region of the Central Highlands at the beginning of the twentieth century, describes a gong orchestra of the Ede as being made up of a big drum which he calls *ngor* (*h'gor*); two or three big flat gongs—depending on the wealth of the owner of the orchestra, although a regular gong set generally has two—called *thiar*; five *knah* flat gongs arranged in ascending size; and three *ching* bossed gongs. The modern gong orchestra differs from this only in the number of *knah* gongs, of which there are six instead of five, and the number of *thiar* (*čar*), of which there is one instead of two. I was told during my fieldwork that in ancient times gongs were purchased separately and gong orchestras did not have a standardized number of elements, which could vary according to the wealth of the owner of the orchestras. Most people could only afford the basic elements of an essential gong orchestra, but wealthy people could add additional elements, such as more *čar*, after the minimum number of gongs necessary for an orchestra had been acquired.

During my fieldwork and conversations with friends, I noticed that even though a gong orchestra consisted of all the above-mentioned elements, during actual playing I rarely saw the *ana*, *mông*, and *čar* gongs, which traditionally hang to one end of the bench. When I asked them the reason, my consultants gave elusive answers. Some of them told me that these gongs had a less important role, namely copying the pattern of the gongs placed on the bench, while others told me that they were only played in the context of very important rituals and that since 1975 (when the whole country was unified) these rituals were celebrated less often. Others told me that they no longer play these gongs because they had been sold or even stolen. In addition, even though the *h'gor* drum is still generally included as part of the ensemble, it can also be omitted.

The two gongs placed at the two opposite ends of the line (the *mdŭ* bossed gong and the *knah* flat gong) mark the beat and the off-beat (or vice versa), while the others play what can be loosely defined as the melody. The five remaining flat gongs can be divided into two groups, the "*khôk*" group (*khôk, hluê khôk, hluê khôk diet*) and the "*h'liang*" group (*h'liang, hluê h'liang*) (see Figure 8.4). Each group plays the same rhythmic-melodic pattern, and they intertwine together to create a complex interlocking polyphonic effect.

Figure 8.5 is my transcription of an Ede gong piece commonly called *Tông Mang*. The order of the gongs arranged vertically on the score corresponds to the order in which the gong players are seated on the bench. *Knah* and *mdŭ*, at each end of the line, play the beat and the off-beat, while the rhythmic-melodic patterns of the "*h'liang*" and "*khôk*" groups intertwine. On this occasion *h'gor*, the double-headed drum, was not part of the ensemble.

The musical scale used by the Ede is a hexatonic scale. As the bossed gong *mdŭ* duplicates the sound of one of the other gongs, I have not included it in the scale in Figure 8.6. In addition it is muted by being played on a cushion, so its sound is not very clearly defined.

The Ede claim to derive their approach to gong ensemble playing, as well as their musical scale, from another instrument, a mouth organ called *ding năm* (which literally means six bamboo tubes). In a similar way to the process described by Nicolas (2010, 2011), according to whom metal instruments in Southeast Asia are usually based on pre-existing instruments made of easily available materials, such as bamboo or wood, the gong playing of the Ede is based on the *ding năm* (see Figure 8.7). This ancient instrument

Figure 8.4: *Čĭng* ensemble of the Ede people (Vincenzo della Ratta).

Tong Mang

Figure 8.5: Indicative transcription of *Tông Mang*, a piece of Ede gong music (Vincenzo della Ratta).

Figure 8.6: Example of the hexatonic scale of an Ede ensemble I recorded during my fieldwork. Its tuning is suitable for writing in the western notation system (Vincenzo della Ratta).

is made of six bamboo tubes inserted into a gourd that are mirrored by the six basic *čing knah* flat gongs of the ensemble (the *mdŭ* bossed gong, as well as the other gongs played outside the bench, were evidently conceived as additional elements). The *ding năm* player alternatively closes and opens the holes of the tubes (each of which has the same name as one of the six basic gongs) in order to create a polyphony based on the combinations of two or more sounds from the different tubes. The way in which the gong ensemble functions is very similar to this basic conception.

Nowadays there are three distinct occurrences within which the Ede play gongs. These are traditional rituals, neo-traditional ceremonies, and extra-traditional events. Traditional rituals are occasions when living people communicate with the *Yang*, the spirits of their traditional religion. The Ede

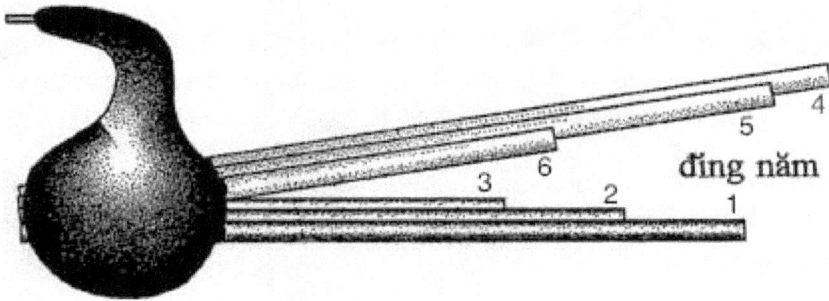

Order of the tubes of the *ding năm* with their relative musical notes.		
1	Ana\Knah	B
2	H'Liang	D
3	Hluê H'Liang	F#
4	Khôk	G
5	Hluê Khôk	A
6	Hluê Khôk Diet	E

Khôk   I lluê Khôk   Ana\Knah   I l'Liang   I lluê Khôk Diet   I lluê I l'Liang

Figure 8.7: The *ding năm* mouth organ (Vincenzo della Ratta; and Kersalé 2000: 31). Used with permission of Buda Records.

practice a wide variety of rituals, some of which—such as mortuary rituals (see Jouin 1949) and some agricultural rites (see Maurice 1951)—involve gong music.[3] Certain Ede traditional rituals are drastically changing (such as weddings, which are now increasingly celebrated in the Vietnamese way), while others are disappearing. Among the latter are rituals connected to the agricultural cycle, which used to be among the most important rites celebrated by the community, but which are now disappearing due to changes in traditional agriculture, as well as the beliefs associated with it.

Neo-traditional celebrations can be defined as a modification of the ancient traditional rituals, maintaining some traditional elements and functions, although the purposes for which they are celebrated are not closely connected to traditional customs. Neo-traditional celebrations include state-organized celebrations, which were instituted during the French colonial period. One of the best examples of them is the so-called *Palabre du serment*, "a ceremony in which village chiefs and other influential men from the province of Darlac swore an oath of allegiance to the French" (Salemink 2003: 83). This ceremony was invented by Léopold Sabatier, the French Resident of Darlac, by modifying an Ede traditional ritual called *Mnam thun ian prong* (see Besnard 1907: 78), and therefore resulted, together with other similar measures extensively adopted by the French colonial authorities, in the "inventions of traditions for political goals" (Salemink 2003: 85).[4]

Even though this ceremony was discontinued many years ago, the present authorities have maintained a similar strategy towards the Ede people. An example of this is the "Festive Day of National Unity" (*Ngày hội đại đoan kết toàn dan tộc*), which I personally witnessed in 2012 in a village of the province of Dak Lak, on the occasion of celebrations for the "82nd anniversary of the foundation of the National United Front of Vietnam" (*Kỷ niệm 82 năm ngày thành lập mặt trận dân tộc thống nhất Việt Nam*). Following a series of speeches by party cadres and local authorities, Ede traditional music was played on a stage. An Ede man played the *ding năm* mouth organ and sang traditional melodies, and then a group of Ede elders played gong music in front of the audience. The guests (in order of importance) were invited to drink the ritual liquor. On this occasion I recorded *Tông Mang*, the piece which is transcribed in Figure 8.5. As Ama H'Loan explained to me, this is a well-known traditional gong piece played on many different occasions and therefore, as far as I can determine, the state authorities simply instituted the ritual, while the music remained unaffected. I have been unable to determine what kind of music was played during the *Palabre du serment*, but it seems likely that traditional gong music was also used for this ceremony.[5]

Celebrations in which traditional elements and practices have been incorporated within the Catholic liturgy also belong to the category of neo-traditional rituals. Through the promotion of dialogue between the local culture and official Catholic doctrine—a process known as "inculturation" and which started following the Second Vatican Council (1962–65)—elements and practices belonging to the traditional religion were integrated into the practices of the local Catholic Church. The activity of Catholic missionaries among the Ede began in the 1950s, reinforced by the arrival of the Benedictine sisters of Vanves (France) in 1954, who founded a convent in the area of Buon Ma Thuot, which was moved to Thù Đức, in the outskirts of Saigon, in 1967. Two nuns, Sœur Colomban and Sœur Boniface, stayed on in the area north of Buon Ma Thuot, where they lived in communion with the

Ede and established a cooperative village which lasted until 1975, when they were expelled from Vietnam (Dartigues and Guillemin 2009: 148). Although Sœur Colomban reports some activities related to the inculturation process among the Ede,[6] I do not have any data concerning this process as regards gong music. As I was informed while visiting a church in the proximity of Buon Ma Thuot, Ede gong music is rarely played during Catholic celebrations, but mostly on important liturgical occasions, such as Christmas or Tet, the Vietnamese New Year. I was told, although I have never actually heard it being played, that the gong music played in the context of these celebrations does not substantially differ from traditional gong music, similarly to the way gong music is used within what I have defined as state-organized celebrations. Ede gong music has probably been left untouched within these rituals due to its marked rhythmical characteristics, which make it essentially incompatible with the canons of western music. However, even though the actual form of traditional gong music has probably not been affected by the above-mentioned process of the invention of rituals, its meaning and the way in which it is conceived has certainly been changed due to the different context in which it is played.

Unlike neo-traditional rituals, extra-traditional events can be defined as all those occasions that, although unconnected with traditional and ritual contexts, adopt ritual elements associated with them. I will now analyse in detail performances held for tourists, which can give us a good insight into this category.

Buon Ako Dhong

The village of Buon Ako Dhong is in Dak Lak province, just three kilometers from the center of Buon Ma Thuot, the biggest and richest city of the Central Highlands. Its longhouses, constructed with expensive materials of a very high quality, and surrounded by gardens in a rather incongruous European style, are very different from those of most villages. The "Ako Dhong village," as it is called in the *Lonely Planet* guidebook, attracts many tourists who come here for "a pleasant break from the downtown din," to quote the words of the guidebook, as well as to get a taste of the traditional Ede culture. Like several other villages in the Central Highlands where tourists are admitted, Buon Ako Dhong has profited from the UNESCO declaration.

Ama Y'Pi, the leader of the troupe of performers to which Ama H'Loan belongs, owns one of these longhouses. Although he belongs to the Mnong people (an Austroasiatic or Mon-Khmer speaking ethnic group), Ama Y'Pi can speak Ede and Vietnamese fluently, as well as French, as I soon discovered.[7] After Ama H'Loan had passed on my request, Ama Y'Pi kindly gave me permission to witness one of the troupe's performances, and I was allowed to sit to one side of the longhouse with my recording equipment.

The troupe consisted of eleven performers, most of whom seemed to be between fifty and sixty years old. There were also some particularly elderly members, such as Ama H'Loan, who were clearly respected by the others as the most learned and experienced concerning Ede traditions. There was only one younger male member, a youth around twenty years old who, as Ama H'Loan later told me, had been admitted to the troupe because of his particularly fine voice. The troupe also included three young dancing girls, who also occasionally sang.

The brand new longhouse where the tourists were received was used exclusively as a venue for holding performances. Ama Y'Pi's modern house, constructed with bricks and cement, stood directly behind it. That night a bus arrived with twenty or more French tourists. They were welcomed and invited to sit on mats arranged along one side of the longhouse. A jar of rice wine was placed in the middle of the house, as it is the traditional practice to drink rice wine while gongs are played. A selection of traditional tunes was performed, played with gongs and other traditional instruments, such as *čĭng kram* (bamboo gongs), *tăk ta* (a free reed aerophone), *ding năm* (a mouth organ), and *ding buôt* (a flute), which were often accompanied by singing. A simple introduction to the traditional culture and customs of the Ede was provided by Ama Y'Pi in Vietnamese and the tour-guide translated this into French. The presence of electric lights, video recordings, cameras and their flashes created an atmosphere that was very unlike that of a traditional context. Nevertheless, one rarely has the opportunity of listening to Ede traditional music played with these old instruments. The younger generations are more attracted to modern music and these traditional instruments are nowadays played, mostly by elderly people, only in some remote areas of the region. What we were witnessing was therefore a rather rare and special event, for the audience as well as for me.

As I mentioned earlier, the Ede language does not have a generic term for music, but instead it specifies the action of playing a particular instrument (for example beating the gongs, *tông čĭng*) or singing. The Ede practice several forms of vocal expression. The generic term for singing is *mmuiñ* (*muynh* or *munh*), but this word can also refer to traditional story-telling (*khan*)[8] or to the recitation of customary law (*phat kdi*) (see Sabatier and Antomarchi 1940).

Other terms that refer to singing are: *kưt*—usually accompanied by the *ding buôt* flute; *čŏk hia*—a lament directed to a dead person (see Jouin 1949); *aê rêi* (*airay*, or *aray*)—involving two alternating voices, usually accompanied by the *ding năm* mouth organ or another instrument; and *iêô Yang mdijê* (or *yêo Yang*)—a chant or recitation used for worshipping in a ritual context (see Maurice 1951).

The first of these, *mmuiñ*, is generally used to convey ideas and personal opinions, while *kưt* is often chosen to communicate emotions, although it is sometimes hard to make a clear distinction between *mmuiñ* and *kưt*.[9] Instead *aê rêi*, a chant sung alternately by a man and a woman (although one of the voices can also be substituted by an instrument), is used to express feelings of love towards a person, living or dead (Tô Đông Hải 2004: 355–58). All of these oral expressions are based on a particular "expressive form made of rhythmic verse … which are symbolic preambles expressed as metaphors" (Kersalé 2000: 21), called *klei duê*. It involves some aesthetic and functional features, within which the rhythm and assonance of the words are fundamental aspects. The verses, improvised by the singer, emphasize correspondences and symmetries between consonants and vowels, and they employ metaphor, comparison, hyperbole, as well as various other expressive devices.

Figure 8.8: Interior of the longhouse. Ama Y'Pi providing an introduction to the Ede culture (photo by Vincenzo della Ratta).

A few samples of vocal music were performed that night, giving the audience an insight into the vocal expressions of the Ede. I was particularly intrigued by a song played with a guitar and sung by two choirs (male and female), consisting of the five youngest members of the troupe, which was presented as an Ede *chanson d'amour*. This song, known as *Buôn Dur Kmăn*, is based on a traditional *aê rêi* form, to which a verse-chorus musical structure and fixed lyrics had been added. The version of *Buôn Dur Kmăn* that I listened to that night was basically a western-style pop-song, strongly influenced by western musical canons, as regards its tonal harmony, formal structure, the presence of two choirs, and the accompanying instrument. Also, the lyrics referred to an event that was far from the established customs of the Ede people. The song was about a group of boys going to another village to court the local girls, as was also implied by the presence of both male and female choirs. Anyone unfamiliar with Ede traditions might consider this a perfectly innocent pretext for a romantic song or a love story, but, as Ama H'Loan explained to me, in traditional Ede society, a group of boys or men going to another village without asking its chief for permission would very probably be interpreted as an aggressive act and might even lead to conflict between the villages concerned.

Even though I did not explicitly question the troupe on this matter, I believe that *Buôn Dur Kmăn* was included in the performance because throughout Vietnam it is considered, or at least presented, as a traditional Ede song. In fact, *Buôn Dur Kmăn*, as well as several other songs of this kind, belongs to a repertoire of so-called "folk-songs" (*dân ca*) pertaining to ethnic minority groups that have been "corrected" (*chỉnh lý*) as regards some of their characteristics (Nguyễn Thuyết Phong 1991: 4), such as their lyrics and formal structures, in order to make them "more modern and, therefore, more palatable to the modern socialist masses" (Meeker 2013: 35). More generally, this repertoire can be associated with what has been defined by Arana (1999) as "neotraditional music" (*nhạc dân tộc hiện đại*), a new kind of music that she describes as

> a nationalist art form that is modern yet traditional and folk-derived; artistic yet politically aligned; and distinctly Vietnamese while incorporating the "progressive" and "universally accessible" traditions of Europe, the Soviet Union, and China, as well as the "tribal" or "indigenous" traditions of the non-Viet ethnic minorities living within Vietnam's borders and belonging to

Figure 8.9: A group of young people performing *Buôn Dur Kmăn* (photo by Vincenzo della Ratta).

Malayo-Polynesians, Sino-Tibetan, Thai, and Mon-Khmer lan-guage families. (Arana 1999: 49).

The show also included a dance performance. The Ede consider dance to be a very particular phenomenon, as it is only performed on occasions when gongs are played. That evening, three young female dancers executed a tradi-tional Ede dance, called *gru ewu*. This special dance was normally performed exclusively in the context of rituals such as the funerals of important persons or tomb abandonments, but unfortunately the practice of dancing *gru ewu* has now almost disappeared and it is rare to see it even within its traditional context. It was performed only by women, who are the leading figures of the matrilineal Ede society, and never by men. On this occasion the three girls stood in a circle and mimicked the graceful movements of the *gru*, a heron-like bird. They then slowly took a few steps to the side in a counter-clockwise direction, and once again moved like a *gru*. This dance requires some practice in order to be synchronized and harmonious and it can only be performed by sufficiently trained dancers.

The dance performance was conceived as a sort of medley, in such a way that this first dance was immediately followed by another dance practiced by a neighboring ethnic group, the Jarai, which belongs to the same linguistic family as the Ede people. This Jarai dance, called *soang arap* or simply *soang*, is also traditionally performed by women who hold each other's hands and move slowly in a counter-clockwise direction. I was rather surprised to see it being danced in that context, accompanied by the typical Ede gong ensemble. Presumably this dance was included in the show because the *soang arap* is a group dance, and it is relatively easy to perform. It was also particularly appropriate for performing at the end of the show as it gave the troupe the opportunity to invite the audience to get up and take part in the dance together with the performers. It would certainly have been very difficult for foreigners to participate in a more complex dance like the *gru ewu*.

After this last dance the tourists said their goodbyes, left the longhouse, and took the tour bus back to their hotels in Buon Ma Thuot. I spent some more time with Ama H'Loan and the others, drinking what was left of the rice wine and discussing their performance.

Figure 8.10: Ama Y'Pi (standing on the left) watches Ama H'Loan (seated to the left) drinking ritual wine from a jar together with the tour guide and another performer (photo by Vincenzo della Ratta).

Extra-Traditional Events

The performance I have summarized above consisted of a selection of Ede traditional music and dance, together with a Jarai dance and a modern song strongly influenced by western musical canons. Unlike the other contexts in which gongs are played (i.e. traditional rituals, and neo-traditional celebrations), extra-traditional events—of which performances held for tourists constitute a good example—are the result of a few basic processes that I will now underline. In doing so, I will refer to the studies conducted by Evans (1985) and Salemink (2003). Even though both authors made reference to the wider context of the Vietnamese cultural policy in the Central Highlands, in my opinion their analyses and reflections are also highly relevant to the smaller context of the performance under consideration in this study.

First, I noticed that the repertoire of the performance seems to closely reflect a process that Evans (1985: 142) defined as "selective preservation." This is the process by which some parts of a tradition are deliberately preserved while others are rejected. Obviously, the Ede performers had to choose what was and what was not suitable for presentation to an audience of foreign tourists. In a one-hour performance it was obviously impossible to present the whole range of their traditions, which would nevertheless still have been a decontextualized representation. As a consequence of this kind of process, the younger generations involved in such performances learn only a limited and selected portion of their tradition, while the other portion, which is not chosen for representation, is forgotten and falls into disuse.

Another process involved in performances such as these is that of "folklorization." As stated by Salemink (2003: 278), by *folklorizing* particular aspects of a culture the expressive and aesthetic characteristics of the culture are stressed, while the correlated cognitive and ethical aspects are denied. This process involves a de-contextualization of cultural phenomena, which alters their original function and significance. No funeral or tomb abandonment was being celebrated at the longhouse that night, but on that occasion a group of tourists were shown how the *gru ewu* dance is performed. In this case, the aesthetic aspect of gong music had substantially replaced its sacred function, thus giving the impression that this was a form of music just like any other, simply to be heard and enjoyed in the context of a show or performance.

In addition, the process of hybridization is a prominent factor in practices related to performances of this kind. On the occasion that I witnessed the Ede culture, which was intended to be the central attraction of the show, it was presented together with features borrowed from other cultures: that of the Jarai people and of the western musical tradition. The dance of the Jarai, together with their gong set, is now occasionally adopted by the Ede for their rituals in some parts of the northern territories, which neighbor those of the Jarai. A similar discourse applies to the use of western canons within the music of the Ede. Singing in unison, once inconceivable, is now a part of everyday life for younger members of the community, as well as the use of vocal polyphony in order to embellish a melody, which they tend to associate with the use of tonal harmony. The same considerations apply to the guitar, an instrument that is now much more widespread than traditional instruments, such as the *ding năm*, that are now becoming increasingly rare. Alongside all of these processes a more western conception of music is gradually entering Ede culture, starting from the very concept of "music," since, as I previously mentioned, in the Ede language there is no term corresponding to the word and concept of "music" as it is understood in the West.

However, although performances made for tourists are "often one more form of 'invented tradition' or 'strategic inauthenticity' where what is presented to tourists is a partial, incomplete and distorted version of a past that never was" (Gibson and Connell 2005: 267), the event that I witnessed that night, performed by talented traditional musicians, constituted an accurate picture of the present state of Ede music, in which old and new approaches coexist and are blended together.

Conclusions

In this chapter, I have showed how the music of the Ede people has been transformed until the present day, from their traditional music and rituals, first by the use that the colonial administration made of them, followed by the current government of the Socialist Republic of Vietnam, and finally by the way they are represented in the present-day free-market context. From being conceived as an extemporaneous expression of the feelings of the individual, with improvised words, the vocal music of the Ede has increasingly been influenced by western culture, including the use of tonal harmony, pre-established vocal parts, new formal structures, and new musical instruments that do not belong to Ede traditions.

In addition, the culture of gongs has been subjected to a similar process, although some of the influences that it has undergone derive from a similar ethnic group. The use of the dance of the Jarai (*soang arap*) denotes an analogous process of hybridization. Also the reduction of the gong line-up used in the *čĭng* ensemble of the Ede—a process that many of my consultants told me dated back to 1975, when Vietnam was unified—is an important development, but the most drastic change is certainly the increasing desacralization of this type of music, as it modifies the very way in which it has traditionally been conceived: from being a sacred form of music used to communicate with the supernatural world, to music that is listened to simply for enjoyment.

The current desacralization of the gongs is deeply rooted in a wider process of dramatic change of many of the *-scapes* constituting the Central Highlands (Appadurai 1996), involving physical, ecological, economic, infrastructural, demographic, social, and cultural features (Salemink 2012a: 130). Besides this, in line with a policy of eradicating *primitive habits* (Norton 2002: 74), traditional rituals in which gongs were played had been labeled as *superstition* by the central government and consequently discouraged and, in some cases, even prevented (Evans 1992: 291; Logan 2010: 194). All of this has therefore had a deleterious impact on traditional culture.

This was the situation when UNESCO declared the "Space of the Gong Culture" as a World Intangible Cultural Heritage. Although UNESCO's intention was to safeguard and promote the rapidly disappearing culture of gongs, one effect of the declaration was that the gong culture entered a process of "heritagization," that is, the elevation of particular objects and practices to the status of a heritage that has to be preserved (Salemink 2012b: 282). While this process can confer respect and dignity onto a cultural practice, it also involves its instrumentalization, with the result of reifying and objectifying it. This process is extremely contradictory as it

> celebrates the local, the unique, the specific, the authentic, but brings in the global which according to UNESCO is the major threat to cultural diversity. In order to combat some of the negative effects of globalization, more globalization is called forth, and local communities are subjected to its outside interventions. (Salemink 2012b: 286)

"Selectively preserved," "folklorized," "hybridized," and "heritagized," the gong culture of the peoples of the Central Highlands—as well as their music (vocal and instrumental) and culture in the widest sense of the term (including dance and everything that can be performed or displayed)—is also *spectacularized.* A noteworthy example of this is the First International Gong

Festival of Pleiku, which was organized in connection with the UNESCO declaration in November 2009, and at which I was present.

At the opening ceremony, the gong music of the various indigenous cultures of the Central Highlands as well as from other Southeast Asian countries was put on display. Folk-songs, spectacular dances and magnificent choreographed performances based on the traditional imagery of the Central Highlands were performed on a stage, which was embellished with various distinctive elements of indigenous traditional cultures (stilt houses, sacrifice poles, jars of rice wine, etc.). Fireworks and elephant parades alternated with official speeches by party cadres and government officials. National and international scholars were invited to assist, while the whole event was broadcast on national TV. The intention of the organizers was to celebrate and honor the sacred paraphernalia and ritual activities associated with traditional beliefs (such as gongs, sacrifice poles, and ceremonial dances), but they had been transformed into the elements of spectacular choreographic performances in a way that might have seemed somewhat disrespectful to the adherents of these religious practices.

As I have pointed out, nowadays there are three categories of events within which the Ede play gong music: traditional rituals, neo-traditional celebrations, and extra-traditional events. Thus, despite its transformations, the gong culture has not disappeared and continues to exist, traveling in old and new directions, some of them utterly unforeseen. Besides its new developments, gong music is still played in the context of traditional rituals that continue to be celebrated in the remote areas of the Central Highlands. Awareness of their existence remains limited, however, as the region of the Central Highlands is still a restricted area that is off-limits to outsiders and it is isolated from the eyes of ethnomusicologists, anthropologists, and the amateur enthusiasts of gong music. In fact, in the Central Highlands there is the paradoxical situation of a region endorsed by UNESCO as a World Intangible Cultural Heritage, but that is kept apart from global attention. If there is any hope of keeping the "Space of the Gong Culture" alive it is necessary to encourage and facilitate access to the culture of the gong to all interested parties, as well as to safeguard and support the ongoing celebration of traditional rituals involving local communities. This would help to prevent interference from outside and any consequent spectacularization. In fact, an approach of this kind is explicitly promoted by the UNESCO 2003 Convention for the Safeguarding of the Intangible Cultural Heritage (Blake 2009; Marrie 2009).[10]

Acknowledgements

As it would take up too much space here to name all the friends and consultants who contributed in so many different ways toward the successful completion of my research in the Central Highlands of Vietnam and to whom I am extremely thankful, I will only mention those whose help was absolutely essential to my task. I especially wish to thank Madame Lương Thanh Sơn, at that time the director of the Dak Lak Museum of Ethnology of Buon Ma Thuot, and Nguyễn Bích Tuyền, a member of the staff of the museum who accompanied me on my journeys and acted as my translator, as my work would certainly have been more difficult and problematic without their valuable assistance and support. I would also like to thank Peter Bellwood and Patrick Kersalé, who kindly allowed me to use materials for this study. I would also like to express my deepest gratitude to Ama H'Loan, Ama Y'Pi, and their families for their kind hospitality and helpfulness, which not only made my academic research possible but also provided me with some profoundly rewarding and enjoyable human experiences.

About the Author

Vincenzo della Ratta, PhD, has a particular interest in the gong music of the Austronesian peoples of Southeast Asia. This led him to conduct fieldwork in the Central Highlands of Vietnam and in East Kalimantan (Indonesian Borneo), where he concentrated on the music and culture of the Jarai, Ede, and Dayak Benuaq ethnic groups. Vincenzo della Ratta studied and played gamelan music for over six years, in Indonesia and Italy. He has published several articles on his research, and released two albums of his field recordings.

Notes

1   The term "Montagnards" ("people of the mountain")—collectively referring to all indigenous ethnic groups of the Central Highlands—became commonly used instead of the Vietnamese term "Mọi" ("savages," "barbarians"), when the French needed political support from minority groups. With the advent of the Americans, the term "Yards" (shortening of "Montagnards") or "Highlanders" became widespread. Today the Vietnamese officially refer to them as "Thượng," which means

"mountain people." In spite of the many linguistic differences between them, all indigenous ethnic groups refer to themselves as "Sons of the mountain."

2   Hickey (1982b: 25) describes an Ede ("Rhadé Kpa") gong ensemble as consisting of the same elements.

3   For a comprehensive list of Ede rituals, see Maurice (2002).

4   The text enunciated by Sabatier at the *Palabre* can be found in Sabatier (1930). For information on the *Palabre du serment* as well as on the life and activity of Sabatier in Vietnam, see Dubois (1952).

5   Hickey (1982a: 306), who defines this ceremony as "a mixture of French drama and highland tradition," states that "there were the usual rows of jars and music from gongs and drums."

6   For more information about the activity of Sœur Colomban (Françoise Demeure) and Sœur Boniface, see Demeure, n.d.

7   Buon Ako Dhong is the village where Sœur Boniface and Sœur Colomban lived from 1967 to 1975.

8   The *Klei Khan Dam San* (*La chanson de Damsan*, Sabatier 1933), and the *Klei Khan Kdam Yi* (*Le chant épique de Kdam-Yi*, Antomarchi 1955) were among the first *khan* of the Ede to be translated in French and published.

9   Maître (1909: 132) describes the *muñ* (*mmuiñ*) as a *popular song* ("chansonnette populaire") and the *koït* (*kŭt*) as a *sort of quasi sacred liturgical chant* ("une sorte de chant liturgique quasi sacré"). As regards their musical characteristics, he states that the *muñ* and the *koït* do not substantially differ from each other, and that the low prolonged shout that opens the *muñ* is the only real difference between the two forms. Maître provides translations into French of some texts of these songs.

10 Art. 15 of the UNESCO's 2003 Convention for the Safeguarding of the Intangible Cultural Heritage reads: "Within the framework of its safeguarding activities of the intangible cultural heritage, each State Party shall endeavor to ensure the widest possible participation of communities, groups and, where appropriate, individuals that create, maintain and transmit such heritage, and to involve them actively in its management." Art. 13 (d, ii) invites each State Party to adopt measures aimed at "ensuring access to the intangible cultural heritage while respecting customary practices governing access to specific aspects of such heritage" (UNESCO 2003).

References

Antomarchi, Dominique. 1955. "Le chant épique de Kdam-Yi." *Bulletin de l'Ecole Française d'Extrême-Orient* 47(2): 590–616.
   https://doi.org/10.3406/befeo.1955.4175
Appadurai, Arjun. 1996. *Modernity at Large: Cultural Dimensions of Globalization.* Minneapolis and London: University of Minnesota Press.

Arana, Miranda. 1999. *Neotraditional Music in Vietnam*. Kent, OH: Nhac Viet.

Bellwood, Peter. 1995. "Austronesian Prehistory in Southeast Asia: Homeland, Expansion and Transformation." In *The Austronesians: Historical and Comparative Perspectives*, edited by Peter. Bellwood, James J. Fox, and Darell Tryon, 103–18. Canberra: Australian National University Press.

Besnard, Henri. 1907. "Les populations Moï du Darlac." *Bulletin de l'Ecole Française d'Extrême-Orient* 7: 61–86. https://doi.org/10.3406/befeo.1907.1888

Blake, Janet. 2009. "Unesco's 2003 Convention on Intangible Cultural Heritage: The Implications of Community Involvement." In *Intangible Heritage*, edited by Laurajane Smith and Natsuko Akagawa, 45–73. London and New York: Routledge.

Dartigues, Laurent, and Alain Guillemin. 2009. "L'action des religieuses catholiques au Viet Nam (De l'âge religieux à l'âge idéologique)." In *Démocratie, Modernité et Christianisme en Asie*, edited by Guillaume Arotçarena, Paul Jobin, and Jean-François Sabouret, 143–54. Paris: Les Indes Savantes.

Demeure, Françoise (Soeur Colomban). n.d. *Montagnards du Vietnam*. http://www.dieumaintenant.com/montagnards.html (accessed October 25, 2018).

Dournes, Jacques. 1977. *Pötao: une théorie du pouvoir chez les Indochinois Jörai*. Paris: Flammarion.

Dubois, Pierre. 1952. "Notes sur L. Sabatier, résident du Darlac (1913–1936)." *Revue d'Histoire des Colonies* 39(137): 35–62. https://doi.org/10.3406/outre.1952.1175

Evans, Grant. 1985. "Vietnamese Communist Anthropology." *Canberra Anthropology* 8: 116–47. https://doi.org/10.1080/03149098509508574

—1992. "Internal Colonialism in the Central Highlands of Vietnam." *SOJOURN: Journal of Social Issues in Southeast Asia* 7: 274–304. https://doi.org/10.1355/SJ7-2E

Gibson, Chris, and John Connell. 2005. *Music and Tourism: On the Road Again*. Clevedon, Buffalo and Toronto: Channel View Publications. https://doi.org/10.21832/9781873150948

Hauteclocque-Howe, Anne de. 1987. *Les Rhadés: une société de droit maternel*. Paris: Éditions du CNRS.

Hickey, Gerald C. 1982a. *Sons of the Mountains: Ethnohistory of the Vietnamese Central Highlands to 1954*. New Haven, CT: Yale University Press.

—1982b. *Free in the Forest: Ethnohistory of the Vietnamese Central Highlands, 1954–1976*. New Haven, CT: Yale University Press.

Hood, Mantle. 1980. "South-East Asia." In *The New Grove Dictionary of Music and Musicians*, edited by Stanley Sadie, vol. 17: 762–67. London: Macmillan.

Human Rights Watch. 2002. *Repression of Montagnards: Conflicts over Land and Religion in Vietnam's Central Highlands*. https://www.hrw.org/reports/2002/vietnam/ (accessed October 25, 2018).

—2011. *Montagnard Christians in Vietnam: A Case Study in Religious Repression*: https://www.hrw.org/report/2011/03/30/montagnard-christians-vietnam/case-study-religious-repression (accessed October 25, 2018).

Jouin, Bernard Y. 1949. *La mort et la tombe. L'abandon de la tombe. Les cérémonies, prières et sacrifices se rapportant à ces très importantes manifestations de la vie des autochtones du Darlac.* Paris: Institut d'Ethnologie.

Kersalé, Patrick. 2000. *Viet-nam: anthologie de la musique Ede; Vietnam: Anthology of Ede Music.* (Liner notes) Buda Records 92726-2.

Logan, William. 2010. "Protecting the Tay Nguyen Gongs." In *Cultural Diversity, Heritage and Human Rights: Intersections in Theory and Practice*, edited by Michele Langfield, William Logan, and Mairead Nic Criath, 189–207. London and New York: Routledge.

Maître, Henri. 1909. *Les régions Moï du Sud Indo-Chinois. Le plateau du Darlac.* Paris: Plon.

Marrie, Henrietta. 2009. "The UNESCO Convention for the Safeguarding of the Intangible Cultural Heritage and the Protection and Maintenance of the Intangible Cultural Heritage of Indigenous Peoples." In *Intangible Heritage*, edited by Laurajane Smith and Natsuko Akagawa, 169–92. London and New York: Routledge.

Maurice, Albert-Marie. 1951. "Trois fêtes agraires Rhadé." *Bulletin de l'Ecole Française d'Extrême-Orient* 45(1): 185–207. https://doi.org/10.3406/befeo.1951.5517

——2002. *Croyances et pratiques religieuses des Montagnards du centre-Vietnam.* Paris: L'Harmattan.

Meeker, Lauren. 2013. *Sounding out Heritage: Cultural Politics and the Social Practice of Quan ho Folk Song in Northern Vietnam.* Honolulu: University of Hawaii Press. https://doi.org/10.21313/hawaii/9780824835682.001.0001

Nguyễn, Thuyết Phong. 1991. "Ethno-Historical Perspectives on the Traditional Genres of Vietnamese Music." In *New Perspectives on Vietnamese Music*, edited by Thuyết Phong Nguyễn, 1–19. New Haven, CT: Yale Center for International and Area Studies.

Nicolas, Arsenio. 2010. "Aspects of Music Research in Asia in the Twenty-First Century—Connections between Mainland Asia and Island Southeast Asia." Paper submitted to the First Mekong Basin Congress of Music and Cultural Diversity for Sustainable Development. Thailand: Nakhon Phanom.

——2011. "Early Musical Exchange between India and Southeast Asia." In *Early Interactions between South and Southeast Asia: Reflections on Cross-Cultural Exchange*, edited by Pierre-Yves Manguin, A. Mani, and Geoff Wade, 347–70. Singapore: ISEAS Publishing.

Norton, Barley. 2002. "'The Moon Remembers Uncle Ho': The Politics of Music and Mediumship in Northern Vietnam." *British Journal of Ethnomusicology* 11: 71–100. https://doi.org/10.1080/09681220208567329

Sabatier, Léopold. 1930. *Palabre du Serment au Darlac. Assemblée des chefs de tribus. 1er Janvier 1926.* Hanoi: n.p.

——1933. "La chanson de Damsan. Texte et traduction." *Bulletin de l'Ecole Française d'Extrême-Orient* 33: 143–302. https://doi.org/10.3406/befeo.1933.4619

Sabatier, Léopold, and Dominique Antomarchi. 1940. *Recueil des coutumes Rhadées du Darlac (Hdruôm hră klei duê klei bhiăn đuum)*. Hanoi: Imprimerie d'Extrême-Orient.

Salemink, Oskar. 2003. *The Ethnography of Vietnam's Central Highlanders: A Historical Contextualization, 1850–1990*. Honolulu: University of Hawaii Press.

—2011. "A View from the Mountains: A Critical History of Lowlander-Highlander Relations in Vietnam." In *Upland Transformations in Vietnam*, edited by Thomas Sikor, Nghiem Phuong Tuyen, Jennifer Sowerwine, and Jeff Romm, 27–50. Singapore: NUS Press.

—2012a. "Is There Space for Vietnam's Gong Culture? Economic and Social Challenges for the Safeguarding of the Space of Gong Culture." In *South-East Asia: Studies in Art, Cultural Heritage and Artistic Relations with Europe*, edited by Izabela Kopania, 127–34. Warsaw-Torun: Polish Institute of World Art Studies and Tako Publishing House.

—2012b. "The 'Heritagization' of Culture in Vietnam: Intangible Cultural Heritage between Communities, State and Market." Keynote speech, Fourth International Conference on Vietnamese Studies: Vietnam on the Road to Integration and Sustainable Development, 268–91. Hanoi: Vietnamese Academy of Social Sciences and Vietnam National University.

Tô Đông Hải. 2004. "Âm nhạc dân gian Êđê". In *Vùng văn hóa cồng chiêng Tây Nguyên*. Nhiêu Tác Giả, 322–60. Hanoi: Viện văn hóa–Thông tin.

UNESCO. 2003. "Text of the Convention for the Safeguarding of the Intangible Cultural Heritage." https://ich.unesco.org/en/convention (accessed October 25, 2018).

—2005. "Space of Gong Culture" on the UNESCO Representative List of the Intangible Cultural Heritage of Humanity. https://ich.unesco.org/en/RL/space-of-gong-culture-00120 (accessed October 25, 2018).

Part III

The Politics of Intangible Cultural Heritage

Introduction to Part III

Sarah M. Ross
Hannover University of Music, Drama, and Media, Germany

Cultural mapping has been recognized by the United Nations Educational, Scientific and Cultural Organization (UNESCO) as a central technique and tool for cataloging the diversity of tangible and intangible cultural assets of communities worldwide. It is thus inseparably linked to the concept of intangible cultural heritage (ICH), and in particular to the UNESCO Convention for the Safeguarding of the Intangible Cultural Heritage, which was adopted by its member states at the General Conference of UNESCO on October 17, 2003, and which came into effect in April 2006. As of 2017, 175 states have ratified the Convention and thereby implemented the Convention into national law.[1] This means that those national governments that ratified the Convention are now legally bound to designate and empower organizations that will "ensure the survival and vitality of ... living local ... and regional cultural heritage in the face of increasing globalization and its perceived homogenizing effects on culture" (Kurin 2007: 10).

The primary objective of UNESCO's Convention is thus the safeguarding of both traditional and modern intangible cultural heritage of various world cultures. Within this context, the definition of ICH includes:

> practices, representations, expressions, knowledge and know-how that communities recognize as part of their cultural heritage, [and which are] constantly recreated by communities in response to their [changing] environment, their interaction with nature, and their history, providing them with a sense of identity and continuity. (UNESCO 2013)

Against this background, the cultural heritage of a community or society is considered as not having a fixed form, but as an ever-changing cultural expression (UNESCO 2013; Yim 2004: 10). By safeguarding the intangible cultural heritage of a community, not only a society's cultural diversity and creativity can be encouraged, but also contemporary challenges of sustainable development can be met, such as social cohesion, education, or the sustainable management of natural and cultural resources (ibid.).

In order to achieve the aim of safeguarding intangible cultural heritage, UNESCO put up legal settings allowing and promoting the sustainable safeguarding of ICH, and furthermore developed various strategies and institutional infrastructures that enable states worldwide to document and archive their cultural heritage professionally, such as the *List of Intangible Cultural Heritage in Need of Urgent Safeguarding.*[2] In doing so, public knowledge and support for the Convention's concepts and objectives shall be endorsed (Kirshenblatt-Gimblett 2004: 53–54; see also UNESCO 2013). However, as anthropologists Barbara Kirshenblatt-Gimblett (2004) and Dawnhee Yim (2004) state, there are several challenges in the realization of the Convention's primary aims, which are not only limited to the former dichotomy between tangible and intangible heritage,[3] but rather concern UNESCO's long-lasting focus on masterpieces only, rather than on the masters themselves and their specialized skills needed for the actual performance of, for example, particular musical traditions (Kirshenblatt-Gimblett 2004: 53, 55; cf. Yim 2004: 11).[4] Thus, the earlier understanding of intangible cultural heritage, which was at times accompanied by an essentialist rhetoric on the disappearance of an allegedly authentic folk culture, first of all supported scholars and institutions to document and preserve a record of disappearing traditions, rather than to identify the causes for their vanishing and to "[support] the conditions necessary for cultural reproduction. This means according value to the carriers and transmitters of traditions, as well as to their habitus and habitat" (Kirshenblatt-Gimblett 2004: 53). This approach is reflected in a variety of ways in the following chapters.

The prelude is made by Gerda Lechleitner. In her chapter "Historical Voices Reloaded: Rethinking Archival Reponsibilities in Relation to Intangible Cultural Heritage," she discusses, against the background of the CD-edition of *Historical Collections*, the role of the Phonogrammarchiv in Vienna in reference to intangible cultural heritage. The history of this institution, spanning more than one hundred years, is analyzed regarding the perception of history and cultural memory. In doing so, Lechleitner addresses the following questions: What were the considerations of the early archivists? What was their strategy for collecting cultural expressions like music and languages from all over the world at the end of the nineteenth century? And how do we assess today those documents from our point of view?

Not only in everyday life but even more so in policy-related contexts, intangible cultural heritage takes on a variety of meanings in contemporary societies, which is reflected in the diversity of discourses and challenges concerning the realization of the Convention by different nation-states via their politics. Against the background of ethnomusicological case studies, Marzanna Poplawska and Marc-Antoine Camp et al. focus in their chapters on the variety of translations and interpretations of intangible cultural heritage that ensue after the conventions are ratified and implemented (Bendix, Eggert, and Peselmann 2013: 11). The Convention asks its state parties to cooperate with the groups and communities (the owners of intangible cultural heritage) in identifying ICH and drawing up inventories. However, given the timing of the ratification of the Convention, the construction and identification of intangible cultural heritage becomes a value-laden ideological project, and thus a never-ending act of a politics of inclusion and exclusion, as well as of power, as Kristin Kuutma illustrates (Kuutma 2012: 42).

Marzanna Poplawska discusses, in her chapter "Intangible Cultural Heritage and Policy Making in Poland," the process of creating and implementing appropriate policies for the protection of the intangible cultural heritage in Poland. In doing so, she states that it is not an admirable fact that Poland was one of the last states in Europe to ratify the 2003 UNESCO Convention. She thus investigates the reasons for this eight-year deferment and reluctance to introduce and fulfill the requirements of the same. Even though in November 2005 the Polish Ministry of Culture begun to function as the Ministry of Culture and National Heritage, and founded in 2011 the National Heritage Institute, the UNESCO Convention is still awaiting more concrete actions in Poland. While policies and ways of protecting tangible cultural heritage were already available since 1962, the country's intangible cultural heritage has either been neglected or its inherent fluidity and predominant lack of physical form prevented the creation of appropriate protection strategies. Despite the lack of governmental action, some civic and academic initiatives have been undertaken. On the basis of those initiatives, Poplawska investigates the obstacles that ethnomusicologists face in joining the policy-making process and explores the strategies for overcoming these difficulties. She further analyzes the advantages and possible dangers of creating lists of intangible cultural properties, as well as problems in forming appropriate criteria for recognizing the enlisted items.

In regard to such ideological issues, in their jointly written chapter "Mapping and Representing Musical Diversity in Switzerland: The Role of Artists, Ethnomusicologists, and Officials," Marc-Antoine Camp, Brigitte Bachmann-Geiser, David Vitali, Dieter Ringli, and Patricia Jäggi turn their attention to the concept of intangible cultural heritage, as discussed in Switzerland since the country's ratification of the UNESCO Convention in 2008. In doing so, they demonstrate that Switzerland, with its small size and relatively small population, offers valuable insights into the complexities of negotiating the concept of intangible cultural heritage. After Switzerland's ratification of the Convention, governmental agencies began to implement the obligations and recommendations, and published, in 2012, a national List of Living Traditions (http://www.living-traditions.ch). The establishment of this list was managed through several steps of negotiations, involving representatives from cultural groups, cultural anthropologists, ethnomusicologists (the authors themselves), and officials from state agencies. The process sought to find a comprehensive definition of intangible cultural heritage, suitable to accommodate diverse views on cultural traditions in Switzerland. One main question that arose during this process was how to represent cultural traditions and the concept of intangible cultural heritage to a wider public. The chapter thus reflects on the construction process of "living traditions" in Switzerland from varying perspectives, and presents features of its outcome with a special focus on sounds. In particular, the authors each focus on a specific topic, while providing a retrospective view on a similar collection of musical and cultural traditions, disseminated by a state agency for promoting Switzerland's image abroad (Brigitte Bachmann-Geiser); providing insights into the establishment of the "List of Living Traditions in Switzerland" (Marc-Antoine Camp); showing the creation thereby of a virtual soundscape of musical traditions in Switzerland (Patricia Jäggi); evaluating the inclusion and exclusion of musical traditions (Dieter Ringli); and reporting on the current state of political agreement concerning the concept of intangible cultural heritage in Switzerland (David Vitali).

The closing chapter by Sarah Ross, "Tracing the *Minhag Ashkenaz* in Swiss Synagogue Music: Advocates of Intangible Cultural Heritage Meet Agents of Cultural Sustainability," discusses how the concepts of intangible cultural heritage and cultural sustainability are interconnected within the context of the Jewish musical heritage of Switzerland. In doing so, she addresses not only the dissonant awareness and recognition of Switzerland's Jewish cultural heritage on the part of Swiss policy makers, which hampers the process of documenting, researching, promoting, and, finally, safeguarding

Jewish (musical) heritage in Switzerland, she moreover points to the fact that minority/diaspora groups, like the Jews of Switzerland, are only involved in the implementation of the Convention when they do not contradict the intentions of the governmental cultural policy. Thus, Ross promotes the idea of cultural sustainability, compared to that of cultural heritage, as it describes the discursive and dynamic processes of continuing and passing down (and not simply preserving) intangible forms of cultural expressions. In doing so, the model of cultural sustainability outlines a bottom-up movement emerging right from the heart of a community, rather than a top-down movement that is directly linked to the politically instructed realization of the UNESCO Convention for the Safeguarding of the Intangible Cultural Heritage.

Within the context of ethnomusicological studies presented in this part of the book and addressing the politics surrounding ICH, critical discourses about the sociocultural effects of politically-driven heritage-making become apparent, which not only focus on the categorization, political implementation, and instrumentalization of ICH undertaken by a number of experts and engaged stakeholders, but that moreover emphasize that intangible cultural heritage encompasses in equal parts particular cultural practices *and* a whole society's approach to these practices: cultural heritage means practices *and* discourses, history *and* historical culture, tradition *and* traditional culture (Tauschek 2013: 24).

Notes

1   See state parties to the Convention for the Safeguarding of the Intangible Cultural Heritage: http://www.unesco.org/eri/la/convention.asp?KO=17116&language=E (accessed February 23, 2016).

2   As the 2003 UNESCO Convention for the Safeguarding of the Intangible Cultural Heritage points out in Article 12, each state signing the declaration "shall draw up, in a manner geared to its own situation, one or more inventories of the intangible cultural heritage, present in its territory and monitor these." https://ich.unesco.org/en/convention (accessed October 25, 2018).

3   In 2003, the Convention for the Safeguarding of the Intangible Cultural Heritage was drafted, which involved several discourses regarding the differentiation of tangible and intangible cultural heritage.

4   Since 2001, the *Proclamation of Masterpieces of the Oral and Intangible Heritage of Humanity* has been introduced by UNESCO. The objective of this program is to raise awareness on intangible cultural heritage and encourage local communities to protect them and the local people who sustain these forms

of cultural expressions (see Grant 2014: 30–31; "UNESCO Issues First Ever Proclamation of Masterpieces of the Oral and Intangible Heritage," http://www.unesco.org/bpi/eng/unescopress/2001/01-71e.shtml (accessed August 6, 2015).

References

Bendix, Regina F., Aditya Eggert and Arnika Peselmann. 2013. "Introduction: Heritage Regimes and the State." In *Heritage Regimes and the State*, edited by Regina F. Bendix, Aditya Eggert, and Arnika Peselmann, 11–20. Göttingen: Universitätsverlag Göttingen. https://doi.org/10.4000/books.gup.366

Grant, Catherine. 2014. *Music Endangerment: How Language Maintenance Can Help*. Oxford, New York: Oxford University Press.
https://doi.org/10.1093/acprof:oso/9780199352173.001.0001

Kirshenblatt-Gimblett, Barbara. 2004. "Intangible Heritage as Metacultural Production." *Museum International* 56 (1–2): 52–65.
https://doi.org/10.1111/j.1350-0775.2004.00458.x

Kurin, Richard. 2007. "Safeguarding Intangible Cultural Heritage: Key Factors in Implementing the 2003 Convention." Inaugural Public Lecture, Smithsonian Institution and the University of Queensland MoU Ceremony, November 23, 2006. *International Journal of Intangible Heritage* 2: 9–20.

Kuutma, Kristin. 2012. "Communities and the Contested Politics of Representation." In *The First ICH-Researchers Forum The Implementation of UNESCO's 2003 Convention: Final Report*. Osaka: International Research Centre for Intangible Cultural Heritage in the Asia-Pacific Region (IRCI). 42–51.
http://www.irci.jp/assets/files/2012_ICH_Forum.pdf (accessed February 23, 2016).

Tauschek, Markus. 2013. *Kulturerbe: Eine Einführung*. Berlin: Reimer Verlag.

UNESCO. 2013. "Intangible Cultural Heritage." Paris: UNESCO.
http://www.unesco.org/culture/ich/doc/src/20435-EN.pdf
(accessed May 24, 2015).

Yim, Dawnhee. 2004. "Living Human Treasures and the Protection of Intangible Culture Heritage: Experiences and Challenges." *Icom News* 4: 10–12.
http://archives.icom.museum/pdf/E_news2004/p10_2004-4.pdf
(accessed October 15, 2018).

Chapter 9

Historical Voices Reloaded: Rethinking Archival Responsibilities in Relation to Intangible Cultural Heritage

Gerda Lechleitner

Introduction

A cultural manifestation, as soon as it is collected or stored, becomes historical rather quickly. The role of archives is to preserve and make accessible documents (either in written form or as audio-visual documents) for knowledge production and memory. "Tradition" or "heritage" are constructed keywords for remembering cultural manifestations. UNESCO's efforts strive for the same goal. Thus, the following discussions seek to point out similarities and differences in the approaches of archives (specifically focusing on the Phonogrammarchiv of the Austrian Academy of Sciences), and UNESCO's activities in the assessment of respective outcomes.

The website of UNESCO's Intangible Cultural Heritage differentiates between three lists comprising different specifications: the List of Intangible Cultural Heritage in Need of Urgent Safeguarding, the Representative List of the Intangible Cultural Heritage of Humanity, and the Register of Good Safeguarding Practices (UNESCO 2008). This line-up might be perceived as a virtual museum arranged chronologically and by national states. The cultural activities are listed, described in their outstanding value and illustrated additionally with photos or sound and video examples. Thus, the oral traditions and expressions, performing arts, social practices, rituals, and festive events are "fixed" like documents, and fulfill to some extent a similar role as artifacts in museums or documents in an archive. The connection to—or, more suitably, the cooperation with—museums or archives emerges in fact more closely, because the application form to include an item on the Intangible Cultural Heritage List asks for the respective historical background, and for specific documentation including sources, literature, and documentation. Finally, the inclusion of the respective item on the List assumes quite a lively insight of the chosen item, thanks to its additional documentation.

Besides UNESCO's definition, the term "intangible heritage" also emerged in discussions about the function and impact of museums and exhibitions in the first decade of the new millennium (cf. Beier-de Haan 2005). This term—surprisingly in that context—is "imported" from a discourse about global cultural policies and new orientations (cf. Kramer 2009). UNESCO stated that cultural heritage is not limited to material manifestations, but also encompasses living expressions and traditions inherited by countless groups and communities worldwide from their ancestors and transmitted to their descendants, in most cases orally (UNESCO 2003, article 2). In that sense, intangible heritage must be seen as a category incompatible with the definition of museums or archives, that is, institutions which preserve and present "objects" or (as in sound archives) "sound documents." Today, the goal of museums and archives is to make understandable the entireness of human action by connecting tradition and modernization. In arranging specific "objects" in an exhibition, or in commenting on the collected sound recordings in the Vienna Phonogrammarchiv's CD publication, the visitor or user is "guided" to gain a more general idea about a world's culture. It is the contrast between the static of the tangible and the floating of the intangible heritage that has to be bridged and will be discussed in order to shed light on the responsibility of archives.

The importance of intangible heritage (following UNESCO's Convention, article 1, 2003) should raise awareness on three levels—locally, nationally, and internationally—and, moreover, of today's "challenge" of globalization. On the one hand, we have to face a world marked by a global culture and multicultural lifestyle while on the other there is the search for different cultural activities, setting boundaries between "the own" and "the other," evident, for example, in discussions about (multiple or manifold) identities (cf. Grupe 2005; Ceribašić and Haskell 2006). Certainly, these are two competing systems. The UNESCO Convention (2003) responds to the situation by emphasizing intangible cultural heritage, and addresses the need for safeguarding, while ensuring respect and raising awareness of that heritage, which in turn provides the global village with "a touch" of diversity.

The title of this chapter, "Historical Voices Reloaded," points to the importance of historical considerations. Why is the past, such as the past in cultural or musical action, so important? Why are we connected to the past, yet sometimes more and sometimes less? Seeger (2010: 16 et seq.) proposed a meaningful explanation to describe the different values surrounding present-day (commercial) and historical sound recordings: Commercial products have a "long tail" in the digital economy, that is, a commercial recording is very popular at the moment of publication, becomes much less popular in the course of time, but is still commercially useful long after its creation. In contrast, research sound archives, such as those in Vienna, Berlin, or Paris, do not produce popular recordings, but rather carefully preserve recordings produced as part of research, ensuring that the sounds remain available for the long term. Such recordings could be considered to have "a long tail," contrary to commercial recordings. Audiovisual archives often notice that their oldest collections are of greatest value both to researchers and members of the communities that were recorded. Their value appears to increase with age, and thus might be regarded as the opposite of commercial recordings. One of the reasons could be that such recordings have usually comprised currently practiced traditions. In time, their importance increases because languages or traditions change, and thus they become increasingly important for scholars, communities, and the public. In that sense, Seeger (2010: 17) speaks about the reverse of the "long tail" idea, showing that archival recordings often become more important long after their creation.

As previously mentioned, the application form for the inclusion of an intangible heritage item includes documentation with reference to sources, literature, and documents (see Austrian Commission for UNESCO 2015), through which archives become "players," while the "long tail" enjoyed by historical collections means they gain the interest and respect of society. This is thus the point where considerations about intangible cultural heritage and the role of archives meet. In the following, these aspects will be addressed, while discussing audio-visual archives as places of historical sources, as bearers of responsibility vis-à-vis the performers and their descendants, and as partners of UNESCO in respect of intangible cultural heritage.

Audiovisual Archives as Places of Historical Sources

In the late nineteenth and early twentieth centuries, it was not obvious that sound recordings should be archived; they might have been recorded for creating a "text" and then discarded, rather than saved. As we clearly know, it is extremely difficult to redo unique audio recordings, since we cannot reconstruct an instrumental performance, nor can we reconstruct a particular way of singing or speaking or telling a story. For a long time, songbooks were collected, first comprising only texts, then also melodies, and it would indeed be interesting to know how these songs were sung at the time. Sound recordings thus gained importance, although they capture only "one version" or "one moment of reality."

Set against this background, the founding idea of the Phonogrammarchiv of the former Imperial Academy of Sciences in 1899 conveys a farsighted approach. Its founding members, which included physiologist and first director Sigmund Exner, and physicists Franz Exner and Victor von Lang, together with the philologists Wilhelm von Hartel, Richard Heinzel, and Vatroslav Jagić (cf. Exner 1900: 1) underlined the importance of the invention of sound recording, which, they argued, should be used for scholarly research. Thus, sound recordings, which allowed repeated and controlled evaluations of acoustical phenomena such as rhythm, accent, timbre, melodies, and scales, provided the necessary basis for a wide and new range of disciplines such as linguistics or ethnomusicology. The founding members advocated the preservation of those recordings, which would be useful for further research, but could also be of interest to the descendants of the people featuring on the recordings (Exner 1900: 1). Strategies were thus developed to increase the collections of recorded music, triggering, among others, recording expeditions to Croatia, Brazil, and the Isle of Lesbos in 1901, or inviting specific performers to the archive. The visionary, even if unachievable goal was to build a collection of languages and music from around the world. The resultant collections of music recordings up to the beginning of the tape era comprise ca. 4,000 recordings, so in 1999, and one hundred years after the archive's foundation, UNESCO included these collections as "documents of universal significance" in the World Register of its "Memory of the World" Program (UNESCO 1999).

Archival Responsibilities

The Phonogrammarchiv's collections have been the result of focused research on specific subjects, and its key duties are to produce, collect, catalogue, preserve (in the long term), and make accessible audiovisual documents. Its work meets the requirements of the "Memory of the World" Program (Edmondson

2015), in which historical collections have been included: the recordings are preserved in the long term, and they are registered and accessible in the database and online catalogue. Moreover, a multi-media publication of the archive's audio-CDs with data CD and booklet (see Phonogrammarchiv 2015) of its complete historical collections is under progress. The entries in the database and online catalogue reflect the original documentation being brought up to date. The publication offers the possibility of more in-depth discussions that can be read in the comments and checked against the sound recordings and original documentation. The archive's preoccupation with these collections opens new insights into the history of its research, ideas and strategies underpinning the institution, while rethinking activities and their consequences.

UNESCO

UNESCO has formulated various conventions for cultural affairs. The general idea behind all of them is to protect, safeguard, and promote cultural heritage. The Memory of the World Program (1992) states that "the world's documentary heritage belongs to all, should be fully preserved and protected," and "should be permanently accessible to all," which are requirements fulfilled by the Phonogrammarchiv via the registered historical music recording collections included in UNESCO's Memory of the World Program in 1999. "In Africa, when an old man dies, it's a library burning," stated Amadou Hampâté Bâ (1901–1991), a Malian writer and ethnologist, at the UNESCO Convention in 1960. Based on a West African proverb that refers to oral traditions, this statement evokes the importance of memory by a musician, genealogist, storyteller, historian, and myth maker, who conveys a strong sense of culture and community, and thus helps to keep (African) traditions and sensibilities alive, as has been done for centuries. Yet today, the prevailing opinion is often that such abilities and knowledge will be lost, thus archives and museums have taken on the function of keeping heritage intact. To highlight the relationship between archives and UNESCO, and their relatively similar approach and awareness, three examples will help towards further critical reflections. The starting point will be the history and collection policy of the Phonogrammarchiv, and the illustrated book about perspectives on living heritage (Freland 2009).

Capturing the Intangible: Perspectives on the Living Heritage

Capturing the Intangible: Perspectives on the Living Heritage is the title of Freland's (2009) extensive and richly illustrated book presenting the ninety intangible cultural heritage elements inscribed in the Representative List since it came into operation in 2003. The book, while comprising extraordinary photographic material and short, concise texts, reflects the beauty and wealth of the world's living intangible heritage. The book lends the feeling of undertaking a journey into various intangible heritage communities, encountering the joy that communities have in practicing intangible heritage, and realizing the pain when heritage becomes endangered. The book also conveys the communities' devotion to transmitting and revitalizing their heritage. Some of the headlines of this UNESCO publication, at times somewhat sounding like advertising slogans, are used to initiate discussion about archival "static" documents, in contrast to living cultural activities. The chosen examples focus on the significance of sound recordings for both the respective communities and the scholarly world.

In the introductory chapter, the author highlights that "many aspects of intangible cultural heritage are under threat, endangered by factors such as globalization, cultural homogenization, and lack of appreciation and understanding" (Freland 2009: 13). This observation is not completely new, since around 1905–07 researchers already recognized that the world's culture would be Europeanized and homogenized. Erich Moritz von Hornbostel asserted that ethnographic material had to be collected, which, due to the spread and influence of European civilization, would otherwise disappear and irretrievably be lost (Hornbostel 1905: 95). Similarly, Rudolf Pöch, an ethnologist, anthropologist, and pioneer in modern field research (he used the phonograph, a photo camera, and film camera), described the motivation behind his film documentation and (possibly) sound recordings (see Österreichische Mediathek, online catalogue): "they [the recordings] document expressions of a culture which will vanish with the appearance of European civilization" (Pöch 1907a: 805, my translation). He encouraged other researchers to use the new technology to capture vivid documents of cultures that otherwise would vanish and no longer be available to their descendants (cf. Pöch 1907b: 400). From this, we may conclude that European (Western) archives now host unique and early (or sometimes the earliest) sound documents of entire ethnic groups, which form the historical basis for their eligibility in regards to chosen Intangible Cultural Heritage items. As we know today, we have to deal carefully with those sound documents, while considering the circumstances of how they were made. Although the historical collections of, for instance, the Berlin and Vienna Phonogrammarchiv were included in the register of the Memory of the World program, and are therefore accepted as belonging to the world's documentary heritage, it is up to archivists and scholars to address the background of that research and its consequences.

Pöch's recordings from the Kalahari Desert, which he made in 1908 and were published by Lechleitner (2003), shall serve as an example here. In 2003, the Phonogrammarchiv felt obliged to send a rather large number of recording copies to South Africa, in the sense of repatriation regards their history and heritage. These recordings were preserved in Vienna and then returned as digitalized sounds, along with the original documentation and researchers' comments, fieldwork notes, and general conditions pertaining to the realization of the project. During this process, it turned out that Pöch was not only a "pioneer" in modern field research, but also an ambitious and competitive scholar who cared little about moral and ethic behavior, as Martin Legassick and Ciraj Rassool illustrated in their publication resulting from this project (2000). For instance, in her foreword to the publication, Patricia Davison from the South African Museum explained that "the underlying assumption was that 'Bushmen' and 'Hottentots' were living examples of a primitive and dying race that should be studied before it became extinct." She continued that those outcomes would tell us about colonial power relations and might raise the emotive issue of what should be done to redress past wrongdoings (Legassick and Rassool 2000: v). Legassick and Rassool expressed those circumstances even more unambiguously when writing:

> It is generally assumed that science has a privileged position to decide on its own nefarious past, and that it has this position by virtue of superior knowledge ... It is automatically assumed that the museum continues to be the rightful owner, authority and custodian. (Legassick and Rassool 2000: 102–103)

This critical perspective beyond our (European) point of view and the reactions by the persons concerned might have "shocked" established knowledge, but were indeed necessary in the postcolonial age. Rethinking transmitted history differently contributed to new intercultural appreciation and filled a critical gap of understanding, which is similarly concluded by Freland (2009: 11) in his introductory chapter: "The intangible heritage provides us with a sense of identity and belonging, linking our past through the present, with our future."

Heritage implies a search for the past and, to some extent, legitimates its continuing position in the present, based on the search for a distinct, "authentic" culture, while somewhat ignoring the fact that culture has always been the outcome of contacts, influences, and new creations. Identity is an important concept in our modern, multicultural world. Thus, one early example included in the Intangible Cultural Heritage List was Georgian polyphony, a symbol of Georgian identity, which emerged from the Phonogrammarchiv's preservation of early Georgian recordings in prisoner of war camps during World War I from 1915–16. The First World War "offered" a new kind of "field research" by chance, namely, research in prisoner of war camps. This work at first focused on anthropological studies but then also included sound recordings, featuring prisoners from various ethnic communities of Europe and Asian Russia (the Tsarist Empire). Although the recording and scientific approach at that time were somewhat unethical and are still subject to vehement discussion, the actual appreciation of these recordings by Georgians is especially high. When the ambassador of Georgia in Austria, George Arsenishvili, together with a Georgian delegation, visited the Phonogrammarchiv in 2003, they were overwhelmed by listening to those historical voices. As attendees observed, they were less concerned with the context of the recording situation, but focused more on these recordings as the voices of their ancestors, which clearly reflects the importance of historical records for subsequent generations of people. While the recordings reference their historical background, they also signpost continuity and relevance for cultural "insiders." These sound documents thus evoke self-recognition and identification, while at the same time facilitating continued research.

Identity is about continuity, as customs and rites are passed on by communities' elders. More generally, "culture" and, specifically, intangible heritage may be understood as a system of orientation where identity is continuously formed via processes of remembrance and adopting and assigning meanings (cf. Feichtinger et al. 2006: 11). In times of uncertainty and fragmentation, the idea of continuity is very important, and it seems to be the joint or collective heritage that is appreciated. In this regard, "It is hoped that increased visibility as a result of inscription on the Representative List will aid recognition and appreciation of cultural diversity of various communities" (Freland 2009: 25).

As already mentioned, lists can be seen as virtual museums or archives; the inscriptions are selected by committees and then represent a certain value, including an economic one, such as for touristic activities (cf. Robinson 2009: 82 et seq.). Consequently, cultural activities have an increased visibility, which help to earn recognition and appreciation. One of the key phenomena in this discourse is heritage protection in reaction to endangerment. But the tension between preservation and change, monument and living environment, belongs to the antagonisms of current times. To underline that tension, I hereby quote the writer Galsan Tschinag (b. 1944), a member of the Tuva who is aware of his own tradition but is also shaped by the western world: "The yurt—a Stone Age dwelling. It only survived until today because clever persons have left it to stupid ones as an emergency shelter, and even more clever persons have turned it into a museum artefact worthy of admiration" (Tschinag 2012: 56, my translation). Meanwhile, Freland (2009: 39) explains the appreciation of living heritage as follows: "To safeguard the intangible heritage of the world is to be interested in all the history and culture that enlightens our common destiny, it is to honour life!" (Freland 2009: 39).

Therefore, world heritage conveys a certain status awarded and coined by a committee, yet which cannot negate a western point of view. Thus, scholars, such as those working in archives, have the role to critically question the making of sound documents and the context in which they are made. On the other hand, UNESCO also shows the wonderful, colorful, charming aspects of life via marvelous pictures and charming texts (Freland 2009), but in a static way meant for reading and looking. Yet real life is different—we are driven by economic decisions, fading out (or suppressing) quarrels, pain, and disaster. The book thereby has the purpose to inform about cultural diversity at its best, selectively.

Conclusions

When the idea first emerged to establish a research sound archive, its founders assumed that the preserved sound documents would be of interest to future researchers or to the descendants recorded, without any assumptions around collecting "heritage." In the course of time, however, the recordings have become heritage. UNESCO's Intangible Cultural Heritage lists might thereby be compared to collections preserved in archives, although their intentions and representations differ.

In ethnomusicology (or comparative musicology, as it was previously called), recordings were made to study unknown music, specific melodies, particular scales, and exceptional forms and rhythms (Abraham and Hornbostel 1906; Hornbostel 1913, 1927; Graf 1950, 1967, 1972). Based on these findings, "musical maps" were developed that pointed out general and typical forms, and the distribution of musical "styles." The Demonstration Collection (1963), compiled by E. M. von Hornbostel and the Berlin Phonogrammarchiv, can be seen as such an example and as a first attempt to showcase "intangible cultural heritage," namely, the world's musical diversity. Hornbostel compiled outstanding examples from the Berlin Phonogrammarchiv collections from nearly all parts of the world, from the Far East (e.g. Thailand, Indonesia), Australia to Africa, via South and North America, and to Europe. A variety of ethnic groups with "typical" instruments are represented, for example Sheng/mouth organ from Beijing, and specific music genres, such as yodeling from Switzerland.

Ethnomusicologists have been interested in music as such, and also in the communities and their performance of music, asking questions like "what role has music played for them, and what meaning does music have as a social element?" Hours of sound recordings document activities such as singing, making music, and spoken texts, proverbs etc., as part of oral traditions and fragments of performing arts. As archived items, however, they represent these expressions as "fixed" and unchangeable. Yet the Intangible Cultural Heritage List seems to be a "best of" list, worldwide, although, according to UNESCO, it should not represent the cultural manifestation itself but rather the wealth of knowledge and skills. For me, it has turned out that our world, to a large extent, regards museums and archives as capturing and producing canonized knowledge. Such an approach is "western-based" and has been imposed everywhere, for example by training programs to support musical knowledge. In my view, the Intangible Cultural Heritage lists are compiled in a similar vein, and are thus not an exception in that respect. To conclude, let me return to Galsan Tschinag:

> Don't we often enough advocate a wrong matter while honestly striving to do something good? Aren't we sometimes tormented by the feeling of having acted dishonestly, only to learn—the next moment or after a generation—that this wasn't the case at all? (2012: 79, my translation)

About the Author

Gerda Lechleitner, PhD, works at the Phonogram Archive at the Austrian Academy of Sciences and is curator of the Historical Collections. She is the editor of the CD edition *The Complete Historical Collections 1899–1950* and the Phonogram Archive's Yearbook "International Forum on Audio-Visual Research." Her research focus includes intellectual history around 1900, and the history and development of audiovisual archives and their role as "lieu de mémoire." She is also interested in the significance of (acoustic) historical sources, as well as in music and minorities, and multipart music.

References

Abraham, Otto, and Erich Moritz von Hornbostel. 1906. "Phonographierte Indianermelodien aus British Columbia." In *Boas Anniversary Volume: Anthropological Papers Written in Honor of Franz Boas*, edited by H. A. Andrews and Berthold Laufer, 447–74. New York: G. E. Stechert.

Austrian Commission for UNESCO. 2015. "Bewerbung um Aufnahme einer Tradition in das österreichische Verzeichnis des immateriellen Kulturerbes." http://immaterielleskulturerbe.unesco.at/cgi-bin/page.pl?id=7&lang=de (accessed October 15, 2018).

Beier-de Haan, Rosmarie. 2005. "Jenseits der Dinge. Die Generierung des Intangible Heritage in den 'Gedächtnisorten' Museum und Ausstellung." In *Kulturerbe als soziokulturelle Praxis*, edited by Moritz Csáky and Monika Sommer, 57–76. Innsbruck: Studienverlag.

Ceribašić, Naila, and Erica Haskell, eds. 2006. *Shared Musics and Minority Identities*. Zagreb, Roč: Institute of Ethnology and Folklore Research, Cultural-Artistic Society "Istarski željesniča."

Edmondson, Ray. 2015. "Recommendation concerning the Preservation of, and Access to, Documentary Heritage Including in Digital Form. Implementation Guidelines." (Contract 4500313593). https://en.unesco.org/programme/mow/recommendation-documentary-heritage (accessed December 3, 2018).

Exner, Sigmund. 1900. "Bericht über die Arbeiten der von der kaiserl. Akademie der Wissenschaften eingesetzten Commission zur Gründung eines Phonogramm-Archives." *Anzeiger der mathematisch-naturwissenschaftlichen Klasse der kaiserl. Akademie der Wissenschaften in Wien* 37: 1–6.

Feichtinger, Johannes, Elisabeth Großegger, Getraud Marinelli-König, Peter Stachel, and Heidemarie Uhl. 2006. "Vorwort." In *Schauplatz Kultur–Zentraleuropa: Transdisziplinäre Annäherungen*, edited by Johannes Feichtinger, Elisabeth Großegger, Getraud Marinelli-König, Peter Stachel, and Heidemarie Uhl, 11–14. Innsbruck, Wien, Bozen: Studienverlag.

Freland, François-Xavier. 2009. *Capturing the Intangible: Perspectives on the Living Heritage*. Paris: UNESCO.

Graf, Walter. 1950. *Die musikwissenschaftlichen Phonogramme Rudolf Pöchs von der Nordküste Neuguineas. Eine materialkritische Studie unter besonderer*

Berücksichtigung der völkerkundlichen Grundlagen. Wien: Österreichische Akademie der Wissenschaften, Rudolf Pöch Nachlaß, Serie B: Völkerkunde, Bd. 2.

—1967. "Zur sonagraphischen Untersuchung von Sprache und Musik." *Beiträge zur Kenntnis Südosteuropas und des Nahen Orients* 2: 40–55.

—1972. "Aspekte musikalischer Klangforschung." In *Studia instrumentorum musicae popularis II, Bericht über die Internationale Arbeitstagung der Study Group on Folk Musical Instruments des International Folk Music Council, Stockholm 1969*, edited by Ernst Emsheimer, 47–52. Stockholm: Musikhistoriska museet.

Grupe, Gerd, ed. 2005. *Musiethnologie und Volksmusikforschung in Österreich: Das "Fremde" und das "Eigene"?* Aachen: Shaker Verlag.

Hornbostel, Erich Moritz von. 1905. "Probleme der vergleichenden Musikwissenschaft." *Zeitschrift der Internationalen Musikgesellschaft* 3(7): 85–97.

—1913. "Melodie und Skala." *Jahrbuch der Musikbibliothek Peters* XIX: 11–23.

—1927. "Musikalische Tonsysteme." *Handbuch der Physik* VIII: 425–49.

Kramer, Dieter. 2009. "Immaterielles Kulturerbe, kulturelle Vielfalt und die UNESCO. Eine Herausforderung für die Europäische Ethnologie?" In *Erb.gut? Kulturelles Erbe in Wissenschaft und Gesellschaft*, edited by Karl C. Berger, Margot Schindler and Ingo Schneider, 61–74. Wien: Selbstverlag des Vereins für Volkskunde.

Legassick, Martin, and Ciraj Rassool. 2000. *Skeletons in the Cupboard: South African Museums and the Trade in Human Remains 1907–1917.* Cape Town and Kimberley: South African Museum and McGregor Museum.

Österreichische Mediathek. Online catalogue. https://www.mediathek.at/akustische-chronik/suche/detail/atom/135BBA4F-3BB-0008D-00000B84-135B28B9/pool/BWEB/ (accessed December 3, 2018).

Phonogrammarchiv. 2015. *The Complete Historical Collections.* http://www.phonogrammarchiv.at/wwwnew/edition_e.htm#Gesamtausgabe (accessed October 15, 2018).

Pöch, Rudolf. 1907a. "Zweiter Bericht über meine phonographischen Aufnahmen in Neu-Guinea." *Sitzungsbericht der kaiserl. Akademie der Wissenschaften in Wien. Mathematisch-naturwissenschaftliche Klasse 116/2a*, 801–17 (= 10. Mitteilung der Phonogrammarchivs-Kommission).

—1907b. "Reisen in Neu-Guinea in den Jahren 1904–1906." *Zeitschrift für Ethnologie* 39: 382–400.

Robinson, Mike. 2009. "Moving Heritage Forward: Tourism, the Popular and the Hypermodern." In *Erb.gut? Kulturelles Erbe in Wissenschaft und Gesellschaft*, edited by Karl C. Berger, Margot Schindler, and Ingo Schneider, 75–88. Wien: Selbstverlag des Vereins für Volkskunde.

Seeger, Anthony. 2010. "Looking to the Past and Creating the Future: The Functions and Ethics of Audiovisual Archives in the 21st Century." *Jahrbuch des Phonogrammarchivs der Österreichischen Akademie der Wissenschaften* 1: 13–29. Göttingen: Cuvillier.

Tschinag, Galsan. 2012. *Gold und Staub*. Zürich: Unionsverlag.

UNESCO. 1999. "Memory of the World: The Historical Collections (1899–1950) of the Vienna Phonogrammarchiv." http://www.unesco.org/new/en/communication-and-information/flagship-project-activities/memory-of-the-world/register/full-list-of-registered-heritage/registered-heritage-page-8/the-historical-collections-1899-1950-of-the-vienna-phonogrammarchiv/#c191394 (accessed October 15, 2018).

—2003. "Text of the Convention for the Safeguarding of the Intangible Cultural Heritage." http://www.unesco.org/culture/ich/en/convention (accessed October 15, 2018).

—2008. "Purpose of the Lists of Intangible Cultural Heritage and of the Register of Good Safeguarding Practices." https://ich.unesco.org/en/purpose-of-the-lists-00807 (accessed December 3, 2018).

Recordings

Lechleitner. Gerda. 2003. *Rudolf Pöch's Kalahari Recordings (1908)* (= *Sound Documents from the Phonogrammarchiv of the Austrian Academy of Sciences: The Complete Historical Collections 1899–1950*, general editor: Dietrich Schüller, Series 7, OEAW PHA CD 19). Wien: VÖAW.

Various Artists. 1963. *The Demonstration Collection of E.M. von Hornbostel and the Berlin Phonogramm-Archiv*. Ethnic Folkways Library FE4175.

Chapter 10

Intangible Cultural Heritage and Policy Making in Poland

Marzanna Poplawska

This chapter discusses the process of creating and implementing appropriate policies for the protection of Intangible Cultural Heritage (ICH) in Poland. While portraying the current situation of ICH in Poland, I specifically refer to the models that have been developing since the 1950s and 1960s in Asian countries such as Japan and South Korea. These models may serve as valuable points of reference for creating optimal strategies when dealing with ICH.

The Convention for the Safeguarding of the Intangible Cultural Heritage, which was passed in 2003[1] and went into effect in 2006, recommends that countries and scholars develop inventories of ICH in their territory, as well as work with the groups who maintain ICH to ensure their continued existence (Kurin 2004). In Poland, the major force behind the development of ICH policies is the Ministry of Culture and National Heritage, which (as discussed below)—under the pressure of public opinion (mainly organizations linked to traditional music)—began formulating and implementing ICH policies after ratifying the Convention in 2011. This process, to some degree, was assisted by public consultations. As for the Convention itself, it is surrounded by a discourse of enthusiasts and cautious warners of possible negative impacts, such as standardization or fossilization of ICH (especially when it comes to creating inventories). In Poland, many look at the Convention as a means of advancing and fostering knowledge of traditional culture, a way of stimulating its development and interest in it. Others, especially scholars, dispute the Convention boundlessly, scrutinizing its individual recommendations, inspecting its significance and value in the Polish context, and trying to foresee its consequences. In any case, as Christina Kreps—an established anthropologist theorizing heritage and its preservation—observes, the Convention reflects an important shift in thinking: from a concern for safeguarding tangible cultural heritage to a concern for the protection of the knowledge, skills, and values behind this heritage as well as a concern for the people and social processes that sustain it. It demonstrates the need to value cultural expressions on the local level (in particular), in addition to the global level. It also acknowledges the worth of all different kinds of cultural forms (Kreps 2005: 7). By signing the Convention, the governments acknowledge this focal shift from tangible toward intangible heritage. Nonetheless, the process of changing perceptions and thinking habits poses many challenges. Its beginnings in Poland have been slow. However, since 2013, the process of implementing ICH has accelerated, especially with the many events of the Year of Oskar Kolberg (2014).

Institutions and ICH Politics in Poland

Poland was the 135th country to ratify the Convention, one of the last in Europe to do so—a peculiar fact, considering the country's very location in the heart of Europe. As of May 2018, there are 178 states that ratified the Convention. The Polish ratification took place in 2011, eight years after the Convention was adopted and five years after it went into effect. The signing off of the Convention was proceeded by several administrational changes, which are important in view of the terminology increasingly used in the language of official legislation as well as in the academic discourse.

Firstly, the Polish Ministry of Culture was renamed in November 2005—two years after the Convention—as the Ministry of Culture and National Heritage. In 2011, the Ministry founded the National Heritage Institute, which is a continuation of several different institutions, mainly related to tangible cultural properties. The history of the National Heritage Institute begins with the Center for Documentation of Historical Monuments established in 1962. In 2007, after forty-five years of existence, the Center merged with the Center for Protection of Historical Landscape to form the National Center for Research and Documentation of Historical Monuments. In 2007, yet another institution joined the Center, namely the Center for Protection of Archeological Heritage. In 2011, the Center finally changed its name into the current one, which is far more general and less evidently related to the material/tangible (both cultural/historical and natural) objects. This historical genealogy of the National Heritage Institute is crucial to understanding the perception of it as a proper or improper location for the protection of ICH (something that has been disputed); it is also essential to comprehending the evaluation of its activities, which will become apparent in the subsequent parts of this chapter.

Because of the long-term inaction of the Polish government regarding the Convention for the Safeguarding of the Intangible Cultural Heritage, in December 2010, Jadwiga Rodowicz, a scholar of Japanese theater and—then—a Polish ambassador to Japan, launched a Foundation for Intangible Cultural Heritage in Poland. The mission of the Foundation was to work together with non-governmental organizations, various institutions and individuals to "support, research and develop initiatives in order to protect the ICH in Poland (understood as a historically changeable geographic area)."[2] However, in 2012, Rodowicz was offered a position in the Ministry of Culture and National Heritage, and the Foundation no longer seems active. Perhaps after sparking the initial interest in the Convention, followed by its ratification, the Foundation considered its role fulfilled.

The second initiative—intended to pressure the Polish government to take action—was an open letter to the Minister of Culture and National Heritage (also sent to the Polish Parliament—the Committee on Culture and Media), the President of Poland, and the Polish UNESCO Committee. The letter called for the realization of the Convention, which Poland had ratified a year earlier. Many distinguished scholars, representatives of radio stations, museums, various cultural foundations and associations, ethnographers, and also ethnomusicologists signed the letter.

In response, the Minister undertook several steps to act on the Convention: he established an advising body on ICH, then ordered expert legal reports. Lastly, it was the National Heritage Institute that was charged with the task of preparing the practical aspects of the implementation of the Convention. In turn, the National Heritage Institute (as well as the Minister himself) appealed to the local governments (Marshals) to create in the local administration a position of coordinator for ICH. As of 2013, only one out of sixteen local governments created such a position. In Warmian-Masurian Voivodeship it is held by a fine artist, a member of the Association of Folk Artists.

The National Heritage Institute has branch offices all over the country. These offices were also asked to designate a staff member who would deal with ICH matters. However, the process was very slow as the branch offices were not entirely clear on their role; those made responsible for ICH (administratively) often continue their previous tasks, not taking much initiative regarding ICH. In response to inquisitive public calls, the President of Poland, in 2011, called a public debate. The participants of the debate were scholars and representatives of the Polish UNESCO Committee as well as representatives of different cultural institutions. Apart from the presidential debate, in 2012, two conferences and workshops were organized on the proposed scheme and methods of implementing the Convention: one symposium took place in Warsaw and the other in Lublin. They were especially directed at the NGOs. In October 2014, another workshop for NGOs, cultural institutions, and local governments took place in Sandomierz.[3]

The groups and organizations that have particular interest in the Convention are many—this fact testifies to the vitality of the contemporary folk/folklore scene in Poland. Most of them are affiliated with the Forum for Traditional Music (Forum Muzyki Tradycyjnej), which was established in 2011. On the newly-created website of the National Heritage Institute, there are twenty-two such organizations, mostly foundations and associations; they are identified as representing "performing arts and music traditions." Among the plethora of organizations concerned with folk traditions are the Polish Ethnological Society (Polskie Towarzystwo Ludoznawcze or PTL) and Association of Folk Artists (Stowarzyszenie Twórców Ludowych or STL). The Polish Ethnological Society (founded in 1895) considers as its mission the documentation, development, and popularization of knowledge of historical and contemporary world cultures. Until 2018, it was the only Polish association designated by UNESCO as an expert organization and may be called to evaluate ICH applications.[4]

The year 2013 brought some progress on ICH matters, especially regarding policy making. First, in January, the vice-minister in the Ministry of Culture and National Heritage announced the launch of the application program for ICH.[5] Subsequently, a special website dedicated to ICH was launched as a part of the National Heritage Institute's own website. It compiles relevant information on ICH (in fact, this is the only methodical source of information that can be accessed by the public). The site promises to be continually developed. Among other things it contains information on ICH-related events happening throughout Poland, links to NGOs and other institutions concerned with ICH; it also lists sources and programs of financial assistance to those active in the realm of traditional culture. In concurrence with governmental directives, these are all existing programs that performers and activists in folk culture may consider for application. The information contained on the website was also disseminated among pertinent institutions in a booklet form.

198 *Cultural Mapping and Musical Diversity*

Despite the absence of a widespread promotion of ICH "in the field" (as some of the folklore activists complain), in 2013–2014 several applications were submitted to the National Heritage Institute for consideration. In August 2014, an official celebratory announcement of the first cultural elements that were included on the national list/inventory of ICH took place. The cultural items enlisted include: a disappearing profession (artistic and historical gunsmithy); two Cracow traditions: *lajkonik* (a unique hobby horse custom) and *szopka* (an elaborate nativity scene crib/crèche); river rafting tradition; a procession in celebration of the Body and Blood of Christ in Lowicz; use of the Esperanto language. The first musical cultural element on the national list is the tradition of making and performing of the bagpipes from Podhale (Tatra Mountains, in southern Poland). As of 2018, there are already thirty-two cultural items on the national list, including several musical ones: four types of bagpipes from different regions, Polish national dances, and also the traditions of New Year's caroling, weddings from Szamotuly (Greater Poland), as well as coalminers' celebration of Barborka/St. Barbara's day (Upper Silesia). In November 2018, the first Polish cultural element was inscribed on the UNESCO List—the Cracow tradition of *szopka* making.

Problems and Concerns

It appears that after initial stagnation, ICH matters in Poland are developing more actively. Nevertheless, the general impressions and opinions—as expressed by some of the folklore activists, who are especially interested in the implementation of the Convention—are somewhat downcast.[6] Many problems are seen both in the system, which is still in the making, and in its execution. There is general skepticism and disillusionment as to the extent to which the state will be involved (especially financially), the level of information on the Convention and the opportunities it carries, its execution, the competence of people who will be responsible for it, as well as some ambiguity and general incomprehensibility with the procedures. Some even question the Convention itself: whether, in the Polish context, it has any real/ practical application, whether anything good or useful can come out of it. The validity of designating the National Heritage Institute as the executor of the Convention is also questioned. Furthermore, the team responsible for the procedures concerning ICH is miniscule—in the National Heritage Institute in Warsaw, there are only two staff members (ethnologists).

Looking closer at the competency level of the institutions involved in ICH reveals that it varies throughout the regions. For example, the Polish Folklore Society in Wroclaw (Lower Silesia), an expert organization that comprises ethnologists, does not have any expert on music; the employees of the regional offices of the Institute of National Heritage are for the most part art historians or archeologists. When it comes to local governments, it does happen at times that they have an ethnographer working in their midst (as, for example, in Bialystok).

Among the major complaints is the lack of proper promotion and education about ICH. This, however, will—most likely—change depending on the gradual flow of applications. While the activists believe that the implementation of the Convention may take years, they observe that it is being used—at least to some extent—as a tool for political success. The push for creating the regional and national lists—as tangible effects of the work done—is very strong, while the "real" outcome of securing a spot on the list is yet to be seen. The Ministry repeatedly characterizes the inclusion on the national inventory as an honorary act, not followed by any financial assistance.[7]

Some problems are identified in the application process itself. These concern, for example, the consensus that has to be reached within a given group that submits the application—the questions arise especially about the nature and methods of so-called public consultations, which are a must. Who is to be consulted—an entire village or several villages, where a given tradition occurs? How should this be done, precisely? It is not entirely clear whose responsibility it is to recommend a given cultural element. The National Heritage Institute does not always have answers to such specific questions. There is also the problem of documenting—who is to be charged with this task? Who is going to provide the appropriate resources (especially financial) for that?

In general, the local administration is reluctant to act—either uncertain about what to do, or not giving the problem enough attention. Such an attitude persists even though at times the local government is approached by local cultural institutions, as it was in the case of Lower Silesia, when representatives of the Ethnographic Museum and a few other organizations came forward proposing cooperation.

The state itself does not provide sufficient help and it seems to refrain from any financial responsibility; many of the tasks that should be performed by the state are delegated to others. The advising body to the Minister—which issues recommendations on the applications—comprises nineteen experts out of which only a few deal with Intangible Cultural Heritage (among them are an ethnomusicologist and an ethno-linguist). However, the council may invite outside experts, depending on the nature of a given application.

The UNESCO Convention for the Safeguarding of the Intangible Cultural Heritage is a potential vehicle of change, especially in the field of education, with many people seeing it as an opportunity to educate the larger society about traditional/folk music as well as possibly changing negative, stereotypical opinions on folklore. This issue is indeed urgent, as folk music had been relegated entirely from school programs. As regards possible educational changes, the report prepared for the Institute of Music and Dance (which is another governmental institution created in 2010) gives several examples that might be considered for further application. One of them is the case of Cracow Academy of Music, which founded a new instrumental specialization (2010), i.e. knee fiddle; it includes two historic traditional Polish instruments (*fidel plocka* and *suka bilgorajska*).

Cooperation between different ministries is a requisite in the effective implementation of the ICH. The Ministry of Education, Ministry of Agriculture, and Ministry of Regional Development need to be working closely with the Ministry of Culture and National Heritage, which is primarily charged with ICH matters. Nonetheless, such cooperation seems very hard to achieve. For example, the letter proposing collaboration, sent by the National Heritage Institute to the Ministry of Education, received no response.

Uprooted Communities

Problems of a different nature are faced in regions where continuity of the tradition was interrupted due to World War II and the political shifts, which were its direct outcome. In regions such as Lower Silesia and Warmia and Masuria, the traditional musical locale was entirely displaced. Hence, among their current inhabitants are Polish from Lvov, Vilnius, even former Yugoslavia, as well as natives of Ukraine. Many of them are geographically dispersed and confused as to what kind of heritage they are to cultivate.[8] Issues are raised, for example, as to what kind of regional dress is to be worn by folk groups in Lower Silesia. Often, in the process, "new" traditions are being invented through a negotiation of various cultural traits. Certain regions, as Lower Silesia or Podlasie, are being presented as modern, multi-cultural sites—this image is exploited in education as well as in cultural tourism.

Cultural Tourism

One of the possible problems that might arise in relation to the implementation of the Convention is closely linked to economics—this is the danger of overt commercialization. In the discussions of ICH as well as in its promotion, the often-mentioned benefit is the (very tangible) income to be gained from the development of touristic interest in the cultural elements successfully inscribed on ICH lists (national or UNESCO's). A notable example comes from the Podlasie region, where seven different workshops were established, including weaving, lace-making, culinary art, visual arts, folk ornamentation, and also a song-dance workshop.[9] Eventually some of them, like the weaving workshop, developed to significantly supplement the livelihoods of the people engaged in the traditional activities. This tangible economic possibility, in the time of grave unemployment, especially in some regions, is—of course—of great value, as it creates alternative sources of income. However, caution must be applied when invigorating various traditional activities not to forsake artistic standards and quality.

An unquestionably positive effect of the implementation of ICH is reactivation or revitalization of certain practices as in the case of a unique weaving technique (*perebory*) from the Podlasie region (see Wawryniuk 2010). In 2016, the *perebory* tradition was inscribed on the national ICH List. The

Figure 10.1: Clothing collection based on *perebory* patterns. Source: http://podlasie24.pl/wiadomosci/biala-podlaska/perebory-w-nowej-kolekcji-znanej-firmy-odziezowej-d8d6.html. Used with permission.

Figure 10.2: Traditional *perebory* making. Source:
http://www.echokatolickie.pl/index.php?str=100&id=2689. Used with permission.

weaving technique has also become of interest to the fashion industry—an entire clothing collection was created, inspired by this particular weaving method. This case is an example of making the folk art relevant, creating demand for it, and thereby assuring that it has a place in contemporary life.

Intangible Cultural Heritage in Poland has been usually equated with folk and village culture. Such understanding of this concept has been often debated. Only a few debaters, however, bring to attention the fact that ICH is broader than that. Cultural elements recognized by UNESCO such as the Viennese coffee house culture or Mediterranean diet point to the broader understanding of ICH. Considering this broader application of the term, some speak of Polish *Wigilia*—a unique Christmas Eve dinner tradition—as a potential entry for the UNESCO List. However, these kinds of "national" (or inter-regional) practices generate even more uncertainty, as no one yet is able to determine the way to enroll them on any ICH list.

The greatest danger for ICH is "overprotection" and musealization. Too little time has passed from the formulation of the Convention for the Safeguarding of the Intangible Cultural Heritage to determine the final outcome of its implementation. Optimists hope that with some caution and awareness of the potential dangers, it will be possible to avoid them.

A critical problem in the implementation of the Convention on ICH in Poland is folk culture's overwhelmingly negative associations: for example, with the culture of the poor and uneducated, with so-called *Cepelia*—things of dubious value that are for sale, with the staged and communist-state-promoted folklore as represented in the past by the State Folk Song and Dance Ensemble Mazowsze (Mazovia) or Song and Dance Ensemble Śląsk (Silesia). Despite innumerable examples that contradict such stereotypical images of folk culture, these connotations endure.[10]

Models of ICH Politics

ICH policies formulated by UNESCO were preceded by the policies introduced in Asian countries such as Japan and South Korea. These two states are the pioneers for preserving, protecting and fostering ICH, especially traditional (performing) arts. Therefore, in this section, I briefly discuss their achievements in the realm of ICH. Currently it is the East Asian states that are the leaders in terms of number of cultural items placed on the UNESCO List: China has 39 items inscribed, Japan–21, and South Korea–19 (UNESCO 2018).

Japan was the first country to introduce legislation on cultural property in 1950 through a designation of a special Law for the Protection of Cultural Properties, which were ultimately defined as properties of "high historical or artistic value," including drama, music, and craft techniques (Hyoki 2014).

National recognition is given to the individual owners or holders of a given cultural element, designated as "National Living Treasures." In some cases, the system also recognizes entire groups or organizations. The government provides encouragement and support in the form of financial grants to help protect cultural property and to foster the transmission process, especially training of successors. The holders are often offered the opportunity, venue and resources to perform or exhibit their art. Several institutions are involved in ICH protection. The government, through the Japan Arts Council, organizes special exhibitions, training workshops, and other activities to educate future generations of Japanese traditional artists as well as their practitioners. Very important tasks are research and documentation. In 1968, the Japanese Ministry of Education established a special body called the Agency for Cultural Affairs[11] in order to promote, utilize, and preserve Japanese arts and culture. Moreover, the National Research Institute for Cultural Properties in Tokyo was founded to set in motion policy making for the preservation of ICH in Japan.

As the senior researcher at the Department of Intangible Cultural Heritage at the Institute states, intangible cultural heritage is "embodied, expressed, and ensured by the living people." The aim of the government and the law is specifically "NOT to order the people who hold … [this] heritage to conserve it, BUT to help the people to hand their heritage down to the next generation by themselves" (Hyoki 2014: 32–33).

The Cultural Property Protection Law of Korea was passed in 1962, a decade later. In its basic form, it mirrors Japanese law. Two years after the creation of the law, in 1964, South Korea established a List of Important Intangible Cultural Properties, officially designating specific arts for preservation.[12] The particular items are proclaimed and maintained by South Korea's Cultural Heritage Administration. The support given by the South Korean government is very much similar to the assistance provided by Japanese authorities. The South Korean government sponsors public events as well as overseas performances and exhibitions.

The South Korean government erected a special body, which is the only national, government-sponsored institution in South Korea, charged with the mission to educate, preserve, promote, and develop South Korea's Intangible Cultural Heritage. The National Gugak Center (formerly National Center for Korean Traditional Performing Arts, 1951) is the primary institution of learning for South Korean traditional music. In time it became highly specialized, and developed into five large divisions or areas of activity: education, research, publication, promotion, and performance. Its activity is diverse, and includes workshops of traditional South Korean music designed especially for interested foreigners.

Several Eastern European countries have already implemented systems of identification and selection of cultural elements as well as support systems for their practitioners. This resulted in a number of elements being inscribed onto the UNESCO List. Czech Republic and Slovakia each have five cultural items, Hungary also five, Lithuania–three, Estonia–four, Bulgaria and Romania–seven each (some of these items are shared with other countries). The unquestionable champion is Croatia with fifteen items (UNESCO 2018). In Czech Republic, it is the museums that are charged with the task of creating inventories, researching and describing cultural elements. The fruits of these efforts are publications—books and video recordings, which disseminate knowledge, promote, and elevate interest in Czech traditional culture.[13]

Looking at the extensive experience of Asian countries and accomplishments of Poland's neighbors shows, on the one hand, how much work still needs to be done in Poland regarding ICH. On the other hand, however, it raises hope that such accomplishments are attainable: systematic, coordinated research, whose results would be adequately propagated; dissemination of

Figures 10.3a and 10.3b: Inauguration concert of Oskar Kolberg's Year in National Philharmonic Hall in Warsaw and in Przysucha (Kolberg's place of birth). Photos by Danuta Matloch, MKiDN. Source: http://www.mkidn.gov.pl/pages/posts/inauguracja-roku-oskara-kolberga-4480.php. Used with permission.

knowledge and undertaking of educational efforts that would lead to deeper recognition of traditional/folk culture. Cultural projects either initiated by the European Union administration, or the Ministry of Culture and National Heritage, include European Heritage Days, annually celebrated, which draw attention to regional cultures; the program Heritage Plus, which, although focused on tangible culture, does not exclude ICH; the program Culture Plus-Digitalization, designed to digitalize cultural resources, and hopefully can be extended to include traditional/folk culture. The year 2014 was designated as the Year of Oskar Kolberg,[14] commemorating the 200 year anniversary of his birth—many concerts, symposia, and exhibitions were held, and recordings produced; making traditional/folk culture more visible in media and public life.[15] Hopefully many of these activities will be continued in the future.

Even though the fossilization of ICH is a legitimate concern, the Polish example is a positive one. Concurrently with the traditional/folk cultural scene, there is a very ardent and dynamic scene of folk-inspired music groups that often merge Polish folk with classical and world music (traditional music and instruments from various parts of the world, mostly non-European).[16] The role of Polish public radio and its festival "New Tradition" indisputably has played a major role in shaping the interest in this kind of musical endeavor. For nearly two decades, Polish Radio awards festival prizes to the most promising groups and to the best folk records, also honoring prominent traditional artists.

Essential to ICH politics is the awareness that tradition is subject to change, that it is a dynamic force which cannot be entirely controlled. As long as folk music operates in two modes: the more traditional, where the tradition is passed on mostly unchanged—"as it was" or "as it used to be," and a parallel one, which transforms it and keeps it alive in a form that is often more attractive to young audiences—traditional music will not disappear from the national music-scape. Negotiation between the two modes is certainly highly challenging and demanding.

Conclusions

Considering Poland's rich traditional culture, there are many cultural elements that could become candidates for designation as ICH. Hopefully, the process, which began in 2011 with ratification of the Convention for the Safeguarding of the Intangible Cultural Heritage, will continue to progress with greater speed after the initial procedures (such as translation of UNESCO documents, legal reports, and creating an application form) have been finally put in place, and the first items inscribed onto the national list. Indisputably, the downside is the lack of complex financial assistance as well as some ambiguity in the Convention's execution and practical implementation. While it seems evident that education and transmission shall be the main aims of the Convention's implementation, the emphasis seems to be on administrational resolutions rather than real protection strategies that would result from the formulation of clear laws/obligations instead of mere recommendations for various levels of governance. The activities and efforts that are being undertaken in the realm of ICH are, on the whole, too dispersed; the competences of many institutions overlap, which at times leads to decisional conflicts or downright inaction. What is needed is competent coordination of all efforts and a proper base that would connect them. Databases of regional traditions (that could be easily verified) and clear division of labor in identifying cultural assets are of particular importance.

The comparison with the comprehensive programs functioning in Asia (and also in Eastern Europe) shows that the models being developed by the Polish administration lack decisiveness and, most important of all, sufficient funds. While there are many institutions already involved in the folk scene, there is a general lack of communication, especially among governmental bodies. The National Heritage Institute and its branches have insufficient staff resources to fully deal with ICH, without which administrational efforts can be misdirected, or even futile. The priorities set by the government, unfortunately, do not leave much hope for more money flowing in the direction of folk/traditional culture at the moment. What is optimistic though is the dynamism and true dedication of many individuals working at the grass-roots level within various associations and organizations that care deeply for the future of traditional culture and the humanist values that it contains.

The process of implementation of ICH constitutes a possible venue for dynamic activity of ethnomusicologists as an applied-ethnomusicology venture. They may participate in the application process as consultants or act as advisors to the relevant decision-making bodies. This can be only possible if the institutions with which they are affiliated recognize it as valid, designating time and space for such pursuits.

About the Author

Marzanna Poplawska holds degrees from Warsaw University (MA in Musicology, 1998) and Wesleyan University (PhD in Ethnomusicology, 2008). She has studied and taught in Poland (Warsaw University, Wroclaw University), UK (Durham University), Indonesia (Institute of Indonesian Arts in Yogyakarta), Ireland (University College Cork), and the United States (Wesleyan University, University of North Carolina at Chapel Hill). Her primary interests encompass the musical traditions of Indonesia, Southeast Asia, and Central-Eastern Europe as well as acculturation/inculturation, music and religion, diaspora, and Intangible Cultural Heritage. She is also an active performer of central-Javanese music and dance.

Notes

1 See UNESCO 2003.
2 Foundation for the Intangible Cultural Heritage in Poland—mission statement: http://fndk.livenet.pl/ (accessed August 15, 2012) [web page no longer live].
3 Between 2015 and 2018 several other conferences and meetings were held on the ICH.
4 The Polish Folklore Society is a member of the World Council of Anthropological Associations. As of 2015, it has not yet evaluated any applications submitted to UNESCO. In 2018, UNESCO also accredited the Association of Folk Artists (founded in 1968) and the Serfenta Association (founded in 2006).
5 The vice-minister also holds the position of General Conservator, thus, he is directly connected with the National Heritage Institute.
6 Personal communications, 2013.
7 In terms of finances, the Ministry points to already existing programs, for example, "Education" and "Cultural Heritage"—a part of governmental program "Folk Culture," or the "School of Masters of Tradition." See the website of the

Narodowy Instytut Dziedzictwa ("National Heritage Institute") devoted to ICH: http://niematerialne.nid.pl/Ochrona_dziedzictwa/Zrodla_finansowania/ or the opening announcement of the national ICH list—a press conference "Intangible Heritage—Promotion of Our Identity" (January 1, 2013, Olsztyn): https://www.youtube.com/watch?v=yz3A9nyiLd0 (accessed October 25, 2018).

8 These kinds of concerns were expressed, for example, during the conference on Best Safeguarding Practices, organized in 2013 by the National Heritage Institute (in Olsztynek, near Olsztyn, north-east Poland).

9 This project began with "The Trail of Folk Handicrafts," initiated by the Podlasie Museum in Bialystok in 1994. See http://atrakcjepodlasia.pl/tradycja-i-kuchnia/szlak-rekodziela-ludowego-wojewodztwa-podlaskiego/. Many cultural projects, including traditional singing workshops, are conducted by the Foundation of Podlasie Heritage (established in 2004).

10 To bypass these connotations, there seems to be a general tendency to use the term "traditional culture" in relation to ICH.

11 It was created through merging of the Cultural Bureau of the Ministry of Education and the Commission for Protection of Cultural Properties.

12 See Kang 2005; Yang 2003. For particular cultural items on the ICH list, see Korean Cultural Heritage 2011.

13 See Šimša (2008, 2011); Blahůšek and Vojancová (2011); Blahůšek and Teturová (2012).

14 Oskar Kolberg (1814–1890) was an ethnographer, folklorist, and composer. He is best known for his life's work *Lud* (*Folk*), which is a compilation of folk traditions (songs and customs) from various Polish (and neighboring) regions. The collection consists of over fifty volumes; currently, eighty-six are published, including Kolberg's biography, letters, and various supplements. Oskar Kolberg, *Dziela wszystkie* (1961–2002).

15 The Institute of Music and Dance prepared an extensive report, which summarizes all the activities that took place during the Year of Oskar Kolberg. A website (in Polish and English) was also created for the event: Rok Kolberga 2014: http://www.kolberg2014.org.pl/pl/2014/aktualnosci (accessed April 10, 2019).

16 See, for example, the usage of folk music samples in an album released in 1996 by Grzegorz Ciechowski, a popular rock artist (Panfil and Kotlarz, *Grzegorz Ciechowski: reportaż o kłopotach z płytą "OjDADAna"*).

References

Blahůšek, Jan, and Jarmila Teturová. 2012. *Jízda králů na jihovýchodě České republiky* ("The Ride of Kings in the South-East of the Czech Republic"). Strážnice: Ústav Národní lidové kultury.

Blahůšek, Jan, and Ilona Vojancová. 2011. *Vesnické masopustní obchůzky a masky na Hlinecku* ("Shrovetide Door-to-Door Processions and Masks in the Villages of the Hlinecko Area"). Strážnice: Národní ústav lidové kultury.

Hyoki, Satoru. 2014. "Safeguarding Intangible Cultural Heritage in Japan: Systems, Schemes and Activities." In *A Presentation by the Senior Researcher at the Department of Intangible Cultural Heritage*. Tokyo: National Research Institute for Cultural Properties. http://www.unesco.org/culture/ich/doc/src/00177-EN.pdf (accessed August 15, 2017).

Kang, Kyunghwan. 2005. "Preservation and Protection of Intangible Cultural Properties: Institutional and Policy Measures in Korea." In *Sub-Regional Experts Meeting in Asia on Intangible Cultural Heritage: Safeguarding and Inventory-Making Methodologies, Bangkok.*
http://www.accu.or.jp/ich/en/pdf/c2005subreg_RepKorea1.pdf (accessed August 15, 2017).

Korean Cultural Heritage. 2011. Seoul: Hankookmunhwasa.

Kreps, Christina. 2005. "Indigenous Curation as Intangible Cultural Heritage: Thoughts on the Relevance of the 2003 UNESCO Convention." In *Theorizing Cultural Heritage at the Smithsonian Institution Center for Folklife and Cultural Heritage 2004–2007* 1(2): 3–8.

Kurin, Richard. 2004. "Safeguarding Intangible Cultural Heritage in the 2003 UNESCO Convention: A Critical Appraisal." *Museum International* 56(1–2): 66–77. https://doi.org/10.1111/j.1350-0775.2004.00459.x

Panfil, Monika, and Dariusz Kotlarz. n.d. *Grzegorz Ciechowski reportaż o kłopotach z płytą "OjDADAna"* http://ciechowski.art.pl/wywiad_ojdadana_gw.html (accessed April 10, 2019).

Rok Kolberga. 2014. http://www.kolberg2014.org.pl/pl/2014/aktualnosci (accessed April 10, 2019).

Šimša, Martin. 2008. *Bearers of Folk Craft Tradition I: The Practitioners Awarded by the Minister of Culture of the Czech Republic between 2001 and 2008.* Strážnice: Institute of Folk Culture.

—2011. *Bearers of Folk Craft Tradition I: The Practitioners Awarded by the Minister of Culture of the Czech Republic between 2001 and 2008.* Strážnice: Institute of Folk Culture.

UNESCO. 2003. "Text of the Convention for the Safeguarding of the Intangible Cultural Heritage." https://ich.unesco.org/en/convention (accessed October 25, 2018).

—2018. "Lists of Intangible Cultural Heritage and the Register of Good Safeguarding Practices." https://ich.unesco.org/en/lists (accessed April 10, 2019).

Wawryniuk, Agnieszka. 2010. "Powroty do przeszłości" ["Returns to the Past"]. In *Echo Katolickie*. October 21, 2010.
http://www.echokatolickie.pl/index.php?str=100&id=2689 (accessed August 15, 2017).

Yang, Chong-sŭng. 2003. *Cultural Protection Policy in Korea: Intangible Cultural Properties and Living National Treasures.* Seoul: Jimoondang International.

Chapter 11

Mapping and Representing Musical Diversity in Switzerland: The Role of Artists, Ethnomusicologists, and Officials[1]

Marc-Antoine Camp, Brigitte Bachmann-Geiser, David Vitali, Dieter Ringli, and Patricia Jäggi

The UNESCO Convention for the Safeguarding of the Intangible Cultural Heritage (UNESCO 2003) is extensively discussed in ethnomusicology, since, in many respects, its goals concern and affect the discipline's subject matter. Traditional musics are one of the foci for the safeguarding measures adopted by the international cultural policy instrument. The impact of the UNESCO Convention, however, depends mainly on its implementation on a national level. Considering that the Convention is a "broth spoiled by too many cooks"—an internationally reached consensus with open questions—when it is adopted by individual nations, the concept of intangible cultural heritage is substantiated by each country's specific interests. Rather than an extensive consideration of international policy connected to the UNESCO Convention, we turn our attention here to the concept of intangible cultural heritage, as it has been discussed in Switzerland since the country's ratification of the UNESCO Convention in 2008 (OFC 2015), with the aim of providing a case study of one country's implementation of the UNESCO Convention (and thereby disregarding the fact that cultural practices are mobile and transgress national borders). Switzerland, with its small size and relatively small population, offers valuable insights into the complexities of negotiating the concept of intangible cultural heritage.

The chapter assembles four perspectives on the "List of Living Traditions in Switzerland" (OFC 2012a), the national inventory of intangible cultural heritage developed between 2010 and 2012. These perspectives represent some of the arguments advanced by artists and practitioners of intangible cultural heritage, by ethnomusicologists and other experts, as well as by officials, politicians, and the broader public during the process of national inventorying. Here, these arguments are enunciated on the basis of the individual experiences of the chapter's contributors. To begin, Brigitte Bachmann-Geiser examines the precursors of the concept of intangible cultural heritage, with reference to past research into folk musical elements; David Vitali, responsible for the establishment of the "List of Living Traditions" at the Swiss Federal Office of Culture, reports on the current state of political agreement concerning the concept of intangible cultural heritage in Switzerland; Dieter Ringli analyzes the national list and critically outlines its shortcomings; and, lastly, Patricia Jäggi studies the concept of intangible cultural heritage through an artistic approach to the "List of Living Traditions."[2]

Folk Musical Elements in Swiss Calendrical Custom

The term "intangible cultural heritage" predates the UNESCO Convention of 2003; it has a terminological history of several years (see Camp 2006) and an even longer foundation in the academic traditions of folklore studies, cultural anthropology, ethnomusicology, and related disciplines. It is worth, then, providing a review of the conceptual history, referring to Bachmann-Geiser's fieldwork in Switzerland in the 1970s, and her historical, organological, and particularly iconographic studies, as well as her numerous outreach projects, which aimed to bring "folk musical elements" to the attention of a broader public.[3]

The documentation of intangible cultural heritage is one of the measures mentioned in the UNESCO Convention (Article 2, Paragraph 3; UNESCO 2003) and stands for what ethnomusicologists have undertaken for decades through participatory observation in everyday life, audio-visual recordings of music making, and interviews with practitioners of traditions. While intangible cultural heritage has been rather neglected on the level of international law compared to material cultural expressions, in early folklore studies the reverse was true: the immateriality of singing was a foremost concern, and predated studies on material music culture such as instruments. Starting in the eighteenth century, folk songs were collected and documented all over Europe, while the systematic survey of musical instruments in Europe only became a subject of study in the late 1950s. Taking the seminal 1914 article

"Systematik der Musikinstrumente" by Erich Moritz von Hornbostel and Curt Sachs as a foundation, the ethnomusicologists Erich Stockmann and Ernst Emsheimer launched the idea of creating a manual of European folk musical instruments by publishing a number of methodological articles, the first of which appeared in 1959 (Emsheimer and Stockmann 1959; see also Stockmann 1964). They provided a set of methods for analyzing historical documents and fieldwork data, to be used by researchers in different countries. Each musical instrument was to be described using terminologies, construction technologies, playing techniques, and musical uses, repertory, history, geographical distribution, and social functions. The first two volumes of the *Handbuch der Europäischen Volksmusikinstrumente* were published for Hungary (Sárosi 1967) and former Czechoslovakia (Kunz and Elschek 1974–1983). These publications served as guidelines for Bachmann-Geiser's comprehensive overview of musical instruments in Switzerland (Bachmann-Geiser 1981), in which she described folk musical instruments in the context of, for example, dance music, as children's toys, or as tools to facilitate herdsmen's labor. However, the use of musical instruments in calendric customs was missing in the publications on Hungarian and Czechoslovakian instruments; apparently, during the Cold War, "customs" in countries of the Soviet bloc were not seen as an expression of traditional culture by researchers, since they were often misused to represent political ideas.

Customs that marked the course of the year became an important topic for Bachmann-Geiser from the 1980s onwards (cf. Thalmann 1981; Deutsch and Schepping 1988). The connected inquiries into musical instruments and customs revealed the study of the material aspect of cultural traditions to be inextricable from the many attendant immaterial aspects of their use. Conversely, it makes little sense to neglect material aspects when focusing on intangible cultural heritage (see also Article 2, Paragraph 3; UNESCO 2003). Moreover, Bachmann-Geiser's research revealed that local people often invest a large proportion of their spare time in safeguarding customs, but do not always receive recognition for their engagement. As a form of recognition, she worked to make customs known not only through publishing academic studies, but also through newspaper reports and recordings, and by introducing customs in museums. Of special note are the exhibitions in the Kornhaus Burgdorf between 1991 and 2005 and in the open-air museum Ballenberg since 2010, in which folk musical instruments are presented as a systematic collection and according to their uses and functions. With the DVD *Customs and Traditions in Switzerland* (Bachmann-Geiser 2007), Bachmann-Geiser created a kind of list of intangible cultural heritage, using new possibilities of digital outreach—the content was, for some time, also published online—and addressing an international public by including versions in five languages. The DVD was designed to be sent to television studios abroad and to Swiss embassies all over the world for distribution. Its success was not only due to the diversity of the folk traditions it presents, but certainly also because of the interest in customs generated by the UNESCO Convention of 2003: between 2007 and 2013 there were five editions of the DVD, with a total of 20,000 copies produced. The compilation of audio-visual contents was the result of weeks of archival research in the studios of Swiss Radio and Television in Zurich, Geneva, and Lugano. It was extremely difficult to find excerpts of the selected folk customs that were neither too long nor too short, while simultaneously being gratifying to discover some gems of past recordings.

With this retrospective lens, one can clearly recognize that not only traditions, but also academic concepts about them, as well as forms of outreach are steadily (re-)invented. Old questions on topics such as how to exhibit intangible cultural heritage in its present-day societal constellations are being taken up anew in the current debate on the role of museums in safeguarding intangible cultural heritage in Switzerland (VMS/ICOM 2010).

Intangible Cultural Heritage as a New Field of National Cultural Policy

Several elements researched by Bachmann-Geiser were inscribed in the "List of Living Traditions in Switzerland." One example is the spring tradition of the "Feuillu" in the canton of Geneva, with its singing performances by boys as May Kings and girls as May Queens. This tradition had gained impetus thanks to the song set "Le Jeu du Feuillu" (1900) by the music educator Émile Jaques-Dalcroze, who is said to have been inspired to compose the set by representations of the "Feuillu" itself. It was studied and made known by Bachmann-Geiser, among others, and was chosen by the canton of Geneva as national intangible cultural heritage (OFC 2012c).

According to David Vitali, Head of Culture and Society at the Swiss Federal Office of Culture, the Swiss government initially held a skeptical view on the concept of intangible cultural heritage, but then pursued an engaged implementation of the UNESCO Convention. The implementation aims—according to the Convention's text—at "safeguarding," that is, "ensuring the viability of the intangible cultural heritage, including the identification, documentation, research, preservation, protection, promotion, enhancement, transmission, particularly through formal and non-formal education, as well as the revitalization of the various aspects of such heritage" (Article 2, Paragraph 3; UNESCO 2003). As a national political action, however, implementing all components of this vast catalog of actions would be beyond the scope of the new cultural policy. Rather, it was decided to focus on aspects of valorization and transmission of intangible cultural heritage. To this end, measures could be taken first through the establishment of a national list of intangible cultural heritage, since this is—besides the financial contribution to the Intangible Cultural Heritage Fund and the periodic reporting to UNESCO's Intergovernmental Committee for the Safeguarding of the Intangible Cultural Heritage—a binding obligation for state parties and could therefore easily be enforced (Articles 12 and 25; UNESCO 2003).

However, to establish such a list is not at all an easy undertaking in Switzerland (and probably elsewhere). Accounting for the country's linguistic and cultural diversity, cultural policy in Switzerland is not centralized; the federal constitution gives the twenty-six cantons sovereignty in cultural matters, limiting federal cultural actions by the principle of subsidiarity. The Federal Office of Culture is therefore in the first instance an intermediary agency between the UNESCO Convention's institutions and the cantons, which again give much autonomy concerning the promotion of cultural life to municipalities. Furthermore, civil society is traditionally very strong in Switzerland, with many people being involved in processes of cultural policy. The list was therefore established in a joint venture between cantonal cultural agencies and the Federal Office of Culture, with the participation of experts, such as the University of Applied Sciences and Arts as coordination office, and members of civil society, which were mainly mobilized and represented by the Swiss Commission for UNESCO (for a description of the establishment of the list, see Graezer Bideau 2012 and Camp 2015). The process required a high level of coordination among these participants, when compared to a simple top-down solution. However, it also encouraged the recommended involvement of communities (Article 15; UNESCO 2003), thus managing to fulfill one of the main goals of the Convention. The result of the inventorying process was published in five languages in 2012 via a digital information network, containing documentations of 165 living traditions (OFC 2012a). In addition to the establishment of the inventory, the Federal Office of Culture supported practice-oriented studies and events on the handling of traditional craftsmanship, on the exhibiting of living traditions in museums, on the transmission of living traditions in schools, and on the relationship between living traditions and tourism (cf. OFC 2015).

The aim of the "List of Living Traditions in Switzerland," the cardinal point of action by federal and cantonal authorities, was to raise awareness within the broader public about the varied cultural expressions of identity, as well as its changes under the present conditions of globalization. To designate the elements of intangible cultural heritage inscribed in the list, the term "living traditions" was chosen (however not indisputably). First, this term allows for a distinction between the nationally recognized elements, the "living traditions," and the internationally recognized elements in the UNESCO lists, the elements of "intangible cultural heritage" (although the expression "living traditions" has been used by UNESCO in connection with the concept of intangible cultural heritage). Secondly, whereas "intangible cultural heritage" refers primarily to a legal concept, "living traditions" foregrounds the multiple and changing manifestations, which correspond to the aspect of "cultural diversity." Thirdly, "living traditions" is much easier to communicate to a broader public in comparison to the abstract legal term "intangible cultural heritage."

The "List of Living Traditions in Switzerland" is the temporary result of a consensus on the concept of intangible cultural heritage, which was sought among various participants in Switzerland. As required by the UNESCO Convention (Article 12; UNESCO 2003), the list was reviewed for the first time between 2016 and 2018.

Questions about the List of Living Traditions and its Impacts

Apparently, the political frame was an influential factor in shaping the implementation of the UNESCO Convention in Switzerland. This political frame is even considered as a tradition of its own, referred to in the "List of Living Traditions in Switzerland" as "Consensus-seeking and direct democracy" (OFC 2012a). However, this tradition of consensus seeking is born out of fundamental dissent that is also present in the list. One can ask some critical questions about the list and about its impacts, as does Dieter Ringli, who was not involved in establishing the list in its current state.

When analyzing the "List of Living Traditions in Switzerland," the absence of yodeling is immediately noticeable. The so-called "natural yodeling," characterized by the absence of lyrics, is present in the two entries "Folk Music in Central Switzerland" and "Folk Music in the Appenzellerland

and Toggenburg Regions," but the "yodeling songs" with verses and yodeled chorus are not mentioned. This is surprising, since there is nothing—with the possible exception of cheese and chocolate—that is so commonly associated with Switzerland as this form of yodeling. When traveling outside Europe, it is not uncommon for a Swiss person to be asked: "Oh, you're from Switzerland, can you yodel?" And even to Swiss people who may not like yodeling, this vocal expression is considered "typical" of the country. The special status of the yodeling song is due to the existence of several hundred yodeling clubs around Switzerland, whose members practice on a weekly basis. They are united by the Swiss Yodeling Association, with its more than one hundred years of history, its approximately 20,000 members, and its tri-annual Federal Yodeling Festivals, which currently attract up to 200,000 people. It is difficult to explain why yodeling songs are missing from the list, but one possible reason is the critical views in the 1970s and 1980s of the then very conservative Swiss Yodeling Association and its normative power on yodeling aesthetics (see, for example, Baumann 1976; Zemp 1987). As the yodeling song tradition is still very much alive, evolving, and part of the cultural diversity and identity of Switzerland, its absence from the list is hardly justifiable.[4]

The impact of the list on traditions is another, probably even more important, avenue of inquiry. What does it mean for some regional traditions to be on the list, but for corresponding or similar traditions of other regions to be excluded? The list entry "Glarus Choirs and Orchestras," which encompasses an unarguably impressive past and present practice in one canton, suggests that there is nothing comparable among lay musical activities in Switzerland; however, there are other regions with similar choir and orchestra traditions that could equally claim to be outstanding. Even more astonishing is the representation of the instrumental folk music traditions in the list. Generally, four styles are commonly differentiated in the German-speaking part of Switzerland as a means of regional identity expressions: (1) the Central Swiss style with clarinet, chromatic accordion, piano, and double bass; (2) the Bernese style, often with diatonic accordions in two parallel voices, played a bit slower than in Central Switzerland; (3) the Grisons style, played with diatonic accordion and two clarinets; (4) the instrumental music in the Appenzellerland and Toggenburg regions with hammered dulcimer, double bass, cello, and two violins. All four styles can be considered as lively practiced traditions, but, whereas the first and fourth style are represented in the "List of Living Traditions in Switzerland," the others are missing.[5] If we acknowledge the goal of the list, that is, to "generate recognition for the bearers and practitioners of living traditions" (OFC 2012b), one may conclude that only some musical practices are worthy of safeguarding, and others not. The inconsistency of the list may lead—ideologically speaking—to a distortion of competition and, in the long term, to a reduction of highlighted cultural diversity. The aims of the list would be foiled by the list itself.

Another question arises from the composition of the list: how many years must a cultural practice exist in order for it to be considered a "Living Tradition"? One of the most ubiquitous musical activities is not inscribed in the list: pop and rock music and bands. There are thousands of amateur bands in Switzerland—Ringli being a member of one of them—with musicians aged between ten and seventy years, usually just playing for fun. This musical activity started in the early 1960s, growing steadily in subsequent decades, and becoming an important aspect of the practitioners' cultural identity. Why are pop and rock bands not inscribed in the list, despite the fact that they can look back on fifty years of tradition (quite a long time in the fast-changing twenty-first century)? Do these musical activities lack the exotic thrill of a specific alpine culture, referred to in tourism marketing and characterizing many elements of the list? Although pop and rock practices are present in other countries, too, as the choirs and orchestras are widespread in Switzerland and not only in the canton of Glarus, they represent a vast part of Switzerland's population. And if such living practices among urban and globalized Swiss populations are missing from the list, one might ask: what kind of criteria are required for a musical activity to become a "living tradition" in order to be inscribed in the list?

Thus, the issue of the presumed longevity of musical practices that are recognized as "living tradition" may raise critical questions: if the list had been established 150 years ago, which traditions from today's list would be on it? The answer: almost none. Some of the "living traditions" are social practices that trace back to the Middle Ages, but most of them were revived in a modern form in the second half of the nineteenth or in the twentieth century. In particular, most "living traditions" in the domain of performing arts are recent. For example, the "Amateur Theatre in Central Switzerland" consists of various individual traditions, such as the "Japanesenspiele" in Schwyz, established in 1857, the "Tellspiele" in Altdorf since 1899, and the "Einsiedler Welttheater" with its first performance in 1924. Similarly, instrumental music on the 150-year-old list would include examples such as wind and string instruments, but omit the Schwyzerörgeli, which was invented in the 1890s and came into vogue in the 1920s, and is now considered one of the most characteristic sound markers in Swiss instrumental folk music.

In conclusion, a critical analysis of the "List of Living Traditions in Switzerland" points to a fundamental contradiction inherent in inventorying. The list suggests that a tradition can be captured and fixed for an inventory in its supposed "essence" (Leimgruber 2014), that is, independent of subjective, culturally, and historically specific points of view. But experience shows heterogeneous and unstable points of view, and reveals traditions as constantly changing practices, some going out of style, some new ones coming into existence. The effect of a list, similar to the norm-setting once applied to yodeling practices, may hamper the changing dynamics of traditions and obstruct the changes necessary for them to be passed to the next generations and for assuring their safeguarding. "Tradition" is not a value on its own to be safeguarded; a tradition is valuable as long as it brings people together, unites generations, or encourages debates on cultural identity (for the issue of safeguarding within applied ethnomusicology, see Grant 2012).

Living Traditions in Switzerland: A Sound Collage

Beside the above critical ethnomusicological analysis, there are other ways to approach the effect of the inventorying process. For example, on the German version of the website, the practices represented in the "List of Living Traditions in Switzerland" were grouped into a set of verb pairs (OFC 2012a), such as those describing the above-mentioned tradition of "Feuillu": "dancing and moving," "striking up and singing," and "stopping by and asking." The verbs put an emphasis on the actions involved in practices surrounding intangible cultural heritage, allowing for new groupings of traditions beyond the established ones with their potentially normative effects such as the "domains" of "intangible cultural heritage" in the UNESCO Convention (Article 2, Paragraph 2; UNESCO 2013). Another critical approach to the "List of Living Traditions in Switzerland" was evident in an interview staged by the comedians Vincent Kucholl and Vincent Veillon on "Avalanche Risk Management," parodying the state's valorization of the "living tradition" and its assumed bearers (Kucholl and Veillon 2012). Meanwhile, in her latest outreach project, Bachmann-Geiser compiled a CD of melodies, rhythms, and "noises" of customs, an unusual approach due to its omission of visual aspects. The resultant 53-track CD allows for a solely acoustic experience of traditions of Switzerland during one year (Bachmann-Geiser 2013).

Patricia Jäggi similarly focuses on the acoustic aspect of traditions, but takes an alternative path. With reference to Bachmann-Geiser's CD and other recorded sounds, Jäggi combined the soundscapes of various list elements in a five-minute-long composition (Jäggi 2014). The starting excerpt in this collage of acoustic snippets and fragments is the sound of a puck hit by a "Hornuss" player[6] (see Jäggi 2014 for the traditions used in her sound composition, and OFC 2012a for the descriptions of the respective traditions). Following this opening is both a sequencing and juxtaposition of sounds from carnival and other wintertime traditions, as well as from alpine summer customs, along with vocal sounds produced by humans, horns, and other instruments, as well as sounds from machines and tools of craft production, and natural sounds like the ones produced by a snow avalanche and water waves. Jäggi primarily compiled the sounds according to aesthetic criteria. On the one hand, there are familiar sound elements, for which listeners may recognize differing contexts and uses, for instance bells as indicators of daytime, incidents, and warnings (the fortress bell of the "Munot traditions") and as locators of animals (as in "Animal husbandry and cow fighting"). On the other hand, there is a juxtaposition of cacophony and euphony. The first part of the collage contains sounds from various traditions, whereby hubbub produced by smaller and larger human groups forms an important part of the soundscape. These uncontrollable, dense, and loud sounds contrast with traditions that have a more private and intimate character, and whose acoustic expressions are quieter, probably also more organized, and therefore may be considered harmonious (Jäggi 2014). The collage ends with the softness of a sung lullaby.

For the editing process of the composition, Jäggi relied on ideas by the Soviet filmmaker Sergei Eisenstein. In his early montage theory, Eisenstein talks about montage as a technique where fragments are set in relation to each other to build a syntagma. On their own, these elements are without meaning; it is only through the montage that they attain significance. The process of choosing, selecting, and foregrounding the significant elements is called framing. Framing does not mean that the artist is provided with a pre-established frame in which to include everything. When montage means the temporal or rhythmic organization of fragments, framing refers more to the narrative aspects, such as confrontations between fragments. During the process of montage, fragments are framed through interrelations (Robertson 2009).

Through the musical collage, Jäggi aimed to emphasize the versatility and mutability of a musical tradition. Focusing on the creative or inventive impulses that are intrinsic to traditions, and especially to practitioners of traditions, montage and framing can be seen as a theoretical conception for our understanding of "tradition" (Jäggi 2014). It puts into perspective the steady re-assembling of sensual elements in the course of a practice over time. Above all, the chosen artistic approach to the list may be seen as a manifestation of a "living tradition" itself. Recomposing historical recordings into a collage can be seen as an act of taking up existing material, combining it in new ways, and setting it into a different context. And that is what bearers of traditions do in their practice, thereby constantly renewing those traditions.

Concluding Remarks

To summarize, this chapter calls for a critical consideration of multiple perspectives on the concept of intangible cultural heritage: to study the concept's academic history and research practices; to examine the political processes by which intangible cultural heritage is defined on a national level; to obtain critical experts' views to counterbalance the lobbying for specific interests in political negotiations (e.g. in inventorying); and, finally, to encourage artistic or creative public actions to deconstruct established meanings of traditions. We would like to suggest that effective outreach decisions and government actions in the field of intangible cultural heritage tend toward fixing traditions via declarations of supposed "essences," while historically, culturally, and artistically guided approaches have the potential to deconstruct seemingly inflexible frameworks, counteract tendencies toward petrifying traditions, and thereby supporting cultural policy's valorization of traditional musics. Ultimately, it is crucial to allow a continuous re-defining of "intangible cultural heritage" by including practitioners of traditions and artists, experts like ethnomusicologists, as well as the broader public, politicians, and officials. When dealing with questions of cultural identity, as is the case with the concept of intangible cultural heritage, it is advantageous to let "too many cooks spoil the broth." Only then can we understand essentializing tendencies, while deconstructing potentials as inextricable from each other (cf. Koselleck 1979).

About the Authors

Marc-Antoine Camp received his PhD from the University of Zürich (Switzerland) after studies in historical musicology, ethnomusicology, and anthropology, where he also worked in the Archives of Ethnomusicology.

Since 2008, Camp has been a researcher at Lucerne University of Applied Sciences and Arts. His research and publications focus on music education, the transmission of musical knowledge, and the concept of intangible cultural heritage in Switzerland, Brazil, and China.

Brigitte Bachmann-Geiser, PhD, specializes in organology. Her work includes an inventory of folk musical instruments in Switzerland (1971–1977), a Swiss contribution for the *Handbuch der Europäischen Volksmusikinstrumente*, and conceptualizing expositions (Kornhaus Burgdorf, Freilichtmuseum Ballenberg). She has published several books, over 200 articles, 35 records, and a selection of films about traditional music and musical instruments. Her work has been recognized with awards by the Smithsonian Institute in Washington, DC, the Bernese Cantonal Music Commission, with the Premio Giuseppe Pittrè of Palermo University, and the Walter Deutsch-Preis of the Österreichischen Bundesministeriums für Bildung, Wissenschaft und Kultur. In 2000 she became Honorary Professor at the University of Freiburg im Breisgau.

David Vitali has been, since 2012, the Head of the "Culture and Society" branch at the Swiss Federal Office of Culture, which he joined in 2005. In 2006, he was assigned the ratification and implementation of the "UNESCO Convention for the Safeguarding of the Intangible Cultural Heritage." Vitali studied history and philology at the Universities of Zurich and Oxford. Thereafter, he worked as a researcher at the Bavarian Academy of Sciences and Humanities in Munich and at the University of Zurich (1995–2005), where he obtained his PhD in Philology in 2004.

Dieter Ringli studied musicology and ethnomusicology at the University of Zürich. His 2003 PhD thesis was on traditional Swiss music and he worked as a senior lecturer at the Archives of Ethnomusicology at the University of Zurich until 2008. Since 2001, Dieter Ringli has been a lecturer in the history of music at Lucerne University of Applied Sciences and Arts (Music School) and, since 2008, on aesthetics of popular music and ethnomusicology at the Zurich University of the Arts. He is an active musician in the contemporary folk scene of Switzerland with his band Drüdieter.

Patricia Jäggi has been a researcher at the Music School of Lucerne University of Applied Sciences and Arts since 2012. She completed her PhD at the University of Basel with a study on post-war listening cultures as exemplified by the sounds of Swiss Radio International for a project titled "Broadcasting

Swissness," supported by the Swiss National Science Foundation. Previously, Patricia Jäggi studied cultural analysis, German studies, art history, and general and comparative literature at the Universities of Bern and Zürich. Her research interests are sound studies, anthropology, and ethnography of the senses and of perception, as well as radio anthropology and history.

Notes

1 The authors would like to thank Natalie Kirschstein for her critical and careful revision of the text.
2 This contribution is the result of a panel session at the ESEM Seminar 2013 in Bern. Marc-Antoine Camp, who had been mandated by the Federal Office of Culture to coordinate the establishment of the "List of Living Traditions in Switzerland," organized the panel and edited this text.
3 A new publication by Bachmann-Geiser resumes her research from the 1970s (Bachmann-Geiser 2019).
4 During the first revision of the list (2016–2018), yodeling songs were included (OFC 2017).
5 During the first revision of the list (2016–2018) the Grisons style was included (OFC 2017).
6 "Hornuss" is a traditional game originating in the Bernese region.

References

Bachmann-Geiser, Brigitte. 1981. *Die Volksmusikinstrumente der Schweiz*. Handbuch der europäischen Volksmusikinstrumente I(4). Leipzig: Deutscher Verlag für Musik.
—2007. *Customs and Traditions in Switzerland* (DVD), produced by swissinfo/SRI Webfactory. Bern: Presence Switzerland.
—2019. *Geschichte der Schweizer Volksmusik*. Basel: Schwabe Verlag.
Baumann, Max Peter. 1976. *Musikfolklore und Musikfolklorismus. Eine ethnomusikologische Untersuchung zum Funktionswandel des Jodels*. Winterthur: Amadeus-Verlag.
Camp, Marc-Antoine. 2006. "Die UNESCO-Konvention zur Bewahrung des immateriellen Kulturerbes." *Bulletin GVS/CH-EM* 4: 58–67. www.ch-em.ch/images/stories/pdf/gvs_ch-em_bulletin_2006.pdf (accessed July 27, 2017).
—2015. *Die Erstellung der Liste der lebendigen Traditionen in der Schweiz*. In *Communicating Music*, edited Antonio Baldassarre and Marc-Antoine Camp, 237–51. Bern: Lang.

Deutsch, Walter, and Wilhelm Schepping, eds. 1988. *Musik im Brauch der Gegenwart. Ergebnisse der Tagung der Kommission für Lied-, Musik- und Tanzforschung in der deutschen Gesellschaft für Volkskunde, 1986.* Schriften zur Volksmusik 12. Wien: Schendl.

Emsheimer, Ernst, and Erich Stockmann. 1959. "Vorbemerkungen zu einem Handbuch der europäischen Musikinstrumente." *Deutsches Jahrbuch für Volkskunde* 5: 412–16.

Graezer Bideau, Florence. 2012. "Inventorier les 'traditions vivantes.' Approches du patrimoine culturel immatériel dans le système fédéral Suisse." *ethnographiques. org: revue en ligne de sciences humaines et sociales* 24: 1–29. http://www.ethnographiques.org/2012/Graezer-Bideau (accessed July 27, 2017).

Grant, Catherine. 2012. "Rethinking Safeguarding: Objections and Responses to Protecting and Promoting Endangered Musical Heritage." *Ethnomusicology Forum* 21(1): 39–59. https://doi.org/10.1080/17411912.2012.641733

von Hornbostel, Erich Moritz, and Curt Sachs. 1914. "Systematik der Musikinstrumente." *Zeitschrift für Ethnologie* 46(4–5): 553–90.

Jäggi, Patricia. 2014. "Mashing up Living Traditions." *Norient Magazine* (February 14, 2014). http://norient.com/podcasts/living-traditions-collage (accessed July 27, 2017).

Koselleck, Reinhart. 1979. "Zur historisch-politischen Semantik asymmetrischer Gegenbegriffe." In Reinhard Koselleck, *Vergangene Zukunft. Zur Semantik geschichtlicher Zeiten*, 211–59. Frankfurt am Main: Suhrkamp.

Kunz, Ludvik, and Oskár Elschek. 1974–1983. *Die Volksmusikinstrumente der Tschechoslowakei.* Handbuch der europäischen Volksmusikinstrumente I(1–2). Leipzig: Deutscher Verlag für Musik.

Leimgruber, Walter. 2014. "Kultur und Kulturtheorien: Zwischen De- und Rekonstruktionen." Akademievortrag, Heft XXIII. *Swiss Academies Communications* 9(3). Bern: SAGW.

OFC (Office Fédéral de la Culture, Suisse), ed. 2012a. *List of Living Traditions in Switzerland.* www.lebendigetraditionen.ch (accessed July 27, 2017).

—2012b. "Information: Inventory of Living Traditions." In *List of Living Traditions in Switzerland.* www.lebendigetraditionen.ch/informationen/index.html?lang=en (accessed July 27, 2017).

—2012c. "Feuillu." *List of Living Traditions in Switzerland.* www.lebendigetraditionen.ch/traditionen/00131/index.html?lang=en (accessed July 27, 2017).

—2015. *Patrimoine culturel immatériel.* https://www.bak.admin.ch/bak/fr/home/patrimoine-culturel/patrimoine-culturel-immateriel.html (accessed March 21, 2019).

—2017. *Actualisation—Liste des traditions vivantes en Suisse.* https://www.bak.admin.ch/bak/fr/home/patrimoine-culturel/patrimoine-culturel-immateriel/mise-en-_uvre/actualisation---liste-des-traditions-vivantes-en-suisse.html (accessed March 21, 2019).

Robertson, Robert. 2009. *Eisenstein on the Audiovisual: The Montage of Music, Image and Sound in Cinema.* London: I.B. Tauris.

Sárosi, Bálint. 1967. *Die Volksmusikinstrumente Ungarns.* Handbuch der europäischen Volksmusikinstrumente I(4). Leipzig: Deutscher Verlag für Musik.

Stockmann, Erich. 1964. "Die europäischen Volksmusikinstrumente. Möglichkeiten und Probleme ihrer Darstellung in einem Handbuch." *Deutsches Jahrbuch für Volkskunde* 10: 238–53.

Thalmann, Rolf, ed. 1981. *Das Jahr der Schweiz in Fest und Brauch.* Zürich: Artemis (2nd edn 1983).

UNESCO. 2003. "Text of the Convention for the Safeguarding of the Intangible Cultural Heritage." https://ich.unesco.org/en/convention (accessed October 25, 2018).

VMS (Verband der Museen der Schweiz)/ICOM (Internationaler Musikrat Schweiz). 2010. museums.ch. *Die Schweizer Museumszeitschrift* 5. https://www.museums.ch/publikationen/revue/revue-museums.ch/ (accessed March 21, 2019).

Recordings and Videos

Bachmann-Geiser, Brigitte. 2013. *Der klingende Jahreskreis. Melodien, Rhythmen und Lärm in Volksbräuchen der Schweiz* (Compact Disc). Oberhofen: Zytglogge (CD ZYT 4623).

Kucholl, Vincent, and Vincent Veillon. 2012. "Les risques d'avalanche en Suisse." *120 secondes sur Couleur* 3 (September 18, 2012). Video. www.120secondes.info/videos/les-risques-davalanche-en-suisse-skip-pannatier (accessed July 27, 2017).

Zemp, Hugo. 1987. *A Swiss Yodelling Series: "Jüüzli" of the Muotatal* (2-DVD set of four films: *Yootzing and Yodelling*, 1987; *Head Voice, Chest Voice*, 1987; *The Wedding of Susanna and Josef*, 1986; *Glattalp*, 1986), color, 126 min, Swiss-German with English subtitles. Available at Documentary Educational Resources, www.der.org/films/swiss-yodelling-series.html (accessed July 27, 2017).

Chapter 12

Tracing the *Minhag Ashkenaz* in Swiss Synagogue Music: Advocates of Intangible Cultural Heritage Meet Agents of Cultural Sustainability[1]

Sarah M. Ross

When thinking about intangible cultural heritage, it first of all conjures the problem of discontinuity, and the question of who is going to "stand up" for disappearing musical traditions and cultural knowledge in order to "give back" long-lost voices in honor of past and future generations. Secondly, it brings up the issue of recognizing those who have continuously worked through cultural and social changes, while pursuing musical traditions from their own cultural heritage that otherwise would have disappeared, and thereby striking out in new directions in their roles as so-called "change agents of sustainability" (Dieleman 2008: 117).

Nowadays, the term cultural sustainability is used in a platitudinous way and is regarded by many as "taboo." Nevertheless, sustainability has become an essential part of everyday life, even though its meaning is hardly rooted in societal awareness (cf. Kagan 2008: 15). However, as it turned out during my fieldwork among Jewish communities in the German-speaking parts of Switzerland, the application of the idea of cultural sustainability in the study of Jewish cultural heritage, in general, and of synagogue music, in particular, can indeed be beneficial. Thus, this article discusses how the concepts of intangible cultural heritage and cultural sustainability are inter-connected. The idea of cultural sustainability is preferred here, compared to that of cultural heritage, as it describes the discursive and dynamic processes of continuing and passing down (and not simply of preserving) intangible forms of cultural expressions. In doing so, cultural sustainability describes a bottom-up movement emerging right from the heart of community, rather than a top-down movement directly linked to the politically-charged UNESCO Convention for the Safeguarding of the Intangible Cultural Heritage.

Contemporary musicians, such as François Lilienfeld, whom I met in the Jewish community of Bern in 2013, play a significant role in the continuation of Jewish musical traditions in Swiss communities. Because of the increasing popularity of American and Israeli melodies used nowadays within synagogue services, Lilienfeld has seen the use of Louis Lewandowski's compositions disappear,[2] even though his melodies once made up the largest part of tunes sung within German-speaking synagogue communities in Switzerland. The fear of Lewandowski's vanishing thus has a large impact on Lilienfeld's work: for example, in his arrangement of Lewandowski's scoring of Psalm 92, the original and characteristic organ accompaniment is replaced by an orchestra. In doing so, Lilienfeld tried to make the initial composition for liturgical use richer in sound and more attractive for an average audience, while preserving Lewandowski's musical heritage for the concert hall, as he explained in our interview.[3]

While people like Lilienfeld are now worried about the continuation of Lewandowski's melodies within synagogue services, Lewandowski's compositions were once regarded as a threat. At the beginning of the nineteenth century, the reform movement had a strong influence on the development of Jewish liturgical music within communities in the German-speaking countries of Europe. According to musicologist Abraham Zvi Idelsohn, the liturgical and musical reformation of Judaism became the downfall of synagogue songs, as traditional prayer chants, and modes and melodies used for the cantillation of the Torah, were replaced by "modern music" (Idelsohn 1932: VI), that is, by through-composed choral works by Louis Lewandowski, Samuel Naumbourg, and Salomon Sulzer. Even though Idelsohn regarded the musical impact of this triumvirate as the death of German synagogue music—he wrote "der deutsche Synagogengesang hörte auf semitisch schöpferisch zu sein ... und wurde vollends zu einer Abart der deutschen Musik" ("German synagogue song stopped being creative in a Semitic sense ... and became a [negative] variation of German [art] music")—the works by Lewandowski, Naumbourg, and Sulzer belong to the so-called *Minhag Ashkenaz* (German custom), just as traditional synagogue chants do.

This chapter will thus provide a short discussion on the concept of intangible cultural heritage (ICH) and its applicability within Swiss Judaism and its culture, and then outline the concept of cultural sustainability, followed by discussions of the *Minhag Ashkenaz* within the context of Swiss-Jewish ritual music while providing further musical examples by Louis Lewandowski and Samuel Naumbourg, and outlining how their music is pursued and passed on in contemporary communities in Switzerland. This will be examined against the background of the theoretical concept of cultural sustainability, while showing how cantors, composers of synagogue music, and choirs act as so-called "change agents of sustainability," and thereby contribute to the safeguarding of the Jewish musical heritage of Switzerland. The following explanations are guided by the question of the role played by music makers in the realization of cultural sustainability, and what strategies they pursue.[4] The chapter is based on data collected via numerous interviews conducted with representatives of Jewish communities in Zurich, Basel, and Bern since 2011, which are duly contextualized with historical research.

Applying the Concept of Intangible Cultural Heritage to Swiss-Jewish Cultural Heritage

Since World War II, discussions about the definition of concepts such as tangible and intangible cultural heritage, as well as about the arbitrariness and interrelatedness of these categories, have been led by experts of the United Nations Educational, Scientific and Cultural Organization (UNESCO)[5] as well as independent scholars of different fields of music research, ethnomusicology included.[6] As it would be beyond the scope of this chapter to reproduce these discourses, the following explanations will be limited to the application of the concept of ICH within the context of the Swiss-Jewish cultural/musical heritage.[7]

The Jewish musical heritage of the Surbtal, located in the canton of Aargau in Switzerland, as I have discussed in detail elsewhere (see Ross 2014), lends itself to the challenges of safeguarding Jewish cultural heritage. Here, the Jewish musical traditions of the two Aargovian villages Endingen and Lengnau and other forms of Swiss-Jewish customs and folk traditions became endangered and died out as a direct result of the disappearance of socio-cultural contexts in which they once thrived and as a consequence of a misunderstood and misapplied idea of safeguarding the intangible Jewish cultural heritage of Switzerland (Ross 2014: 120–23; cf. Grant 2012; Lowenstein 1997: 63; Rapp Buri 2008; Stein 2008).

Switzerland ratified the Convention for the Safeguarding of the Intangible Cultural Heritage in July 2008 (see Leimgruber 2010). Since then, much effort has been put into the community-based project Jewish Heritage Path Endingen-Lengnau, which is now part of a larger project called *Doppeltür*,[8] the Jewish Museum Switzerland in Basel, as well as the Archives of Contemporary History in Zurich (here particularly the Image Archives Swiss Jews), which are, by the time of writing, the only projects and institutions that are actively involved in the preservation of Jewish culture in Switzerland. However, within this context, almost all efforts have been put into the safe-guarding of the *tangible* forms of Swiss-Jewish cultural expressions, such as the unique Jewish architecture of Endingen and Lengnau. Thus, spurred by the Convention for the Safeguarding of ICH, only a few Swiss researchers, experts, and activists engaged with the complex challenges of maintaining and revitalizing the cultural heritage of Switzerland's Jewry. Ironically, these enterprises do not include the preservation of Jewish rural folk songs of the Surbtal, let alone other forms of Jewish musical traditions in Switzerland, such as the Western-Ashkenazi modes and melodies of Swiss synagogue music, also labeled *Minhag Ashkenaz* (see also below). The implementation of the Convention in Switzerland "seems mainly to promulgate notions of intangible cultural heritage based on images of past, traditional, fundamentally rural traditions, which can serve as a counter-image to the development of modern society" (Leimgruber 2010: 185). But this view on ICH excludes cultures and cultural forms that are "mobile and transnational, [and which are] medial transmissions of popular culture, [as well as] performative elements of culture." Thus, and with regard to the notion that culture becomes more and more detached from its societal roots, many actors in the field of cultural preservation "feel left out by the way the Convention is being publicized" in Switzerland (see Leimgruber 2010: 185).

Thus, a broader understanding of intangible cultural heritage in Switzerland in general, and of Jewish cultural heritage in particular, encompassing all cultural expressions in which Jewish identities manifest themselves, is missing. The task to sustain Switzerland's Jewish cultural heritage as a living entity that goes beyond mere collection and safeguarding of (in-)tangible artifacts is not yet fulfilled. What is needed is a change in perspective that takes into account those actors (as well as their life spaces and social worlds), who continuously try to sustain the unique Jewish musical (and other oral) traditions of Switzerland (see Kirshenblatt-Gimblett 2004: 53–54). The realization of the UNESCO Convention is even further hampered by political problems and the difficult relationship between Switzerland's Jewry and the Swiss state, and a dissonant awareness and appreciation of Jewish cultural heritage on both sides.

Dissonant Views on Jewish Heritage

Although the cultural achievements of the Swiss Jews are visible, they still negate their existence. As revealed in several interviews,[9] Jews in Switzerland consider themselves as European-Jewish rather than Swiss-Jewish, and tend to identify themselves almost exclusively with the Holocaust, even though the majority of Swiss Jews have not been directly affected by World War II. In addition, Jewish self-conception in Switzerland is still influenced by an attitude that emerged, according to my interviewee H. Mugier,[10] in the 1960s, when people were proud of being Jewish, but wanted to keep their pride to themselves. Thus, it was (and still is) uncommon to reveal one's Jewish identity in public. Although this is gradually changing, with Jewish communities becoming increasingly engaged in dialogues with their non-Jewish neighbors, some Swiss Jews nevertheless have a broken relationship to Switzerland and its culture. This is also based on the fact that the Swiss state does not feel an active commitment to its Jewish population. Consequently, the relationship between Jews and Switzerland is of course a relationship of mutual tolerance, but at the same time also one of noticeable ignorance (see Picard 2014: 14). This leads to a dissonance in awareness and recognition of the country's Jewish cultural heritage, which hampers the documenting, researching, promoting, and safeguarding of Jewish (musical) heritage in Switzerland (cf. Ashworth and Graham 2005: 5).

In Switzerland, with its subsidization of arts and culture, cultural policy, and hence the realization of the UNESCO Convention, are at the discretion of the municipalities and cantons. This means that the federal government plays only "a secondary role in promoting culture, both financially and substantially" (Leimgruber 2010: 182). Consequently, and as Leimgruber further states, "the lion's share of support for culture comes from the cantons and from city governments" (ibid.). In this regard, Urs Staub of the Federal Office for Culture of the Canton of Basel stated in 2013 that Swiss museums, and thus also the Jewish Museum of Switzerland in Basel, have to be centers of excellence and as such have to contribute to Swiss national identity if they want to receive any financial aid (see Bollag 2013). But who decides whether, in this case, Jewish cultural institutions can and do contribute to national Swiss identity? The cantons, which are responsible for the content of the lists, do indeed "rely on proposals made by bearers of intangible cultural heritage," but have the overall authority with regard to the final compilation of the lists of intangible cultural heritage of each canton, and thus have the final say about funding (Leimgruber 2010: 182). Consequently, Jewish culture, which is a cross-cantonal and cross-cultural phenomenon that cannot be categorized by uniform selection criteria of *Schweizer Volkskultur* (see Leimgruber 2010: 183),[11] as well as researchers and activists, are mixed up in a cultural and political context that is characterized by contrary perspectives, along with rather arbitrary interpretations and political applications of the concept of ICH. Furthermore, as Leimgruber states, "diaspora groups [such as the Jews in Switzerland] are being involved [in the realization of the Convention] only if they do not contradict the intentions of the governmental cultural policy" (Leimgruber 2010: 186).

The point to be made here is that all heritage interventions change not only the relationship of people to what they do and how they understand their culture and themselves, but that the change itself, as well as those protagonists who spur it, are intrinsic to the production and reproduction of culture, and thus to the world heritage enterprise (Kirshenblatt-Gimblett 2004: 58–59). Consequently, an alternative perspective on safeguarding the Jewish musical heritage of Switzerland is offered in the following discussion, which emanates from the focus on the concept of cultural sustainability. Doing so, this approach acknowledges the fact that people are not only objects of cultural preservation but also subjects: the fact that they cannot be reduced to their function as mere cultural carriers and transmitters of traditions, but have to be recognized as actively engaged, conscious, and reflexive agents in the heritage enterprise itself (Kirshenblatt-Gimblett 2004: 58). Thus, and by means of the example of the *Minhag Ashkenaz* in Swiss synagogue music, the following part of the article is centered around the meaning of knowledgeable and skilled persons, such as cantors and composers of synagogue music, who—as so-called "change agents of sustainability"—help not only to maintain a particular art of Jewish liturgical music, but to transmit it to others. Thereby, they play an important role in the preservation and continuation of Swiss-Jewish cultural heritage (cf. Yim 2004: 11). This perspective on the preservation of Jewish musical traditions shows how the safeguarding of intangible cultural heritage and the notion of cultural sustainability are interrelated on a personal level.

Cultural Sustainability and Ethnomusicology

The general understanding of the term sustainability refers to a "sustainable development … that meets the needs of the present without compromising future generations to meet their own needs" (World Commission on

Environment and Development 1987: 43). Janet Moore further understands sustainability as "a concept, a goal, and a strategy," whereby the "concept speaks to the reconciliation of social justice, ecological integrity, and the well-being of all living systems on the planet, [while the] goal is to create an ecologically and socially just world within the means of nature without compromising future generations" (Moore 2005: 78). Against the background of this understanding of sustainability, the study of sustainability has emerged in the twenty-first century as a vibrant academic discipline and innovation, which brings together scholarship and practice, global and local perspectives. Emerging from disciplines from across the natural and social sciences, engineering, and medicine, the study of sustainability tries to understand the complex dynamics that arise from interactions between human and environmental systems (Kates et al. 2001; Swart et al. 2002).

In comparison, the term "cultural sustainability" is concerned with actions and issues that affect how communities manifest their cultural identity and sense of place by preserving and cultivating traditions, as well as by developing cultural systems and commonly accepted values. These traditions, cultural systems, values, and shared spaces, which all make up the cultural capital of a community, are at the core of cultural heritage, may it be tangible or intangible. Yet, within current discourses on sustainability, an explicit reference to the safeguarding of cultural heritage is either overlooked or applied simplistically, even though a community's cultural identity and handling of its heritage influences its approach to cultural sustainability: "Cultural heritage connects people to a place that symbolizes the identity and values that provide a sense of belonging on personal and community levels, and the continuance of that heritage [of that cultural capital respectively] is what cultural sustainability is about" (cf. Scammon 2012). Until now, there is no single definition of cultural sustainability that is adequate on its own. With regard to the maintenance of cultural capital (which includes a society's intangible forms of cultural heritage, such as ideas, practices, and musical traditions), David Thorsby (2011) states:

> by failing to sustain the cultural values that provide people with a sense of identity, and by not undertaking the investment needed to maintain the stock of tangible and intangible cultural capital or to increase it ... cultural systems [will likewise be placed] in jeopardy and may ... break down, with consequence of loss of welfare and economic output. (Thorsby 2011: 145)

The concept of cultural sustainability is also viable and relevant for current discourses within ethnomusicology, where the interrelation of music and sustainability has long been recognized (see Grant 2014; Fenn and Titon 2003; Fargion 2009; Petocz, Reid, and Bennett 2014; Titon 2009a, 2009c). Within this context, music sustainability, or the sustainability of music, was first concerned with the documentation of musical traditions feared to disappear. This approach is now referred to as *salvage ethnomusicology*. Since the enacting of the UNESCO Convention in 2003, ethnomusicological approaches have become more pragmatic, now acknowledging "the natural emergence, change and decay of musical traditions as well as the many local and global processes that act upon all music genres" (Grant 2013; see also Grant 2014: 14). In this regard, Jeff Todd Titon (2009b) states in his research blog on the subject of sustainability and music that

> when we consider that certain musics and musical cultures have become extinct, we realize that it is not music as a human resource that is endangered, but rather it is particular musical cultures and practices, which contribute to the diversity of the world's musical resources that are endangered. It is to these musical cultures that sustainability applies. (ibid.)

Yet, when considering music sustainability in its broadest context, it refers to the ability of a music genre to persist without consequences of either a static tradition or a bearing preservation (Grant 2013). In this regard, ethnomusicologists have tried to sustain musical cultures in different ways: first, by collecting and archiving musical and ethnographic data (an approach that does not necessarily sustain musical genres as living cultures); second, by displaying musical cultures at heritage sites (that might lead to a decontextualization of its original performance context and thus to a change in the function and meaning of this music for a certain community); and third, by means of community work in the sense of applied ethnomusicology, and thus by working together on the development of common goals and methods so that communities are enabled to sustain their musical cultures on their own. In this regard, Titon further states: "the term sustainability is better suited than the terms preservation or conservation" (Titon 2009b).

Within ethnomusicology, both intangible cultural heritage and sustainability attracted criticisms, which is due to the fact that there is no standardized ethnomusicological terminology available that reflects the aims and approaches in relation to the preservation, revitalization, and sustainability of music (see Grant 2014: 10–11). Notwithstanding, and as indicated above, I consider the term intangible cultural heritage as inappropriate, as it puts the focus too much on the political and preservationist stance, and thus on music of the past that needs to be collected, documented, and protected, which is a rather *passive act* of safeguarding conducted by specialists. In comparison, the term sustainability refers to an *active process* of enabling people (a community) to pursue their own musical genres and cultures, acknowledging all the transformations and changes it has experienced (cf. Grant 2014: 10, 12). Thus, and with regard to the *Minhag Ashkenaz* in Swiss synagogue music, musical sustainability shall be concerned with sustaining a community's local music style in the present and future (informed by musical traditions of the past), rather than with the mere safeguarding of an assumed authentic style of previous times, which might have disappeared for some reason.

Thus, when understood as neither "basic" nor "applied" research, the study of sustainability in ethnomusicology encompasses both relevant theoretical and educational work as well as pragmatic models of problem solving. In doing so, it serves the need to advance both knowledge and informed action by creating a dynamic bridge between the two (see Clark and Dickson 2003). In the following discussion, I will expand the third way of sustaining music by focusing on the role of so-called "change agents of sustainability."

Change Agents of Sustainability

The term "change agents of sustainability" goes back to the Dutch sociologist Hans Dieleman, and signifies important actors in the implementation and realization of sustainable development in a society. In his article "Sustainability, Art and Reflexivity" (2008), Dieleman "analyzes how sustainability as a societal change process can meet the manifold reflexive practices of artists" and other creative professionals (Kagan 2008: 29). Yet the idea of sustainability is not just about the needs of present and future generations that shall be met through sustainable thinking and action (Brocchi 2007: 6). Rather, and as it turned out in various fieldwork situations, it is about giving the rather conservative concept of (cultural) sustainability a new image, while initiating a more in-depth critical debate on the idea of cultural sustainability. Persons engaged in the cultural sector thus play an important role.

The main question is what role ethnomusicology can play in stimulating, guiding, and facilitating changes in sustainability. Ethnomusicological work, in comparison to other sciences and politics, is not only restricted to

CULTURAL DIMENSION (e.g. cultural variety)		
ECOLOGICAL DIMENSION (e.g. saving natural resources)	ECONOMIC DIMENSION (e.g. preventive economic activity)	SOCIAL DIMENSION (e.g. intrasocial equity)

Figure 12.1: Four-pillar model of sustainability (Sarah M. Ross)

analytical rationalities applied toward understanding reality. On the contrary, ethnomusicology's focus on understanding how people make sense of the world through their music making as it is embedded in their day-to-day experiences predestines it for an applied approach in the study of sustainability, because sustainability is more than just a rational process of the creation of a new world with new institutions, products, processes and relationships, but rather a societal and cultural process. In this context, reasons advocating a cultural change in support of sustainable development do indeed come from (scientific and political) arguments, but they are nevertheless embedded in emotions, convictions, desires and fears, lifestyles, identities, and intuitive notions that are in turn reflected and negotiated within people's music making (Dieleman 2008: 108).

Most discourses on sustainability are nowadays coined by a four-pillar model that understands sustainable development as a discursive process located within the quadrangle of ecology, economy, society, and culture (see Figure 12.1). Culture is seen here as a transverse dimension in which the importance of sustainable development is being negotiated. Applied to the idea of a change agent in sustainability, this means that agents act through cultural strategies of sustainability on a meta-level of social communication. In doing so, they can, for example, activate a sensitization process for the importance and necessity of preserving the *Minhag Ashkenaz* in synagogue music inside the Jewish communities. This is further clarified below.

Defining *Minhag Ashkenaz*

The term *Minhag* literally means "custom," and encompasses all religious and cultural practices accepted and cultivated by a community in a certain geographical region, and thus includes all forms of synagogue music, such as the Torah cantillation, the Jewish prayer modes (*nusach*),[12] the cantorial recitative, and choral singing. The term *Ashkenaz* is originally a medieval Hebrew designation for Germany. More precisely, the term refers to the Jewish culture that has emerged in the Rhineland since the tenth century. With increasing Jewish emigration from Germany throughout the thirteenth and fourteenth centuries, the term was also assigned to communities in Switzerland, northern France, England, northern Italy, and since the sixteenth century also to Jewish communities in Eastern Europe. In the eighteenth-century Polish-Lithuanian Commonwealth, the so-called Ashkenazim developed their own form of Jewish culture and music that was highly influenced by the Chassidic movement (Lotter and Wolffsohn 2000: 79).

In comparison, the term *Minhag Ashkenaz*, strictly speaking, only refers to the religious, cultural, and thus musical traditions of the Jews, who once lived west and south of the river Elbe. This led throughout the nineteenth century to the division between the Western-Ashkenazi Judaism that followed the *Minhag Ashkenaz* and the Eastern-Ashkenazi Judaism that followed the so-called *Minhag Polin* (the Polish custom). The linguistic and cultural boundary mentioned above thus refers to the nineteenth century, and has to be understood as a substitute border that is easily crossed on the scale of popular culture (Lowenstein 1997: 61).

In turn, the *Minhag Ashkenaz* is determined by a variety of local characteristics: language, customs, and liturgical melodies differ in Southwest Germany, and the neighboring states Alsace and Switzerland, from those commonly used north of the river Mosel—such as in North-Rhine-Westphalia and Lower Saxony (ibid.), which explains the so-called *Minhag Alsace-Lorraine* or the *Southern German Minhag*.

In Switzerland, the *Southern German Minhag* used to be only followed in the villages Endingen and Lengnau, which, from the seventeenth to the nineteenth century were the only places in Switzerland where Jews had the permission of permanent settlement. Jews from Alsace and Southern Germany also lived in this region. After the ban on settlement was lifted in 1879, many Jewish families left Endingen and Lengnau, and moved to urban centers in Switzerland (such as Zurich, Basel, or Bern), as well as abroad. They took the Southern German Jewish customs and thus some of their musical traditions with them. Today, some remains of the liturgical melodies that have been sung in the Surbtal can, for example, still be heard in the orthodox Jewish community Adass Yeshurun in Zurich, of which some former families of Endingen and Lengnau became members (see Ross 2014). Here, the pronunciation of the Hebrew language is, along with the actual melodies and the unique dialect called Surbtal-Yiddish,[13] one of the crucial cultural markers of the *Southern German Minhag*. The following example of the 'Hamavdil', a hymn sung at the close of the *Havdalah* ceremony to mark the end of the Shabbat, gives an impression of linguistic features of the *Southern German Minhag* (see phonetic and musical transcription below, Figure 12.2): here, the members of Adass Yeshurun pronounce, for example, the medieval long vowel *a* (â) as a long *o* or *ou*, whereas a lengthened original short *a* remained *a* (cf. Lowenstein 1997: 63; Idelsohn 1932: VII).

Phonetic transcription of the Hebrew chorus:	English translation:
Hamavdil bein k*ou*desh l'ch*ou*l	He who separates between holy and secular,
chatoteinu hu imch*ou*l	May he forgive our sins
zareinu v'chaspeinu yarbe chach*ou*l	Our offspring and wealth,
v'chakochavim balail*ou*...	May he increase like dust and like the nighttime stars...

The *Minhag Ashkenaz* in Swiss Synagogue Music

The *Minhag Ashkenaz* used to be the most popular and widespread style of Jewish rite practiced in Central Europe. Today, it is still followed in just a few communities in Israel, the United States, and the UK. Within the context of Swiss synagogue music, remnants of the Southern German custom can be found today to different degrees in the orthodox community Adass Yeshurun in Zurich (see example above), the Israelite community Basel, and the Jewish community of Bern. Analyses of musical characteristics of the oral traditions of the *Minhag Ashkenaz* are thus based—for the most part—on nineteenth- and twentieth-century manuscripts (such as Idelsohn's "Thesaurus of Oriental Hebrew Melodies," 1932), as well as on audio recordings emanating from ethnomusicology fieldwork or private archives, and empirical data collected through fieldwork among Jewish communities. In comparison to the Eastern

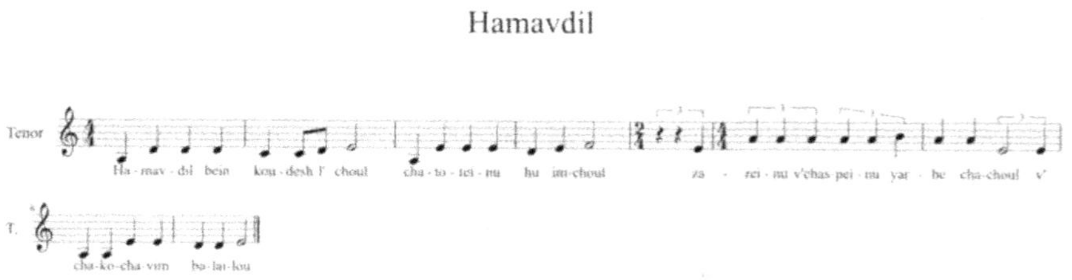

Hamavdil

Figure 12.2: The beginning of 'Hamavdil', as sung at the Adass Yeshurun synagogue in Zurich (transcription by author)[14]

European tradition of synagogue music, the *Minhag Ashkenaz* is characterized by its frequent use of Western major and minor tonality, whereby melodic elements in minor are for the most parts eclipsed, Moreover, a strict rhythmical structure (less rubato than in the *Minhag Polin*), preference for a formal and exulting sentiment in the cantorial recitative (in contrast to the characteristic notion of supplication and lamentation in Eastern European *chazzanut*), frequent use of upbeats, a limited scope for melody, and abstinence from free recitatives as well as from an over-use of melodic ornamentation, are significant features of Southern German synagogue music (cf. Klein 2013: 73–76; Idelsohn 1932: XIII–XV).

Since the second half of the twentieth century, Jewish life in Switzerland was shaped by major social changes: the enforced cultural and social pluralization of the communities, the growing secularization of society, and the increasing Jewish immigration from Eastern Europe, the USA, and Israel led to a partial replacement of local (German) Jewish musical traditions by those of the immigrants. Thus, the musical patchwork of communities in the German-speaking part of Switzerland has become more and more complex. Today, rabbis and cantors act on the interface of Western and Eastern European, and Sephardic and Anglo-American traditions of synagogue music. However, the essential question is: How could the *Minhag Ashkenaz* in Swiss synagogue music—at least to some extent—be preserved, and what are the issues surrounding sustainability in this context? Answers to these questions can be found in the social structures of Swiss-Jewish communities and in their handling of musical heritage, but also, as stated at the beginning of this chapter, in the self-awareness of the cantors, synagogue composers, and choirs as so-called "change agents of sustainability."

Where and How Do "Change Agents of Sustainability" Get Active?

The preservation of the *Minhag Ashkenaz* in Switzerland is made possible by a strong consensus-oriented community culture, such as in the Jewish community of Bern which will be discussed here. The Bernese tradition can be described as ranging somewhere between moderate-Orthodox and carefully liberal, which is due to a respected order of tolerance. The latter impacts on community life so that those members, to whom traditional conventions and habits are important, keep faith in the community, while at the same time welcoming liberally-oriented members. Yet this openness toward liberal ideas is not synonymous with the desire for new, egalitarian Jewish liturgical traditions common among liberal forces (Picard 2014: 30; Gerson 2014: 147).

Therefore it is not surprising that the *Southern German Minhag* is still partially practiced in the Jewish community of Bern. In 1848, Jews from Alsace founded the Bernese community under the name "Corporation of the Israelites in Bern." Until 1874, the synagogue stood under the rabbinate Hégenheim (near Basel), and thus under the leadership of the liberal rabbi Moïse Nordmann.[15] Nordmann, like his successors, among them rabbi Zvi H. Engelmayer (who came from Frankfurt to Bern in 1963), not only brought the *Minhag Ashkenaz*, but also the so-called "jekkische (German) Nusach" to Bern,[16] where it has been maintained to this day. This *nusach* is, however, practiced in parallel with Eastern European and American traditions that have been introduced by the Hungarian rabbi David Polnauer and the American cantor Teron Cohen.

In general, the *jekkische Nusach* is characterized by its frequent use of major tonality, a melismatic opening on the first word, as well as by a final cadence on the 5th pitch (usually a typical 6–5 cadence, see square markers in Figure 12.3), as can be seen in the transcription of the "Barchu" (the call to prayer) by cantor Max Wohlberg (1907–1996). Wohlberg's transcription is in turn based on Louis Lewandowski's version of 'Bar'chu' (see Lewandowski 1871: 14), which is still sung in Bern (see Figure 12.4).

During the last forty years, and due to his preference for Lewandowski's compositions, it was mainly cantor José Kaufmann (in office from 1975 to 2012), who maintained the "German Nusach" in Bern, which is also part of the *Minhag Ashkenaz*. Kaufmann comes from an Orthodox Jewish family from Hesse, who fled to Argentina in the 1930s. He grew up in a German-Orthodox community in Buenos Aires, where he was trained as a religious

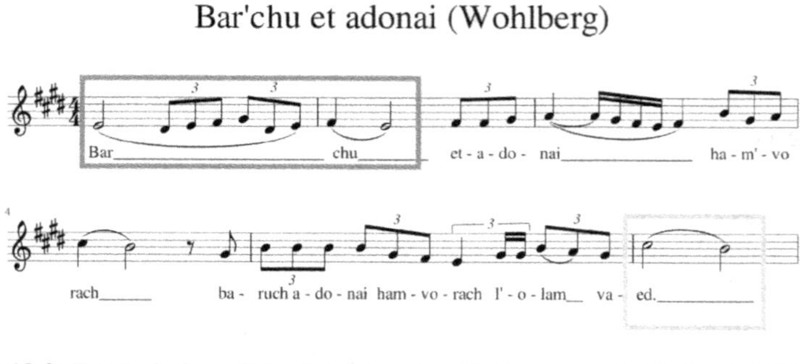

Bar'chu et adonai (Wohlberg)

Figure 12.3: Transcription of 'Bar'chu' by Max Wohlberg, printed in Tarsi (2002: 181).

Määriw L'Schabboss

Figure 12.4: Transcription of 'Bar'chu' by Louis Lewandowski, printed in Lewandowski (1871: 14).

education teacher and cantor. In 1969, he took up his first position as a cantor in Montevideo, and moved to Bern six years later. Because of his background and education, Kaufmann is well acquainted with the Western Ashkenazi tradition of synagogue music (Abelin 2012). Whereas the prayer modes and melodies are maintained by the community itself, who have sung them for the last thirty-five years, the way the Torah is recited, however, has changed since the American-trained cantor Teron Cohen came into office in 2012. Since then, the Western Ashkenazi (German) tradition of Torah tropes, which is hardly used anywhere else, has been replaced by the "American Tradition." As the reading from the Torah is reserved for the cantor, as well as the rabbi and a few men now and then serving as prayer leaders, the majority of the community is not only uninformed about the practice of biblical cantillation, but is moreover unable to pursue this particular tradition. Idelsohn noted in his *Hebräisch-Orientalischer Melodienschatz* (1932: XVI) a few melodic motifs (Torah tropes, see Figure 12.5), which used to be sung in the exact same way by cantor Kaufmann until a few years ago, and that give an impression of the character of the Western Ashkenazi tradition of biblical cantillation.

Not only Lewandowski's compositions, but also the works by Samuel Naumbourg, are of high importance in the musical tradition of Swiss-German communities. This is particularly evident when taking a closer look at the repertoire of the synagogue choirs in Switzerland. At this point, the synagogue choir of the Israelite community of Basel will be discussed as an example.

The Israelite community of Basel, founded by Alsatian and German Jews in 1805, stood under the rabbinate Hegenheim. During the nineteenth

Tabelle der rekonstruierten Pentateuchweise.

Figure 12.5: Motifs of the Southern German Torah trope as printed in Idelsohn (1932: XVI).

century, immigrants from Alsace and southern Germany, and later on also from Eastern Europe, who came to Switzerland in the wake of World War I, shaped the cultural and musical life of the Basel community. Most of the refugees who arrived during World War II had to leave again in 1945. Likewise, these former members of the community left their musical footprints, as Henry Mugier, former prayer leader in Basel and today in Bern, explained it in our interview.[17]

Since 1928, the male choir of the Israelite community of Basel has been documented almost completely, and can look back on eighty-six years of an uninterrupted history and musical tradition.[18] Today, the choir consists of sixteen amateur singers and is conducted by the Israeli Doron Schleifer.[19] The community of Basel is one of few Jewish communities in Switzerland that has a permanent prayer leader and a synagogue choir that supports the cantor's solo every Shabbat. Moreover, the choir succeeded to safeguard both the music of the three great synagogue composers Lewandowski, Naumbourg, and Sulzer, as well as that of local composers Louis Epstein (the son of the Frankfurt cantor Max Epstein who re-established the choir) and others during and after the Holocaust. Particularly, the works by the Bavarian cantor Samuel Naumbourg, who was trained in the mid-nineteenth century in

Munich and later on worked in France and Alsace, is of special significance within the musical tradition of Basel (Schleifer 2013: 7–15).

Thus, the synagogue choir of Basel no longer identifies, for example, the Ya'aleh prayer ("may he arise") as Naumbourg's composition, but now calls it the "Basel tradition," under which title it continues to be passed on.[20] The Ya'aleh is the anthem that precedes the *Selichot* (liturgical poems of penance and repentance), and which follows the evening service on *Yom Kippur* (the day of atonement). The musical notation (Figure 12.6) shows that the melodic voice-leading of cantor and choir is rather simple, followed by imitative passages. Moreover, the cantorial recitative is mostly syllabic, with very little ornamentation and written in a 4/4 time, which is—in contrast to the usual free, non-metric improvisation of liturgical texts (particularly in the Eastern European tradition)—characteristic of Naumbourg's style of composition (see Schleifer 2013: 57).

Naumbourg's intention was to re-establish "the original form" of traditional synagogue song. He wanted to free Jewish liturgical chants from excessive ornaments, with which cantors had overloaded them, in order to display and accentuate their own voices effectively. Naumbourg believed that he had to present the traditional tunes in the new guise of choral arrangements

Figure 12.6: Beginning of 'Ya'aleh' by Samuel Naumbourg (transcription courtesy of the Basel Synagogue Choir).

in order to be able to secure the music's continuance (Schleifer 2013: 37). In retrospect, Naumbourg can thus be considered a "change agent of sustainability." During his time in Munich, he was exposed to two opposing currents in synagogue music, one aimed to preserve the ancient chants of southern Germany, the other aimed at reforming synagogue music by following the example of European church music. These tensions had a great influence on Naumbourg's work. In his song collection *Agudat Schirim* (1874), Naumbourg tried (similar to François Lilienfeld today) to publicize synagogue music as widely as possible by re-arranging it in the format of a piano score. He hoped that the music could more easily be implemented in smaller communities, and would thus be protected in modern synagogues. At the same time, Naumbourg attached great importance to the fact that the communities would sing newer compositions alongside the traditional synagogue chants, and thus pleaded for the coexistence of different traditions (Schleifer 2013: 36–37). The Israelite community of Basel and the Jewish community of Bern, in which the *Minhag Ashkenaz* can be found primarily within the *chazzanut* and the repertoire of the synagogue choirs, now follow a similar strategy of cultural sustainability, as tradition can only result from progress. In doing so, and thus in their role as "change agents of sustainability," they raise consciousness and respect for their communities' own musical heritage, and promote a communal awareness that certain music genres are (going to be) endangered. This is the essential first step in an effort to acquire a comprehensive view of sustainability issues.

Conclusions

It has been the argument of this chapter that, in comparison to the politically driven top-down cultural projects of heritage intervention, such as in the case of the Jewish musical traditions of the Surbtal, the community-driven bottom-up interventions spurred by so-called "change agents of sustainability" are the basic prerequisite to musical sustainability. It has been suggested that Jewish communities in Switzerland shall be enabled to firstly recognize and then to manage and pursue their own musical heritage in order to become independent of Swiss policy-makers and their determination to acknowledge Jewish musical traditions of Switzerland as part of the country's ICH. Otherwise, even well-intended concepts of cultural heritage and associated methods and heritage interventions run the risk of becoming a nonsustainable exercise.

Consequently, and with regard to the safeguarding of the Jewish musical heritage of Switzerland, not only are the general socio-cultural contexts in which the music is practiced relevant, but also the individual actors, such as Samuel Naumbourg or José Kaufmann, François Lilienfeld and the members of the synagogue choirs, who ensure—within the context of this community —that the *Minhag Ashkenaz* keeps its place in the individual and the collective memory of the Swiss Jews, even if supposedly unsustainable influences impact on the communities and their musical traditions. This forces protagonists to navigate changing socio-cultural structures in order to preserve old traditions alongside new ones, and to sustain them for the future. Against the theoretical background of the concept of cultural sustainability, the protagonists can thus be understood as "change agents of sustainability." Cultural sustainability does not mean that traditions are cultivated for nostalgic reasons. It rather means to build a bridge to the past, present, and future by continuing the *Minhag Ashkenaz* in synagogue music. The critical examination of strategies of cultural sustainability opens many topics and research areas outside of Jewish music studies and (ethno-)musicology. According to Dieleman, arts and artists are, with regard to the realization of cultural sustainability, of vital importance, as they bring about a change of perspective on the need for sustainable thinking and acting, namely by helping people to reflect and express themselves and their surroundings, for example through "symbolic meaning" and "signs." Being involved in various social-artistic interventions, and by touching upon people's emotions, intuitions, and visions, artists show that they have the capacities to reflect, stimulate, guide, and facilitate respective social transformation and change, given that sustainability means change (Dieleman 2008: 121). The primary purpose of safeguarding Swiss-Jewish musical heritage may thus be something other than ensuring long-term viability of the music for its own sake. It may be more about the reclamation of music's place in people's personal and public memory. This is why the discourses on preserving ICH should be demystified to make them more acceptable and applicable to local communities.

About the Author

Sarah M. Ross is Professor of Jewish Music Studies and Director of the European Center for Jewish Music at Hannover University of Music, Drama, and Media, Germany. She obtained her PhD in 2010 at the Rostock University of Music and Theatre, Germany. She is the author of *A Season of Singing:*

Creating Feminist Jewish Music in the United States (Brandeis University Press, 2016), co-editor of *Judaism and Emotion: Texts, Performance, Experience* (Peter Lang, 2013), and editor of the book series *Jewish Music Studies* (Peter Lang). Her main fields of research are Jewish music, ethnomusicological gender studies, and music and sustainability.

Notes

1   The article is based on a paper held at the XXIX European Seminar in Ethnomusicology (ESEM) that took place from September 4–8, 2013, in Bern (Switzerland), as well as on a talk held at the Hochschule für Musik, Theater und Medien Hannover (Germany) on January 12, 2015.

2   Louis Lewandowski (April 23, 1821–February 4, 1894) was a Polish composer of Jewish liturgical music who contributed to the reformation of the synagogue service liturgy. His most famous works were composed during his tenure as musical director at the Neue Synagoge in Berlin and his melodies form a substantial part of synagogue services around the world today (see Nemtsov and Hermann 2011: 10–23).

3   Personal interview with François Lilienfeld, October 24, 2012, Bern.

4   As the Jewish communities referred to in this article all follow traditional rite, it is not possible for women to hold a position as rabbi or cantor. The following main protagonists mentioned in this article are all men.

5   Since the General Conference in 2003, the UNESCO Convention for the Safeguarding of the Intangible Cultural Heritage has experienced an extremely rapid ratification, with 161 signatory states in 2014; see http://www.unesco.org/culture/ich/?pg=00024 (accessed May 24, 2015).

6   See Kirshenblatt-Gimblett (2004) and Howard (2012).

7   For a further discussion on the general concept of intangible cultural heritage, see the chapter introduction to this part of the book.

8   Since 2009, this project is part of the canton's intangible cultural heritage program: see *Projekt Doppeltür*: http://www.doppeltuer.ch (accessed October 30, 2018).

9   See e.g. interviews with Gaby Knoch-Mund, Basel, August 2013 and Henry Mugier, Bern, July 2013.

10   Personal interview with Henry Mugier, Bern, July 2013.

11   The term *Schweizer Volkskultur* can in general be translated as Swiss folk culture, but is put in this context on the same level as Swiss intangible cultural heritage (Leimgruber 2010: 183). In this regard, Leimgruber further discusses the oddities of the use of this term with regard to the safeguarding of intangible cultural heritage in Switzerland (ibid.)

12   *Nusach* means "text" or "version" and refers to both the textual structure of synagogue services and to scales and melodic motifs which are sung—without strict

tempo/measure—to the prayer texts. Musicologist Boaz Tarsi defines the term as follows: "By definition, the *steiger* system [*steiger* is an alternative term for *nusach*—SR] does not consist of scales only, but rather constitutes a scalar framework for improvisation on given motifs and other musical characteristics within an intricate network of interrelationships with other musical and extra-musical factors" (Tarsi 2002: 178).

13 Surbtal-Yiddish is a hybrid language consisting of words from Modern High German, Hebrew, Romanic as well as local Swiss-German dialects. Together with the Yiddish language spoken in Alsace and Southern Germany, Surbtal-Yiddish belongs to the so-called Western Yiddish dialects. Today, it is already an almost dead-language that disappeared with the emigration of Jewish families in the nineteenth century.

14 Transcription made by author on the basis of a melody sung by E.B. during personal interview in Zurich, July 2012.

15 The rabbinate Hégenheim, located in Hégenheim, which is a French community in the department of Haut-Rhin in Alsace, existed from 1772 to 1910. Since 1808, the rabbinate was part of the Consistoire Wintzenheim/Colmar. In 1907, the seat of the rabbinate was relocated to Saint-Louis. From 1805 to 1866, the rabbinate Hégenheim was responsible for the surrounding Alsatian Jewish communities, including those of Basel and other places in Switzerland. For further information see http://www.alemannia-judaica.de/hegenheim_synagogue.htm (accessed May 29, 2015).

16 *Jekkische Nusach* is a term that is used by my interview partners.

17 Personal interview with Henry Mugier, Bern, July 2013; see CD-booklet of Chasan Issachar Helman (cantor), Synagogenchor Basel, Michel Uhlmann (conductor), "Ma Tovu—Die lebendige Tradition des gesungenen Gottesdienstes," Synagogenchor Basel (1998): 19–22.

18 See the website of the Basel synagogue choir:
http://web277.login-41.hoststar.ch/Synagogenchor/index.php?option=com_content&task=blogcategory&id=14&Itemid=35 (accessed October 30, 2018).

19 One characteristic feature of traditional Ashkenazi synagogue services (in comparison e.g. to Sephardic services, where no prayer leader exists) is the presence of a cantor leading prayer and song.

20 Cf. track 2 and the CD-booklet of: Chasan Issachar Helman (cantor), Synagogenchor Basel, Michel Uhlmann (conductor), *Ya'aleh*, Synagogenchor Basel (2003).

References

Abelin, Peter. 2012. "Forum Gespräch mit Kantor Jose Kaufmann." *JGB Forum* 91: 2–12.

Ashworth, Gregory John, and Brian J. Graham. 2005. *Senses of Place, Senses of Time*. Aldershot: Ashgate.

Bollag, Peter. 2013. "Vitrinen und Sponsoren: Das Jüdische Museum kämpft um Aufmerksamkeit—und mehr Geld." In *Jüdische Allgemeine: Wochenzeitung für Politik, Kultur, Religion und jüdisches Leben* (August 15, 2013). https://www.juedische-allgemeine.de/juedische-welt/vitrinen-und-sponsoren/ (accessed June 6, 2019).

Brocchi, Davide. 2007. "Die kulturelle Dimension der Nachhaltigkeit." *Cultura21*. http://davidebrocchi.eu/wp-content/uploads/2013/08/2007_dimension_nach-haltigkeit.pdf (accessed June 3, 2015).

Clark, William C., and Nancy M. Dickson. 2003. "Sustainability Science: The Emerging Research Program." *Proceedings of the National Academy of Science USA* 100(14): 8059–61. https://doi.org/10.1073/pnas.1231333100

Dieleman, Hans. 2008. "Sustainability, Art and Reflexivity: Why Artists and Designers May Become Key Change Agents in Sustainability." In *Sustainability: A New Frontier for the Arts and Cultures*, edited by Sacha Kagan and Volker Kirchber, 108–46. Frankfurt am Main: VAS–Verlag für Akademische Schriften.

Fargion, Janet Topp. 2009. "'For My Own Purpose?' Examining Ethnomusicology Field Methods for a Sustainable Music." In *Music and Sustainability*, edited by Jonathan P. J. Stock, 75–93. The World of Music 51(1). Berlin: VWB.

Fenn, John, and Jeff Todd Titon. 2003. "A Conversation with Jeff Todd Titon." *Folklore Forum* 34(1–2): 119–31.

Gerson, Daniel. 2014. "Pluralisierung und Polarisierung. Jüdische Reformbewegungen in der Schweiz 1950–2010." In *Schweizer Judentum im Wandel: Religion und Gemeinschaft zwischen Integration, Selbstbehauptung und Abgrenzung*, edited by Jacques Picard and Daniel Gerson, 99–157. Zürich: Chronos Verlag.

Grant, Catherine. 2012. "Rethinking Safeguarding: Objections and Responses to Protecting and Promoting Endangered Musical Heritage." *Ethnomusicology Forum* 21(1): 39–59. https://doi.org/10.1080/17411912.2012.641733

—2013. "Music Sustainability." In *Oxford Bibliographies in Music*, edited by Bruce Gufstafson. New York: Oxford University Press. https://doi.org/10.1093/obo/9780199757824-0105

—2014. *Music Endangerment: How Language Maintenance Can Help*. Oxford and New York: Oxford University Press.

Howard, Keith, ed. 2012. *Music as Intangible Cultural Heritage: Policy, Ideology, and Practice in the Preservation of East Asian Traditions*. Farnham: Ashgate.

Idelsohn, Abraham Zvi. 1932. *Hebräisch-Orientalischer Melodienschatz*. Leipzig: Breitkopf & Härtel.

Kagan, S. 2008. "Sustainability as a New Frontier for the Arts and Cultures." In *Sustainability: A New Frontier for the Arts and Cultures*, edited by S. Kagan and V. Kirchberg, 14–24. Frankfurt am Main: VAS-Verlag für Akademische Schriften.

Kates, Robert W., William C. Clark, Robert Corell, J. Michael Hall, Carlo C. Jaeger et al. 2001. "Sustainability Science." *Science*, New Series 292(5517): 641–42. https://doi.org/10.2139/ssrn.257359

Kirshenblatt-Gimblett, Barbara. 2004. "Intangible Cultural Heritage as Metacultural Production." *Museum International* 56(1–2): 52–65. https://doi.org/10.1111/j.1350-0775.2004.00458.x

Klein, Amit. 2013. "Singing Their Heart Out: Emotional Excitement in Cantorial Recitatives and Carlebach Nusach." In *Judaism and Emotion: Texts, Performance, Experience*, edited by Sarah Ross, Gabriel Levy, and Soham Al-Suadi, 67–97. New York: Peter Lang.

Leimgruber, Walter. 2010. "Switzerland and the UNESCO Convention on Intangible Cultural Heritage." *Journal of Folklore Research* 47: 161–96. https://doi.org/10.2979/jfr.2010.47.1-2.161

Lewandowski, Louis. 1871. *Kol Rinnah U'T'fillah: Ein- und zweistimmige Gesänge für den israelitischen Gottesdienst*. Frankfurt am Main: J. Kaffmann Verlag.

Lotter, Friedrich, and Michael Wolffsohn. 2000. "Aschkenaz." In *Neues Lexikon des Judentums*, edited by Julius H. Schoeps, 79. Gütersloh: Gütersloher Verlagshaus.

Lowenstein, Steven. 1997. "The Shifting Boundary between Eastern and Western Jewry." *Jewish Social Studies*, New Series 4(1): 60–78. https://doi.org/10.2979/JSS.1997.4.1.60

Moore, Janet. 2005. "Is Higher Education Ready for Transformative Learning? A Question Explored in the Study of Sustainability." *Journal of Transformative Education* 3(1): 76–91. https://doi.org/10.1177/1541344604270862

Nemtsov, Jascha, and Simon Hermann. 2011. *Louis Lewandowski: "Liebe macht das Lied unsterblich."* Jüdische Miniaturen 114. Berlin: Hentrich & Hentrich.

Petocz, Peter, Anna Reid, and Dawn Bennett. 2014. "The Music Workforce, Cultural Heritage, and Sustainability." *International Journal of Cultural and Creative Industries* 1: 4–16.

Picard, Jacques. 2014. "Konfliktuelle Vielfalt und sekundäre Pluralisierung. Zum Werte- und Traditionswandel im Schweizer Judentum." In *Schweizer Judentum im Wandel: Religion und Gemeinschaft zwischen Integration, Selbstbehauptung und Abgrenzung*, edited by Jacques Picard and Daniel Gerson, 11–65. Zürich: Chronos Verlag.

Rapp Buri, Anna. 2008. *Jüdisches Kulturgut in und aus Endingen und Lengnau*, edited by Verein für die Erhaltung der Synagogen und des Friedhofes Endingen-Lengnau. Heidelberg and Ubstadt-Weiher: Verlag Regionalkultur.

Ross, Sarah M. 2014. "Sense or Absence of Nationalism: Searching for a Swiss-Jewish Musical Identity." In *Music and Minorities from Around the World: Research, Documentation and Interdisciplinary Study*, edited by Ursula Hemetek, Essica Marks, and Adelaida Reyes, 115–39. Newcastle upon Tyne: Cambridge Scholars Publishing.

Scammon, Denise. 2012. "Recognizing Cultural Sustainability." https://specialdee.wordpress.com/2012/04/07/recognizing-cultural-sustainability/ (accessed October 30, 2018).

Schleifer, Eliyahu. 2013. *Samuel Naumbourg: Kantor der Französisch-Jüdischen Emanzipation*. Jüdische Miniaturen 136. Berlin: Hentrich & Hentrich.

Stein, Peter. 2008. *Lebendiges und untergegangenes jüdisches Brauchtum: Brauch gestern und heute, Brauch hier und dort, mit besonderer Berücksichtigung der schweizerischen Judendörfer Endingen und Lengnau*, edited by Verein für die Erhaltung der Synagogen und des Friedhofes Endingen-Lengnau. Heidelberg and Ubstadt-Weiher: Verlag Regionalkultur.

Swart, Rob, Paul Raskin, John Robinson, Robert Kates, and William C. Clark. 2002. "Critical Challenges for Sustainability Science." *Science*, New Series 297(5589): 1994–95. https://doi.org/10.1126/science.297.5589.1994

Tarsi, Boaz. 2002. "Observations on Practices of 'Nusach' in America." *Asia Music* 33(2): 175–219.

Thorsby, David. 2011. "Cultural Capital." In *A Handbook of Cultural Economics*, edited by Ruth Towse, 142–46. 2nd edn. Cheltenham, UK and Northampton, MA: Edward Elgar.

Titon, Jeff Todd. 2009a. "Economy, Ecology, and Music: An Introduction." In *Music and Sustainability*, edited by Jonathan P. J. Stock, 5–15. The World of Music 51(1). Berlin: VWB.

—2009b. "Sustainability and Music: China Lecture 1 Summary." http://sustainablemusic.blogspot.ch/2009/11/sustainability-and-music-china-lecture.html (November 21, 2009) (accessed June 3, 2015).

—2009c. "Music and Sustainability: An Ecological Viewpoint." In *Music and Sustainability*, edited by Jonathan P. J. Stock, 119–137. The World of Music 51(1). Berlin: VWB.

World Commission on Environment and Development. 1987. *Our Common Future*. Oxford and New York: Oxford University Press.

Yim, Dawnhee. 2004. "Living Human Treasures and the Protection of Intangible Cultural Heritage: Experience and Challenges." *ICOM NEWS* 4: 10–12. http://archives.icom.museum/pdf/E_news2004/p10_2004-4.pdf (accessed May 25, 2015).

Recordings

Helman, Issachar. 1998. *Ma Tovu—Die lebendige Tradition des gesungenen Gottesdienstes*. With Synagogenchor Basel and Michel Uhlmann (conductor). CD. Basel: Verlag Victor Goldschmidt.

—2003. *Ya'aleh*. With Synagogenchor Basel and Michel Uhlmann (conductor). CD. Basel: Verlag Victor Goldschmidt.

Part IV

Intangible Cultural Heritage: Case Studies

Introduction to Part IV

Sarah M. Ross
Hannover University of Music, Drama, and Media, Germany

> The documentation of intangible cultural heritage is one of the measures mentioned in the UNESCO Convention … and stands for what ethnomusicologists have undertaken for decades through participatory observation in everyday life, audio-visual recordings of music making, and interviews with practitioners of traditions. (Camp et al., this volume)

Following the previous discussions on the politics of intangible cultural heritage, the final chapters of this book contain three contrasting ethnomusicological case studies about various performing arts, including music, dance, singing, and festivals, as one domain of ICH as defined by the Convention. Thus, and according to ethnomusicologist Marc-Antoine Camp, it does not come as a surprise that one unifying element of these case studies is the application of fieldwork as a central research method, through which the authors gradually extract the concepts, expectations, influences, and discourses surrounding the history of musical practices as important cultural assets in need of preservation, and their impact on the UNESCO List of Intangible Cultural Heritage. Beyond that, the ethnographic approach to understanding intangible cultural heritage allows the researcher to position her-/himself within the field, thereby taking a critical and self-reflexive perspective within the context of heritagization of musical traditions.

Questions that guide the chapters in this final part of the book are: How do UNESCO's efforts "interact with preexisting local, regional and state efforts to conserve and promote culture" (Bendix, Eggert, and Peselmann

2013: 11)? How are "cultural and social politics of identity, belonging and exclusion" mediated? (Kuutma 2013: 2). Who defines musical heritage, and who has control over the conceptualization of its stewardship? What concept of musical heritage do performers share, and do they see themselves as an integral part of intangible cultural heritage? Is there an alternative approach to applied work, which puts the focus on the safeguarding of real human well-being and freedom rather than on a constructed vision of ICH?

In order to safeguard the performing arts, most countries that have ratified the Convention have paid considerable attention to their documentation. However, as the following chapters will demonstrate, documenting intangible cultural heritage is only one element of safeguarding. Another important and common focus is the notion that "safeguarding performing arts is not 'freezing' traditions in a certain moment of time, but making those heritages live," as Le Thi Minh Ly (2008) states. Living heritage, in this regard, means that intangible cultural heritage

> lives sustainably and is transmitted from generations to generations thanks to diverse means and conditions. Therefore, "living heritage" is a notion that needs to be conceived and practiced in a thorough manner for the sake of the practicality of the safeguarding of heritage in contemporary life. (Ly 2008: 66)

The authors critically examine the limitations of the concept of ICH, on the one hand, and the measures to implement the Convention in different nation-states on the other. Opening this part is Matthew Machin-Autenrieth's chapter "Flamenco for Andalusia, Flamenco for Humanity: Regionalization and Intangible Cultural Heritage in Spain." There has been a significant increase in the number of musical traditions recognized as intangible cultural heritage, and ethnomusicologists have begun to critically examine the safeguarding of musical traditions and the impact of ICH politics on musical communities. In the Spanish context, as Machin-Autenrieth demonstrates, flamenco is a pertinent case study. Following a failed attempt in 2005, on November 16, 2010, flamenco was recognized as Intangible Cultural Heritage and inscribed in UNESCO's Representative List of the Intangible Cultural Heritage of Humanity. The declaration was met with jubilation, particularly at the institutional level and in the media. However, while flamenco is recognized as a Spanish form of heritage, it is most commonly associated with the autonomous region of Andalusia. As such, the declaration strengthened the Andalusian government's project of "regionalization" and identity building, thereby consolidating flamenco as a cultural marker for Andalusia and a "gift" for humanity. Machin-Autenrieth consequently examines the impact of the UNESCO declaration on regional musical policy in Andalusia, including firstly the circumstances surrounding flamenco's acceptance as Intangible Cultural Heritage in 2010 and its failure in 2005, and secondly exploring the effects of the declaration at an institutional level, with particular focus on Andalusia's own heritage inventories, education system, and culture industry. These effects are contextualized within the wider process of regionalization in Andalusia in the twenty-first century. Finally, by drawing upon ethnographic research conducted in Granada in 2012, he alludes to points of conflict surrounding the declaration, with particular focus on the *zambra*, a local performance style and flamenco sub-tradition, and argues that flamenco's development as heritage runs the risk of stifling local flamenco diversity at the expense of a unified regional tradition.

The subsequent chapter by Thomas Beardslee on "Questioning Safeguarding: Heritage and Capabilities at Jemaa el Fnaa Square, Morocco," discusses the problems that emerged from the Declaration of Masterpieces and the successes of the 2003 Convention (UNESCO 2003). Since then, the UNESCO paradigms of "intangible cultural heritage" and "safeguarding" have become influential concepts in international, national, and local cultural policy. However, as Beardslee argues, "safeguarding" seeks to impose onto the flow of human activity a way of thinking that is better suited to physical sites: culture as a static edifice and under threat of erosion, with safeguarding as a means to "shore up." This results in an awkward fit between theory and practice, leading to projects with unattainable goals, poorly directed resources, and limited benefits for their intended recipients, as Beardslee demonstrates. His chapter is based on one year's fieldwork among open-air performers at Jemaa el Fnaa Square in Marrakech, Morocco. The square was in many ways the genesis of UNESCO's Intangible Cultural Heritage project, and serves as a useful case study to illustrate the effects (or lack thereof) of safeguarding within a community of performers, thereby problematizing the concepts of heritage and safeguarding, and proposing Amartya Sen's and Martha Nussbaum's "capabilities approach" as an alternative framework for dealing with cultural heritage, intangible or otherwise. The capabilities approach seeks ways of enhancing the possible range of choices and abilities of individuals and communities, rather than the prescribing of particular activities. This approach is well suited to projects relating to culture, and its fluid and dynamic nature thereby resists static, prescriptive notions of "heritage." Beardslee further discusses how the idea of capabilities could result in more effective action, addressing both individuals' capabilities deficits and the hopes of those wanting to see their traditions continue.

The final chapter by Zuzana Jurková, "The *Verbuňk* under the Pressure of World Fame," examines the inscription of a Czech performance practice in the UNESCO Intangible Cultural Heritage List, with focus on the so-called *verbuňk*, a contemporary male dance featuring singing. In recent decades, *verbuňk* has not only been shaped by local concepts of tradition, the expectations of various groups of spectators, and the meanings which performers of the *verbuňk* attribute to it, but it has also been influenced by the idea of intangible cultural heritage. In 2005, the Slovácko *verbuňk* (Slovácko is a region in southeastern Moravia) became the first cultural phenomenon in the Czech region to be included in the Representative List of the Intangible Cultural Heritage of Humanity. While this dance has surely existed for a long time, it was only in the past decades that it attracted attention among various folklorists. Moreover, since the mid-1980s, the largest Czech folklore festival—the Slovácko celebrations in Strážnice—featured a contest for the best Slovak *verbuňk* dancer, which is organized by the National Institute of Folk Culture (NÚLK) in Strážnice, a folklore institute publishing academic and popular materials, including those dedicated to the *verbuňk*, and it was here that the initiative for its inscription in the UNESCO List emerged. Subsequently, NÚLK materials and affiliates have further nurtured this regional folklore movement via, for instance, *verbuňk* lessons, which are non-existent in other Czech regions. There is no doubt that these initiatives influence the meaning of the *verbuňk*, including a decontextualized use of the word *verbuňk*, rendering the dance as a kind of invented tradition. Yet, despite the century-long existence of Slovácko folklore in many towns of the Czech Republic, the *verbuňk* is not performed anywhere else, which is why this cultural phenomenon is inseparably connected to a dense network of local culture and tradition.

References

Bendix, Regina F., Aditya Eggert, and Arnika Peselmann. 2013. "Introduction: Heritage Regimes and the State." In *Heritage Regimes and the State*, edited by Regina F. Bendix, Aditya Eggert, and Arnika Peselmann, 11–20. Göttingen: Universitätsverlag Göttingen. https://doi.org/10.4000/books.gup.366

Kuutma, Kristin. 2013. "Concepts and Contingencies in Heritage Politics." In *Anthropological Perspectives on Intangible Cultural Heritage*, edited by Lourdes Arizpe and Cristina Amescua, 1–15. Cham, Heidelberg, New York, Dordrecht, and London: Springer. https://doi.org/10.1007/978-3-319-00855-4_1

Ly, Le Thi Minh. 2008. "Introduction to Performing Arts in the Context of Sustainable Cultural Tourism." In *Safeguarding Intangible Cultural Heritage and Sustainable Cultural Tourism: Opportunities and Challenges*, UNESCO-EIIHCAP Regional Meeting Hué, Viet Nam, December 11–13, 2007, 66–67. Bangkok: UNESCO Bangkok.

UNESCO. 2003. "Text of the Convention for the Safeguarding of the Intangible Cultural Heritage." Paris: UNESCO. https://ich.unesco.org/en/convention (accessed October 15, 2018).

Chapter 13

Flamenco for Andalusia, Flamenco for Humanity: Regionalization and Intangible Cultural Heritage in Spain

Matthew Machin-Autenrieth

> Flamenco is our most genuine cultural identity; it is the art of our
> land, a symbol with which we identify ourselves as Andalusians
> within and outside of our borders.[1]

This statement appears on the website of the *Instituto Andaluz del Flamenco*
("Andalusian Institute of Flamenco"), an arm of the Andalusian government's
Department of Culture. Charged with the development and diffusion of flamenco within and beyond the borders of Andalusia, this agency has come to
represent the ongoing institutional support for flamenco. In recent years, the
Andalusian government has invested heavily in the regional development of
the tradition across three performative practices (song, guitar, and dance),
both as a symbol of identity for Andalusians and as a cultural "ambassador" for the region abroad. The development of flamenco in Andalusia is a
reflection of a wider trend across many of the seventeen autonomous communities of Spain towards the consolidation of distinct regional identities.
In November 2010, the Andalusian "regionalist" project gained an international dimension when flamenco was inscribed in UNESCO's Representative
List of the Intangible Cultural Heritage of Humanity. While this inscription
recognizes flamenco as Spanish cultural heritage, its impact is most keenly
felt in Andalusia. Flamenco's official status as a universal art form is intricately tied up with issues regarding the representation of regional identities
in Spain. The inscription highlights the cultural significance of flamenco for
the Andalusian region despite its relevance for other regions in Spain.

In this chapter, I examine the impact of the UNESCO inscription on the "regionalization" of flamenco (i.e., its development by regional institutions),[2] framed by the wider context of identity politics in Spain. Flamenco's institutional recognition as heritage has been a goal for scholars and governmental personnel in Andalusia since the 1990s, yet only recently has it gained national and international status as Intangible Cultural Heritage (henceforth referred to as ICH). Drawing on theoretical perspectives in heritage studies, I trace the circumstances surrounding flamenco's recognition as ICH, as well as exploring how this status has been instrumentalized by the Andalusian government for social, political, and economic ends. However, the conflation of cultural heritage with geo-political agendas can create points of conflict. Indeed, the ways in which the Andalusian government has capitalized upon the inscription in its own project of regional identity building has received criticism from some quarters. Drawing on field research in Granada, I briefly focus on one case study of the *zambra*—a flamenco genre and context of performance in the Sacromonte neighborhood of the city. Arguably, the *zambra* demonstrates the shortcomings of the Andalusian government's implementation of the UNESCO declaration. By establishing flamenco as a unified, regional, and global art form, the Andalusian government's instrumentalization of the UNESCO declaration may in fact marginalize smaller components of the tradition and effectively curtail its diversity.

Heritage Studies and Regionalism in Ethnomusicology

The study of ICH has become more prominent in ethnomusicology, especially since the ratification of UNESCO's new Convention for the Safeguarding of the Intangible Cultural Heritage of Humanity in 2003.[3] A number of scholars have sought to analyze critically the impact of heritage policy on the safeguarding of musical traditions around the globe. This present volume adds to a growing body of scholarship that has emerged in recent years dealing with the implications of music as heritage in both its tangible and intangible forms (Grant 2012; Graeff 2014; Howard 2012a; Kirshenblatt-Gimblett 1995; Seeger 2009; Wong 2009; Norton and Matsumoto 2019). One important aspect of this field of scholarly pursuit is the ways in which musical heritage is instrumentalized for political purposes, particularly in the context of territorial identity building. In his excellent volume *Music as Intangible Cultural Heritage*, Keith Howard (2012b) argues that top-down institutional approaches have dominated in heritage preservation policies across the region. In East Asia, the process of heritage preservation, Howard contends, has been used for the advancement of identity politics: "Efforts to preserve can be considered ... as a nostalgic appeal to hang onto the way things were, or as a regionalist or nationalist effort to retain a local, regional or state identity against outside infiltration" (2012b: 7–8).

The sub-national region is one context in which the advancement of identity politics through heritage preservation is particularly polemical. Matt Gillan (2012) considers how the Japanese Law for the Protection of Cultural Properties, a forerunner to UNESCO's own policy, has played out in a regional context—the island of Okinawa—considering "a region-led approach to cultural heritage within the framework of national law" (2012: 213). Gillan argues that the local government's implementation of the heritage law has served to consolidate Okinawa's "belonging" to the Japanese nation-state, as well as being used to demarcate regional identity vis-à-vis national identity. I contribute to this regional debate by exploring the impact of UNESCO and national policy in the context of a European region— Andalusia. Flamenco's recognition as ICH at the state level appears to be overshadowed by the Andalusian government's own political interests in the tradition as a marker of regional identity. As such, the inscription has served to strengthen the regional development of flamenco, bringing into focus existing debates regarding the nature of regional and national identities in Spain. As I explore below, the flamenco case highlights issues regarding the implementation of UNESCO policy and the resulting homogenization of musical practices (Graeff 2014).

In addition to the growing body of ethnomusicological scholarship concerning ICH, theoretical perspectives in the wider field of heritage studies are also useful when examining flamenco's status as ICH and its implications for the regional development of the tradition.[4] In the context of flamenco, it is evident that its recognition as ICH by UNESCO is being instrumentalized in the Andalusian context as a form of cultural and economic capital, particularly when it comes to the political significance and touristic appeal of the tradition. As such, the "heritagization" (i.e., the consolidation and promotion of heritage in specific contexts) of flamenco can be viewed as a form of cultural practice (Smith and Akagawa 2009), one that is being utilized in the service of an ongoing regionalist project in Andalusia aimed at strengthening regional identity and promoting it outside of the region. I will consider the ways in which flamenco's status as ICH is intricately tied up with this process of regionalization—that is, the creation of regional institutions within a nation-state and the consolidation of regional identities vis-à-vis the nation.

Before considering the UNESCO declaration for flamenco, it is important to sketch out the regional relevance of the tradition and current governmental efforts aimed at its development.

Flamenco and Regional Identity

The relationship between flamenco and Andalusian regional identity has a long and contentious history, the tradition being closely linked with the emergence of Andalusian regionalism. Since the late nineteenth century, flamenco's relevance as an identity symbol has grown in tandem with calls for greater autonomy within Andalusia, particularly given the tradition's supposed origins in the region.[5] Although flamenco has been and continues to be viewed as a unique manifestation of *Gitano* ("Gypsy") identity (Mitchell 1994; Steingress 1993; Washabaugh 1996), its association with Andalusian identity has always been an integral element of its wider social significance. Indeed, it is difficult to separate flamenco's *Gitano* and Andalusian significance given the conflation of an exoticized Gypsy identity with representations of Andalusian-ness, particularly as a by-product of nineteenth-century European Romanticism (Charnon-Deutsch 2004). Up until the start of the Spanish Civil War in 1936, flamenco was viewed as a unique component of Andalusian identity, a view that was advanced by a number of notable Andalusians including Manuel de Falla (1876–1946), Federico García Lorca (1898–1936), and the "father of Andalusian regionalism," Blas Infante (1885–1936).[6]

With the onset of the Civil War in 1936 and Francisco Franco's (1892–1975) ascension to power in 1939, flamenco's regional associations were suppressed as it became repackaged as a national tradition. In the new nationalist social order, flamenco was "carefully cultivated, cosmetically retouched, and strategically orchestrated in such a way as to present an image of flamenco as a component of Spanish national identity" (Washabaugh 1996: 162). When Franco died in 1975, Spain went into a swift process of political and social transition. The question of regional autonomy that had begun in the nineteenth century and reached its zenith in the Second Republic (1931–1939), moved center stage as decentralization went hand-in-hand with Spain's transition to democracy. As a result of the decentralization process, seventeen autonomous communities were created with varying degrees of power,[7] with Andalusia gaining its autonomous status in 1981. Initially, flamenco had less of a role to play in "official" representations of Andalusian identity given its former associations with the Franco regime (Washabaugh 2012: 83). However, as the dust settled on Spain's nationalist past, the representation of regional cultural distinctiveness has resurfaced as a prominent element of Spanish politics.

Since the 1990s, the Andalusian government has started to invest in the regional development of flamenco, particularly through state-funded festivals and educational policies (Gutiérrez Mate 2010; López Castro 2004; Washabaugh 2012: 85–89). This process is part of a wider ongoing regionalization project in Andalusia, aimed at consolidating autonomous powers and reinforcing regional identity (Machin-Autenrieth 2015, 2017a). The institutional endorsement of flamenco culminated in 2005 with the creation of the Andalusian Institute of Flamenco. This agency was specifically designed for the development and dissemination of flamenco, and coordinates the flamenco activities of all other governmental departments. In 2007, flamenco was also included in the revised Andalusian Statute of Autonomy, granting the government "exclusive competency" (*competencia exclusiva*) over the development of the tradition (Junta de Andalucía 2007).[8] This inclusion can only be understood within the wider context of identity politics in Spain. Around this time, a number of regions in the country were seeking further devolution of autonomous powers and greater recognition of regional identities in what some scholars have referred to as a "second wave of decentralisation" (Keating and Wilson 2009; see also Delledonne and Martinico 2011). Since the new statute, the Andalusian government has invested a significant amount of resources in developing flamenco across the public domain as a marker of regional identity both within Andalusia and abroad. The recognition of flamenco as ICH, while acknowledging the tradition's "universal" status, underwrites this ongoing project of regional identity building.

Flamenco for Andalusia, Flamenco for Humanity

Prior to the 2010 inscription, flamenco had already started to be established as a form of heritage according to national and regional legislation.[9] In 1985, the *Patrimonio Histórico Español* ("Spanish Historical Heritage") register was implemented where elements of tangible heritage were recognized as *Bienes de Interés Cultural* ("Assets of Cultural Interest"). Subsequently, regional autonomies were permitted to develop their own heritage laws and catalogs given Spain's decentralization. Like Gillan (2012) has shown in the Japanese context, the Andalusian government embraced a regional approach within the wider framework of national heritage policy, and in 1991 it adopted its own heritage law, the *Ley de Patrimonio Histórico de Andalucía* ("Historical Heritage of Andalusia Act"), with elements being included in the *Catálogo General del Patrimonio Histórico Andaluz* ("General Catalogue of Andalusian Historical Heritage"). However, despite an increase in international rhetoric surrounding ICH during the 1990s and early 2000s, the Spanish government was slow to recognize intangible forms of heritage in its own heritage policy, instead focusing on tangible, monumental, and aesthetic elements (Zabala 2013). This perpetuated an "authorized heritage discourse" that characterized much of UNESCO's own heritage policy prior to the implementation of ICH and from which UNESCO sought to move away (Smith 2006; Smith and Akagawa 2009: 3).

Since the 1990s, a number of scholars have sought to raise the profile of flamenco as heritage according to the Historical Heritage of Andalusia Act (Cruces Roldán 2001, 2002; García Plata 1996). A key problem, however, has been how to recognize flamenco according to legislation that is heavily biased towards tangible forms of heritage (Cruces Roldán 2002). In 1999, the flamenco scholar and advisor to the Andalusian government, Cristina Cruces Roldán, facilitated the recognition of recordings by the singer Niña de los Peines (1890–1969) as *Bien de Intéres Cultural*. Nonetheless, this small step forward in flamenco's recognition as heritage did not address issues regarding the reconciliation of the intangible with the tangible. Following the declaration of the recordings, Cruces Roldán (2001, 2002, 2014) wrote extensively regarding both the intangible and tangible components of the flamenco tradition, arguing for a more fluid perception of heritage that would enable a pluralistic practice such as flamenco to be recognized according to Andalusia's existing heritage legislation. Underscoring the regionalist rhetoric at this time, Cruces Roldán argued that flamenco's recognition as heritage was necessary "in order to know and value [it] as a fundamental identity marker of our culture and, therefore, as a common heritage of all Andalusians" (2002: 193).

With Andalusia's new Statute of Autonomy in 2007 came amendments to existing heritage legislation that facilitated the incorporation of intangible elements and paved the way for flamenco's recognition as ICH by UNESCO in 2010, as well as its inscription in the regional heritage list (see below). It is important to recognize, however, that the 2010 inscription was not the first attempt. In 2004, a nomination was put forward for flamenco's recognition as ICH under the former Masterpieces of the Oral and Intangible Heritage of Humanity convention. This nomination was not just for flamenco, but rather a joint application for flamenco and Arab-Andalusian classical music from North Africa (*música andalusí*), traditions believed to have originated in Muslim Spain or "al-Andalus" (711–1492). This application received joint support from the Andalusian government and the governments of Algeria, Morocco, and Tunisia (Cruces Roldán, personal communication, April 30, 2012; Paetzold 2009; Washabaugh 2012: 94). However, as Washabaugh notes, the nomination did not meet UNESCO's stringent criteria at that time: "Specifically, UNESCO back then, required evidence that flamenco music is a homogeneous cultural phenomenon conserved from the past but threatened with extinction in the present, and potentially beneficial for all humankind in the future" (Washabaugh 2012: 94).

The second application for flamenco was submitted in August 2009 and approved by UNESCO on November 16, 2010 under the new convention, a day that is now recognized in Andalusia as *Día del Flamenco* ("Flamenco Day"). The 2003 Convention consists of two primary lists that attempt to reflect the breadth of intangible heritage worldwide (UNESCO 2003). The first is the List of Intangible Cultural Heritage in Need of Urgent Safeguarding in which traditions at risk of disappearing are included, with more attention being paid to immediate safeguarding measures. The second is the Representative List of the Intangible Cultural Heritage of Humanity, which consists of well-established traditions that represent the global diversity of heritage and that raise awareness of the importance of ICH.[10] Flamenco was included in the second list given its existing vitality as a tradition and its international reach. The flamenco application consisted of a detailed nomination file explaining how the tradition meets UNESCO's criteria for recognition as ICH (UNESCO 2010), a video documentary, a portfolio of representative photographs, and 300 letters of support from flamenco communities.[11]

When analyzing the nomination file, it is interesting to uncover the identity politics permeating the text. As a state party that has ratified the UNESCO Convention, Spain put forward the nomination for flamenco as one of its most representative forms of ICH particularly at an international level. However, as is outlined in the nomination file itself (UNESCO 2010), ICH policy in Spain has been devolved to the regional governments so that they can advance their own cultural representations within the framework of national and international heritage policy. As such, the flamenco nomination file refers to the fundamental role of the regional governments of Andalusia, Extremadura, and Murcia in designing and implementing the declaration. Yet, at the helm is the Andalusian government with the region being described as the "heartland of flamenco" and the majority of the safeguarding and development strategies pertaining to Andalusia and/or being implemented by the Andalusian government (UNESCO 2010). Despite acknowledging the wider roots of the tradition in other regions of Spain and its inextricable connection to the *Gitano* community, the detailed breakdown of safeguarding measures demonstrates the monopoly that the Andalusian government has over flamenco's heritagization (UNESCO 2010: 9–16). However, flamenco is also described as a "socially responsible art form" that attests to the diversity of heritage worldwide (UNESCO 2010: 7). It is constructed as a truly universal tradition which, given its supposed roots in Andalusia's multicultural heritage, embodies a respect for tolerance and diversity at a local and a universal level.

This dual-track construction of flamenco for Andalusia (as a culturally-embedded tradition) and for humanity (as a universal art form) was also reflected in the promotional strategies for the UNESCO inscription. The Andalusian government invested heavily in marketing campaigns prior to the inscription both within the region and abroad. On Andalusian public television a flamenco series called *El Sol, la Sal, el Son* ("The Sun, the Salt, the Sound") was released the day before the inscription as recognition of flamenco's nomination. Moreover, the Andalusian Institute of Flamenco initiated a promotional campaign called *Flamenco Soy* ("I am Flamenco") that aimed to raise the profile of flamenco's nomination as ICH and to receive signatures of support within Andalusia and beyond. The campaign encapsulated the ethos behind the UNESCO inscription—it reinforced the Andalusian roots of the tradition reflected in its institutional support and "regionalist" rhetoric, as well as acknowledging the universal reach of the tradition in the campaign's international marketing strategies.

Implementing the UNESCO Inscription

For Andalusian institutions and the flamenco community, the inscription was regarded as a resounding success. It consolidated and strengthened the existing institutional development of flamenco, and was viewed by the Andalusian government as an extension of the tradition's inclusion in the Andalusian Statute of Autonomy in 2007. Immediately following the inscription, there was an abundance of media reports (including the Andalusian Institute of Flamenco's own publication *La Nueva Alboreá*) expressing jubilation over the announcement and its relevance for Andalusia. The then Andalusian President, José Antonio Griñán, even came forward to recognize the success of the inscription and flamenco's role as a marker of regional identity for citizens and abroad.[12] The institutional commitment to flamenco following the inscription is best exemplified by the first international conference on flamenco held in Seville in November 2011 (not surprisingly, this event coincided with "Flamenco Day"). Organized by the Andalusian Institute of Flamenco, the conference attracted a number of prominent scholars, some of whom have had roles in the institutional development of flamenco. Using the UNESCO inscription as a basis, the conference was intended as a forum to debate the structure of the flamenco industry and how it could be developed further in light of the tradition's status as ICH.

The conclusions of the conference were published online by the Andalusian Institute of Flamenco in the *Libro Blanco del Flamenco* ("White Paper for Flamenco"),[13] a policy framework that is arguably the most tangible representation of institutional support for the tradition following the UNESCO inscription. The *Libro Blanco* outlines three target areas for the consolidation of flamenco as a culture industry and a symbol of regional identity within Andalusia and beyond: (i) the strengthening of the institutional framework for flamenco, including greater interaction between public and private spheres; (ii) the conservation of flamenco and its recognition as heritage according to existing policies; and (iii) the diffusion and promotion of flamenco as a lucrative culture industry within and outside of Andalusia. Development strategies that fall into these three areas are diverse, and some measures were already being implemented prior to the UNESCO inscription. Here, I will focus on three particular strategies that have received more attention since the inscription: heritage policy, education, and the flamenco festival circuit.

As discussed above, the 2010 inscription was not the first official recognition of flamenco as heritage. The recordings of Niña de los Peines marked a turning point in flamenco's status as heritage according to existing national and regional frameworks. As a result of changes to Andalusia's own heritage policy in the 2007 statute and the UNESCO inscription, flamenco is now starting to be included in Andalusia's own regional heritage list. The inscription requires that state parties ensure elements of heritage are recognized and cataloged according to national heritage policies. In the Spanish context, the central government has been relatively "hands-off," leaving the Andalusian government free to harness its own autonomous powers in the preservation of heritage in order to integrate flamenco according to existing legislative frameworks. Following the UNESCO inscription, a handful of flamenco forms/sub-genres have been recognized as *Bien de Interés Cultural* such as the *Escuela Sevillana de Baile* ("Sevillian School of Dance"), a particular style of dancing that is unique to Seville. While seemingly an act of symbolic recognition, these internal heritage declarations seek to ensure that these smaller components of the tradition continue to be developed in educational, performance, and academic contexts across the region.

In terms of education, the UNESCO inscription has strengthened an existing initiative to integrate flamenco across all levels of the Andalusian public educational system. Keenly aware of the power of early education in the transmission of a particular ideological position and identity, Andalusian officials and scholars have sought to embed flamenco in the regional social consciousness through educational means. Since the 1980s, there have been calls to include flamenco in the educational system following the devolution of powers to Andalusia.[14] However, this endeavor has frequently met with opposition from teachers and there has been a lack of agreement on exactly how flamenco should be integrated into the educational system (Washabaugh 2012: 85–89). In part, the rejection of flamenco in the educational context stems from negative stereotypes surrounding the tradition, particularly its perceived historical links to prostitution, drinking, and social marginality (Cristina Cruces Roldán, personal communication, April 30, 2012). The UNESCO inscription, therefore, is seen as a way of dissociating flamenco from its negative stereotypes given its international status as a form of human heritage. In May 2014, the *Orden por la que se establecen Medidas para la Inclusión del Flamenco en el Sistema Educativo Andaluz* ("Agenda for Establishing Measures for the Inclusion of Flamenco in the Andalusian Education System") was finally published having been drafted in 2011.[15] Citing flamenco's status as ICH as a guiding principle, this document outlines a number of initiatives including the publication of resources for teachers, the creation of an online portal for flamenco education (which has recently been completed[16]) and extracurricular activities such as workshops. It is still too soon to assess the extent to which these measures will advance flamenco's integration into the Andalusian educational system, but it is apparent that the tradition is a key point of focus in the ongoing project of regional identity building particularly through educational means.

The impact of the inscription is most keenly felt in the development of flamenco as a culture industry, particularly in terms of the consolidation of the tradition's existing festival circuit and tourism. In the safeguarding measures section of the nomination file, one of the main areas of focus is the development of festivals within and outside of the region. The file states that approximately 12.5 million euros will be spent on the consolidation and development of Andalusian and international festivals.[17] At the regional level, a large portion of the funding has been directed towards two large-scale performance circuits, namely *Flamenco Viene del Sur* ("Flamenco Comes from the South") and the *Ballet Flamenco de Andalucía* ("Flamenco Ballet of Andalusia"). These productions showcase the biggest names in the industry and are seen as the flagship events of the Andalusian Institute of Flamenco. They are held across all the major cities of Andalusia and as such use flamenco as a way of unifying the eight provinces of the region. At an international level, the UNESCO inscription underscores the continued development of European and American festivals, using the ICH "branding" as a way of legitimizing the increased internationalization of flamenco as a universal art form and as a way of promoting Andalusian culture abroad through tourism.

The UNESCO inscription has played an important role in consolidating the notion that flamenco embodies universal human values of democracy, tolerance, and creativity. Yet, the declaration is also underwritten by the concept of flamenco's relevance for Andalusian culture and identity: a "home-grown" product of the region that radiates out to the rest of the world as a form of universal heritage. Despite flamenco's roots in other parts of Spain, Andalusia has emerged as the crucible of the tradition's artistic creativity. As such, while the inscription packages flamenco in the guise of a universal art form, it will in fact serve to legitimize an ongoing regionalist project aimed at developing flamenco as a central symbol of Andalusian identity. The heritagization of flamenco establishes the tradition as a form of cultural capital (in the mobilization of regional identification) and as a form of economic capital (in the development of the culture and tourism industries). Like Gillan's (2012) research in the Okinawan context, flamenco's declaration as ICH is intricately involved in regional politics and the struggle for autonomous self-representation within a decentralized state. The Spanish and Japanese examples put into question an established understanding of heritage within the context of the nation-state, necessitating a deeper look into the complex dimensions of national vis-à-vis regional politics in the heritagization process.

Points of Conflict

This interplay between heritage and regional politics carries with it a number of contentious issues, some of which were apparent during my field research in Granada.[18] While the flamenco declaration is still relatively recent and its full impact is yet to be understood, a number of narratives emerged during my fieldwork that revealed ambivalent responses to the inscription that also reflect wider concerns regarding the regionalization of flamenco. One ongoing issue is the lack of recognition of other Spanish regions (most notably Extremadura and Murcia) in the development of flamenco, with the Andalusian government having effectively monopolized the industry. Within Andalusia itself, however, the relevance of flamenco for conceptions of identity is often problematic. For some Andalusians (like many Spaniards in general), flamenco is not considered to be part of their personal identification and they fear that the UNESCO inscription will only serve the Andalusian "nationalist" cause,[19] further ingraining flamenco into the regional consciousness and obscuring other readings of Andalusian identity and culture (Machin-Autenrieth 2015). Flamenco artists, producers, and aficionados also have their own concerns. Some people I interviewed criticized the monopoly of the Andalusian government over the flamenco industry that in effect marginalizes certain artists and provinces, a process that they believe will be exacerbated by the UNESCO inscription.

The inscription also raises issues surrounding exactly what type of flamenco is being supported. The flamenco tradition in its three main performance mediums (song, dance, and guitar) is immensely diverse, consisting of a plethora of "mini"-styles called *palos* that consist of their own lyrical, musical, and kinaesthetic features. These *palos* are often associated with particular locations (within and beyond Andalusia) and/or artists, and can also be grouped into larger categories such as the *cante jondo* ("deep song") repertoire.[20] Arguably, flamenco can also be understood as being comprised of different sub-genres, distinct "mini"-traditions that trace a continuum between Andalusian folk traditions and flamenco itself.[21] One pertinent example is the *zambra*, a performance context and genre of flamenco unique to the Sacromonte neighborhood of Granada. As a performance context, the *zambra* refers to a number of traditional caves that scatter the hills of Sacromonte where *Gitano* communities have performed to predominantly tourist audiences since the nineteenth century. As a genre, the *zambra* (or more usually the *zambra gitana*) refers to a re-enactment of traditional *Gitano* wedding rituals, comprising numerous choreographed group dances that depict various stages of the wedding.[22] For some scholars and aficionados, the *zambra gitana* is placed outside of the flamenco canon due to its folkloric characteristics and group dances.

As a performance context, the *zambra* survives and is the prominent face of the flamenco tourism industry in Granada.[23] The various caves in the

Sacromonte neighborhood, usually linked to *Gitano* families, stage performances to audiences from around the world in an intimate setting that proves
to be a unique experience for those who attend. Audience members sit around
the edge of the cave with musicians seated at the back and the dancers performing in the middle, integrating the audience members into the space of the
performance. However, I quickly learnt that the majority of the performances
in these caves consisted of the typical repertoire that can be found in any
performance venue in Andalusia and beyond.[24] Very few artists perform the
traditional *zambra gitana*, instead opting for popular *palos* that attract audiences and that are deemed more "virtuosic" or "creative." Nonetheless, some
artists do hold onto the *zambra gitana*, viewing it as a distinct manifestation
of the flamenco tradition that is unique to Granada and more specifically
Sacromonte and its *Gitano* community.

The decline of the *zambra gitana* is a result of numerous social and
cultural forces. In part, it stems from devastating floods in Sacromonte in
1963 and the forced evacuations of *Gitano* communities, which negatively
impacted on the flamenco industry of the area. During the 1990s, tourism
began to blossom again in Sacromonte and with it came a resurgence in flamenco performances. However, the newer generation of artists was attracted
by and trained in modern flamenco styles, and despite continuing the lineage
of Sacromonte's *Gitano* community they now usually shun forms associated with the *zambra gitana*. Instead, they embrace flamenco as a "world
music," inspired by the creativity and virtuosic innovations of artists such as
Paco de Lucía (1947–2014). The survival of the *zambra gitana* is interesting
when it comes to the UNESCO declaration and reveals some of the contradictory aspects of heritagization. Of course, the decline of the *zambra gitana*
is not the result of the UNESCO inscription as it began to deteriorate prior
to flamenco's recognition as ICH. And indeed as Catherine Grant (2012)
has noted, scholars in the field of heritage studies frequently debate whether
forms of heritage that are in decline need to be saved at all. Drawing on
the Vietnamese *ca trù* as a musical example, she alludes to the "ecological"
problem in heritage preservation—that is, whether it is desirable (and indeed
ethical) to preserve traditions that are in decline or let them fade naturally,
rather than keeping them alive artificially.

This debate was apparent in my own interactions with musicians and aficionados in Granada, and the revival of the *zambra gitana* has its advocates
and its detractors. What strikes me, however, is where the *zambra gitana* fits
within the parameters of flamenco's status as ICH. Flamenco is a diverse
tradition that comprises many distinct performance styles associated with an

array of social, cultural, and geographical contexts. To recognize a "single" flamenco as ICH, therefore, is potentially problematic. In a conversation with Cristina Cruces Roldán, she alluded to the idea that any one component of the flamenco tradition could be recognized as ICH according to UNESCO's criteria:

> I always think that in place of flamenco, the *soleá* could be sub-mitted to the list; the *soleá de Triana* that is a thousandth of the whole song, guitar, and dance of flamenco, no? However, it would be sufficient. Because UNESCO's criteria isn't a criteria of quan-tity, but of quality (personal communication, April 30, 2012).[25]

Perhaps, then, the UNESCO inscription for flamenco is too wide reach-ing; the tradition is simply too diverse to warrant recognition as a single ICH. Yet, it has been recognized by UNESCO and arguably, therefore, its status as a unified heritage will only continue the wider homogenization of the tradition that some would argue has been occurring since flamenco broke onto the world music scene in the 1970s. Gradually, distinct and local man-ifestations of the flamenco tradition, like the *zambra*, are being replaced by a unified, Andalusian flamenco whole that is not necessarily the sum of its constitutive parts. The vision of the Andalusian government that underlines the implementation of the UNESCO inscription is that of a unified regional tradition. Local readings of flamenco artistry may therefore struggle to find a "voice" within the wider scene if they do not conform to the Andalusian, and by extension "universal," image of the tradition. However, the Andalusian government's recognition of different components of flamenco as *Bien de Interés Cultural* goes part of the way towards recognizing flamenco's inter-nal diversity. Significantly for the discussion here, there have also been calls to include the *zambra* on the Andalusian heritage list even though this has yet to be fulfilled. Nonetheless, the peripheral position of the *zambra gitana* in the flamenco canon (some disregard its status as flamenco altogether) means that it is likely to be denied the safeguarding measures that it needs.

A related issue in the safeguarding of traditions such as the *zambra* is an apparent discrepancy between the top-down process of heritagization and bottom-up attempts to integrate communities in the safeguarding of heritage (itself a prominent criteria for UNESCO's recognition as ICH). In the case of the *zambra*, a handful of people in the Sacromonte community are ded-icated to preserving, documenting, and safeguarding the *zambra* both as a context and a genre. Most notable in this respect is the *Gitano* singer, poet, and scholar Curro Albaicín, who is involved in community-based preservation projects for documentation related to the *zambra* (and Sacromonte in general) and in the continuation of traditional forms of the *zambra gitana*. This endeavor is tied up with his own nostalgia for the *zambra* and the neighborhood of which it is a part, and their significance for conceptions of local identity. In an interview with Curro, he was critical of the institutional development of flamenco and claimed that he has received no support from Andalusian institutions in preserving local flamenco heritage in Sacromonte, even following the UNESCO inscription (personal communication, May 9, 2012).[26] This calls into question the nature of the UNESCO inscription and the supposed requirement of integrating communities in the process of heritage preservation. While the flamenco nomination file had widespread support from artists, culture workers, and aficionados, certain communities (such as Sacromonte) appear to have fallen by the wayside. Given the precarious state of the *zambra gitana*, the UNESCO inscription has brought into focus grievances and narratives of marginalization that had been lingering under the surface.

Conclusion

In this chapter, I have examined the circumstances surrounding the UNESCO inscription and flamenco's recognition as heritage according to international, national, and regional policies. Flamenco is caught up in a complex web of multi-level politics that reflects wider calls for the greater recognition of regional identity within a decentralized Spanish state. The flamenco example demonstrates the need to look beyond the nation-state as the primary actor in the heritagization process. Heritage declarations are inextricably linked to intersecting local, regional, national, and international politics. I have argued that the regional level within nation-states is integral to a full understanding of heritage declarations and their implementation. However, as I have shown, there are question marks over the instrumentalization of heritage for political agendas such as regional identity building. Using the *zambra* as a case study, I have argued that the UNESCO inscription may in fact sideline local manifestations of the tradition, as Andalusian institutions focus on the consolidation of a unified regional flamenco packaged within its universal status. Overall, the inscription has strengthened the existing institutional development of flamenco, thus consolidating it as a lucrative culture industry and a symbol of identity. However, what this case study shows is that when musical heritage is utilized in the service of identity politics, points of conflict may arise that deserve close analysis.

About the Author

Matthew Machin-Autenrieth is a Senior Research Associate at the Faculty of Music, University of Cambridge and the Principal Investigator for the European Research Council-funded project "Past and Present Musical Encounters across the Strait of Gibraltar" (2018–23). For more information on the project, see: www.musicalencounters.co.uk. He completed his Master's degree and PhD in Ethnomusicology at Cardiff University. Following his studies, Machin-Autenrieth was appointed as a Leverhulme Early Career Fellow at the University of Cambridge (2014–17). He has taught ethnomusicology at both undergraduate and postgraduate levels at the University of Cambridge, Cardiff University, and the University of Plymouth. He has written numerous publications spanning flamenco, regional identity, heritage studies, and intercultural music making, including the monograph *Flamenco, Regionalism and Musical Heritage in Southern Spain* (Routledge, 2017).

Notes

1   Instituto Andaluz del Flamenco, https://www.juntadeandalucia.es/cultura/aaiicc/centros/instituto-andaluz-de-flamenco (accessed June 11, 2019). All translations from Spanish are my own.
2   I borrow the term "regionalization" from political geography to account for the process of decentralization within a nation-state and the consolidation of regional identities by autonomous regional institutions. See Schrijver (2006). For more on the regionalization of flamenco specifically, see Machin-Autenrieth (2015, 2017a: 35–48).
3   This replaced the former Masterpieces of the Oral and Intangible Heritage of Humanity convention. The new Convention came into force in 2006 with the first elements being included in 2008 (this included ninety traditions that had previously been included on the Masterpieces List). For more information on the history of the UNESCO Convention, see Aikawa (2004); Aikawa-Faure (2009); Smith and Akagawa (2009).
4   The literature regarding ICH has boomed in recent years, particularly following the 2003 UNESCO Convention. For an overview of current debates in the field of heritage studies, see Aikawa (2004); Aikawa-Faure (2009); Bendix (2009);

Bendix, Eggert, and Peselmann (2012); Kirshenblatt-Gimblett (2004); Smith (2006); Smith and Akagawa (2009).

5   Here, I offer a cursory overview of the historical relationship between flamenco and Andalusian regional identity. For a more thorough analysis of this relationship, see Chuse (2003); Manuel (1989); Mitchell (1994); Washabaugh (1996, 2012). For sources in Spanish, see Cruces Roldán (2002, 2003); Grande (1979); Manuel Gamboa (2005); Steingress and Baltanás (1998); Steingress (1993, 1998a, 1998b, 1998c, 2002).

6   García Lorca and Falla viewed flamenco as a distinct *gitano-andaluz* ("Gypsy-Andalusian") tradition that represented a universal human spirit. For more on their involvement with flamenco, see Christoforidis (2007) and García Gómez (1998). Blas Infante was a leading figure in the struggle for Andalusian autonomy during the early decades of the twentieth century. He viewed flamenco as a uniquely Andalusian tradition that was rooted in the region's multicultural history (Infante 2010 [1915], 2010 [1929–1933]; Cortés Peña 2001).

7   For more information on the history and development of Andalusian autonomy in particular, see Cortés Peña (1994, 2001); Gilmore (1981); Moreno Navarro (1977, 1993); Newton (1982).

8   There was great controversy surrounding this declaration and the Andalusian government was criticized for appropriating flamenco for its own political ends. These criticisms were most notable in Extremadura and Murcia, two regions that have prominent flamenco scenes and important roles in the historical and stylistic development of the tradition (Machin-Autenrieth 2017a: 39–42).

9   In chapter 4 of my monograph, I offer a more detailed discussion of some of the aspects covered in this section (Machin-Autenrieth 2017a). For another discussion of the UNESCO inscription, see Cruces Roldán (2014).

10   There is also a third list called the Register of Best Safeguarding Practices where UNESCO's state parties are able to put forward specific case studies of their own safeguarding practices for ICH.

11   All of the application materials can be accessed on UNESCO's website, http://www.unesco.org/culture/ich/index.php?1g=en&pg=00011&RL=00363 (accessed April 4, 2019).

12   In particular, see the interview with José Antonio Griñán in issue 16 of *La Nueva Alboreá* (Agraso 2010), https://www.juntadeandalucia.es/cultura/flamenco/content/la-nueva-alboreá (accessed April 4, 2019).

13   The entire *Libro Blanco del Flamenco* can be accessed at https://www.juntadeandalucia.es/cultura/flamenco/content/libro-blanco-del-flamenco (accessed April 4, 2019).

14   For more on the educational development of flamenco, see Gutiérrez Mate (2010); López Castro (2004); Washabaugh (2012: 85–89).

15   For the complete agenda, see Junta de Andalucía (2014).

16 See http://www.juntadeandalucia.es/educacion/webportal/web/portal-de-flamenco (accessed April 4, 2019).

17 The economic crisis in Spain, and particularly Andalusia, has meant that funding for flamenco has diminished in the years following the UNESCO inscription.

18 Field research for this chapter was conducted in Andalusia (predominantly Granada) in 2012, with follow-up fieldwork in 2015 and 2016.

19 The term "nationalist" was used by a number of my interlocutors, referring to the idea that the Andalusian government is adopting policies reminiscent of Catalan or Basque nationalism, emphasizing Andalusia's distinctiveness as a supposed "nation." Some people I talked to even likened the Andalusian government's development of flamenco to *nacionalflamenquismo*, a term often used to describe the Franco regime's instrumentalization of flamenco in the construction of a unified and exportable national identity.

20 For more information on *palos*, see Manuel (2010).

21 I acknowledge the complexities in any classificatory description of the flamenco tradition and its stylistic derivations. There are many debates regarding how flamenco and its constitutive *palos* and sub-genres should be categorized, which are beyond the scope of this chapter. Rather, I wish only to introduce a generic understanding of flamenco classification as way of exposition.

22 For a thorough understanding of the *zambra* and the flamenco scene in Granada more generally, see Albaicín (2011); Cabrero Palomares (2009); Martos Sánchez (2008); Molina Fajardo (1974); Navarro García (1993).

23 For an analysis of the relationship between the *zambra* and tourism in Granada, see Machin-Autenrieth (2017b).

24 More specifically, the type of repertoire is essentially the same as that found in *tablaos*, a performance venue dedicated to flamenco spectacles that are usually aimed at tourist audiences, rather than the intimate performance setting of traditional *peñas*.

25 The *soleá* is a *palo* that belongs to the *cante jondo* repertoire. The *soleá de Triana* is a "sub-palo" or stylistic derivation of the *soleá* that comes from the Triana neighborhood of Seville.

26 Since I have conducted research for this chapter, Curro Albaicín is now (2019) spearheading a petition to have the *zambra* recognized by UNESCO as Intangible Cultural Heritage and has gained some support from local institutions in Granada.

References

Agraso, Aida Rodríguez. 2010. "Con este declaración ratificamos un compromiso recogido en nuestro Estatuto." Interview with José Antonio Griñán in *La Nueva Alboreá* 16: 28–29.

Aikawa, Noriko. 2004. "An Historical Overview of the Preparation of the UNESCO International Convention for the Safeguarding of the Intangible Cultural Heritage." *Museum International* 56(1–2): 137–49.
https://doi.org/10.1111/j.1350-0775.2004.00468.x

Aikawa-Faure, Noriko. 2009. "From the Proclamation of Masterpieces to the *Convention for the Safeguarding of Intangible Cultural Heritage.*" In *Intangible Heritage*, edited by Laurajane Smith and Natsuko Akagawa, 13–44. London: Routledge.

Albaicín, Curro. 2011. *Zambras de Granada y flamencos del Sacromonte: una historia flamenca en Granada.* Córdoba: Almuzara.

Bendix, Regina. 2009. "Heritage between Economy and Politics: An Assessment from the Perspective of Cultural Anthropology." In *Intangible Heritage*, edited by Laurajane Smith and Natsuko Akagawa, 253–69. London: Routledge.

Bendix, Regina F., Aditya Eggert, and Arnika Peselmann, eds. 2012. *Heritage Regimes and the State.* Göttingen: Universitätsverlag Göttingen.
https://doi.org/10.4000/books.gup.348

Cabrero Palomares, Francisco. 2009. *Granada en clave—enclave de flamenco.* Granada: Tleo.

Charnon-Deutsch, Lou. 2004. *The Spanish Gypsy: The History of a European Obsession.* Pennsylvania: Pennsylvania State University Press.

Christoforidis, Michael. 2007. "Manuel de Falla, Flamenco and Spanish Identity." In *Western Music and Race*, edited by Julie Brown, 230–43. Cambridge: Cambridge University Press.

Chuse, Loren. 2003. *The Cantaoras: Music, Gender, and Identity in Flamenco Song.* London: Routledge.

Cortés Peña, Antonio Luis. 1994. "El último nacionalismo: Andalucía y su historia." *Manuscrits* 12: 213–44.

—2001. "Nacionalismo/regionalismo andaluz ¿una invención de laboratorio?" *Historia Social* 40: 137–51.

Cruces Roldán, Cristina. 2001. *El Flamenco como patrimonio: anotaciones a la Declaración de los Registros Sonoros de la Niña de los Peines como Bien de Interés Cultural.* Seville: Ayuntamiento de Sevilla.

—2002. *Antropología y flamenco: más allá de la música*, Vol. 1. Seville: Signatura Ediciones.

—2003. *Antropología y flamenco: más allá de la música*, Vol. 2. Seville: Signatura Ediciones.

—2014. "El flamenco como constructo patrimonial. Representaciones sociales y aproximaciones metodológicas." *PASOS: Revista de Turismo y Patrimonio Cultural* 12(4): 819–35. https://doi.org/10.25145/j.pasos.2014.12.060

Delledonne, Giacomo, and Giuseppe Martinico. 2011. "Legal Conflicts and Subnational Constitutionalism." *Rutgers Law Journal* 42(4): 881–912.
https://doi.org/10.2139/ssrn.1824210

García Gómez, Génesis. 1998. "Volksgeist y género español." In *Flamenco y nacionalismo: aportaciones para una sociología política del flamenco*, edited by Gerhard Steingress and Enrique Baltanás, 193–206. Seville: Universidad de Sevilla, Fundación el Monte.

García Plata, Fuensanta. 1996. "El flamenco y las políticas de protección, conservación y difusión del patrimonio cultural andaluz." In *El flamenco: identidades sociales, ritual y patrimonio cultural*, edited by Cristina Cruces Roldán, 149–64. Seville: Consejería de Cultura.

Gillan, Matt. 2012. "Whose Heritage? Cultural Properties, Legislation and Regional Identity in Okinawa." In *Music as Intangible Cultural Heritage: Policy, Ideology, and Practice in the Preservation of East Asian Traditions*, edited by Keith Howard, 213–28. Farnham: Ashgate.

Gilmore, David. 1981. "Andalusian Regionalism: Anthropological Perspectives." *Iberian Studies* 10(2): 58–67.

Graeff, Nina. 2014. "Experiencing Music and Intangible Cultural Heritage: Some Thoughts on Safeguarding Music's Intangible Dimension." *El Oído Pensante* 2(2). http://ppct.caicyt.gov.ar/index.php/oidopensante/article/view/4802 (accessed April 4, 2019).

Grande, Félix. 1979. *Memoria del cante flamenco*. 2 vols. Madrid: Alianza Editorial.

Grant, Catherine. 2012. "Rethinking Safeguarding: Objections and Responses to Protecting and Promoting Endangered Musical Heritage." *Ethnomusicology Forum* 21(1): 31–51. https://doi.org/10.1080/17411912.2012.641733

Gutiérrez Mate, Rubén. 2010. "¿Se aprende flamenco en el sistema educativo andaluz?" *Revista de Investigación sobre Flamenco/La Madrugá* 3: 1–8.

Howard, Keith, ed. 2012a. *Music as Intangible Cultural Heritage: Policy, Ideology, and Practice in the Preservation of East Asian Traditions*. Farnham: Ashgate.

—2012b. "Introduction: East Asian Music as Intangible Cultural Heritage." In *Music as Intangible Cultural Heritage: Policy, Ideology, and Practice in the Preservation of East Asian Traditions*, edited by Keith Howard, 1–21. Farnham: Ashgate.

Infante, Blas. 2010 [1915]. *Ideal andaluz*. Seville: Fundación Pública Andaluza Centro de Estudios Andaluces.

—2010 [1929–1933]. *Orígenes de lo flamenco y secreto del cante jondo*, 125th anniversary edn. Seville: Junta de Andalucía.

Junta de Andalucía. 2007. *Estatuto de Autonomía para Andalucía*. Seville: Parlamento de Andalucía. http://www.parlamentodeandalucia.es/opencms/export/portal-web-parlamento/contenidos/pdf/PublicacionesNOoficiales/TextosLegislativos/ESTATUTO_AUTONOMIA_2007.pdf (accessed April 4, 2019).

—2012. *Libro blanco del flamenco*. Seville: Instituto Andaluz del Flamenco. https://www.juntadeandalucia.es/cultura/flamenco/content/libro-blanco-del-flamenco (accessed April 4, 2019).

—2014. "Orden de 7 de mayo de 2014, por la que se establecen medidas para la inclusión del flamenco en el sistema educativo andaluz." *Boletín Oficial de la Junta de Andalucía*, May 28, 2014. https://www.juntadeandalucia.es/boja/2014/101/ (accessed April 4, 2019).

Keating, Michael, and Alex Wilson. 2009. "Renegotiating the State of Autonomies: Statute Reform and Multi-level Politics in Spain." *West European Politics* 32(3): 536–58. https://doi.org/10.1080/01402380902779089

Kirshenblatt-Gimblett, Barbara. 1995. "Theorizing Heritage." *Ethnomusicology* 39(3): 367–80. https://doi.org/10.2307/924627

—2004. "Intangible Heritage as Metacultural Production." *Museum International* 56(1–2): 52–65. https://doi.org/10.1111/j.1350-0775.2004.00458.x

López Castro, Miguel, ed. 2004. *Introducción al flamenco en el currículum escolar.* Madrid: Universidad Internacional de Andalucía.

Machin-Autenrieth, Matthew. 2015. "Flamenco ¿Algo Nuestro? (Something of Ours?): Music, Regionalism and Political Geography in Andalusia, Spain." *Ethnomusicology Forum* 24(1): 4–27. https://doi.org/10.1080/17411912.2014.966852

—2017a. *Flamenco, Regionalism and Musical Heritage in Southern Spain.* Farnham: Ashgate.

—2017b. "The Zambra, Tourism and Discourses of Authenticity in Granada's Flamenco Scene." *MUSICultures* 43(2): 157–79.

Manuel, Peter. 1989. "Andalusian, Gypsy and Class Identity in the Contemporary Flamenco Complex." *Ethnomusicology* 33(1): 47–65. https://doi.org/10.2307/852169

—2010. "Composition, Authorship and Ownership in Flamenco, Past and Present." *Ethnomusicology* 54(1): 106–135. https://doi.org/10.5406/ethnomusicology.54.1.0106

Manuel Gamboa, José. 2005. *Una historia del flamenco.* Madrid: Espasa.

Martos Sánchez, Emilia. 2008. "La zambra en Al-Andalus y su proyección histórica." *Espiral. Cuadernos del Profesorado*, vols 1–2. https://core.ac.uk/download/pdf/154261757.pdf (accessed April 4, 2019). https://doi.org/10.25115/ecp.v1i2.871

Mitchell, Timothy. 1994. *Flamenco Deep Song.* New Haven: Yale University Press. https://doi.org/10.2307/j.ctt1xp3s6b

Molina Fajardo, Eduardo. 1974. *El flamenco en Granada: teoría de sus orígenes e historia.* Granada: Miguel Sánchez.

Moreno Navarro, Isidoro. 1977. *Andalucía: subdesarrollo, clases sociales y regionalismo.* Madrid: Manifiesto Editorial.

—1993. *Andalucía: identidad y cultura (estudios de antropología andaluza).* Málaga: Editorial Liberia Ágora.

Navarro García, José Luis. 1993. *Cantes y bailes de Granada.* Málaga: Editorial Arguval.

Newton, M. T. 1982. "Andalusia: The Long Road to Autonomy." *Journal of Area Studies* 6(3): 27–32. https://doi.org/10.1080/02613530.1982.9673577

Norton, Barley, and Naomi Matsumoto, eds. 2019. *Music as Heritage: Historical and Ethnographic Perspectives*. Abingdon: Routledge.

Paetzold, Christopher. 2009. "Singing Beneath the Alhambra: The North African and Arabic Past and Present in Contemporary Andalusian Music." *Journal of Spanish Cultural Studies* 10(2): 207–23. https://doi.org/10.1080/14636200902990711

Schrijver, Frans. 2006. *Regionalism after Regionalisation: Spain, France and the United Kingdom*. Amsterdam: Amsterdam University Press. https://doi.org/10.5117/9789056294281

Seeger, Anthony. 2009. "Lessons Learned from the ICTM (NGO) Evaluation of Nominations for the UNESCO *Masterpieces of the Oral and Intangible Heritage of Humanity*, 2001–5." In *Intangible Heritage*, edited by Laurajane Smith and Natsuko Akagawa, 112–28. London: Routledge.

Smith, Laurajane. 2006. *The Uses of Heritage*. London and New York: Routledge.

Smith, Laurajane, and Natsuko Akagawa, eds. 2009. *Intangible Heritage*. London: Routledge. https://doi.org/10.4324/9780203602263

Steingress, Gerhard. 1993. *Sociología del Cante Flamenco*. Jerez: Centro Andaluz del Flamenco.

—1998a. "El cante flamenco como manifestación artística, instrumento ideológico y elemento de la identidad cultural andaluza." In *Flamenco y nacionalismo: aportaciones para una sociología política del flamenco*, edited by Gerhard Steingress and Enrique Baltanás, 21–39. Seville: Universidad de Sevilla, Fundación el Monte.

—1998b. "Ideología y mentalidad en la construcción de la identidad cultural (casticismo, ideal andaluz y psicología cotidiana en el flamenco)." In *Flamenco y nacionalismo: aportaciones para una sociología política del flamenco*, edited by Gerhard Steingress and Enrique Baltanás, 165–91. Seville: Universidad de Sevilla, Fundación el Monte.

—1998c. *Sobre flamenco y flamencología (escritos escogidos 1988–1998)*. Seville: Signatura Ediciones.

—2002. "El flamenco como patrimonio cultural o una construcción artificial más de la identidad andaluza." *Revista Andaluza de Ciencias Sociales* 1: 43–64.

Steingress, Gerhard, and Enrique Baltanás, eds. 1998. *Flamenco y nacionalismo: aportaciones para una sociología política del flamenco*. Seville: Universidad de Sevilla, Fundación el Monte.

UNESCO. 2003. "Text of the Convention for the Safeguarding of the Intangible Cultural Heritage." Paris: UNESCO. https://ich.unesco.org/en/convention (accessed April 4, 2019).

—2010. *Nomination File no. 00363 for Inscription on the Representative List of the Intangible Cultural Heritage: Flamenco*, 5th session in Kenya (UNESCO). http://www.unesco.org/culture/ich/index.php?lg=en&pg=00011&RL=00363 (accessed April 4, 2019).

Washabaugh, William. 1996. *Flamenco: Passion, Politics and Popular Culture*. Oxford: Berg.

—2012. *Flamenco Music and National Identity in Spain.* Farnham: Ashgate.
Wong, Isabel. 2009. "The Heritage of *Kunqu*: Preserving Music and Theater Traditions in China." In *Intangible Heritage Embodied*, edited by Helaine Silverman and D. Fairchild Ruggles, 15–35. New York: Springer. https://doi.org/10.1007/978-1-4419-0072-2_2
Zabala, Labaca. 2013. "La protección del patrimonio etnográfico en España y en las comunidades autónomas: especial referencia al País Vasco y Andalucía." *RIIPAC: Revista sobre Patrimonio Cultural* 2: 105–48.

Chapter 14

Questioning Safeguarding: Heritage and Capabilities at Jemaa el Fnaa Square, Morocco

Thomas Beardslee

Like many others who decide to study ethnomusicology, I entered graduate school with notions of doing applied work. The desire to study, think, and write about music was certainly there, but I also wanted to *do* something, to somehow act to make the world a better place. I suspect that a majority of those working in ethnomusicology (or any ethnographic field, really) harbor similar impulses. We work closely with people—live with them, play music with them, and in the case of the native ethnographer, are them. In our field-work, we cultivate reciprocal bonds of trust and caring with those we study, trying our best to understand the lives they live, and the music they make. The desire to help is a natural result of this process, which brings to light not only the musical worlds of those we study, but also the deprivations and injustices they (and we) face. But the question remains as to what exactly to do, and what should be our guiding rationale when creating our own applied projects, or participating in the projects of others. This chapter will discuss this question, challenging one of its most common answers—the preservation of musical heritage—while offering an alternative approach based on the work of economist Amartya Sen, among others. I will argue that the focus of applied work should be the safeguarding of real human well-being and freedoms, rather than the safeguarding of a constructed vision of "intangible cultural heritage."

There are, of course, a healthy number of ethnomusicologists who have discussed and/or conducted applied ethnomusicology along lines other than that of preservation, such as Daniel Avorgbedor's study of the ways in which to aid music-making in the face of depleted human resources (1992); Anthony Seeger's work in helping the Suya record their music and negotiate land disputes (2008); Gregory Barz and Judah Cohen's work with HIV in Africa (Barz and Cohen 2011); and Svanibor Pettan's work with music and conflict resolution (2008). As Rebecca Dirksen discusses in her survey of applied ethnomusicology, ethnomusicologists embrace many aims other than preservation: disaster relief, conflict resolution, human rights, medicine and healing, and others (Dirksen 2011). But in our conferences, round tables, listservs—and, of course, writings—the narrative of preserving tradition still appears and re-appears, if perhaps toned down to less grandiose terms of support, enabling, or empowerment (Beardslee 2014).

The most internationally well-known set of applied projects in the area of the preservation of living practice comes from UNESCO, and the Intangible Cultural Heritage (ICH) safeguarding regime it has pursued in a variety of forms since the mid-1990s. My discussion of the topic of preservation is largely based on research performed at Jemaa el Fnaa Square in Marrakech, Morocco, which in some ways was one of the sites of the ICH program's genesis. The Square is the performance space for a huge population of *hlay-qiya*, street performers in a wide variety of genres who work in the *halqa*, a circle made up of the audience.[1] The *hlayqiya* run the gamut of what would be loosely considered "traditional" performance genres in the Marrakech area, including Berber and Arabic-language music, *Gnawa* (a syncretic Afro-Moroccan genre), snake charming, fortune-telling, acrobats, Saharan medicine sellers, magicians, and a great many others. They work mostly in the large central area of the Square, with open-air restaurants, orange juice stands, and countless knick-knack vendors surrounding them.

Figure 14.1: Abdelhakim Khabzaoui, with *halqa* members Ahmed (left) on *tarija* and Abderrahim (right) on *darbuka* (photo by Tom Beardslee).

The Square was the hub of economic life in Marrakech for centuries, and in the present day is also the hub of its tourist trade. While the inter-city bus station and taxi ranks have been banished elsewhere, the Square remains the jumping-off point for tourists with both its own attractions and its central proximity to all other tourist sites in the Marrakech *medina* (old city). It draws not only a healthy contingent of foreign tourists but also large crowds of Moroccans from elsewhere in the country. Finally, it remains an affordable afternoon's or evening's entertainment for Marrakechis from all over the city, who stream into the Square on foot, taxi, or city bus around sundown. The Jemaa el Fnaa, while often bemoaned as a site that has succumbed (or is succumbing) to the demands of the international tourist trade at the expense of its local "authenticity," remains a multilayered site that addresses the desires of a wide variety of visitors, from the Belgian tourist seeking mystery to the medina resident seeking a bowl of soup, an hour's distraction, and a bag of fresh mint to bring home for tea.

The site and its performers were declared a UNESCO Masterpiece of the Oral and Intangible Cultural Heritage of Humanity in 2001.[2] This represented a continuation of the Jemaa el Fnaa's long history of designation as a Moroccan cultural site, beginning with a colonial decree of protection in 1921, followed by a royal decree in 1957 and declaration as a UNESCO World Heritage site (as part of the Marrakech medina) in 1985 (Borghi 2004; Skounti 2012; Beardslee 2014). Following the declaration, a scattered assortment of safeguarding activities took place at the Square. Many of the activities focused on the storytellers, who (to judge from both talks with those involved in the project and from the storytellers' prominence in the literature generated by it) were deemed by those who initiated the heritage project to be the most important and endangered aspect of the heritage at Jemaa el Fnaa. A youth awareness program brought them into a few schools, and many of their stories were recorded. A booklet in French and Arabic was printed, describing the heritage present at the Square (with special emphasis given to the storytellers), and was also distributed to schools throughout Morocco. Various heritage concert festivals have also taken place at the Square, organized by the local government and heritage associations.[3]

I spent a total of a year at the Square between 2010 and 2012 (with several follow-up trips in the years since), conducting both classic participant-observation-interview research as well as doing a quantitative livelihood survey among the *hlayqiya*.[4] I wanted to know the answers to a number of questions regarding the impact of the UNESCO declaration, the performers' concepts of themselves as heritage, and the sort of structures that supported and detracted from the performers' capabilities to achieve the goals they valued, musical or otherwise. The declaration was in 2001, and many of these activities took place from 2003 to 2006. By the time I arrived at the Square in October 2010, it was apparent that this complex of activities had not only not accomplished any of the stated safeguarding goals but had also failed to contribute significantly to the lasting well-being of the performers or audiences. The storytellers that were the project's principal focus were (and remain) almost entirely absent from the Square, and none of the many performers I spoke with over the research period or since has reported any lasting benefit from the UNESCO declaration. I believe the storytellers, and the performers at the Square in general, were failed by this set of activities, but not because of a lack of effort or good will on the part of those who worked on their behalf. They were let down, ironically, by the *raison d'être* and framing concept of the projects themselves: the idea of heritage safeguarding.

The Problems with Heritage

Adopting a critical stance toward heritage production is hardly a new thing, and the tacit assumptions and misunderstandings of traditional culture that are embedded in the intangible cultural heritage model (and the dysfunctions that can result from them) have been discussed in depth by a number of authors, including Barbara Kirshenblatt-Gimblett (1995, 2004), Dorothy Noyes (2006, 2011), and Jean-Loup Amselle (2004). For the purposes of this discussion, I would like to focus on several problematic aspects of intangible heritage:

Heritage is a mode of (meta)cultural production, not an item waiting to be discovered

Much of the discussion about ICH in the UNESCO literature and elsewhere rests on the idea that heritage exists on its own out in the wild, waiting to be discovered and inventoried. This renders invisible the creative process that is part and parcel of intangible heritage. To quote Barbara Kirshenblatt-Gimblett, "heritage is a mode of cultural production in the present that has recourse to the past" (Kirshenblatt-Gimblett 1995: 369). A heritage "practice" is created out of selected traits, albeit possibly through a process that involves extensive consultation with the population of interest. When we talk about a "culture" or a "practice" for the purposes of documentation and study, we collapse an observed array of behaviors into a package suitable for discussion: Karnatak music, Appalachian fiddling, Moroccan storytelling. We create borders, we simplify complexities, we create an object that may be discussed, documented, and safeguarded.

This bordering and simplification creates disjunctures when heritage becomes policy, between the heritage as created (in a safeguarding plan, for example) and the endlessly messy, variable, and complex world of human interaction. A practice as described is a thing—it has a name, stable characteristics that define what it is (and is not), and a line between who does and does not engage in it. But when we are looking at what people actually do, what we are actually seeing is not a concrete "thing" at all. Rather, it is an emergent property of the decisions and actions of many individuals, each with their own set of influences and goals. The practice becomes a bordered whole *only within the confines of our description*. As Dorothy Noyes points out in her study of the Patum festival in Catalonia, applying these imagined borders to a real-life practice inevitably excludes integral aspects and participants while including others, at the same time rendering invisible a practice's interconnectedness with the rest of the world (Noyes 2006).

Heritage production often requires very different skills than the activities that serve as its objects

One of the other pertinent flaws in the ICH paradigm is the idea that the approach is inherently more democratic: everyone has ICH, and safeguarding it is a process that all may potentially participate in. This is far from the truth, in that the creation of ICH requires a specific set of relatively difficult-to-obtain skills: inventorying and the preparation of dossiers require literacy (for UNESCO purposes in French or English), computer skills, and potentially a university education and access to an accrediting institution such as a university or ministry of culture. Thus the process places power/knowledge over one group of people in the hands of another group, creating an "intangible" variation of what Laurajane Smith refers to as the "authorized heritage discourse"—a version dressed up in the language of community stewardship and a valorization of "traditional" culture, but one that shuts out many just as effectively (Smith 2006: 28). To be fair, UNESCO works to close this gap through a number of means, including working with local NGOs and holding capacity-building workshops in order to equip a wider group of people with the tools to participate in the heritage-building process. However, this merely widens the circle of potential heritage-makers without erasing the underlying border between those who are able to actively participate in the process and those who are not.

The UNESCO ICH safeguarding process also does a couple of other things: it places the ultimate authority to nominate practices for addition to the safeguarding lists in the hands of the Member-State governments (gloss- ing over potential conflict between state and population concerned) *and* requires the creation of a safeguarding plan and an administrative body to oversee it—a bureaucratic organism that all will not have equal access to, and one that will have sway for an undefined length of time.[5] As Dorothy Noyes puts it, "Zeitgeists come and go, but bureaucracy is forever" (Noyes 2006: 43).

Heritage is an intrinsic "good"

The idea of cultural "loss"—that people can lose or regain their culture—also rests on a notion of cultural identity that connects practices to people on an unconscious level, be it on a quasi-genetic foundation or a Herderian fit of natural environment and practice. As Udo Will and William Benn Michaels point out, "If we speak about lost culture or lost identity, there has to be some way of explaining how what people actually do and practice does not consti- tute their real identity, but what has been practiced in the past does" (Michaels 1992: 683; Will 2008: 27). If a practice can be lost and later regained—and for that "regaining" to be inherently good for you—there must be an innate connection between person and practice at a level deeper than mere lived experience and conscious thought: who you think you are is not necessarily who you are. To assume that what people other than yourself did before you were born is a part of your own past is to assume a thread of culture that runs between your own experience and theirs, something "in the blood" in the same manner previously assigned to race.

It is generally agreed that culture is learned; if you have never done some- thing, never engaged in an activity, you cannot lose it—you never had it in the first place. To say that a group of people have lost an item of cultural heritage (and could find it again through safeguarding and revitalization efforts) is to imply that there is a connection between it and them on a level outside their lived experience. The ICH discourse employs this essentialized view of culture, albeit encased in several layers of doublethink that clearly try to leave some rhetorical distance between the idea of "cultural" heritage and racial or ethnic heritage (Kirshenblatt-Gimblett 2004; Noyes 2006). The authors of UNESCO materials and instruments are clearly not unaware of the implications of the heritage concept and its potential to be used as fodder for claims based on race, and for the celebration of heritage to be taken as a prescriptive statement on what particular activities are "good" for people based on their ethnic affiliation—much emphasis is placed on the community's recognition of heritage as such:

> intangible cultural heritage can only be heritage when it is recognized as such by the communities, groups or individuals that create, maintain and transmit it—without their recognition, nobody else can decide for them that a given expression or practice is their heritage. *What is Intangible Cultural Heritage?* (UNESCO 2009)

This quote, clearly intended to inject conscious decision-making into the discourse in order to counteract this essentialized view of heritage, still fails to address the problem. First, if the practice is already something that people recognize as important, then why does it need to be preserved? This question points to the unspoken implication in this quote: there are people who should be practicing this heritage, but are not. If people are not engaging in a practice, what basis is there for saying that they should, other than making a connection with an inherited, essential nature? To accept this as a fact would be to place ourselves in shark-infested ideological waters, in that it implies a pre-determination of personal characteristics based on cultural affiliation, genetic makeup, geographic origin, or phenotype.

Intangible Cultural Heritage at the Jemaa el Fnaa

In the case of the Jemaa el Fnaa, the problems with the mechanics of the heritage-making process were acutely visible in a number of ways, chief among them the lack of any direct involvement of the performers affected by the declaration. The dossier was prepared (with help from the Moroccan Ministry of Culture) by les Amis de la Place, an association of scholars, artists, and local businesspersons, among them Juan Goytisolo (a well-known Spanish author) and Ouidad Tebba (currently Dean of the Faculty of Letters and Human Sciences at Cadi Ayyad University). The performers were certainly consulted in the process—a survey was conducted with the performers working there at the time, and several of the storyteller's biographies appeared in the booklet produced by UNESCO as part of the project and distributed to schools throughout the Marrakech region (Skounti, Tebbaa, and Nadim 2005). But they played no creative role in the making of the UNESCO ICH "version" of the Jemaa el Fnaa, relegated instead to the role of objects. Again, this was not a case of deliberate disregard—when I spoke with Ouidad Tebbaa and others about the creation of the UNESCO dossier and the formation of the project, it was clear that these people cared very much about the Square and its performers, and were working to do their best by them. But as stated before, the process necessarily excludes the direct input of those without the requisite skills. The *hlayqiya*—often non-literate, usually not formally educated beyond a few years, and not possessing political or academic clout—were not in a position to work directly on the dossier or participate actively to make their voices heard in the heritage-building process.[6]

As a result, the descriptions of the Square and the safeguarding plan based on it bear almost none of the voices of the performers, nor do they address their very real concerns about the Square, its uses, and their own needs and futures. Instead, these materials and projects bear the stamp of those directly involved in their creation; their nostalgias, desires, and visions of the Jemaa el Fnaa, and their ideas about what actions should be taken. In the materials produced as part of the UNESCO project (including a booklet, a book published by Tebbaa, Mohammed Faiz, and several photographers (Tebbaa et al. 2004), and assorted entries on the UNESCO website), the performers appear in photographs as nameless archetypes, with the exception of a handful of performers the authors felt to be particularly significant. Performers in less "traditional" genres (many of whom have been at the Square for decades) were omitted, such as the groups that play more modern folk/popular music.

Most importantly, the projects and the resources allotted to them (including $153,000 in funds-in-trust from the Japanese government) were directed at this heritage vision, rather than at the performers themselves: the recording of storytellers' tales, the photographing of the Square, the holding of colloquia about the Square's heritage, the making of the booklet, and the awareness-raising campaign in Moroccan schools. When Goytisolo, Tebbaa and the other members of the Amis de la Place found themselves unable to continue with the project due to their own lack of available time or energy, the remaining funds were returned to UNESCO. Aside from a small group of storytellers who did benefit somewhat, the allotment of these resources was a unanimous sore point among the performers. Their objections highlight an important difference between their viewpoints about the locus of the heritage in question and that of the Amis: in the vision of the Square created for the UNESCO project, the performers are *bearers* of heritage, who inherit it, carry it, and pass it on. But time and again I heard *hlayqiya* describe *themselves as part* of the Square's heritage, rather than mere bearers—hence a fair amount of anger about the funds being directed to things like booklets and colloquia, and eventually returned to UNESCO rather than disbursed among the *hlayqiya*.[7]

In the end, what the people involved with the safeguarding at the Jemaa el Fnaa were left with was a largely disappointing result—the practice of storytelling at the Square continued its decline, the performers benefited little if at all, and performers (and to some extent the members of the Amis, as far as I could tell) were left disillusioned by the experience. While it could be argued that this was somehow the result of other factors (such as insufficient funding and a general lack of coherence and efficiency in the administration of the project), I lay the blame squarely at the feet of the guiding principle: the safeguarding of intangible cultural heritage. I have discussed a number of reasons why this approach was flawed: it aims at unattainable goals (the preservation of cultural practices), it is based on bad theory (an essentialized, bounded concept of cultures and practices) and despite its ostensible focus on the practitioners of heritage, it still writes them into the process as bearers, objects with little personal agency (Kirshenblatt-Gimblett 2004; Skounti 2008).

But criticism is not sufficient, and beyond the necessary identification of the problem serves to do little beyond vent steam and generate snarky academic prose—more needs to be done than to merely complain. In the beginning of this chapter I spoke about the bonds of mutual trust and caring we build in the process of our fieldwork, and the desire to reciprocate the kindnesses we are shown. Mere complaint does not address the desire to act that these feelings generate. But if the ICH paradigm doesn't work for us, how do we make a plan to help that uses the skills and expertise we have to offer? And what, exactly, should be our goal?

The Capability Approach

The answers to this question are to be found, I feel, when we look beyond cultural practices and cultural groups as stable things to be preserved and protected, and start looking at the factors that affect individuals' abilities to participate in and work together with others in the building and maintenance of a socio-cultural world that they wish to live in. To explain this rather new-agey statement, I return to the definition of performance practices (i.e. music, dance, storytelling, and so on) I mentioned earlier: "practices" as emergent properties of the interactions of many individuals. Each participant possesses a mind of their own and concepts of the world that, while they may at times closely resemble those of the others they interact with, are never quite identical. The world that results changes constantly and appears differently depending on the participants and the vantage point from which it is viewed. For an analogy/example, there is the Square's performing area (see Figure 14.2), which features a remarkably stable layout and schedule of performing, vending, begging, and walking spaces. While it does shift, one can very often find the same performer or vendor in the same few meters, year in and year out. The "map" of this layout exists in its entirety in no fixed place—not on a drawing on the local administrator's wall, nor in markings on the interlocking tiles of the Square, or even in the mind of a particular person. Instead, it is created and re-created in the interactions between those who go there, each of whom knows a part of it. A given *hlayqiya* or vendor usually knows his or her portion they occupy very well and a certain amount about the rest, and the whole structure at any given moment is the end result of these many visions of the space coming together. This "map," in turn, is only one visible physical aspect of the emergent property that is the Square. There are a great many such structures (sound, income strategy, repertoire, types of patron) overlaid and intertwined there. There is no "thing" with defined boundaries to preserve in this phenomenon and to try to do so would require willful ignorance of its complexity.

What is needed is a way of thinking about the issue that better accounts for the emergent, un-bordered quality of human activity. As an alternative to heritage preservation as a framework and starting point for our actions—be they projects we undertake ourselves or ones in which we choose to participate—I am reaching somewhat outside our normally-traveled theoretical territory to propose the Capability Approach, initially developed by economist Amartya Sen (1999) as an alternative approach in welfare economics.

Capabilities and Functionings

Sen developed the Capability Approach (CA) in light of the inadequacy of income as a proxy indicator of well-being, and of the pure focus on enhancing income figures (such as per-capita income and gross domestic product) in development efforts. In measuring how well-off someone is, income does not tell the whole story: African-Americans, for example, despite earning

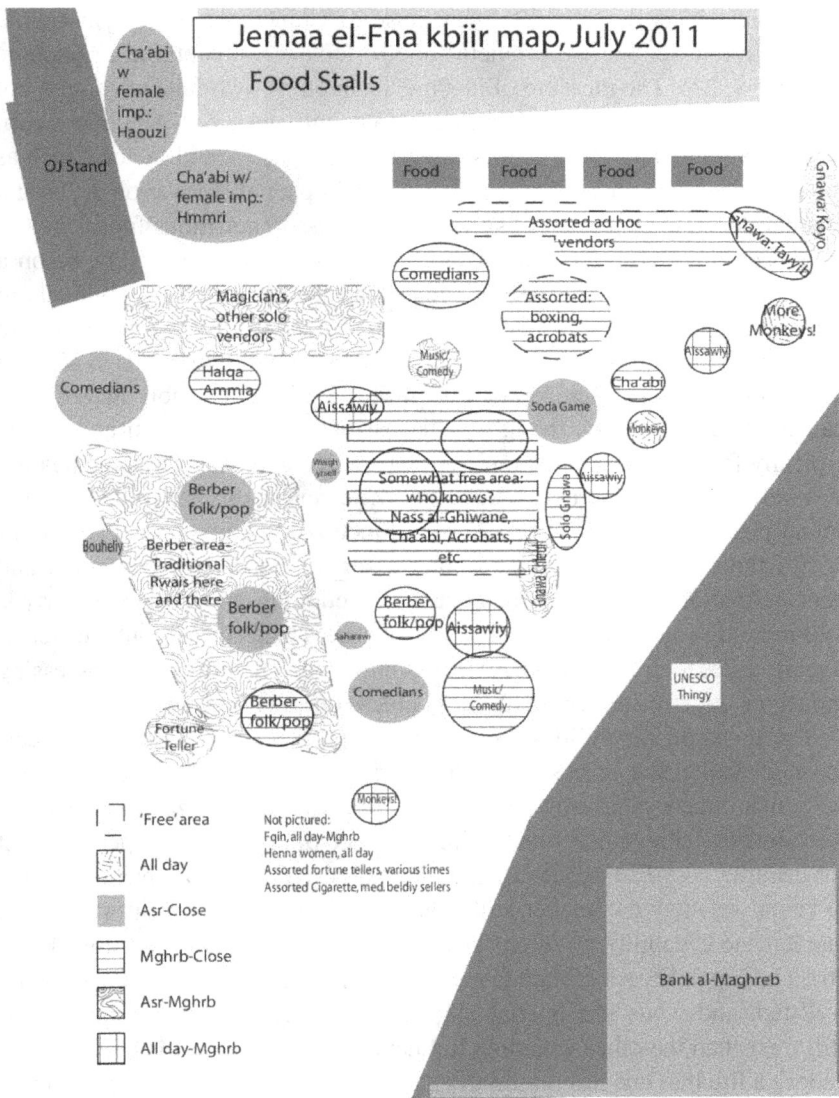

Figure 14.2: Map of approximate performance spaces and times they are found throughout the day, as demarcated by prayer times; drawn by the author.

an absolute income far higher than those of Chinese or Indians in Kerala State, have lower life expectancies due to factors not captured by income (Sen 1999: 23). The measure of income taken on its own fails to capture not only relative disparities in income within a country (African-Americans earn less on average than other census categories) but also social factors, such as those stemming from entrenched racism, the impact of the war on drugs and inequalities in the educational system, and access to nutritious food.

Instead of placing the evaluative emphasis on resources, utility, or on a list of inalienable rights, the CA focuses on the abilities of individuals to achieve the things and to live the lives that they value. The CA refers to these valued beings and doings as functionings, and the freedoms to achieve them as capabilities (Sen 1999). Functionings can conceivably include any valued state or activity, though in discussions of the CA, Sen and others typically focus on basic functionings such as living a long life, being healthy and well-nourished, learning to read and write, and so on. Capabilities are the actual possibilities to achieve a chosen functioning, a sort of holistic package of the resources, rights, and other assorted social, environmental, and personal factors necessary to achieve the functionings they value. Poverty is thus not only conceived in terms of lack of access to resources, but the lack of opportunities to turn available resources into valued functionings: possessing money or other resources is worthless unless one has the opportunities.

The focus on capabilities, rather than on particular functionings, reflects the high value Sen places on agency and choice. Instead of stating that a particular functioning must be achieved, the CA emphasizes people's real freedoms to achieve that functioning. In place of stating that a person must eat healthily, it asks the question of whether or not the person has the choice of being well-fed: the hunger-striker and the famine-sufferer both starve, but one has the capability to avoid starvation and the other does not (Sen 1999: 76). The capability set of the hunger-striker includes the functioning of being well-fed, and while she is choosing not to pursue this functioning, she is still freer than the other who does not have that capability. It is the ability to choose a life that one has reason to value, and the individual agency that this involves is the thing to be preserved—capabilities have intrinsic value. At the same time, capabilities can also be instrumental in that they are necessary for the achievement of functionings that permit still other capabilities: a minimum ability to be healthy and safe is necessary in order to go to school and become literate, and a minimum level of schooling can in turn be necessary to participate in the economy and democratic process, and so on.

Sen's approach has been very influential in the field of international development, including serving as the basis for the UN's Human Development Index, which augments measurements of income with measurements of life expectancy, levels of education, and inequality. It has been elaborated and expanded upon by other scholars such as Martha Nussbaum,[8] Sabina Alkire, Ingrid Robeyns, and Paul Anand et al., who have addressed such topics as ethics, women's rights, and issues of measurement and application (Nussbaum 2001; Alkire 2005, 2007; Robeyns 2005; Anand, Santos, and Smith 2004).

In the context of our discussion of ICH, we can view the CA as an alternate method of framing the question of what we want to preserve, and how we go about preserving it. With the flaws discussed earlier in mind, and when placing the emphasis on capabilities, we turn the issue on its head: instead of thinking about ways to help people maintain their culture, we can think about ways to help them *create* it. Culture is not something that is received, borne, and then passed on like a magical relay baton. Like the "map" of the Square discussed earlier, culture is continuously created in a process of emergence. People use existing materials, to be sure, things that they have learned and that have meaning for them—but they use and re-assemble them in response to current conditions and in new ways. To quote Dorothy Noyes, "Folklore does not stop just because print, mass media, and digital media arrive. Practitioners adapt to new communicative environments while often continuing to make strategic use of the older ones" (Noyes 2011: 41).

The question for the ethnomusicologist or other scholar looking to do applied work would then be whether or not the population of concern has the capabilities to participate in the kinds of performance practices (a term I am using as an umbrella for kinds of activities that tend to interest us, such as music, dance, drama, storytelling and so on) that they would choose. These capabilities are in turn a function of other capabilities—in order to participate in a practice, one needs at least a minimum ability to do other things: to be healthy, to make a living, to associate with others, to be safe, to have political agency, to be educated. The question of whether or not people have the capability to participate in performance practices might be answered by asking other questions in a variety of other areas:

1. **Livelihood**: The capability to make a livelihood, borrow and save, and have access to capital
   a. Do people (or their guardians, in the case of children or other dependents) have the ability to make a living in a safe, healthy, dignified, and sustainable manner?

    b. Do they have access to credit and savings instruments?

    c. Do they have access to the necessary forms of capital, both in terms of their means of financial income and their capability to engage in performance practices?

    d. Are there adequate social safety nets present to cushion shocks to livelihood?

2. **Association**: The capability to associate with others freely

    a. Do people have the ability to seek out and associate with others with whom to perform?

    b. Do people have the capability to be treated (and to treat others) with dignity, mutual respect, and equality?

    c. Do performers have access to an audience, and vice-versa?

    d. Do people have the time and freedom from undue stress necessary to associate with others?

    e. Do performers have an available physical space (performance, rehearsal)?

    f. Do people have access to transportation?

3. **Safety**: The capability to both be and to feel safe

    a. Are people reasonably free from physical threats—from violence, accidents, and natural disaster?

    b. Are they able to live without the stress and anxiety created by the presence of physical threats?

4. **Health**: The capability to live a long and healthy life

    a. Do people have access to clean and adequate food, water, and shelter?

    b. Do performers have real access to preventive, palliative, and curative medical care? Is there an adequate social safety net that ensures the presence of these types of care?

5. **Political agency**: The capability to exercise some control over one's environment

    a. Do performers have access to their political representatives, and have a voice in matters that concern them?

    b. Do they have freedom of speech and opinion?

6. **Education**: The capability to learn both about performance and the world in general

    a. Do people have access to the formal and informal education and instructional opportunities that enable performance capabilities and capabilities in general?

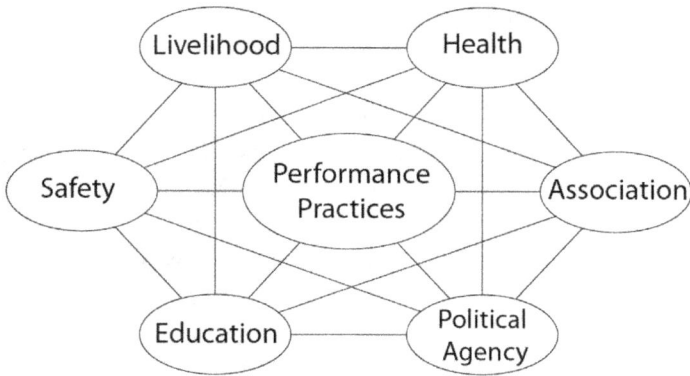

Figure 14.3: A web of mutual influence; drawn by the author

This list is not intended to be comprehensive or universal—as Sen (2004) emphasizes, any sort of list-making must be a flexible operation, reacting to the circumstance it is applied to. This list is developed for this case study, while in another circumstance it may make sense to group sub-categories differently, or add entirely new ones—if speaking of children, for example, one might add emphasis on the capability to play. It is also placed in no particular order of importance—and might, in fact, be better represented as a web of mutual influence (see Figure 14.3).

Again, asking these questions implies a reorientation from the practices themselves to the people who engage in them; it is not the practices that are to be safeguarded, but rather the capabilities of people to engage in them. Obviously, people are resilient, and we make music, dance, and tell stories under all sorts of conditions where the answers to the above questions would be in the negative. But it is difficult to argue that diminished capabilities in other areas do not affect the capability to engage in performance practices: one can be too ill to sing, too unsafe to gather with others, too busy with factory work to learn how to dance, or actively forbidden by one's government to tell stories in one's native language.

Capabilities and the hlayqiya

The capabilities questions that would likely concern us as ethnomusicologists can be framed in a couple of ways: first (and most obvious) is to look for ways to enhance the capabilities of a given group of individuals to engage at a basic level in the sorts of "musicking" they would choose, and to investigate what instrumental factors are present or lacking, such as security, space, health, and physical capital. One might seek out populations whose capabilities to engage in valued musical functionings, or at times to even formulate an idea of what those functionings might be, are curtailed by their circumstances—refugee camp populations come to mind as extreme examples, as do victims of slavery or child labor. In a second frame, we might look at capabilities gaps in general in a population we are already studying, and ask how our own insights gained in our research might be used to address these gaps.

In regards to the *hlayqiya*, we have a mixed bag. One might look at the existence of the Square as evidence that the capabilities to perform exist, and that life in Marrakech and Morocco in general provides at least the minimum level of the necessary instrumental capabilities—enough "yes" answers to the above list. The Jemaa el Fnaa itself can be seen as one huge supporting structure—a public space that provides a performance space and an enthusiastic, generous audience. It allows the *hlayqiya* to practice their arts, make a living, and associate with each other. It is a place where performance is learned as well, and many *hlayqiya* in a variety of genres described the Square as a "madrasa" (a school) where they learned a great deal about repertoire and performance practice. And (certain events aside) the Jemaa el Fnaa provides a safe—if a bit intense at times—place for the audience to participate in these practices.

The *hlayqiya*'s lives, however, remain fraught with gaps in capabilities that limit their abilities to lead the lives they wish to lead, and to engage in performance practices in the manner and extent they would choose. The informal social networks of the Square provide some minimal mutual-aid cushion for catastrophes, but income shocks—such as that resulting from the April 28, 2011 terrorist attack on the Square—still result in drastically reduced capacities to achieve certain functionings, such as living in good health and providing for children's education. For example, the meager incomes of the *hlayqiya* severely limit their access to medical care, and most do without the preventive and much of the curative or palliative care those reading this chapter likely take for granted (Beardslee 2014).[9] I frequently observed cases where ill health prevented *hlayqiya* from working at the Square—both a strain on income and the general happiness of people who for the most part genuinely loved their work.

There is current talk of the local government providing a system of limited health insurance, a catastrophe fund, and a micro-lending organization for the Square's performers. The possibilities of this actually coming about, however, are hampered by the *hlayqiya*'s lack of political agency. Up until recently, the performers have had little to no negotiating power with the local government, and no say in what happens to their own work space. In addition to the intrinsic value of this capability failure, this impacts the lives and livelihoods of the *hlayqiya* in a number of ways, such as the increasing use of the Square by the local government for large public concerts and events such as the Marrakech Film Festival that interfere with the *hlayqia*'s use of the space and put a dent in their livelihoods. Hopes for a remedy to this lack of political agency can be seen in the increasingly organized artists' associations that started to form in the years following the UNESCO declaration, giving the *hlayqiya* the ability to strike or otherwise demonstrate and negotiate as a group. Indeed, in 2013 the various associations did manage to form a coalition and strike for several days, until some promises of social assistance for the performers were extracted from the city government (which have yet to materialize, but the *hlayqiya* I spoke with seemed unsurprised at this and willing to hold more strikes if necessary). Ultimately, this fostering of group feeling among the *hlayqiya* and a sense of their own importance to the larger picture of the Marrakech economy may be the most significant and lasting legacy of the 2001 declaration.

Thus the official declaration of the Square as an important piece of Moroccan and world ICH has undoubtedly helped with some of the capabilities gaps amongst the *hlayqiya*, and it would be incorrect to say that heritage activities cannot aid, empower, and attract resources to a vulnerable population. However, in this particular case these benefits came to the *hlayqiya* indirectly, as a byproduct of the declaration and the activities that followed it, rather than as a part of the project. Fourteen years later, the lives and capabilities of these performers—to live healthy lives, to educate their children, to be adequately represented in matters regarding their workspace—remain largely unchanged.

Working with the CA in mind, it would seem that a good point of focus for any intervention would be the enhancing of their capabilities of political agency, improving the abilities of the *hlayqiya* to interact constructively with their local government. If there is to be hope of addressing the other capabilities gaps they face—to live long, healthy lives, to educate their children, to have control over their working space—they need the power and means to make collective demands. Giving financial and logistical assistance to the nascent performers' associations would seem to be a good way forward: the performers themselves have already put a great deal of work into forming these associations, and the Moroccan government (at both national and local levels) seems to actively encourage the formation of associations, offering financial incentives for their creation and development.

Conclusions

I am calling for a different orientation in our applied work, a different thing to safeguard: not the practices we construct as intangible heritage, but the real freedoms to participate in the emergent process of culture. People are incredibly resilient, and we *do* make culture in circumstances of poverty, disease, war, oppressive governments, and other conditions of capabilities deprivation. But our primary goal in our applied work should be to work towards a world in which we do not have to. At the same time, I am not pretending that it is possible to simply drop the idea of heritage in applied work, and I feel—for reasons that are a bit outside the scope of this chapter—that there is no other real way for organizations like UNESCO to work differently than they currently do. While many ethnomusicologists do applied work in other areas, many of our opportunities will involve heritage. We will find ourselves working with folklife centers, heritage institutes, ministries of culture, and groups of people that we care about that are concerned with the survival of their ways of life. But in any circumstances we find ourselves working we can always stand to re-evaluate our goals, and what I am calling for in introducing Sen's concept of capabilities is a shift in focus from practices to people, and from the promotion of our constructions of performing practice to the capabilities of individuals to shape their world.

About the Author

Thomas Beardslee, PhD, is a professional musician and music teacher living in Brussels, Belgium. His current professional and research interests concern practical applications of his doctoral research on the Sen/Nussbaum capabilities approach, including music and capabilities in refugee populations. He also performs regularly on guitar, pedal steel, oud, and banjo throughout Belgium and elsewhere in Europe.

Notes

1 The term *hlayqiya* (sing. *hlayqi* or *halaqi*) means "of the *halqa*."
2 The Jemaa el Fnaa was later enrolled into the Representative List of the Intangible Cultural Heritage of Humanity in 2008, along with the other Masterpieces that were declared in 2001, 2003, and 2005 prior to the entry into force of the 2003 Convention for the Safeguarding of the Intangible Cultural Heritage (UNESCO 2014).
3 Many of the activities proposed in the safeguarding plan that most directly concerned the performers were never undertaken in the end, such as a website, storytelling contests, and a pension fund for aged performers. In contrast, the proposed activities that concerned the physical site (such as reductions in number of illuminated signs, re-routing of car traffic, demolishing of undesirably modern buildings), which had strong implications for the Square's "authentic" appearance and thus its value as a tourist attraction, were all carried out in full.
4 The survey was administered to forty respondents (just over 10% of the total estimated population of *hlayqiya* at the Square) among representatives of all genres performing regularly on the Square during the research period. It covered questions of income, expenses, savings, and access to health care and education.
5 UNESCO has been working in recent years to expand the role of local NGOs in the nomination and dossier preparation process, something a few participating Member States were not particularly happy about in the drafting of the 2003 Convention (Ahmed Skounti, personal communication; Hafstein 2004: 148).
6 This statement about the performers' levels of education is based on survey data I collected as part of my dissertation research.
7 Understanding and communication between the *hlayqiya* and the Amis was so poor that most performers I spoke with had simply assumed the money had simply been pocketed, either by the Amis or by the local government.
8 Nussbaum's contributions are significant enough that the CA is often referred to as the Sen/Nussbaum Capabilities Approach.
9 *Hlayqiya* income in 2011 averaged between 18,000 and 32,000 Moroccan dirhams a year (1600–3200 Euros), varying widely by genre (Beardslee 2014).

References

Alkire, Sabina. 2005. "Subjective Quantitative Studies of Human Agency." *Social Indicators Research* 74(1): 217–60. https://doi.org/10.1007/s11205-005-6525-0
—2007. "Choosing Dimensions: The Capability Approach and Multidimensional Poverty." Chronic Poverty Research Center Working Paper 88.
http://www.chronicpoverty.org/publications/details/choosing-dimensions-the-capability-approach-and-multidimensional-poverty1/ss (accessed October 20, 2018).

298   *Cultural Mapping and Musical Diversity*

Amselle, Jean-Loup. 2004. "Intangible Heritage and Contemporary African Art." *Museum International* 56(1–2): 84–90. https://doi.org/10.1111/j.1350-0775.2004.00461.x

Anand, Paul, Cristina Santos, and Ron Smith. 2004. "The Measurement of Capabilities." In *Poverty, Capability, and Measurement*, edited by Paul Anand, Cristina Santos, and Ron Smith, 283–310. Oxford: Oxford University Press. https://doi.org/10.1093/acprof:oso/9780199239115.003.0017

Avorgbedor, Daniel K. 1992. "The Impact of Rural-Urban Migration on a Village Music Culture: Some Implications for Applied Ethnomusicology." *African Music* 7, no. 2 (January 1, 1992): 45–57.

Barz, Gregory F., and Judah M. Cohen. 2011. *The Culture of AIDS in Africa: Hope and Healing through Music and the Arts.* Oxford University Press.

Beardslee, Thomas. 2014. "Questioning Safeguarding: Heritage and Capabilities at the Jemaa El Fnaa." PhD dissertation. Columbus, OH: Ohio State University.

Borghi, Rachele. 2004. "Riflessioni Sul Senso Del Luogo: Il Caso Della Piazza Jamaa Al Fna Di Marrakech." *Bollettino Della Società Geografica Italiana* 3: 745–64.

Dirksen, Rebecca. 2011. "Power and Potential in Contemporary Haitian Music: Mizik Angaje Cultural Action and Community-Led Development in Pre- and Post-Quake Port-au-Prince." Conference Paper, Society for Ethnomusicology& Congress on Research in Dance, Joint Annual Meeting, Philadelphia, PA.

Hafstein, Valdimar. 2004. "The Making of Intangible Cultural Heritage: Tradition and Authenticity, Community and Humanity." PhD dissertation. Berkeley: University of California.

Kirshenblatt-Gimblett, Barbara. 1995. "Theorizing Heritage." *Ethnomusicology* 39(3): 367–80. https://doi.org/10.2307/924627

—2004. "Intangible Heritage as Metacultural Production." *Museum International* 56(1–2): 52–65. https://doi.org/10.1111/j.1350-0775.2004.00458.x

Michaels, Walter Benn. 1992. "Race into Culture: A Critical Genealogy of Cultural Identity." *Critical Inquiry* 18(4): 655–85.

Noyes, Dorothy. 2006. "The Judgment of Solomon: Global Protections for Tradition and the Problem of Community Ownership." *Cultural Analysis* 5: 27–56.

—2011. "Traditional Culture: How Does It Work?" *Museum Anthropology Review* 5(1–2): 39–47.

Nussbaum, Martha C. 2001. *Women and Human Development: The Capabilities Approach.* Cambridge: Cambridge University Press.

Pettan, Svanibor. 2008. "Applied Ethnomusicology and Empowerment Strategies: Views from across the Atlantic." *Muzikoloski Zbornik* 44(1): 85–99.

Robeyns, Ingrid. 2005. "The Capability Approach: A Theoretical Survey." *Journal of Human Development* 6 (March): 93–117. https://doi.org/10.1080/146498805200034266

Seeger, Anthony. 2008. "Theories Forged in the Crucible of Action: The Joys, Dangers, and Potentials of Advocacy and Fieldwork." In *Shadows in the Field:*

New Perspectives for Fieldwork in Ethnomusicology, edited by Gregory F. Barz and Timothy J. Cooley, 271–88. New York: Oxford University Press.

Sen, Amartya. 1999. *Development as Freedom*. New York: Knopf.

—2004. "Capabilities, Lists, and Public Reason: Continuing the Conversation." *Feminist Economics* 10(3): 77–80. https://doi.org/10.1080/1354570042000315163

Skounti, Ahmed. 2008. "The Authentic Illusion." In *Intangible Heritage*, edited by Laurajane Smith and Natsuko Akagawa, 74–92. New York: Routledge.

—2012. "The Red City: Medina of Marrakesh." In *World Heritage: Benefits Beyond Borders*, edited by Amareswar Galla, 82–93. Cambridge: Cambridge University Press.

Skounti, Ahmed, Ouidad Tebbaa, and Hassan Nadim. 2005. *La Place Jemaa El Fna: Patrimoine Culturel Immateriel de Marrakech, Du Maroc, et de l'Humanite*. Rabat, Morocco: UNESCO.

Smith, Laurajane. 2006. *Uses of Heritage*. New York: Routledge. https://doi.org/10.4324/9780203602263

Tebbaa, Ouidad, Mohammed Faiz, Antoine Lorgnier, Charles Rossignol, and Hassan Nadim. 2004. *Place Jemâa El Fna, Marrakech*. Geneva: Collection Evasion.

UNESCO. 2009. *What Is Intangible Cultural Heritage?* Paris: UNESCO. https://ich.unesco.org/en/what-is-intangible-heritage-00003 (accessed November 5, 2015).

—2014. "UNESCO Culture Sector—Intangible Heritage—2003 Convention: Lists of Intangible Cultural Heritage and Register of Best Safeguarding Practices." http://www.unesco.org/culture/ich/index.php?lg=en&pg=00011 (accessed November 5, 2015).

Will, Udo. 2008. "'In the Garden of Cultural Identities Silk Flowers Quickly Grow Roots': On the Logic of Culture, Race and Identity in Postmodernist Discourse." *European Meetings in Ethnomusicology* 12: 18–36.

Chapter 15

The *Verbuňk* under the Pressure of World Fame[1]

Zuzana Jurková

Czechs and foreign tourists alike consider the Czech Republic a paradise of historical architecture. This is hallmarked by the fact that twelve of its monuments have been proclaimed UNESCO World Heritage Sites, the first of which was inscribed in 1992. In comparison, the register of Czech elements on the UNESCO Intangible Cultural Heritage List is shorter and more recent; there are five entries. The first of them, the Slovácko *verbuňk* or "dance of the recruits," was inscribed only in 2005.[2]

In order to highlight the multi-layered perception of a music genre inscribed into the UNESCO List, I address the contemporary form of the *verbuňk* in this chapter. I am specifically interested in the influences that shape this form: the discourse that surrounds the history of the *verbuňk* (and thus the question of how the historical sources related to it are used); the expectations of the audience—both locals and non-locals; the values that young *verbuňkers* project onto it; and the mechanisms of preserving it. Since the *verbuňk* is presented primarily as *traditional* dance, and since I understand tradition—in agreement with, for example, Glassie (2003: 192–93)—as "volitional, temporal action," as "an integral component of culture," I believe that comprehension of those influences makes it easier to understand that volition in a concrete culture. The *verbuňk* was inscribed on the UNESCO Intangible Cultural Heritage List in November 2005.[3] And as the inscription of the *verbuňk* was initiated and administratively prepared by former *verbuňkers* in an environment closely connected to the *verbuňk*, I am also interested in how such "volitional ... action" (Glassie 2003: 192–93) influences the further existence of the phenomenon.

Today, the *verbuňk* can be found in southeast Moravia, where it originated in two different contexts. The first is local celebrations, such as "hody"
(feasts) and weddings, for example; the second are competitions of young
men—the *"verbuňkers."* The video,[4] to which I refer in the following text,
captures the winner of the competition for the best dancer of the Slovácko[5]
verbuňk of 2013,[6] Jakub Tomala (b. 1983). The atmosphere of the competition, which is also important for the subsequent discussion, is quite evident
from the video.

One of the usual features of good anthropological texts is intersubjectivity, "the method of connecting as many perspectives on the same data
as possible,"[7] permitting the creation of a more vivid picture. Therefore, in
the following, I combine three perspectives. The first one, the voice of an
anthropologist from Mars, is actually "twofold" because it presents both
positioning—"all the subjective responses that affect how the researcher sees
data" (Stone Sunstein and Chiseri-Strater 2007: 131)—and a perspective
of non-local spectators at the numerous folklore festivals in Slovácko. By
means of a "voice of history" I want to show both how elements of preserved
historical sources are used in today's (re)constructions of the *verbuňk* and the
institutional mechanisms that supported its preservation and the UNESCO
listing. The "voices of *verbuňkers*" are surprisingly homogeneous; however,
a special role and authority belong to Karel Pavlištík (b. 1931), one of the
founders of regular competitions and an initiator of the inscription. In conclusion I will try—again from an intersubjective perspective—to find out more
about the influence of the UNESCO listing.

The Ethnomusicologist from Mars

The first voice in this intersubjective polyphony is the voice of an ethnomusicologist from Mars. By this term I refer to Bruno Nettl's *Heartland
Excursions* (1995), and also more freely to Oliver Sacks's *An Anthropologist
on Mars* (1995). Both authors make reference to the distant planet in the
sense of cultural "distance" of the researcher to the society under investigation, thus the insufficiency of his/her cultural competence. In Nettl's case, it
is about a learned distance, while Sacks discusses the perspective of the autist
Temple Grandin. That ethnomusicologist is me, and Mars is Prague, about
250 kilometers west of Strážnice.

As a child of Socialist Czechoslovakia, and like all of my peers in kin-
dergarten and later in elementary school, I learned "folk songs": simple,

predictable symmetric melodies with naïve rural texts. Singing them, rather fun at the age of six, became later less and less bearable. References in songs to "little geese" and "little sheep," which people practically never encountered in a country where private agriculture did not exist, made it a matter entirely disconnected from my life, some sort of false idyll, just like the "happy" youth depicted on political posters. One issue, however, was essential about folk songs: in the upper grades, we learned mainly about their connection to Czech history, particularly the preservation of national values and language at a time when Czechs lived in parts of Austria and/or the Austro-Hungarian Empire (until 1918). Therefore, we learned that folk songs often inspired Bedřich Smetana (1824–1884) and Antonín Dvořák (1841–1904), the founders of Czech national music.

The fact that after graduation from high school I applied to study ethnography and folklore at the university was definitely not connected to my interest in folk music, and the studies themselves did not stimulate it at all. Nevertheless, they confirmed in me the idea of folk songs closely connected to the past, among other factors, because the whole program was mostly conceived as the study of history. During my studies within the framework of this historic approach, we also read the book by famous biologist and amateur folk music researcher Vladimír Úlehla (1888–1947), *Živá píseň (Living Song)*, which was almost fifty years old at that time.[8] It is a comprehensive music ethnography (833 pages) of prewar Strážnice, one of the centers of Slovácko, a region in southeast Moravia. *Živá píseň* enchanted me with its descriptions of how enormously varied that small town seemed, but especially its plentiful cymbalom bands, singing, and dancing. The book ends with poignant fears by the author about the future, and I internalized the idea that his fears would be realized and that the cymbalom bands and the culture connected to them would disappear from daily life.

I have been to Strážnice several times, and the open-air museum on the outskirts and the picturesque exhibition of musical instruments in the local castle museum confirmed the feeling of connection between music and the past. The architectonic appearance of the town, spoiled by a socialist shopping center, seemed to emphasize that this past was irretrievably lost, as was the past of living, spontaneous performances of local music by local musicians.

However, I did not forget *Živá píseň*, and decades later I read it with my students as exemplary music ethnography. Their enthusiasm was no less than mine, but they were more diligent. Using social networks, they contacted their peers in Slovácko, and from these virtual contacts it was already clear that a stratified local culture exists there. During follow-up research, we were constantly fascinated not only by the high percentage of the population there connected with the active performing of music—from solo singers through (predominantly male) choral formations, various instrumental groups playing both a local and an international repertoire, to the psy-trance formation PSCrew—but also, for example, by the density of music publishers.[9] Those who later joined the faculty field research, continued our initial enthusiasm without exception. We also witnessed the *verbuňk*: both at "feasts" and in its competitive context in subregional rounds and at a Strážnice finale; despite its importance, it is far from the only manifestation of local cultural specificity.[10] In any case, we discovered a land unknown to us—*terra incognita*—where people danced and sang together or at least used local musical elements of the past in a way that was meaningful to the participants; they often combined their activities with expressions such as "earlier" or "traditionally." Their approach corresponded perfectly to Glassie's (2003: 192) concept of tradition as "the means of deriving the future from the past."[11]

Voice of History

Let the second voice be the voice of historical data, as are presented today in connection with the *verbuňk*. The term *verbuňk* itself (from the German *werben*, that is, to canvass, take on, recruit) refers to the context of the recruitment of young men into the army. It took place in the Habsburg Monarchy (part of which was also the land of the Czech Crown) until 1781, after which general conscription was introduced; one of the sources of today's *verbuňk* is thus the genre of recruitment dances, which presumably arose around the middle of the eighteenth century.[12] The first music notation explicitly labeled as *verbuňk* comes from the so-called Gubernial collection of 1819 (No. 330),[13] and the song is said to be from the environment of village celebrations, so-called "hody" (feasts),[14] during which we still find the *verbuňk* today. The *verbuňk*, like any other phenomenon, is not isolated—we find choreological, musical, and functional similarities in Hungarian (*verbunkos*) and Slovak (*odzemek*) male dances. Incidentally, the songs to which the *verbuňk* is danced today are called new Hungarian (folk) songs; their relation to Hungarian songs is unsurprising in view of the co-existence of the Czech lands and Hungary in the Austro-Hungarian monarchy until 1918.

The first filmed documentaries with related dances from Slovácko come from the 1920s and 1930s: in the (still silent) film of J. Palouš, the Mardi

Gras "cifrování" was captured, namely, improvised dance figures of young male dancers proceeding informally through the villages in 1921 or 1922.[15] This is exactly the *cifrování* which is the basis of today's *verbuňk* improvisations. Interestingly, in Palouš's film the male dancers often form couples.[16] One decade later,[17] in Vladimír Úlehla's film *Mizející svět* (*Disappearing World*), the *verbuňkers* dance individually in a characteristic tavern setting. Accompanying music is heard, but there is no singing. In the mid-1940s, Josef Lachmann and Jiří Ferenc captured the *verbuňk* in an outdoor setting— in the context of a wedding,[18] this time already with the dancers singing.

From written and film sources, it is clear that individual elements of the dance-song genre, today called *verbuňk*, have been found on the territory of South Moravia for at least two centuries. But at the same time, it is also evident that today's style of performing (which is also precisely described in connection with the inscription on the UNESCO List) was constituted only in the second third of the twentieth century. Despite this, in the surrounding folkloristic discourse (as in many other cases, referring to tradition, where the ancientness is emphasized),[19] the dance is repeatedly linked to history two centuries older.[20] If the main features of today's performance style of the *verbuňk* can be tracked at least to the 1940s, we do not know much from that time about its local expansion and/or locally specific variants, which are, in a contemporary competitive context, considered very important. Today, in any case, the *verbuňk* is spread primarily through the relatively small territory of Slovácko in the most southeastern part of the Czech Republic.

The basic characteristic features are solo male improvised dance[21] connected with singing.[22] The solo character is preserved even when several dancers dance at the same time, and even then it is clear that every dancer dances without regard to the others.[23] Here improvisation means that the dancer chooses from given *cifry* ("figures"); the choice and sequence are up to him, correspond to his personality, but understandably also reflect various influences of his teachers, successful dancers, and so on.

The dance is preceded by the verse of a song, the tune of which is of the so-called new Hungarian-type. The song's formal structure is not completely constant but a four-line structure is always characteristic and its second half is repeated, sometimes only by the accompanying band. The second line can be melodically identical to the first one or a fifth higher. In any case the melody has a relatively broad compass, frequently over an octave. The texts of the songs often, but not always, deal with the army and military themes. A good example is the song on the video:[24]

I already have to join the army
To whom will I leave you here.
Will I return alive from battle
Or will I lose my head somewhere
God alone knows.

A steel saber will slash
And the white coat will turn red.
The boy is lying. Oh, my God, nobody will help him any more.
Not the general himself.

The first verse of the song is followed by a slow dance. After it, the *verbuňker* either sings a second verse (as in the case of the example on the video) or performs a fast dance. Good dancers are expected to use different figures in the slow and the fast parts.[25]

Both the dance and the singing have a certain rudimentary competitiveness about them: the singing with regard to a broad melodic range, in the higher positions of which the *verbuňker* often reaches his vocal maximum (and recalls the ethnomusicological tenet about the "athletic approach" in Western music);[26] the dance, mainly in the fast part, by the execution of complicated figures. Therefore it is not surprising that the initiative of *verbuňker* competition arose in Slovácko.

In July 1946 in Strážnice, one of the Slovácko centers and the very same city that is the venue of Úlehla's book *Živá píseň*, a folklore festival took place; it was later called the International Folklore Festival of Strážnice.[27] From the beginning, it was conceived as a nationwide folklore celebration, although it was and clearly is closely connected to the region of Slovácko. The organizational center of the festival was originally in the Regional Center of Folk Art, which was gradually transformed from a regional institution[28] to the National Institute of Folk Culture under the direction of the Ministry of Culture in 1990.[29] As part of the Strážnice festival there were competitions for the best Slovácko *verbuňk* dancer, irregularly at first and yearly since 1986. The initiators of these renewed competitions are two regionally important personalities, former recognized performers of the *verbuňk* and other dances—Karel Pavlištík[30] and Jan Miroslav Krist.[31] Both of them held various important positions in the festival structure. The latter was also professionally connected with the National Institute of Folk Culture (NÚLK).

From this environment—the festival and NÚLK—also came the impulse to have the *verbuňk* inscribed on the UNESCO List of Intangible Cultural

Heritage.[32] In November 2005, the *verbuňk* (as the first phenomenon of this kind in the Czech Republic) was proclaimed as a Masterpiece of the Oral and Intangible Cultural Heritage of Humanity.

In the second decade of the new millennium, the Strážnice competition has been preceded by six or seven regional rounds.[33] The lower age limit of the competitors is fifteen years; no upper limit has been established.[34] In Strážnice, the selective round and the finals take place during the festival. It is possible to summarize the rules approximately as follows: the successful dancers from the regional rounds and from the previous year proceed to the selective round; then nine to eighteen of the dancers, including the winner of the previous year's competition, winners of the regional competitions, and winners of an audience survey proceed to the finals.[35] Their performances are evaluated by a jury whose members have been (previously) successful dancers. As for the singing, the purity of intonation, dialect, and general expression are judged; the dancing is judged by the difficulty, quantity, variety, execution, and sequence of the figures (*cifry*) in regard to the regional dance style, spatial arrangement and gradation, and also the general level of expression.[36] The folk costume is also part of the evaluation—both its regional affiliation and its being "traditional" costume with no adjustments for dancing.[37] Winning is purely a matter of prestige, unconnected to any financial reward.

Thus, if Glassie's statement that "tradition is … a result of scholarly interest" (Glassie 2003: 192) sounds surprising to some, the above paragraph agrees with him: scientific (folklorist) institutions have a basic share in the form of today's *verbuňk*. At the same time, however, it is necessary to repeat that many of the involved folklorists are local natives and active musicians and dancers. Therefore this tradition is both a product of folklorists and grass-rooted "temporal action."

The Voice of the *Verbuňkers*

And there is a third voice—the voice of the *verbuňkers* themselves and those who, in some other way, are connected to today's *verbuňk* dancing. After the Strážnice finale in 2013, I spoke with four participants aged between eighteen and thirty-two.[38] I was interested in several subjects. The first of them had to do with the backgrounds and circumstances of a young man becoming a first-rate *verbuňker*. My respondents all began at the age of six or seven in local folklore circles attended by approximately half of their schoolmates. (It is unnecessary to mention that similar folklore circles did not exist on the

Figure 15.1: A singing *verbuňker* (photo by Zuzana Jurková).

Prague "Mars" of my time and so neither was there the basic background where a child would take a certain style/genre for granted.)

In the upper grades of school, that is between the ages of eleven and fifteen, a decision about folklore is usually made: some youths continue—maybe after a break of a few years—in an "adult" dance group; others play in cymbal or wind bands, and some stop actively performing folklore. Family tradition connected with folklore groups (not necessarily with the *verbuňk*),[39] and a local music school or music teacher who could markedly steer his pupils, are also important for decision-making. When I mentioned the question of talent (which should not be important in such an environment where the involvement in music-dance production of everyone is desirable, see Turino 2008), the respondents convinced me that participation in groups has nothing to do with it. "Everyone dances as well as he can. People in bands/circles learn and do it for fun: those who can dance (in competitions); those who can't, maybe support us. That's how it works."[40]

As has been said, the *verbuňk* is danced in an environment of local celebration, including feasts. According to musician and former *verbuňker* Tomáš, it is obvious that if young people want to be together they learn the skills that allow them such social connections.[41]

Figure 15.2: Fans/supporters (photo by Zuzana Jurková)

The second topic that interested me was motivation: Why do young men in Slovácko not play soccer or computer games (like their Czech counter-parts), but instead practice demanding dancing and singing several times a week? At first, my respondents' answers mainly contained the word "fun." Later, however, they specified: "In the past, boys danced the *verbuňk* because they wanted to show who was the greatest lady-killer, who got the best gal. And why not return to those traditions?"[42]

The high value that *verbuňkers* attribute to these contests is another important feature of the *verbuňk* scene. First of all, the competitions force the dancers to build up their technical quality, which, according to them, indis-putably grows (and—implicitly—gives rise to further good *verbuňkers*). Secondly, during the competitions the respectful jury[43] decides on the quality of the *verbuňkers*, which affords them incontestable social status.

Under the Pressure of World Fame?

Finally, I was interested in a question that leads to a broader application: Did anything change after a phenomenon—in this case, the *verbuňk*—was inscribed in the UNESCO List?

My *verbuňkers* all agreed that they were glad when many people, not just the locals, learned about their traditions (this word was used relatively frequently). At the same time, however, it seemed that for them this question was not particularly important.[44]

Karel Pavlištík, the key figure in the restoration of regular competitions, writes:

1) The entry strengthened the prestige of activities leading to preservation, of which the competition for the best dancer of the Slovácko *verbuňk* has been playing an important role for 28 years … and has raised the interest of the media and the cultural public…;

2) It contributed to the intensifying of concrete support of community representatives, cultural and social institutions, mainly local efforts at the preservation and development of that dance in regions where the *verbuňk* exists;

3) Systematic professional and amateur documentation of the development of the *verbuňk* in the various environments of its contemporary existence continues;

4) What is most important is that, as a result of the above-mentioned preservation activities, the number of *verbuňk* dancers is growing;

5) The number of ways of handing down the *verbuňk* is increasing; among them, the support and interest in the active mastering of the *verbuňk* by young dancers is very important.[45]

That question of how the *verbuňk* was influenced by its inscription onto the UNESCO List, and what this inscription actually means for the *verbuňk* (Blahůšek et al. 2010: 7), also interested folklorists at the National Institute of Folk Culture. Five years after the inscription of the *verbuňk* onto the UNESCO List, they wrote to the mayors[46] of Podluží,[47] one of the six sub-regions of Slovácko. Of the nineteen mayors, fifteen answered. To a direct question about changes in the social context of *verbuňk*, some of the mayors answered that there weren't any. Such answers, however, could be read in various ways, for example, as a certain pride in one's own tradition: "After recording the dance, we did not realize … any great shift … The bases must be OUR (understand) OWN … Our—now very numerous—youths … learn the *verbuňk* from each other or in families and with siblings" (Blahůšek et al. 2010: 63). The second group acknowledge a certain emotional response: "I think that for us it means … a certain feeling: on one hand, a sort of pride and, on the other, perhaps also a bit of satisfaction that UNESCO is interested and manages to value such a thing as dance from one little region" (Blahůšek et al. 2010: 64). My *verbuňker* respondents perceive it similarly.

Answers to the question about what concrete steps the community supported for the preservation of the *verbuňk* vary. The answer that the community does not support activities connected to the *verbuňk* is the exception. Most frequently the events, linked with the folk costume tradition, are organized by the youths themselves; support on the part of the community consists, for example, of paying rental for the hall; or elsewhere the community contributes in case the event has losses. In other cases, communities substantially contribute to the charges connected with various "traditional" celebrations and emphasize the possibility of involving everyone, not just chosen individuals (Blahůšek et al. 2010: 66). Finances come either directly from the budgets of the communities or the communities look for financing from several sources (in combination with local sponsors, grants from county sources, etc.).

Outlook

Returning to an intersubjective perspective is not simple. The National Institute of Folk Culture (NÚLK) in Strážnice continues to publish older scores and sound sources; nevertheless the essential ones related to the *verbuňk* are already well known. It is thus impossible to imagine a substantial change in the construction of *verbuňk* tradition. One basic aspect of the present and the near future seems to be the close connection of active dancers (and their biggest fans from folklore ensembles) and specialists in folklore institutions. This connection functions through seminars and workshops for dancers, interaction of successful dancers and specialists on competition juries and, at the same time, the informal authority that folklorists usually have among dancers. Thus, there has not been a "schism," a disconnection of the living phenomenon of the favorite dance from academic discourse—nor does it endanger the near future.

My answer from the viewpoint of a Martian ethnomusicologist is quite hesitant. On one hand, it seems that the (relatively recent) inscription itself did not have any fundamental influence on the performance practice of *verbuňk*. Besides the observations of the mayors, given above, this is also indicated by the intensive interest of the dancers and the visitors of the competition at the Strážnice festival, their interest being substantially older than the inscription on the UNESCO List, and the broader general growth of interest in folklore.

On the other hand, I am a little worried about the strict competition criteria, which do not correspond to the use of the *verbuňk* in informal community life.[48] I can imagine separating the *verbuňk* as a competition discipline from the *verbuňk* as an accepted expression of Slovácko youth. If such worries are justified, only time will tell.

About the Author

Zuzana Jurková studied ethnology and musicology at the Philosophical Faculty at Charles University and at the music conservatory in Brno. She is Professor and Head of the Institute for Ethnomusicology at the Faculty of Humanities of Charles University, focused mainly on the research of musics of minorities (*Voices of the Weak* 2009; *Sounds from the Margins* 2013). She concentrates on Romani music (with several publications and an Open Society Fund grant in 1996–98), the history of Czech ethnomusicology (for her PhD and a Fulbright scholarship in Bloomington in 1998) and, in recent years, urban ethnomusicology (*Pražské hudební světy* 2013; *Prague Soundscapes* 2014). She has been awarded numerous international grants, including a Fulbright Research Fellowship (Indiana University Bloomington) and Ruth Craword Mitchell Fellowship (University of Pittsburgh).

Notes

1   Research for this chapter was supported by the Faculty of Humanities, Charles University Prague, Grant SVV 267 701/2013.
2   For more details see the official UNESCO web page:
    https://en.unesco.org/countries/czechia (accessed November 22, 2018).
3   See the UNESCO web page, https://ich.unesco.org/en/RL/slovacko-verbunk-recruit-dances-00147 (accessed November 20, 2018). According to it, the *verbuňk* was proclaimed part of the Intangible Cultural Heritage in 2005 and inscribed on the Representative List of Intangible Cultural Heritage of Humanity in 2008.
4   *Jakub Tomala Popovice*, https://www.youtube.com/watch?v=3gkc8VMjZ6w (accessed November 20, 2018). Posted by David Buchta.
5   Sometimes the term Slovak Moravia is used in English for this region.
6   Already in 1998, when Tomala was fifteen, he was the winner of the Jury of Seniors. In 2009, 2010, and 2013 he won first place in the competition; in 2011 he earned second place and in 2012 third place.
7   Stone Sunstein and Chiseri-Strater (2007: 131). Here I use the term "intersubjectivity" in the sense of a method of writing a text and not in the sense common

in philosophy and psychology—and sometimes ethnomusicology—that is, as psychological relations between and among people. For this concept see Mason (2014).

8   The book was originally published in 1949, shortly after Úlehla's death. In 2008, a reprint was published together with a CD of fifteen recorded songs. The book was co-published by the National Institute of Folk Culture in Strážnice, NÚLK, and Danaj, who recorded the musical examples.

9   For more details, see Jurková (2012).

10 Here again I refer to Glassie (2003: 192), who characterizes tradition as "a result of differences among cultures." Another similarly striking manifestation, attracting broad attention, is the Ride of the Kings, inscribed on the UNESCO List in 2011. For more details, see https://ich.unesco.org/en/RL/ride-of-the-kings-in-the-south-east-of-the-czech-republic-00564 (accessed November 20, 2018).

11 For this concept of tradition see also, e.g., Shils (1981). For a "traditional" interpretation of very contemporary phenomena such as, e.g., the above-mentioned Slovácko hip-hop, see Savage (2011).

12 See, e.g., Blahůšek et al. (2006) or http://festivalstraznice.cz/media/soutez-verbiru/ (accessed November 20, 2018). This is the web page of the National Institute of Folk Culture (NÚLK), to which I will repeatedly refer. This is an umbrella institution for varied events connected to the *verbuňk*, including the most official ones.

13 Moravian and Silesian songs in this collection were published in Vetterl and Hrabalová (1994).

14 For more details, see Krist (2000).

15 These historical films are available on the DVD *Lidové tance z Čech, Moravy a Slezska* VI. *Mužské taneční projevy: Verbuňk na Horňácku* (Folk dances from Bohemia, Moravia and Silesia VI. Male dances: Verbuňk in Horňácko).

16 According to the notations, eyewitnesses still corroborate this pair practice in the 1930s.

17 The Czech film database presents the year of origin as 1932 (premiere April 7, 1933); http://www.fdb.cz/film/mizejici-svet/12614 (accessed September 30, 2014); the accompanying text to DVD *Lidové tance…: Verbuňk na Horňácku* dates the film to 1933 (p. 33).

18 The film *Horňácká svatba* (*Horňácko Wedding*) is from 1944.

19 Numerous examples are presented by, e.g., Hobsbawm (1983).

20 On the above-mentioned web page of the National Institute of Folk Culture (NÚLK) there is written, e.g.: "Ethnomusicologists date the origin of the *verbuňk* on our territory to the first half of the eighteenth century." This same formulation is used in the official application to the UNESCO List, viz. Blahůšel et al. (2006: 15). The unprovability of the ancientness of the local variants corresponds to the testimony of our respondent from Slovácko, 76-year-old FH, according to whom many local variants of folksongs were created by so-called cultural officers. These were, mainly in the 1950s and 1960s, employees of local businesses who

organized leisure musical activities for the workers. They aimed to make folk ensembles' performances as original as possible. Therefore they created "local variants." For more details see the website Ethnomzikologie.eu: https://etnomuzikologie.eu/wp-content/uploads/2018/11/Fratisek-Hruby_About-life-and-music.pdf (accessed November 22, 2018).

21 From the choreological point of view called "hopping."

22 In the literature (e.g., Blahůšek et al. 2006: 15) the formulation "with an introductory song" was found; nevertheless, today we often find that the dancer interlocks singing and dancing (see below).

23 For example, the intermissions of the Strážnice festivals are called "Free Rings" when all the dancers and/or interested people are invited to the stage. Even during the dancing of dozens of *verbuňkers* the distinct solo character is apparent.

24 See note 4.

25 See DVD *Lidové tance z Čech, Moravy a Slezska VI.: Verbuňk na Horňácku* (Folk Dances of Bohemia, Moravia and Silesia VI: Verbuňk in Horňácko).

26 Today in the competition one can notice the enthusiasm of the audience for the highest singing notes.

27 For more details about the festival see Pavlicová and Uhlíková (1997: 204–205).

28 In 1956, established as the Institute of Folk Culture.

29 See the web page of the National Institute of Folk Culture: http://www.nulk.cz/historie-nulk/ (accessed November 20, 2018).

30 Born 1931 in Uherský Brod, he graduated in ethnography from Charles University. Since his studies, he was a member of various dance ensembles and later an instructor of folk dances. He worked as a choreographer and was a member of the program committee of the International Folk Festival in Strážnice. Since 1995 Pavlištík is president of the senate of the festival. For more details see Pavlicová and Uhlíková (1997: 89).

31 Jan Miroslav Krist (1932–2007) was dancer in several Moravian ensembles and subsequently worked as choreographer and dramaturge. From 1953 he was an author and member of the program council of the International Folk Festival in Strážnice and its senate. From 1991, he was employed in the NÚLK. For more details see Pavlicová and Uhlíková (1997: 61–62).

32 According to Blahůšek et al. (2006: 9), administration for the nomination started preparations in 2002. The two above-mentioned dancers were members of the four-member working group.

33 See competition rules at the website Mezinárodní folklórní festival Strážnice: http://festivalstraznice.cz/media/statut-souteze/ (accessed November 19, 2018).

34 Ibid.

35 Ibid.

36 Ibid.

37 Ibid.

38 Such a relatively wide range of ages may seem surprising. However, an overview of the participants of all of the contests since 1986, shows that 2013 was

not exceptional. In 1986 the oldest dancer was 40 years old; the youngest was exactly twenty years younger. And for several years in a row, one of the oldest participants, Ladislav Jagoš (b. 1952), repeatedly earned first place, and, since 1992, has been a member of the expert jury (Blahůšek et al. 2010).

39 We came to similar conclusions in Hluk; see Jurková (2012).

40 Jan H., 19, university student.

41 Tomáš thus intuitively reacts to Bourdieu's concept of cultural capital; however, he does not consider it as an instrument of exclusion, but, on the contrary, as an instrument of social inclusion.

42 Jaroslav Š., 32, psychologist.

43 The respect of the jury is connected to the fact that it is primarily composed of former successful dancers.

44 Field notes, Zuzana Jurková, June 29, 2013.

45 Email correspondence, Zuzana Jurková to K. Pavlištík (July 25, 2013). In the region it is actually possible to find various types of dance courses meant for a varied public (which understandably cannot substitute systematic training); see e.g. an online news web page *Novinky.cz*, http://www.novinky.cz/vase-zpravy/ zlinsky-kraj/uherske-hradiste/4431-26541-do-taju-slovackeho-verbunku- zasveti-zajemce-ve-specialnich-kurzech-v-kunovicich.html (accessed November 1, 2014), and a website of regional news *Jižní Morava* (South Moravia), http://www.jizni-morava.info/kalendar-akci/900_313775_kurz-verbunku (accessed October 11, 2014). For children's *verbuňk* dancing, see e.g., https:// www.youtube.com/watch?v=jXOeJeYoDDI, from 11:30 (accessed October 12, 2014).

46 The reasons why the addressees were mayors and not, for example, leaders of folklore circles are numerous. The main one is that the agenda connected to the inscription specifies institutions responsible for the care of the phenomenon. On the local level these are the town and community authorities of Moravian Slovakia (Blahůšek et al. 2010: 56).

47 The most southern part of Slovácko neighboring on Austria and Slovakia. Its center is Břeclav.

48 What seems most striking to me is the emphasis on local pronunciation, which is simply not usually respected.

References

Blahůšek, Jan, Jan Miroslav Krist, Jana Matuszková, and Karel Pavlištík. 2006. *Slovácký Verbuňk, mistrovské dílo ústního a nemateriálního dědictví lidstva* ("The Slovácko Verbuňk, Dance of Recruits, the Masterpiece of the Oral and Intangible Heritage of Humanity"). Strážnice: Národní ústav lidové kultury.

Blahůšek, Jan, Petr Číhal, Romana Habartová, Petr Horehleď, Magdalena Maňáková, Jitka Matuszková, Alena Karel, Alena Schauerová, and Jarmila Vrtalová. 2010.

Slovácký verbuňk: Současný stav a perspektivy. ("The Slovácko Verbuňk: Contemporary Situation and Perspectives"). Strážnice: Národní ústav lidové kultury.

Glassie, Henry. 2003. "Tradition." In *Eight Words for the Study of Expressive Culture,* edited by Burt Feintuch, 176–97. Urbana: University of Illinois Press.

Hobsbawm, Eric. 1983. "Introduction: Inventing Traditions." In *The Invention of Tradition,* edited by Eric Hobsbawm and Terence Ranger, 1–14. Cambridge: Cambridge University Press. https://doi.org/10.1017/CBO9781107295636.001

Jurková, Zuzana. 2012. "Ethnomusicological Paradigm as a Question of Life and Death (of Tradition)." In *Musical Traditions,* edited by Pál Richter, 71–88. Budapest: HAS Research Center for the Humanities.

Krist, Jan Miroslav. 2000. "Verbuňk na Kyjovsku." In accompanying text to DVD *Lidové tance z Čech, Moravy a Slezska,* řada II, díl 1. Strážnice: Národní ústav lidové kultury.

Mason, Paul. 2014. "Creative Subjectivity in Performance." *Culture Matters: Applying Anthropology* (July 7, 2014). https://culturematters.wordpress.com/2014/07/07/creative-intersubjectivity-in-performance/ (accessed November 30, 2015).

Nettl, Bruno. 1995. *Heartland Excursions.* Urbana and Chicago: University of Illinois Press.

Pavlicová, Martina, and Lucie Uhlíkova. 1997. *Od folkloru k folklorismu. Slovník folklorního hnutí na Moravě a ve Slezsku.* Strážnice: Národní ústav lidové kultury.

Sacks, Oliver. 1995. *An Anthropologist on Mars.* New York: Knopf Doubleday.

Savage, Steve. 2011. "Introduction." In *Bytes and Backbeats: Repurposing Music in the Digital Age by Steve Savage,* 1–19. Ann Arbor, MI: University of Michigan Press. https://doi.org/10.3998/mpub.3432847

Shils, Edward. 1981. *Tradition.* Urbana and Chicago: University of Chicago Press.

Stone Sunstein, Bonnie, and Elizabeth Chiseri-Strater. 2007. *FieldWorking: Reading and Writing Research.* Boston and New York: Bedford/St. Martin.

Turino, Thomas. 2008. *Music as Social Life: The Politics of Participation.* Chicago: University of Chicago Press.

Úlehla, Vladimír. 1949. *Živá píseň.* Praha: František Borový.

Vetterl, Karel, and Olga Hrabalová. 1994. *Guberniální sbírka písní a instrumentální hudby z Moravy a Slezska z r. 1819.* Strážnice: Národní ústav lidové kultury.

Films and Videos

Horňácká svatba. Film directed by Josef Lachmann and Jiří Ferenc, 1944.

Jakub Tomala Popovice. Video: https://www.youtube.com/watch?v=3gkc8VMjZ6w (accessed November 20, 2018). Posted by David Buchta, 2014.

Lidové tance z Čech, Moravy a Slezska VI.: Verbuňk na Slovácku. DVD. Ústav lidové kultury Strážnice, 2003.

Mizející svět. Film directed by Vladimír Úlehla, 1932.

Index

225–43, 251–54, 256–58, 260–71,
279–96 *see also* cultural heritage
  dissonant heritage 67, 73
  heritage management 67–68, 78
  heritage production 67, 282–83
  heritage studies 67–68, 257–58, 268,
    271n
  inconvenient heritage 67, 74
  and musical traditions 251, 257
  national heritage 55, 177, 194–200,
    261–62, 264
  National Heritage Institute (Poland)
    195–200, 206, 207n
  negative heritage 70, 79n
Holy Land 108
Hornbostel, Erich Moritz von 19, 31n,
  186, 190
Howard, Keith 1, 6, 257–58
hybridity 4, 26, 37, 39–40, 47, 235n
hybridization 35, 37–40, 43, 45, 47, 60,
  163, 165

Idelsohn, Abraham Zvi 91–92, 108–21,
  226, 236, 239–40
identity 4, 32n, 35–51, 54–64, 92, 113,
  123–42, 175, 187–88, 215–18, 220,
  229, 231, 251–54, 256–71, 284 *see also*
  hybridity
  and continuity 69, 175, 188
  cultural identity 35, 59, 217–18, 220,
    231, 256, 284
  diversity and fragmentation of 54
  hyphenated identity 38, 40, 47
  and politics 257–58, 260, 262, 271
  regional identity 216, 256–58,
    259–60, 264–65, 270, 271n, 272n
ideology/ies 25, 27, 57, 69, 75
inclusion 3–4, 14, 38, 177–78, 182–83,
  199, 260, 263, 314n *see also* diversity
indigenity 3, 5, 14–15, 17n, 54, 123–24,
  146–50, 160, 166, 167n
intangible cultural heritage 1–8, 15,
  168n, 175–79, 182–83, 186, 190, 203,
  210–20, 225–43, 251–54, 279, 282,
  285, 287
Intangible Cultural Heritage (UNESCO)
  16, 79n, 96, 104, 146–47, 150, 165–66,

168n, 175–79, 186, 188–90, 194–207,
210–20, 225–43, 251–54, 256–57,
262–71, 279, 299, 300, 306, 311n
  and commercialization 201
  and conflict 3–4, 7, 206, 253, 257,
    266–71, 284
  and documentation 14, 182–83, 185,
    197, 203, 211, 214, 232, 251–52,
    270, 282–83, 309
  and fossilization 194, 205
  and inventorying 211, 214, 218, 220,
    283
  and musealization 2, 202
  and musical traditions 3–4, 176, 178,
    252
  policy of 59, 67, 71, 78–79, 182,
    194–207 (Poland), 203 (Japan,
    South Korea), 210–20, 225–43
    (Switzerland), 256–71 (Andalucia,
    Spain), 283
  and regionalization 252–53, 256–71
  resolutions of 3
intersubjectivity 301, 311–312n

Jabotinsky, Ze'ev 117
Jewish music *see also* Idelsohn;
  Switzerland
  Hamavdil 236
  Lewandowski, Louis 226–27,
    238–40, 244n
  Minhag Ashkenaz 225–43
  Minhag Polin 235, 237
  Naumbourg, Samuel 226–27, 239–43
  Nusach 234, 238, 244–45, 245n
  Southern German Minhag 235–36,
    238
  Sulzer, Salomon 226, 240
  Ya'aleh prayer 241, 245n

Kulturhistorische Schule 23–25, 31n
Kulturkreise 23–24, 28–29
Kulturkreislehre 15, 23

landscape 1, 3–6, 14, 22, 55, 87–92,
  96, 111–12, 123–42 *see also* cultural
  landscape; environment
  and musical style 91

www.ingramcontent.com/pod-product-compliance
Lightning Source LLC
Chambersburg PA
CBHW070554270326
41926CB00013B/2313